A Poet's Prose

A Poet's Prose

SELECTED WRITINGS

OF LOUISE BOGAN

With the Uncollected Poems

Edited and with an introduction by Mary Kinzie

Swallow Press / Ohio University Press

Athens

Swallow Press / Ohio University Press, Athens, Ohio 45701
www.ohio.edu/oupress

Jacket/cover photo by Harris & Ewing Studio, ca. 1945, and frontispiece photo, May 28, 1922, in Grinzing, Austria, courtesy Amherst College Archives and Special Collections by permission of the Trustees of Amherst College.

12 11 10 09 08 07 06 05   5 4 3 2 1

Library of Congress Cataloging-in-Publication Data
Bogan, Louise, 1897–1970.
  A poet's prose : selected writings of Louise Bogan : with the uncollected poems / edited and with an introduction by Mary Kinzie.
    p. cm.
  Includes bibliographical references and index.
  ISBN 0-8040-1070-6 (cloth : alk. paper) — ISBN 0-8040-1071-4 (pbk. : alk. paper)
  I. Kinzie, Mary. II. Title.
  PS3503.O195A6 2005
  811'.52—dc22
                    2004029395

Contents

POETRY APPENDIX

Uncollected Poems

Unpublished Poems and Drafts—Dated Works

Unpublished Poems and Drafts—Undated Works

Sources and Acknowledgments

Fiction

"*Keramik*," *The American Caravan*, ed. Van Wyck Brooks, Alfred Kreymborg, Lewis Mumford, and Paul Rosenfield (The Literary Guild of America; Little & Ives, 1927); "Winter Morning" and "Art Embroidery," *The New Republic* (March 14 and 21, 1928). "Soliloquy," *The Second American Caravan* (editors as above; Macauley, 1928). The following stories and sketches appeared in *The New Yorker* and are reprinted with permission: "Hydrotherapy" (June 27, 1931), "Sabbatical Summer" (July 11, 1931), "Zest" (October 24, 1931), "Journey Around My Room" (January 14, 1933), "The Short Life of Emily" (May 6, 1933), "The Last Tear" (July 22, 1933), "Conversation Piece" (August 12, 1933), "Coming Out" (October 14, 1933), "Dove and Serpent" (November 18, 1933), "Letdown" (October 20, 1934), and "To Take Leave" (January 26, 1935). Three previously unpublished pieces are reproduced by permission of the Amherst College Library, where the Louise Bogan Papers are kept: "Not Love, but Ardor" (dated by LB May 1934), "Saturday Night Minimum" (dated 1935), and "Whatever It Is" (dated spring 1936). The uncollected published fiction and poetry was gathered for private circulation in *Uncollected Poetry and Prose,* coedited by Marshall Clements and David Stivender, in 1975.

Journals and Memoir

Except where noted in the text, all the material in this section can be found in the Amherst College Library. Some excerpts from the journals, edited by Ruth Limmer, also appeared in *Antaeus* 27 (1977) and *The New Yorker* (January 30, 1978) and in Ruth Limmer's "mosaic," *Journey Around My Room: The Autobiography of Louise Bogan* (Viking, 1980), abbreviated JAMR.

Letters

Ruth Limmer, ed., *What the Woman Lived: Selected Letters of Louise Bogan, 1920–1970* (Harcourt Brace Jovanovich, 1973), abbreviated WTWL; and the Amherst College Library.

Criticism

Robert Phelps and Ruth Limmer, eds., *A Poet's Alphabet: Reflections on the Literary Art and Vocation,* by Louise Bogan (McGraw-Hill, 1970), abbreviated PA. Individual essays and reviews originally appeared as follows: **W. H. Auden:** brief mention, *The New Yorker* (April 7, 1934); *The Dog Beneath the Skin, The New Yorker* (October 12, 1935); *Letters from Iceland, The Nation* (December 11, 1937); *Oxford Book of Light Verse, The New Yorker* (December 24, 1938); *The Double Man, The New Yorker* (April 12, 1941); *For the Time Being, The New Yorker* (September 23, 1944); *Collected Poetry, The New Yorker* (April 14, 1945); *The Age of Anxiety, The New Yorker* (July 26, 1947); *Poets of the English Language, The New Yorker* (March 17, 1951); *The Shield of Achilles, The New Yorker* (April 30, 1955); *The Criterion Book of Modern American Verse, The New Yorker* (March 1, 1957); *Homage to Clio, The New Yorker* (October 8, 1960). **Charles Baudelaire:** *Flowers of Evil, The New Yorker* (May 3, 1947). **Elizabeth Bowen:** *The Death of the Heart, The Nation* (January 28, 1939). **Colette:** *Chéri, The New Republic* (April 13, 1930). **Ivy Compton-Burnett:** *Darkness and Day* (1951), PA. **"Detective Novels"**: originally "The Time of the Assassins," *The Nation* (April 22, 1944), retitled by Ruth Limmer for PA. **Isak Dinesen:** *Winter's Tales, The Nation* (June 26, 1943). **T. S. Eliot:** *Collected Poems, The New Yorker* (May 23, 1936); *The Family Reunion, The New Yorker* (April 15, 1939); *Four Quartets* (1943), PA. **Gustave Flaubert:** *L'Education sentimentale, The Nation* (October 3, 1942). **"Folk Art"**: originally "Some Notes on Popular and Unpopular Art," *Partisan Review* (September/October 1943), retitled by Ruth Limmer for PA. **André Gide:** *Imaginary Interviews, The Nation* (October 28, 1944); *Journals 1889–1913, The Nation* (October 18, 1947); *Journals 1914–1927, The Nation* (June 5, 1948). **Johann Wolfgang von Goethe:** on the work and influence, *The New Yorker* (September 17, 1949). **"The Heart and the Lyre"**: on American women poets, *Mademoiselle* (May 1947). **Henry James:** *The Princess Casamassima, The Nation* (April 23, 1938);

The Later Phase (on James, by F. O. Matthiessen), *The Nation* (December 23, 1944); *The Bostonians, The Nation* (December 1, 1945). **Juan Ramón Jiménez:** *Selected Writings*, trans. H. R. Hays, *The New Yorker* (February 8, 1958). **James Joyce:** *Finnegans Wake, The New Yorker* (May 6, 1939); *A Skeleton Key to "Finnegans Wake"* (by Campbell and Robinson), *The Nation* (August 19, 1944). **Philip Larkin:** *The Less Deceived, The New Yorker* (September 13, 1958); *The Whitsun Weddings, The New Yorker* (April 10, 1965). **Federico García Lorca:** *Lament for the Death of a Bullfighter, The New Yorker* (September 25, 1937); *The Poet in New York, The New Yorker* (June 1, 1940). **Robert Lowell:** *Lord Weary's Castle, The New Yorker* (November 30, 1946); *Life Studies, The New Yorker* (October 24, 1959); *For the Union Dead, The New Yorker* (April 10, 1965); *Near the Ocean, The New Yorker* (May 20, 1967). **Marianne Moore:** on Moore's intellectual lineage, titled for PA with LB's phrase "American to Her Backbone," *Quarterly Review of Literature* 4:2 (1948). **Ezra Pound:** *Cantos LII–LXXI, The New Yorker* (November 9, 1940); *The Pisan Cantos, The New Yorker* (October 30, 1948); *Rock-Drill 85–95 de los Cantares, The New Yorker* (September 1, 1956). **Dorothy Richardson:** on Horace Gregory's biography of Richardson, *The New York Times Book Review* (August 27, 1967). **Wallace Stevens:** *The Auroras of Autumn, The New Yorker* (October 28, 1950); *Collected Poems*, reviewed with *Poems 1923–54* by E. E. Cummings, *The New Yorker* (December 11, 1954). **Caitlin Thomas:** *Leftover Life to Kill, The New Yorker* (October 12, 1957). **W. B. Yeats:** *Collected Poems, The New Yorker* (April 7, 1934); *Oxford Book of Modern Verse, The New Yorker* (November 14, 1936); on the life and work, *Atlantic Monthly* (May 1938); on Yeats's death, *The Nation* (February 25, 1939); *Last Poems and Plays, The New Yorker* (June 1, 1940); *Collected Poems, The New Yorker* (October 20, 1951). Notes and drafts of many of LB's reviews and essays from 1936 on were donated by the poet to Princeton University in 1952. Sources for individual essays were often traced with the help of Claire E. Knox's excellent bibliography *Louise Bogan: A Reference Source* (Scarecrow Press, 1990).

Poems

Published during LB's lifetime: "A Night in Summer," *The Jabberwock* (Girls' Latin School, 1911–12); "The Betrothal of King Cophetua," Boston University *Beacon* (December 1915); "The Young Wife," *Others* (December

1917); "Survival," *The Measure / A Journal of Poetry* (November 1921); "Elders," "Resolve," "Leave-Taking," and "To a Dead Lover," *Poetry* (August 1922); "Decoration," "A Letter," "Words for Departure," "Epitaph for a Romantic Woman," and "Song" ("Love me because I am lost"), *Body of This Death,* by Louise Bogan (Robert M. McBride, 1923); "Pyrotechnics," *The Liberator* (May 1923); "The Stones" and "Trio," *The Measure* (June 1923); "The Flume," *Dark Summer,* by Louise Bogan (Charles Scribner's Sons, 1929); "Old Divinity," "For an Old Dance," "The Engine," "Gift," and "Hidden," *The New Yorker* (December 14, 1929; February 1, 1930; January 3, 1931; May 28, 1932; and February 15, 1936); "New Moon," *The Nation* (August 7, 1937); "Untitled" ("Tender and insolent"), *Poetry* (October 1937); "The Catalpa Tree," *Voices: A Journal of Verse* (September/December 1951).

Posthumous publication: "Portrait of the Artist as a Young Woman," "Leechdoms," "When at Last," "The Castle of My Heart," and "December Daybreak" appeared with some differences in JAMR; "Fantasy," "Letter to Mrs. Q's Sister," and "Love Severally Rhymed," in *TriQuarterly* (Fall 2004). All poems unpublished during LB's life can be found in the Louise Bogan Papers of the Amherst College Library, and are reproduced with permission.

To Northwestern University I owe thanks for a research grant and a quarter term of leave during the anthology's completion. The help of my research aides Mary South, Chris Shannon, and, most of all, John Dony, was indispensable in the transcription and proofreading of manuscripts.

The staff of Swallow Press / Ohio University Press have been patient and supportive; I am especially grateful to the director, David Sanders, for recognizing the need to bring a selection of Louise Bogan's prose back into print, and to Nancy Basmajian for her astute copyediting.

Finally, I would like to express my gratitude to Daria D'Arienzo, John Lancaster, and the entire staff of the Amherst Library's Archives and Special Collections department for their generous attention and assistance in the completion of this anthology.

Editor's Note

Louise Bogan's ellipses (mid-sentence as well as end-sentence) are shown in the texts by three spaced dots, as was her practice. In the journals, memoirs, and letters, where for economy's sake I have had to compress, deletions of less than a paragraph are shown by ellipsis points in brackets [. . .]; editorial gaps of a paragraph or longer are indicated by the colophon ~. In the criticism, unless otherwise noted, all ellipses are LB's. All numbers in LB's prose have been spelled out except for addresses, dates, times of day, exact numbers over one hundred, and exact sums of money. One exception, in the letters, are numbers for centuries. A comma has been added after the penultimate item in a series. Spellings of words with correct alternatives have been regularized to accord with LB's apparent preference (e.g., theatre, naïveté, débris, metre, façade); capitalization and italics have been treated similarly (e.g., Symbolist, Romanticism, the Unconscious, *décor, vers libre*). In all the prose, except as noted, insertions in brackets are the editor's.

Abbreviations

LB   Louise Bogan

RL   Ruth Limmer

PA   *A Poet's Alphabet: Reflections on the Literary Art and Vocation,* ed. Robert Phelps and Ruth Limmer (McGraw-Hill, 1970).

WTWL   *What the Woman Lived: Selected Letters of Louise Bogan, 1920–1970,* ed. Ruth Limmer (Harcourt Brace Jovanovich, 1973).

JAMR   *Journey Around My Room: The Autobiography of Louise Bogan,* a "mosaic" by Ruth Limmer (Viking, 1980)

EF   *Louise Bogan: A Portrait,* by Elizabeth Frank (Columbia University Press, 1986).

Books by Louise Bogan

POEMS

Body of This Death
Dark Summer
The Sleeping Fury
Poems and New Poems
Collected Poems, 1923–1953
The Blue Estuaries: Poems, 1923–1968

CRITICISM

Achievement in American Poetry, 1900–1950
Selected Criticism
A Poet's Alphabet: Reflections on the Literary Art and Vocation

LETTERS AND MEMOIR

What the Woman Lived: Selected Letters of Louise Bogan, 1920–1970
Journey Around My Room: The Autobiography of Louise Bogan

TRANSLATIONS

—with Elizabeth Mayer:

The Glass Bees, by Ernst Jünger
Elective Affinities, by Johann Wolfgang von Goethe
The Sorrows of Young Werther and *Novella,* by Johann Wolfgang von Goethe

—with Elizabeth Roget:

The Journal of Jules Renard

ANTHOLOGY

—with William Jay Smith:

The Golden Journey: Poems for Young People

Louise Bogan in Her Prose

Louise Bogan was, according to the English poet W. H. Auden, one of "only four American poets" (the others were Marianne Moore, Laura Riding, and T. S. Eliot), and one whose poetic career, as he told her in 1941, when she was forty-four, was "only just beginning." But he also wondered whether her "disgraceful neglect" by critics hadn't begun to blur her realization of her own lyric gift. In the shadow of this neglect, which made composing poetry a struggle for Bogan, she nevertheless fashioned herself into a writer of prose of incomparable liveliness, poignancy, and intelligence. It is to this mission and this career that the present anthology bears witness.

That said, it is true that writing prose was also, for her, a difficult task. The autumn before she died, Louise Bogan at last severed her connection with *The New Yorker* magazine after thirty-eight years as its poetry reviewer. "I've *had* it," she wrote in late 1969 to her friend Ruth Limmer: "No more pronouncements on lousy verse. No more *hidden* competition. No more struggling *not* to be a square. Etc." Contemporary verse on the whole had begun to seem frivolous to this poet who had created, among other daring impersonations, the haunting revision of the myth of the Gorgon (for in her poem "Medusa," Bogan's narrator is both victim and monster), while the effort to place herself in sympathy with work of lesser intensity—given that she was the author of such magisterial lyrics as the brief "Song for a Lyre" and of the mature free-verse meditation "After the Persian"—became too demeaning. But Bogan's decision to make this break was also the result of having struggled, for almost all of those thirty-eight years, against a yet more humbling resistance to completing the work at hand. To this resistance she applied the most skillful enticements, while spending herself against it with efforts that often seem superhuman. Yet, for reasons having to do with her lower-middle-class Irish background and limited formal education (about which she was both bitter and proud), and owing as well to the psychological aftermath of her childhood in a family chronically derailed by a regal, unsatisfied, and mercurial mother, Bogan's career as a literary journalist—no less than her life as an artist and a woman—was vexed and persistently undermined.

Louise Bogan, born in 1897, grew up in mill towns in Maine, New Hampshire, and Massachusetts. Her father, Daniel, worked as a copy clerk and then foreman and sometime inventor at paper mills and bottling factories. His employment made him nominally white-collar, but close to the boundary between Protestant privilege and the not-quite-respectable Irish Catholic economy into which he had been born. As a result, Bogan nursed a strong grudge against "nice" people, with their well-bred voices and their obtuse prosperity, while passionately envying the clean and well-ordered decency of households like the Gardner family's, until praise was wrung from her: "Blessed order!" she cried out at the end of her long sketch of Mrs. Gardner; "Blessed thrift."

Until Louise was seven, her own family often lived in rooms in working-class hotels and somewhat seedy boardinghouses; the family's social world was small. Louise adored her brother Charles, twelve years older then she, who was stalled in an oedipal connection to their mother, drinking to escape, and escaping only toward the end of World War I, when he was killed in action in France. The family's move to Boston in 1909 had meant substituting, for the closed, small-town horizon the Bogans had known before then, a grayer, thronged, and more patchwork life on the fringes of urban poverty in a new apartment development. Although Louise was able to attend the college-preparatory Girls' Latin School, with help from a female benefactor, and flourished there as a young scholar for five years, her need to escape from her passionate and overwhelming mother, Mary (called May), was as strong and tumultuous as her brother's had been. After her successful freshman year at Boston University, she gave up a fellowship for the following year to Radcliffe, eloping in 1916 with a German emigré, Curt Alexander, who was then a corporal in the U.S. Army. She followed her husband in April 1917, after the start of the war, to his posting in the Canal Zone. Here her daughter and only child, Maidie (Mathilde) Alexander, was born. The marriage foundered on the sexual attraction that seemed to have been all that joined them. They had neither books nor ideas in common. "We played *cards!*" Bogan confessed.

The couple separated soon after the end of the war, in 1919, by which time they were at Fort Dix in New Jersey. Bogan took an apartment on West Ninth Street in New York, and periodically left Maidie with the child's Bogan grandparents. Louise had begun to earn a small reputation as a poet, having joined a literary circle that gathered first around Alfred Kreymborg's publication *Others,* then around the magazine *The Measure.* She met two of her lifelong friends, Edmund Wilson and Rolfe Humphries, during the early 1920s, while supporting herself piecemeal by clerking in Brentano's bookstore, working at a branch of the New York Public Library (where Marianne Moore held a more exalted position), and, with poets Léonie Adams and Louise Townsend Nicholl, cataloguing for a Columbia University anthropologist she had met through Ruth Benedict. On the death of her estranged husband from pneumonia in 1920, she received a widow's pension, and on this she went to live in Austria, and to write. She later observed that the distance from the American scene was a godsend because, given the transatlantic mails, she could not hear back very quickly from editors to whom she sent work, and hence did not try to base new writing on past approval.

In Vienna, she lived through a crucial period of solitude and self-testing in an atmosphere of evacuation or abandonment spread out against the backdrop of Baroque ornamentation. She walked down the broad *Alleen,* along the parks, and through the high-ceilinged salons of the house where she rented a room, as if she were the child in a fairy tale from which everyone of her own age and likeness had disappeared. It was a period of inward turning, sharply contrasting with the gregariousness of the previous few years in Greenwich Village. She explored her loneliness and her new identity in verse ("Portrait of the Artist as a Young Woman," a poem she put down two decades later but held back from publication; it is given here in the poetry appendix) and also in memoir (one of her fictional questionnaires that treats this period begins with a vast question, which her earlier need for love from the mother who so worked against her had made negligible: "Have you ever sought God?" The question should have been, "Have you ever sought love?"). It was in such writings that she pursued what would be the lifelong task of working through her past. Her mood is both open and baffled, as she faces the mysterious devastation of her childhood.

Bogan published her first volume of poems, *Body of This Death,* in 1923, shortly after her return from Vienna to New York, the same year she met the poet and novelist Raymond Holden. Her second volume, *Dark Summer,* appeared six years later, in 1929, by which time she and Holden had married. Although it was her longest and most intense erotic relationship, Holden's romantic self-indulgence and Bogan's pathological jealousy eventually made the union a nightmare (with her daughter Maidie caught in the middle between desperate parents—no matter how hard Bogan tried to avoid the pattern that had caused her so much suffering when she herself was young). The poems Bogan wrote during the 1930s were collected in 1937 as *The Sleeping Fury.* This "fury" was also Medusa, a Gorgon of jealousy, but now with her rage wept out. Indeed, the decade that followed was a dead zone for her verse writing. Bogan suffered its loss profoundly, while attempting to understand it as the pattern of the lyric poet's life. She was able to write again in 1948, the release-point being "Song for the Last Act," a poem that came forth as a response to meeting T. S. Eliot, in which Bogan puts down, in terms of music, one of her most impressive tropes for suffering in art as the saying of what cannot be said: "The staves are shuttled over with a stark / Unprinted silence." But after *The Sleeping Fury* only a handful of new poems accompanied the three "new and collected" volumes she published, in 1941, in 1954, and in her final collection, *The Blue Estuaries,* in 1968.

The periods of greatest poetic outpouring were the twenties and thirties —and these were the decades of greatest change for her: the flight from her parents, marriage, and the rapid recoil from the rashness of that union; the birth of her child; her sexual and professional liberation in New York; her first husband's death; the first European awakening (in Austria) and the second, in 1933, in Salzburg, Provence, and Italy, on a trip that coincided with the disintegration of her second marriage. Nevertheless, 1933 gave her an electrifying vision of Europe, for she encountered Renaissance painting, sculpture, and ornament in a way that made it her own. Like Hyacinth in *The Princess Casamassima,* Bogan's encounter with Italian art convinced her that certain objects formerly unknown to her should be preserved at all costs. But the opening of horizons was accompanied by disastrous closings, for this decade was marred by two periods of psychiatric hospitalization, in 1931 and 1933, for depression marked by obsessive and paranoid inclinations—or, as Bogan would write in her journal, tearless sorrow.

It was during her long recuperation between 1933 and 1934 that Bogan began work on an autobiographical narrative, which she sometimes thought of as leading to a book, under the title *Laura Daley's Story.* (Like Edgar Allan Poe, whose single long work of fiction he launched under a name with the same metrical pattern as his own—*The Narrative of Arthur Gordon Pym*—Bogan maintained the syllables and "Irish" of her own name for her protagonist, although she reversed the stresses.) Never finished, the narrative was taken up again in 1958 and 1959, while Bogan was at the MacDowell Colony (an artist's retreat in New Hampshire), and again in 1965, when she reworked a large portion of the 1933 notes. Among the somewhat masked revelations in her journals is the fact that her mother had love affairs in which rather sinister "familiars" connived; that she took Louise to some of her assignations, then left her behind in strange hotel rooms when she went about the town with the "other"; and that Bogan became blind for several days when she was five or six years old. All the while loving and fearing her, an innocent Louise was drawn into her mother's marital betrayals. We also see in these journals a household on the razor's edge, never far from hysteria, penury, and profound domestic disorder. May Bogan's death in 1936 (when Louise was almost forty) brought into focus the restrictions under which her mother had lived—not least, that of becoming middle aged, as her daughter then was, and seeing her energy and beauty fade.

Middle age for Bogan was marked by that further loss, already touched on, which took imaginative shape as the shrinking of the broad current of poetic life—although, ironically, one of her greatest lyrics celebrates the trope of its diminishment as a tiny stream, which is now only "Softly awake, its sound / Poured on the chilly ground" ("Song for a Lyre"). The poem responds to an outrageous, amusing, but soon cooled-off affair with the young poet Theodore Roethke ("Twenty-six years old, and a frightful tank," as she wrote to Edmund Wilson in June of 1935, exhibiting her fondness for diction, albeit typically in the context of well-managed word order and rhetorical buildup, that falls between coarseness and hilarity). Another poem in trimeters, the unpublished "Love Severally Rhymed," which is probably from the same time (it appears in the poetry appendix), employs a similar image of contraction in the life-stream, whose movement has been shrunken down into a mere modifier (both *poured* and now *running* being participial adjectives): The late stream is "Shallow, as in a dyke, / Running in a dream."

Both poems give us a picture of a poet who looks closely, closely listening, too, even to so quiet a sound as the chilly earth's absorption of a bit of water, under the autumn night. Bogan *was* a careful observer, in the way childhood teaches us to be. When she tries to recall in a 1934 journal her first memory of her mother, she admits that it comes in much later than her learning the "rain in the gutter, the mud and the sodden wayside leaves." Indeed, "[t]he grain in a plank sidewalk certainly came through more clearly" to her than did the actions of adults or of other children.

Sometimes ravished by the great as well as the common surfaces and half-obscured proportions of the object world and of the natural one, and at other times disturbed by the mysteriousness of the patterns whose meanings are never single and seldom exhausted, Bogan's instinct in both poem and prose, and in both formal-discursive and more personal-meditative vein, was to inspect and query the accidental surfaces of the moment in such a way that depths became visible, although perhaps not easy to bear: "What would they do if she began to cry: large, hot tears, from the eyes on her protruding head?" People passed "like water, each figure a moving hollow, rolling parallel to the shore." "The willows . . . let fall into foaming water a mist of reddening boughs."

Louise Bogan's fictions, never collected before, raise setting to a role equal in importance to that of character, while characters are faced, not with a fully dramatized conflict or an agon of ignorance that must be met with an ordeal of self-confrontation, but with insights that briefly illuminate a little of the path before them before the light goes out. Joyce had the idea that an epiphany or sudden burst of insight came at the high point of his own stories, but Bogan's characters aren't led up to such points: They *begin* in just such jaggedly perceptive states. Consider how the central figures of two stories from 1933 have to struggle to maintain an "ordinary" perspective because something below the surface has long been troubling their lives. Mrs. Tracy in "Conversation Piece" is drowning in a life of banal pleasantry (perhaps she is even becoming a little daft with it). Mrs. Read, to whom belongs the final moment of melancholy in "The Last Tear," is habitually too self-aware for the meditation about her daughter's being taken over by "nice" people to serve as more than a confirmation of her own misfired attempt to help her daughter Claire enter a more carefree life; instead of savoring her child's prospects, Mrs. Read is most struck by the extent to which Claire has wound up a rather dull and climbing girl, and this insight puts the seal of failure on her own life.

But because Bogan disbelieved that narratives of intimate self-revelation could have any merit—she wanted to create, she wrote to the novelist William Maxwell, not to confess—she often goes only a little way into the events in the lives of the many characters in whom she sees part of herself. What she was left with were the moods and fevers of small, clear moments, within a larger atmosphere of tension produced by reticence only partly in sympathy with itself, and by feeling that is always, of necessity, actively in excess of the occasion. Suffused with yearning, heated by curiosity, under orders from their frightened delight in patterns that *almost* speak out, Bogan's stories of spinsterish Emily Hough and the aging Viennese collector who cannot stay warm and the ruthless and romantic young girl whose drawing teacher disappoints her give heightened form to the charged fixations of Bogan's own thought.

At the same time, Bogan's gift for dialogue in stories like "Whatever It Is," "Conversation Piece," and "Not Love, but Ardor" accurately places her people in time and with reference to each other. Unlike Hemingway's dialogue, Bogan's is not the sort that implies a drama of suffering through the bravado of secrecy, but the kind that grounds an entire code of curiosity and freely sustained interpersonal imbeddedness. "Whatever It Is" illustrates the knack of presenting, entirely through the quotation of a letter, a little corner of a world with enormous *background*—kinships, friendships, former and future affections that might have been part of a larger novelistic situation or *donnée,* yet which, for all their brevity, seem curiously complete. This is why social satire comes readily to her aid.

Her satiric portraits are usually both intuitive and merciless—Duncan MacNeil, for example, in "Sabbatical Summer," who has hopeful standards and tender appetites but no heart. Duncan is easily cowed by the intrusion on his Manhattan summer of a wealthy aunt, whose pushy insistence on his help in ordering a complete edition of Trollope's village novels bound in ooze morocco with moiré *doublures* ruins Duncan's new romantic friendship. For although he despises the aunt's manners, he is something of a fussy collector himself, and it is finally his own prickly good taste that, provoked by the aunt whose effect on him he does not fully grasp, dissuades him from taking any further his infatuation with Sigrid, a somewhat bohemian flower child whose weirdly ornamented clothes are "not entirely clean." We and the author can sympathize with both the girl and Duncan—in fact, Bogan shared Duncan's fondness for walking down staircases into large formal rooms like the lower gallery in the American wing at the Metropolitan—but we do not see these characters continuing into their lives very far past the close of the story. Even when she crafts a penetrating verbal tableau for her characters—as when the letter writer in "Whatever It Is" notes that Evelyn catches her husband with the unlikely Margaret ("'It was Horace's embrace. Margaret was in it, but it was his'")—Bogan seems on the whole more comfortable with complexity of flavor than complexity of motive.

Mrs. Tracy, the lens figure whose perspective leads us through "Conversation Piece," is presented more sympathetically than Duncan or the letter writer, for we never see her from an external vantage; she is the primary observer of the varieties of climbing and clever, half-cultivated badinage on the part of the couple named Williams who have invited her and her husband for drinks. The genius of their portrayal lies in the shift to indirect discourse. Here is Mr. Williams barreling down on Mrs. Tracy; they had been speaking about the Nordic versus the less ambitious New England fashions of cooking fish:

"My friend, Knud Swenson, the pianist, has told me all about Scandinavians and fish," Mr. Williams went on. "Do you know Knud?" No, she didn't know him. "Grand fellow; plays Mozart beautifully. Odd thing, for a Scandinavian to play Mozart so well, isn't it?" She agreed. "You'd think that there'd be too much of that heavy saga business in them, wouldn't you? Are you fond of Mozart?" Very fond. "Do you play the piano at all?" A little. Did Mr. Williams play the piano? Yes, Mr. Williams played. It was unusual to find a male American who played the piano well, Mrs. Tracy had found. That was true, Mr. Williams agreed. If he hadn't gone to school in Leipzig, he probably never would have played the piano. Did Mrs. Tracy know Leipzig? No, she didn't.

In the end, however maddening, Mrs. Tracy's inertia is more appealing, or at least less appalling, than Mr. Williams's zeal, because it is not in her to preen.

A more active observer emerges in the female companion in "Saturday Night Minimum," whose acquiescence to the man is yet sharply critical of his self-love, his admiration for his own elegant spoken syntax and for the effect he thinks he must be having on the room about him; the protagonist notes down those "quick little licks his eyes gave . . . as his sentences formed their balance, led up to their verb," then gathered up their conclusions. Something of Bogan's disdain for the intellectual, "the fine nervous flower of the bourgeoisie," finds its way into this sketch.

A third sort of sketch at which Bogan excelled is based on one concerted twist of style, whether within the small circle of an urban mood-piece such as "Winter Morning" (tightly reined in by the frame of one long, solitary sentence) or in a more objective array of images of a tiny population engaged in self-denying busy-ness (she shows us, in "Art Embroidery," the many women in a department store, just as it opens, heading to the trays of aniline wools and samples of Italian hemstitching). "It is the season," the speaker of another city piece, "Soliloquy," tells us, "when joints of pipe in excavations are wiped with hot lead, and when brown crusty garlic appears in thin bent wooden boxes in the fruit-store windows." It is as if the amusing prehistoric look of excavation sites and the faintly pitiable chips of dry autumn garlic provided satisfaction all the deeper as the phrases modifying them, somewhat out of logical synch with each other ("wiped with hot lead"; "brown crusty garlic") sent out only small sparks of an intuition that would be soon lost. Then suddenly, like a flame across the page, comes a statement of fact too terrible to be embellished by what has the feeling of style: "Once I saw a child try to kiss its mother's cheek, while she beat him off with screams." Hidden in plain view, the reverberant sentence stands at the center of "Soliloquy," yet nothing in the somewhat exploratory rhetoric of the whole leads either up to, or, afterward, away from it. It is a stricken place. No recognition, no cleansing, no recovery is possible from the shocking, involuntary gesture of a mother's hysteria and the implied desolation of the child.

Other prose sketches turn on similarly involuntary, disturbing sentences, which the narrators always carry about with them, unforgettable, as Bogan writes in "Dove and Serpent," "because we cannot understand them, and because they are of no use." Bafflement is the beginning of the doubts and uncertainties peculiar to the artist. The child-narrator of this closely autobiographical sketch is attempting to "read" the designs held in place by the adults about her. The entire story is based on the inscrutability of these patterns, acts, and objects, which do not appear to include the child who watches (the greatest uncertainty being generated by those closest to her: "My mother," she admits, "went about her life with an air of great secrecy"). Secondarily troubling are the things at the house of neighbor Mrs. Parsons (the son's sword and a string-dispenser in the shape of a doll in a paper skirt), which rebuff the child's scrutiny: "The sword had a tasseled belt twisted around its handle. The doll's little feet under the paper skirt, the string appearing from the middle of a rosette in its sash, its bisque head and real hair and small mouth open in a smile—this was a problem I could not solve." (We discover from the journals that there *was* a neighbor named Mrs. Parsons, also that the family in the well-ordered house were actually called Gardner, and that it was indeed Jack Leonard who terrified the children.) Another insoluble riddle is this same Leonard's quotation of the paradox from Matthew 10:16, when Jesus advises the twelve about the world into which he is sending them: "'We must be wise,' he said to my mother. 'We must be as wise as the serpent and as gentle as the dove.'" With these, the first words the child had ever heard from Mr. Leonard that were not profane, the frightening neighbor closes up his knife and lays a perfectly peeled apple on the kitchen table. Danger clings to the knife even as it is closed, to the mouth from which, it is hinted and feared, curses might at any moment shoot forth; but most of all danger hovers over the untrustworthy mother, who unaccountably bestows charity upon so mad and unsavory an old man.

"Dove and Serpent" also contributes its autumnal images to Bogan's lifelong meditation on that period in the fall that seems to have been "saturated through with a strange, chill, almost intolerable air of grief," but one that, instead of imposing on the soul the "agony that it seems to foreshadow and presage," instead leads to "a strange and piercing joy." "[E]verything in the town went wild in autumn and blew about the streets." As winter looms, families close off little-used areas of the house; the chill that falls releases something in her imagination: "The upper rooms smelled of cold plaster and cold wood. The parlor was shut; the piano stood shut and freezing against the wall." Every time a piano appears in Bogan's notes and sketches, something of herself is projected, as well as the premonition of a way of life that is passing. She was clearly one of those solitary temperaments whose earliest companions were things, whose inscapes spoke to her soul. Later, she recognized the thrilling human achievement of ornamental design, coming to believe that the *hand* must cry out, with its own expression, as well as the heart. Pattern is the link between the two, and the order of the life to which it is given to create the pattern. Thus, even simple actions take on an aura that is almost artistic, because suggestive of the gesture of design. Bogan maintained a fondness for certain plain images that suggest an alternative life, into which she might (but does not) step: women hanging out laundry in the sun, for example, had early associations with wind in autumn, later on overlaid with the sight of women lifting their wash to the lines on rooftops visible from the psychiatric hospital in Manhattan where she was being given hydrotherapy. "Clotheslines always stir my heart," she wrote William Maxwell. Even in some of her fragmentary poems that meditate on aging, the room to which the narrator may climb will not be sorrowful or lacking in amenity if there be but solitude and a few groceries and a narrow bed, also a desk, and the sight of women pinning garments to a clothesline on a distant rooftop.

As an artist of prose, tempering elevation with the rush and flair of immediate speech (like Henry James), and then, like another of her favorite authors, André Gide, taking up prose in order to surprise, worry through, and gauge her insight into some odd, new element in herself, we see Bogan also testing the pertinence of word and phrase against the discoveries opened by earlier styles. Time and again, we feel her tracing the periodic sentence-frame high-spiritedly hammered up by Bacon and Browne, made majestic by Gibbon and personal by Swift, testing the point at which she can drive it in a new experimental direction—even, or perhaps especially, by trimming it back. As she wrote in a letter to an aspiring review writer in 1948, one must write with the ear. "This 'writing with the ear' is really the best technical practice you can give yourself. Remember that the reader's attention span is usually v. short. I *cut* and *cut* my sentences, right up to the last version; always keeping the adjectives down to a minimum and the adverbs practically down to zero. The *verb* can do so much!"

Taking her own advice, Bogan tended to discard the just-finished draft and go back to the beginning, on a fresh sheet of paper. She liked to feel the arguments in the sentences opening up beneath her pen as her arm moved across the page; this physical rhythm, and the palpable piling up of newly finished pages, she found both helpful to the fresh springing of her ideas and essential to the honest crispness of the style of any piece she undertook to compose. "I do love the thought running uniform and true throughout the balanced sentence," she wrote in 1940 to her friend, the critic Morton Dauwen Zabel. Her book-length study of twentieth-century American poetry from 1951 came into its final form when she had turned away from earlier versions and set about to recompose all one hundred pages of her exposition *from the beginning.* As for her working method, she wrote her prose out *longhand* "to keep the tone flowing and natural," as she said of her translation of Goethe's *The Sorrows of Young Werther* (produced in collaboration with Elizabeth Mayer). Not only did she come to trust the tempo at which prose emerged from the hand, she also claimed to be able to move forward through successive versions toward ever greater depth of insight. "You must teach the Unconscious to flow into the channel of writing," she wrote in one of her few "how-to" explanations, in a 1933 journal, and that channel had to be mediated by the hand that held the pen.

Bogan brought the brief review into high profile as a form open to both learning and argument (and she could say more in five hundred words than most writers can in five thousand), and she took stands: She pointed out works she thought misdirected (*Finnegans Wake,* for example). She did not refrain from negatively reviewing the work of friends (like the poet Allen Tate). Nor did she fail to acknowledge the weak spots in writing of which she was nevertheless quite fond (such as the fiction of Elizabeth Bowen) or the crotchets of the masters whose achievement she considered profound (Henry James stands out in this regard). To Bogan also goes the credit for bringing James back into prominence as a reader's rather than a scholar's storyteller, highlighting the works to which she herself was partial, the lesser-known middle-period novels *The Bostonians, The Awkward Age, The Tragic Muse,* and the daring tragedy of the artist with a social conscience and an unbreakable devotion to truth, *The Princess Casamassima*. Bogan wrote (*against* the views of critics like Van Wyck Brooks and Stephen Spender) that James employed his protagonist, the illegitimate artisan Hyacinth, as "a cool and undistorting mirror" inserted "between the dark and violent world of the disinherited on the one hand and the preposterous world of privilege on the other." As for whether James's presumed snobbery prevented him from accurately portraying the depressed social classes, Bogan argues, as someone who has seen them firsthand, that in this novel James proves his knowledge of "the relentless mechanisms of poverty—poverty's *minutiae*." But James was first and foremost someone who saw into the heart. That human beings in the work of such an artist are paradoxes to themselves requires a fine touch to accommodate the necessary self-masking: "she bears a grudge," observes Bogan of James's princess, who is actually Christina Light from his earlier novel *Roderick Hudson* —a grudge "against society strong enough to force her into repudiation of everything her trained taste fully values." Pages of analysis have been concentrated in these few, corrosive drops.

Bogan was also adept at pinpointing far-reaching cultural phenomena, and indicating what they might mean for poetry. Insight often took the form of the prose epigram—for example, "The artist, as one Marxian critic has pointed out, does not function in a vacuum. Neither does he function out of a vacuum. Poetry is an activity of the spirit . . . and it withers if that nature is denied, neglected, or negated" (from LB's contribution to Harold E. Stearns, *America Now* [Scribner's, 1938]). Her impulse was always to fight for the individual against the large-scale program, and to face whatever difficulties life threw in her way. The epigram gave her a form for dramatizing that struggle: "At my present age [sixty] one is permitted hope but not *ambition*"; "Form hurts. It brings in anguish, along with sublimity"—some of these bordering on the *maxime,* a harsh or paradoxical truth: "One needs the help of the imagination to die"; "It is some comfort to remember that all the persons of genuine wickedness I have known in my life have been as stupid as dogs." She mused early in World War II that too much efficiency "attracts bombs." When the *maxime* pertained to art, the tailoring of insight to author sometimes obscured the surprising rightness, also the risk taken, in the compression, when contrasted to the epigram about general experience; only those who know something of the writer can estimate the depth of the risk. In the polished perfection of Elizabeth Bowen's fiction, the long tediums of lived experience, which are the province of prose fiction, are largely absent: "The *longueurs,*" Bogan observed, "are deleted to such an extent that they are missed." It seemed to her that Robert Lowell played the double role of misfit and leader—"*poète maudit* and *chef d'école*"—and in this cleverly turned comment took account of Lowell's privilege as well as his genius. About James Joyce there is for her the suspicion that in *Finnegans Wake* he himself may not have known what he was doing: "There is nothing whatever to indicate that Joyce has any real knowledge of the workings of the Subconscious, in sleep or otherwise. Carroll has far more intuition than Joyce into the real structure of the dream"—a statement that might temper the excesses of the many academic groomers of Joyce who assume the contrary. Then there is the pithy statement of terrifically complex, deeply absorbed, minutely examined, and long-percolated knowledge about culture and art. Bogan comments on a more than accidental link between two apparently unconnected events on the timeline of history: namely, that James's late novel *The Golden Bowl* was written in the same year as the French composer Claude Debussy's *La Mer,* which Bogan called "one of Impressionism's triumphs," implying that the James novel was another. Bogan's essay on Goethe concludes with the observation that the most extraordinary artistic evocation of Goethe's "power and poetic range" comes not from another writer, but "through the fifty-one songs written to his lyrics by Hugo Wolf." It almost jolts us to be reminded how powerfully Wolf's songs have responded to the language of yearning and sorrow in Goethe's lyric poems, and how seldom literary artists have responded in kind to Goethe's poetic *oeuvre*. Of Emily Dickinson she observed that, during a period of radical evangelicalism, Dickinson "set herself against the guilt and gloom inherent in this revivalism, but not before the visionary accounts of conversions had opened a dark door in her imagination. It was the mystic's door." So complementary are the exactness of insight and the sharpness of expression that one does not for a moment doubt that Bogan had stood at this same door.

Bogan was not only a great metrical poet but one whose employment of both free verse and *vers libéré* provided her with enormous artistic power; she knew when, and how, to loosen out her line. She recognized in the hatred of form a "typical bourgeois notion" that opened the way to the false democracy of folk art. She believed strict obedience to the demand to break old conventions became "as hampering as any rigid meter when it rules out *any* return to form." She also believed the line of feeling had to be visible beneath all those waves of experiment. This allowed her to discriminate between great works like "Little Gidding" and the somewhat sad rumblings of the "Rock-Drill." As for the periodic cry that poetry was dead, Bogan traced this plaint to the Sunday book section where the professional "middle" operates: "The middle wishes poetry to throb . . . under the historic processes without a break," deaf to the fact that "poetry of a lyric order disappears for a century at a time." At the same time, she was alert to the freshness of certain innovators whose gifts were not strictly lyrical. Bogan was one of the first American critics to notice and review W. H. Auden, who did so much to "break down artificial barriers of form and tone," and she remained intellectually and emotionally responsive to writers as different from one another as Isak Dinesen, Caitlin Thomas, and Dorothy Richardson; her taste in poetry kept her open to Valéry as well as Yeats, to Juan Ramón Jiménez as well as T. S. Eliot. She liked the detective novel and the directness and simplicity of Colette, but she also relished the stylized dialogue-novels of Ivy Compton-Burnett, the broad cultural sweep of Flaubert's *L'Education sentimentale* (which she thought a devastating portrayal of the intellectual as an obsessive hobbyist), and *The Bostonians'* exact social atmosphere of "post-Abolition idealism" and fragmentary cults, both revolutionary and dogmatic. One artist frequently opened her understanding of another (as Yeats helped her understand Lorca, because it seemed to her that both came from countries still rooted in a peasant tradition, with a middle class that had fully developed only within their lifetimes).

However different the artists of whom she wrote, the intimacy of Bogan's criticism reminds us of the style of a journal or letter, while the fact that the letters are written by someone clearly educated and high-principled also brings the genres together. In addition, writers far removed from her sensibility clearly nourished her and sparked coincidences between her own preoccupations and theirs, as when she discovered in Charles Baudelaire's poems the same "look and feeling of those times of day and of those turns of the seasons when the city's sadness is, as it were, distilled and the full, cold mystery of existence leaks through into our consciousness." We might be reading a meditation rather than a review-essay.

Blending between categories presents pleasurable interplay in much of the prose Bogan produced. In addition to the urban sketch, Bogan is responsible for giving new weight to another interesting hybrid—the questionnaire. In part indebted to Socratic probing, in part to the more conversational dialogues of Valéry, and influenced too by often impertinent promotional queries from the press, the book club, the reading group, and the academy, Bogan's questionnaire dramatized, in the questions as well as the answers she devised, her disdain for confession and for gossip when it took the place of ideas, upholding against the glibness of the marketplace her belief in the poet's terrible struggle. She wrote her Scribner's editor, the poet John Hall Wheelock, in 1935, when a women's group asked for her profile, that she would let down her guard only so far as "to let the comfortable creatures know that it is out of poverty, fear, and disaster that poetry grows." Thus, her apparently direct response to the *Partisan Review*'s queries about models and influences is a work of exact and impassioned prose about a partially hidden subject (the very terms of the questionnaire), reaching almost instantly the points on which her belief ran counter to the editors': the limited array of American writers of worth (since they asked, she chose James over Whitman); the meanness and neuroses of liberals; and the dubious value of politics and parties: "The true artist will instinctively reject 'burning questions' and all 'crude oppositions' which can cloud his vision or block his ability to deal with the world," meanwhile remaining the only source of the world's true freedom, and the only figure who can endure it and understand what it costs.

When Bogan took the questionnaire inward, to a more expressive form (because hers were the questions), she adhered to her own advice that, except for the novel, which requires the dry patches and *longueurs* of unfolding, all literature must be succinct, sharp edged, and *dramatic*.

> *Have you ever been alone, before this? Can you remember?*
>
> It is hard for me to remember anything by an act of will. . . . But when I was not alone, I had a dream of nourishing loneliness. I saw it all, including the time of day falling through the windows. I sat in a chair, a book upon my knees. There was no time of which I was the product or for which I waited. I looked upon this vision with joy. I can no longer. . . .
>
> *You did not note architecture, or the weather?*
>
> Yes, I noted these always. I saw the afternoon shadows deeply strike through the Baroque windows, as I had seen them fall, in my childhood, deeply slant and fall, drawing the eye inward into unimagined interiors. . . . I noted the excesses of plaster and the beautiful horizontal reticences of wooden shutters. I saw the shadows lengthen to such a degree that the ground had no more place for them.

It would be hard to name another poet in the twentieth century for whom the variety of modes of expression outside verse were so forcefully present, and for whom the essay and letter, like the memoir and questionnaire, permitted so urgent and satisfying a summons to her always evolving understanding of history and humanity. These modes relied as well on her openness to the exact shades of season, time of day, and impending or lifting weather. Her narrators speak both in journal and story from a protected vantage about unprotected suffering and equally imposing joy. (This is what distinguishes her journals from mere diary.) In the letters as well, the voice is often only a few steps away from the turmoil recorded, but the fact that there is a record at all proves an advance in mastery over the rawness of life. Shape is achieved at a remove that is both enabling and instinctive.

Occasionally in journals there will be thumbnails like those in the letters —on Mabel Dodge, Viola Meynell (whose fiction Bogan believed in and tried to get published in the United States), and Ernest Hemingway, whom she described in language more barbed than that of even the most negative views expressed in any essay. Nevertheless, this candid and virulent paragraph on Hemingway's "decadent, stupid, and even a little obscene" admiration for bullfighting has behind it a fuller force of presenting argument than do similar passages in her letters. Journal writing did not require the author to excuse or, by standing ready to pay for her views, implicitly soften them; the letters did. Even gentler ruminations needed their grounding. But when she records in her notebook the flaws of spirit in the self-important, or the somber yet exciting turn to the autumn equinox, Bogan can pick up the thread of the old conversation with herself without the offhand but nevertheless deflecting and excusing provisos that lie behind the letter writer's role as impresario of a more public self.

During the last fifteen years of her life, the letters become more explanatory and less high-spirited, just as the impulse to get things down in journals seems to taper off. Her fiction ceased with the thirties. The desire to fathom intensity has cooled. One reason for the change in the letters may be that she is writing, for the most part, to people younger than herself—new friends, not those who helped *her* grow as she helped them. The exchanges with Theodore Roethke, and later with William Maxwell and aspiring poet May Sarton, trace a declining arc—a less unguarded intimacy and a more pronounced withholding of self—which parallels the absence of reciprocity, for she could give these younger writers far more (more help, more wisdom, more proof of an artist's tried and accustomed power) than they were able to give her. A motherly instinct came into play, particularly with William Maxwell, who also awoke unwelcome desire in Bogan, which she sublimated into interest in his fiction, and into a lightly charged and kindly affection that made more poignant the complex background, which she had worked through so painfully, behind the want of sustaining maternal resources in her own life. Psychotherapy had helped her to understand and, in part, to forgive, but, as she wrote to Zabel, such self-exploration "can only cure, it cannot console."

The poems Louise Bogan left behind are castoff material, either juvenilia or published but uncollected work, or poems once collected but not reprinted in *The Blue Estuaries,* or drafts (dated and undated) that remained in assorted states of incompletion. Bogan would have surmised that what she left behind might one day see print, but I doubt she would approve. Work that was still under weigh, or which exhibited some excess she had been unable to correct (as in the longest poem she ever wrote, "The Flume"), or poems that were still somewhere in the stages of a sketch, do not reveal the poet at her zenith. These poems do, however, show the return of themes from the major lyrics in the disguise of incomplete transformation; the group as a whole fills out the picture of Bogan's gifts as she struggled to forge them with intense feeling. Pleasantly, occasionally, the verbal gestures we know from her approved canon repeat themselves in unaccustomed form, with a new drama, as when in "Three Sonnets in Autumn" the speaker commends change and the great shifts of cloud and "symbols of running dark and night" under the sign of passion. It is as if the past, when time was so clearly passing "most intent in its groove," were more glorious without the very figure who made the present come alive—this "you, who, half darkened, half in light, / Stymied, forsaken, hold me now in love." In "Man Alone," a poem she did collect, Bogan would play another game with time, now mistrusting the present lover from the vantage of future betrayal: "your infatuate eye / Meets not itself below: / Strangers lie in your arms / As I lie now." The poet has sketched the character of a man (probably Holden) who needed always to see himself reflected in the books he read and the women he made love to. Both poems pose the paradox of imaginative release within a frame of collapsing time in which passion is about to cease, or was never set free into the portended, and fiercely desired, present tense.

It is also a great pleasure to witness some of Bogan's experiments with the verse line, as she relinquishes to expression all the time it needs, until a line seems almost to waver like a tall forest tree. Consider the splendid fourteeners that do *not* split into four-and-three: "Tears were shed, sobbed to wild herbs in a field, whatever their causes"; "Perhaps the secret voice you hear under your mouth was all I could keep" ("The Catalpa Tree"). Her long lines more typically imply a context of shorter ones, whose rhythmical contrasts she orchestrates well, helping her test an idea as it builds. As early as 1917, in "The Young Wife," we see Bogan working out the risky dynamic in loosened stanzas. In tighter ones, her control is still more arresting, since feeling is sufficiently exact to be instantaneous with the saying. Here are the final two stanzas of the three-stanza "December Daybreak," composed in 1967. Trimeter lines predominate, very short dimeter lines punctuate, and against both rise up the comparatively unexpected yet satisfying lengths of the two thoughtful pentameter and hexameter lines:

> But the dream shoots forward to a future
> We shall never see;
> Therefore, in December's night, at the beginning of the morning
> We must give over and be
>
> Once again the ignorant victor
> Or the victim, wise
> Within those proven but broken circles of wisdom
> By which the living live
> And the dead rise.

(from "December Daybreak")

Her anti-adverb strictures aside, Bogan's genius with the adverb and adverbial-prepositional phrase is evident throughout these drafts and discarded poems, combined with her fondness for certain verbs whose intuited wishes the adverbial extensions obey—*pour, set, span, swing, seal, rise, cast, shut*—and the adverbial extensions of which come close to defining Louise Bogan's expressive signature: *give out, count out, give over, give into, pour out from, die out from, rise by, beat under, strike short, drag back, weep downward, seal to, kiss to, make to, stir to.* Not infrequently, the verb serves also as a noun, as when Bogan tells the stone in the heart of the woman in "The Flume" to let her sharpen herself like a blade against it: *Give her whet to the blade.* Nor are the adverb-phrases always as odd as the perceptions guiding them: leaves fall in ravines, *through bitter smoke.*

At the same time as a signature implies a contract with control, the lexical grain and the slant of her syntax point past control to a half-reluctant conversation with a force beyond art and beyond the arena within which art becomes a publicly recognizable endeavor; here she encounters the fitful but unmistakable face of her own daemon. "The universe swings up against my sight." Those qualities that make her lyric *oeuvre* pure and dramatic (rather like a cross between George Herbert and Charles Baudelaire, with streaks of an aggressive parsimony of spirit resembling Emily Dickinson's) also give to Bogan's prose directness of effect alongside a mysterious hesitancy, as if the writer were inching backward toward an abyss, whose edge, from many earlier approaches, the author already almost-knows.

All readers of Louise Bogan are indebted to the poet's first literary executor, Ruth Limmer, and to Bogan's biographer, Elizabeth Frank. The Pulitzer was, quite properly, awarded to Frank in 1986 for *Louise Bogan: A Portrait*. There are few better literary biographies, for the simple reason that thinking like an imaginative writer is not within the reach of most historians, however expert their scholarship. Frank's effort is the more remarkable in light of the fact that all the manuscripts of Bogan's poems prior to 1929 were destroyed in the Hillside fire, when the farmhouse she and Raymond Holden had restored burned to the ground, and when one recalls how fiercely reticent Bogan was about what she called in 1961 the "outright narrative" of her life, with its "rough and vulgar facts": The poet "represses" then absorbs this narrative, Bogan wrote, until, she insisted, "The repressed becomes the poem." And indeed Frank has dared to trace the line of life under the exertions and indirections of the poetry. Although, as she admits, "To read the poems as autobiography violates their privacy, and their formal presence," nevertheless it "completes their sense."

Ruth Limmer took seriously an executor's responsibility to keep the author's work before the public. She arranged for the publication of three separate volumes of prose: Bogan's essays (which were already in press, coedited with Robert Phelps, at the time of Bogan's death in February 1970); her letters; and a biographical sampler incorporating some of the journals, which Limmer styled a "mosaic." The fact that all of these works have long been out of print was the spur for assembling *A Poet's Prose: Selected Writings of Louise Bogan*.

What follows is limited by the fact that selections from three books, two of them longer than four hundred pages, plus the uncollected fiction and poetry had to appear in one book. Some choices were difficult, but all were guided by a desire for breadth in both topic and tone. The letters were hard to excerpt because they are often partial scripts for the ongoing drama of her friendships: Light spots count as strongly as the dark, and have been woven into the rhythms of their lives. The long journals describing Italian art could not be represented, nor could the scores of lists she kept of the many hundreds of books she was about to get from the library, or was then in process of reading; the breadth and voracity of her reading, and the energy with which she trained herself to speak to a general public, proves itself in her critical writing. Precisely because her skeins of association between artists are so revealing, the criticism was yet harder to limit. So to those who regret as I do the absence of the long essays on Emily Dickinson, on Frost, and on formal poetry; of any of the pointed and informative chapters from *Achievement in American Poetry;* of the work on Rilke's spiritual ethos in his prose; of the essays on Eluard, surrealism, and European poetry; of the essays on mythology—to these readers I can only suggest that the essays included here, if not as well known, are as informed and pointedly eloquent. It remains to be seen whether readers might work out for themselves what Bogan had to say about absent figures like Virginia Woolf and Stefan George and Hart Crane; and whether they might extrapolate from the letters included here to the many hundreds of others, like those to her daughter, that mix advice about grooming and diet with directions about getting the apartment floor waxed and the curtain rods repaired. Bogan lived in the world, and faced the banal, as everyone must. ("*How* I hate to dust!" she wrote, with ingenious emphasis.) But it seemed more to the point, given Louise Bogan's feelings about the nearness of financial disaster despite her frugality, that the present volume give the letters she wrote to Rolfe Humphries and Morton Zabel in 1935 about being evicted from her apartment, and that there be excerpts from one of the most interesting *continuous* sequences of letters, written in a veritable maelstrom of paranoid anxiety from Ireland in 1937 to Zabel and Edmund Wilson, in which Bogan drives herself to render her onrushing mental state as it responds to the shifting backgrounds of place. Also that the letters here reflect something of the arc of her life, the hospital stays, the deaths in her immediate family, the honors she was late in receiving, her unceasing efforts to proceed with a feasible schedule of review work on demand. It is also something of a shock to hear what Bogan has to say late in her life on popular figures like the actress Jeanne Moreau and her "concupiscent" affect in

Louise Bogan in Her Prose

Jules et Jim, on cultural phenomena like Susan Sontag on pornography, or the merits of John Updike's novel *Rabbit, Run.* She wrote scathing indictments, often laced with hilarity, of academic icons like John Crowe Ransom and of artistic ones like Martha Graham, whose impersonations, in dance, of Clytemnestra and Emily Dickinson (the latter holding one toe toward heaven) the poet notes with sharply described and derisory delight. Louise Bogan was the sort of person her friends were always hastening to recommend things to. I for one wish I could have pressed into her hands the works of García Márquez and Primo Levi and Iris Murdoch and Merleau-Ponty on Cézanne and Anne Carson and J. M. Coetzee—just to see how she would take them up and turn them to the light and make them new, and in so doing reveal herself afresh.

Mary Kinzie
September 2004

A Poet's Prose

I

Fiction

Keramik

FOR THE first time that summer the gentleman at the table next the lattice was dining alone. His face was tanned like good moroccan leather. The bridge of his curved, fleshless nose was peeled from the sun. The shaven hair at his ears and at the back of the bald skull matched his fine gray flannel shirt almost perfectly. His cuff links were moonstones set in silver. He wore two rings, a cat's eye set in platinum, and a platinum band striped with diamonds, on the little finger of his left hand. The brown, nervous old hands spread the paper money fanwise on the cloth. One waiter from a group that lounged in a corner, their heads together as though they were conspirators in a matter of great import, slid toward him, astonishingly alert suddenly. "*Arrangez,*"[1] the gentleman said to him, and rose stiffly from his chair.

It was getting dark earlier and the splayed leaves of the chestnuts were sallow and dried, immediately above the lights.

In the courtyard near the kitchen, waiters passed and repassed, bearing silver dishes on napkins, the whole length of their forearms. They carried them with a strange swinging motion, as though in this way only not one drop of the precious gravy would be spilled, not one leaf of the salad disturbed. The little *chambres séparées* were filling up gaily. Above the absurd steep roof hung the fresh and ordered stars.

It was nearly autumn. There could be no doubt of it any longer. The vase in the motor was stuffed with stringy asters. Then, what seemed to be whole heaps of leaves rushed under the wheels. Of course, they never swept the streets any more. Girls and young men walked by, holding each other close, in the chilly evening. The barrow of the fruit woman at the corner of Bellaria Street was full of apples. Cherries and plums were over. The gentleman, balancing his chin upon hands clasped over a stick, on the gray cushions of the perfect motor, had reason to feel cold.

The big stone hallway smelled of damp plaster and soap. It was unreasonable to expect Anna to have lighted a fire, he thought, sliding his hand along the thin iron rail of the curving stairway. No one built fires in these frugal times because of one dismal September day.

It was half-past eight. An hour ago Else had still been waiting for him. He thought of her sitting sideways at her dressing table, glancing furtively at her small powdered face in the mirror, becoming restless and unhappy. Her lapis beads grazed that lovely hollow of her collarbone, that always shone freshly, pearlily, like a groove of a shell.

By now she had become angry, had ordered a cab, and was lifting hors d'oeuvres delicately between her fork and spoon from their platter to her plate, in that other garden that amused her, where so many English came, and there was music.

But it pleased him most to imagine her waiting for him, she and her shadow in the mirror, half mournfully looking down at her low-heeled slipper and thick silk stockings, and drawing her long gloves through her hands.

The gentleman inserted the heavy key into the lock of a door on the third landing. He held himself stiffly erect from his hips. His body, under the gray coat, was solid and alive. But the legs were thin: they seemed to dangle from the hips. They were spare old legs that would ache in the approaching autumn.

All the veiled lights in the silken room flashed on as ever. Thank heaven for that! The sconces on either side the couch, the lovely dyed shade on the table beneath the portrait, the tiny lamp in the alcove beside the bed: all alive and the same. Here, too, it was quite warm. He drew off his gloves with a relieved puff of breath.

The bright figurines in their shelved glass case blinked with glazed reflections. The gray and mauve girl gathered her curiously designed hair away
from her neck and breast. Her raised arms and leaning body were beautifully
unrelated arcs. The peasant in the red cap, on hands and knees, looked into
the eyes of a doe that stood trembling before him. The gentleman's stick
struck lightly against the glass box, and all the figures rattled faintly.

Anna had laid out dressing gown and lounging suit across the embroidered linen coverlet of the narrow bed. The dressing table, shaded by a screen
from the lamp, still twinkled here and there from the diminished light at
the window. Some woman had shuddered at all those tortoise-shell boxes
and distorted scent-bottles, set in their silver brocade tray. She had said that
it was like the horrible table in a theatre, where an old woman watches girls
powder their faces and necks, and gropes with hatred after the coins they
leave in her basket.

The woman in the portrait above the gleaming table and its lamp stared
at him, while he rubbed eau-de-cologne under his bony hawk's nose and
brushed his cropped gray hair. She sat in an oak chair, and watched him. She
and the playbill that bore her name and hung, framed in narrow black on
the wall opposite, were whole, in the half-darkness. He felt refreshed and
warmer. Surely a gentler breeze had come up. The chill might die out before morning. He undid the window and opened it outward. The trees below
were parted and closed again by that gentle wind. There they were, the vir-
tuous dead woman he had never met, and himself, in the gray silk rooms. And
there was that girl, out beyond in a garden where there was music. She was
finishing her coffee now, and listened to the violins with shining lashes closed
over deep eyes.

They were no longer his affair, women, dead or alive. The woman hidden
in the dark oils of her portrait had loved the man who had once lived in these
rooms. An actress, very gentle, very sensitive. She had killed herself because
of the breaks and pauses in the midst of love, the faltering between kiss and
kiss. Unfortunate: driven and destroyed by nothing. Caught and crushed between words, kisses, farewells: handsful of air, nothings.

The cherry brandy made a bright funnel-shaped spot in the solid liqueur
glass. Here was reality! The panatela, that too, and the cat's eye set in platinum, evil and mud-green, on the brown knotted finger. He put the tray with
the square bottle, the cigar-box, and the one glass, on the table before the
couch. The room quivered and shone. The smoke from his cigar rose in reflection in the mirror between the windows.

He had taught them all something and had learned nothing in return. There was always more to teach. They were all so much at sea, so stupid or so given to dreams. With each new lover their lives stopped or began. With him they were greedy, or chattering, or vain,—freer than a younger man could make them. They all had been so brief that they were perfectly, sharply outlined. They never thought themselves insecure, although tomorrow they were gone. All brief, save that one wise, quiet girl.

The thin, big-eyed Russian,—he had taught her to sit immobile, to move her eyes only, to play with trifles in her sharp fingers, to smile. When she moved her head the loose skin on her neck wrinkled too easily. The woman from Bucharest, long-waisted, firm-bosomed, had eaten too briskly. He had cured her of that. The hard-legged young French blonde had talked too much, opening her mouth widely over her crowded teeth. They had all learned something before he sent them away.

The sallow leaves fell down upon the tables in the garden. Had she taken her heavy wrap, or did she sit there shivering, while some young man, an acquaintance newly discovered, perhaps, or a stranger, delighted with those cool eyes, held a match shielded in his hand for her long cigarette?

She had not needed to come to him for knowledge. She had always been wise. She corrected his praise, sometimes, but took all that was due her with simplicity. His taste, so unfailing in all matters of fitness and beauty, included her. Therefore she held herself confidently with him and was at ease.

SHE LEANED against the gently curved cover of the inlaid chest. Her ivory shawl swept the reddish wood that was the color of a violin. Flowers, fruit, urns, and naked children were abruptly hidden by the ivory skirt that swept down to the thin, pure feet and ankles. Her hair was as pale as wheat over the square forehead, warmer with yellow in the heavy coil at her neck. Her amber beads, strung on red silk, hung down along her slight bosom and waist and thighs,—bright, weightless, almost to her knees.

The cigarette in her fingers went to ash. Not once did she raise it to her lips. She was inlaid against the blue window, intagliated into the dusk. Weeks would pass: the last leaves would skip over the paved courtyard, and snow would go by in white currents. She sat there leaning forward, bending forward from the curved wood, her body secure and desireless, her cigarette in spark and ashes.

Chords struck at random in some room out beyond beat against his hollow old heart. The brandy seemed to lie there, still holding its red funnel shape, in the block of his breast as in the liqueur glass.

She leaned forward, curved like a plume. His ears at once heard and said the music.

IN HER street the lights of a café are very bright under their grotesque shades. A piano spins out a fast wiry song. She fumbles in her bag for the portieress's money. But the young man has it already in his hand. He pushes the bell. The portieress wakens slightly, sleeps again. At the third ring she moves herself gently from her husband and leans down for her shoes.

"I must see you again soon."

"I am busy. You would have to telephone."

"We could go to the country some afternoon before it gets too cold. To that restaurant near the little artificial lake, some afternoon for tea, before the end of the month."

"You could telephone."

"You will forgive me if I tell you that I think you are beautiful?"

"Yes, yes."

"To have seen you again tonight! Let me telephone tomorrow."

"You are impatient."

"We have the same interests. We could do so many things together."

He kisses her hand, fervently, on the seams of the white glove. Her face and hair are one silver pallor in the shadow. Something not her heart is beating,—something like pity, like revenge, in the middle of her body. Her thoughts give quick runs and mimic theatrical gestures while she listens and knows how cold she is.

"I had an old lover. That is over now. 'I kiss your heart!' he said once to me." This disturbing acrobatic notion whirls in cartwheels around her brain.

THE SONG goes on and on, behind the chestnut leaves' lax fingers. The nuts in burred cases lie also on the stems. In spring the towering flowers had hung like little sponges in the rain.

The old body, tanned to the waist, and patched with graying hair, faces the woman lost in dark oils. The Schubert song links itself to the fans, combs, crests of the piano notes. Over and over: increasing forgetting, begun. The

powders and salves on the dressing case are closed in upon their own perfume. Who will use them again? Some woman brought in from the street in
winter, whose southern skin is cracking from the cold.

One figurine, blended out of the light, holds flowers in a spatulate hand
against his glazed breast. One sits upright, arms crossed on chest, like a gun-
ner on a caisson.

Voice and piano climb through the broken measure. The voice cries out
full and whole, hung on a strong breath.

He hears that voice. The lamplight burns on the sheets. He hears it and
gives it back and praises it and lets it fall into the well of his old heart, cooler
than women's wisdom, or passion, or chastity.

[1927]

Keramik: German for ceramics. The title refers to the porcelain figures the wealthy, aging
Viennese gentleman collects.
1. *"Arrangez"*: "Sort this out."

Winter Morning

OVER THE carefully arranged rhomboids and stars of the nut-shop windows: the pale pistachio border, the mixed center of butternut and walnut,
the crisp almonds looking their rich taste; over the lingerie stores, narrow
in cardboard boxes, hung with cheap crisp chemises all cut from the same
pattern, flattered with lace, colored like candy, with here and there a shift
of transparent chiffon black as the spots on dice; over chain grocery stores,
piled with canned pineapple and tomatoes and blocks of efficient soap; over
the windows where faded bergère[1] and damask are brightened by the flash
of glass full of silver leaves and flowers; over the closed mouths of garages,
behind which elevator and ramp rise through the dust in plaster angles of a
mechanical dream; over the fenestrated towers that shoot upward from the
eye, bent backward from the vision, balanced on narrow steel, but firm as
though buttressed by the very earth's iron kernel, springing upward as
though never to fall, and littered, throughout their shelved floors, by desk,

chair, telephone, water cooler, typewriter in interminable, incredible number; over the wide market streets, where boxcars and trucks now shunt out their fresh loads of meat, greens, yellow fruit, eggs; over empty theatres, the ceilings bent like rococo foreheads in sleep, above the dark cavern; over the sleekly packed apartments, whose doormen must soon come back to be seen behind the grilled doors like captured admirals; over the disorderly packed tenements, their fire escapes twisted about and downward like chains; over the elevated, whose patterned rails will fall in light and shadow, in the afternoon, upon the trucks and automobiles beneath, fleeing with them; over the elevated stations, with wooden-scalloped eaves, wherein the coal is almost burned out in the potbellied stove; over the shooting galleries and photographers' windows, lighted with a cold green glare, like the sun in hell; over stone horse and fountain; over women advancing with palms into the sky, deliberate, heroic, their bronze dresses blown out behind them by a wind always coming from the same quarter; over museum and newsstand, prison and subway entrance; over food, drink, bed; over the glut and the lack; it is winter morning. The horned head of a steam shovel called Bucyrus or Thew takes its first bite of earth and rubble and lets it fall; claps its flat mouth after it. The first red-hot rivet flies across from the forge to the bucket. From the blue acetylene torch, the first jet of sparks rockets down, rebounds and dissolves through the empty framework of girders.

[1928]

1. bergère: deep armchair.

Art Embroidery

THE ELEVATOR lets out a wheel of women. Here they are, on the fifth floor, in a garden of bright permanence, blooming with cushions, artificial flowers, piles of aniline wools, bleak wide lengths of linen stamped with repeated and intolerable blue designs. Here are towels full of cross-stitch, patchwork already cut out and put into bags ("a revival of the art of our grandmothers"), intricate canvas squares ready for high-bred needlepoint. Come and graze, good women. The cotton has been carded, the wool spun; the dyes are fast and the needles sharp and of great variety. Graze and forget time and love, hearty children, and the anatomy of the house. Here are gauzy lamp-shades, and the materials for their manufacture; you can veil every heartless sprig of electricity in your house with these. Sit here at this table and learn how to make a baby jacket with a pebbly surface. Or a pillow all of silk petals, or a fine rug garlanded about with roses, or a fire screen, with a conventional bouquet, nature twice removed, to be contrived by the crafty thread. Have you tried, you less ambitious, a bridge-cover with hearts and spades, a cover for hot biscuits, tea napkins with Italian hemstitching? Our grandmothers never knew about Italian hemstitching.—There are moments when embroidery is enough. There is time you do not need: prepare to clothe the bones of rooms with doily and rug and pillow; the bones of time with stitches that can be kept or thrown away, as you prefer.

To push through this female crowd is difficult. These backs and arms and sides have a terrific solidity. They are heavy—wider at the feet than at the head. They have clean gloves, obstinately bright glances (a veil pulled over the sagging lines that have been creased by animal pain, and by grief more deep than the flesh can remember; over the dull eyes so used to door and window, table, bed and chair, the curtain raised in the morning, the lamp lit at night, the known faces pressed again and again into the eyes), slightly perfumed bosoms, neat shoes. They can wait, three deep, shoulder to shoulder, at the counters under whose glass the cotton and silk lie pressed like keepsakes. Tons of machinery, enough to crack them all to bits, rock behind the walls, over the ceiling, under the floors. A beginning autumn day rushes toward its early evening; the clocks champ minutes and strike all in a row; today is never again; it is late; everything should begin. They have the linen in the hand now; the purse is opened; the money is paid. Now they have stitches for tomorrow, put in to clothe the hours. They have time.

[1928]

Soliloquy

HOW CAN you be sure, my good girl, in the favor of maturity and the half-dignity of bridled affection, that this is not your place, here under the hoarse rails and in front of the bridge ramped securely to the shore with intricate bulk and solidity? Cigarettes yellow the teeth and grief hardens the heart, and the day will come, don't be certain that it will not, when a good sleep, with your chin on your collar bone, leaning against the radiator in the Periodical Room, that warms you down to your paper shoes, will prove the most beneficent straw in the fat sheaf. Sleep in the day, a rug of sleep, hairy and heavy, pulled by the will up over the forehead, while beside you, beyond the double interference of window glass and balustrade, people pass, to be seen from the corner of the eye (were it open), like water—each figure a moving hollow, rolling parallel to the shore. Grasp, now as then, the penny of poetry in the pocket, though it cannot be spent for mature ends, or even minted out of the grown-up nature, in the brilliance of its piteous copper. It is the season when joints of pipe in excavations are wiped with hot lead, and when brown crusty garlic appears in thin bent wooden boxes in the fruit-store windows. It is the hour when harrowed women push their idle men out into the street, to walk up and down, not speaking to the child whose hand they hold. The child drags a little behind, and swings its small handbag in the shape of a suitcase. Determined to be itself under the muffler and stocking cap, lagging behind, pulling the man's hand backward, swinging its box. You can wander up and down, too, in this street where white iron beds show in the corners of the windows. That's a sizeable fur collar that you wear—walk in it up and down, and play that long game of forgetting, as though there were not enough lumber in the heavy mind, struck out of remembrance. Forget everything the moment that it happens: that's an excellent method of getting down a street, or up a stair, or into a house. Forget Bodwell's: the barroom downstairs, and the bloody collar that made such an impression upon your young eye when you saw it lying in the gutter, one Sunday morning. Forget those faces stuck to the heart like leeches, that you would wish to multiply into many, but which remain so few. Go in more for metaphor, that cloak, that subterfuge, and less for wincing. "It is like—" "It is like—": that's the way to get out from behind that proud visage, that hearty, indelible sneer.

Play at the hydrants getting up and walking at you, or invent one of those series of unrelated objects, that might do you proud, one of that swarm bred of
Rimbaud's billiard table at the bottom of the lake. Why were you not taught
the jargon of the metaphysician's impotence, or the philosopher's despair?

The streetcar goes looping up the bridge. Mere juggler's sleight. As
simple as the tread of the legendary crew locked into the zodiac's rim: up;
Crab, Lion, Gemini, Aquarius, Ram. Up and over me. Once I saw a child try
to kiss its mother's cheek, while she beat him off with screams. How any
terrified adult can be blamed, after that. You will break my hand off at the
wrist, you lag so far behind. A garden, looking between dahlia stalks, cindery,
full of old sunflowers and golden glows, facing the sun that walked down hill
with you, to the wooden barn stuck over with advertisements. Who said that
he had kissed the deaf-mute girl, behind the rusted tin sheath of an enormous
signboard, at the edge of town, on Saturday night in the rain?

This is a well-bred rock garden. It has been to the best schools. It received a cane with a diamond ferrule on the occasion of its engagement. It
breeds only in wedlock, and owns stock in bonded companies. In 1880 it was
planted, from seeds dropped under a glass bell by shell-roses. I will show you
all my rocks. At heart I am not a moralist. At heart I am a dropped smock
fit for any quatrain of Swift's. But when I am tired I like to shop for clothes,
and when I am hungry, I approve of patting on the head the defenseless, the
docile deer. I also like to pretend that I am living in everywhere I have ever
lived, at the same time. Do have some tea out of these cups of Florentine
leather bought in that charming shop run by the gentlewoman with the
blue teeth. Upstairs I have love enclosed in a parenthesis. The feudal idea
really sprang from the merchandising of sprockets and cams. Keep your relatives out of my way. They were brought up under a bureau. I don't approve.

Come home; come home. To the white iron bed and the scolding
mother, the white dish of meat and potatoes on the table under the gas.
There's a fire in the stove.

Be now, pure miracle. The dark rises and the rain falls. Within and without water speaks with two voices.

[1928]

Hydrotherapy

SHE OPENED the door and went in. This was the second time; she wasn't so frightened and she had come up alone. The long mirror again faced her, but she did not look into it. She had taken a vow against mirrors.

The fat nurse who winked, to point up casual remarks, said "Good morning," and the Swedish woman who was so expert with the hose said "Hello." She took off her wrapper and nightgown in a cubicle. Exactly like a bathhouse, except for the absence of sand and spiders. She wrapped herself in the sheet.

And again the fat nurse who winked said, as she handed over the paper cup of water: "Here's your cocktail. It's the only thing that's free around here, so why not have two?" Always the obedient patient, she took two. People needed to have their stock jokes appreciated in this world.

Two women were already baking in the cabinets. Their heads, wrapped around the throat with towels, protruded from the enamel boxes, and looked quite heated. Well-done. Unexpectedly, both of them smiled. She smiled back. The fat nurse gave her a chair and a tabloid. "Now just wait a while and read the scandals." She (the fat nurse) winked.

She sat beside a marble slab and a hopper full of salt. The sun shone brightly through one window on the rows of tubs, ordinary tubs, standing side by side, drawn up with parade-ground precision, and on the one extraordinary tub that had a wooden rim and was shaped like an enormous keyhole. The excessively pretty girl who was almost well of sleeping sickness buttoned the strap of her bathing suit and stepped into the keyhole tub. How odd that sleeping sickness should attack excessively pretty girls, and that a tired psyche should be her own lot. The girl began to do exercises under water. Ten years of sleep would be what she herself would choose. But no. Tonic baths for an aching heart. She sneered quietly down at the scandals.

HER CABINET was ready. The stool, as usual, was too high, so while the nurse adjusted it, she stood looking into the bright tin interior, at the heat and brightness pouring from the electric bulbs which studded the sides. She didn't care for this a great deal. The cold towel went around her neck.

She stepped up and sat down; the sheet slid off and she shut her eyes as the nurse closed down the flaps. It was frightening to see those flaps close.

Her hands were cold on her knees. She was terrified again. The pretty girl slowly raised a pretty right leg. That was ridiculous, of course, and she should laugh or cry. What would they do if she began to cry: large, hot tears, from the eyes in her protruding head? Let her out and slap her on the back? Keep her in till she melted? My God, the liberties people took with you when your heart broke! Fiends in human form, lightly disguised as hydrotherapists, inducted you into cabinets. Soon it would be so hot that she would cry out automatically. Not really, though. Too proud.

As a matter of fact, she began to feel better. All of her below the neck relaxed. She put her chin down on the towel and looked out the window. Someone was hanging out clothes on a roof. How sunny it was! What fun it would be to expect sleeping sickness next week, and meantime to float away, preferably on the wings of love, out of hydrotherapy into life. To drift away on pinions, and assist the woman on the roof at her clothes-hanging. To sail toward sleep, every morning at nine-thirty sharp. To give the heart, the psyche, a treat, an aërial adventure. To stand on a roof with a mouthful of clothespins.

THE NURSE pulled the flaps back. She was hot. The sheet was hotter. She walked over to the table dotted with dials and coiled with hose, and down to the shower. The needle-spray steamed. She walked into it. It crackled; it hit her at once sharply and delicately; subtly it changed temperature. Then the hosing began, from nape to heels, and that changed temperature too. Quite suddenly, it became icy cold, right at the waistline. "Turn around," said the Swedish nurse, and the spray hit her full in the diaphragm. All good comes from the diaphragm, according to the yogis. She had time to think of that before she lost her breath. She threw up her arms and squealed. "Turn around." She lost her breath again.

"All right." It was over. The Swedish nurse handed her a towel. "You feel good, eh?" Being a Swede, did she try to avoid the letter "j"? Why couldn't Swedes be comic, and include the letter "j"? "Hello," "Turn around," "You feel good, eh?" No chance there. She liked the Swedish nurse. She never would think of laughing at her. But she really should be warned against any tendency to build up a defense mechanism against the letter "j." It would get her in time.

She was rubbed dry. And suddenly, for a little moment, for a fraction of a clock-tick as she leaned against the wall to balance herself while she put her feet into her slippers, she felt very strange. Just for a split second, as she caught the eye of the fat nurse who winked, she stopped suffering.

[1931]

Sabbatical Summer

DUNCAN MACNEIL was always glad to tell people just why his father wasn't a millionaire. Something, a long time ago, had gone wrong with the parental hardware business. Duncan had gone to Harvard, but shortly thereafter he had had to go to work. Not to day labor, it is true, nor even to the leveling and deadening grind of the white-collar, non-professional classes. Duncan had a profession. He taught English literature in a day school in Cleveland. After five years of this, by hard practice of thrift, he was able to take what he was pleased to term a sabbatical summer in New York. He wanted to observe life, to make interesting contacts, and to study music. He was very fond of music. He even could perform: his rendition, on the piano, of Brahms was adequate if a little lax.

HE CAME to New York early one June. It was a year when the municipal government had taken it into its head to tear up large sections of the principal streets. Also, an unprecedented amount of tearing-down and building-up seemed to be going on in the building trades. Duncan was promptly thrown into a state which partook of fear and ecstasy. He had bad dreams, at night, in the Harvard Club, of Cleveland suddenly rising up on end and letting its population slide into Lake Erie. He wakened, early in the summer mornings, to the sound of riveting. It was New York all the time.

How his situation pleased him! He dressed and went out to inspect life, excavations, steam shovels, steel-hoists, concrete mixers, and Ingersoll Rand drills, before breakfast. He knew a few people, whom he looked up, after his passion for building and wrecking had somewhat died down. His father's failure to become a millionaire naturally limited his range. The people he knew were not rich enough to live coolly while the city by degrees became hotter and hotter. Their apartments were not exactly remarkable for long pale vistas of parquet, for terraces a hundred yards long, for the sound of cool glasses echoing in large, shadowy halls, for lovely women reduced by perspective into enchanting doll-like figures. One man he knew had a Korean butler, but his apartment was extremely small. Everything was hot and near at hand. People sat on a divan and smoked into each other's faces. There was nothing really elegant about that. It was too bad about Duncan's father.

He looked about for an apartment of his own. He needed a piano, and a place where he could make cocktails and tea. He must practice Brahms, heat or no heat, and soon he might meet some nice girl who had little or no prejudice against visiting a gentleman's rooms. The rooms, when he found them, were not entirely satisfactory. The piano was very large (it took up all the space in the bedroom), but a faint tinge of pampas grass and dusty peacock feathers tainted the air. However, the kitchenette was equipped with glasses, a cocktail shaker, and a nursery icebox. Duncan was really very happy. He was a resident of New York.

Now he could range freely. He unpacked his books and his music. He put the photograph of the girl he had loved and lost (whose father, curiously enough, *was* a millionaire) on the desk. The photograph lent quite a tone to the room. The girl was astride a hunter in the very act of clearing an extremely elegant hedge. You couldn't see her face very clearly, but her hat and raised elbows contained every element of chic. He tried a little Czerny on the piano. He hung his four impeccable summer suits in the closet.

THEN, FOR weeks, nothing happened. Even the man with the Korean butler went out of town. He did not meet any elegant women, or any dowdy ones. The piano began to bore him. He took to haunting museums, which, after all, were spacious, cool, and full of luxurious objects. And then finally, as an impossible climax to a dreary procession of days, his aunt from Cleveland came to town and it became his duty to show her around.

This was indeed a blow. His aunt was perhaps the dullest woman alive. She was set in bourgeois tradition as in a vise. (Duncan, in spite of his respect for the concomitants of money, never thought of himself as a member of the bourgeoisie. He was an artist.) She was much richer than the rest of the family, and didn't for a moment let you forget it. She heckled salespeople in shops, she sent food back in restaurants, she talked incessantly. She knew interminable pointless stories of provincial social life. She would want to go to all the dullest places. What a dismal break! Duncan, one exquisite July morning, went down to her hotel with a perfect hash of hateful feelings in his heart.

She was as bad as ever. She sat in the lounge of her small but exclusive hotel, in a hard high hat—undersized, rapacious, stupid, and powerful. He was in for it. She started off at once. One of his ridiculous female cousins was to be married. She had come to New York for the express purpose of buying wedding presents. Duncan damned her heartily and took her out into the lovely weather. He wanted to stamp on her excellent custom-made shoes, to bash in her execrable hat, to tear her fur scarf from her neck. For she was wearing a fur scarf. Two denatured-looking baum martens nipped one another's tails around her shoulders, and looked up at him with atrocious glass eyes. They had hard black noses. He wanted to stamp on them and on her.

She wanted, of all things, a set of Trollope. In fine binding, it went without saying. Crushed calf or ooze morocco, horrible moiré *doublures,*[1] edges as gilt as hell. The bookstore, a small and exclusive one, was only a step away. He found the place. In the politest way possible, he almost shoved her through the door.

An extremely odd-looking girl came toward them. At first, in the gloom engendered by thousands of fine bindings, ranged on shelves and in cases, he couldn't quite make her out. She was rather small, slender, and perfectly blonde. Her hair was the rarest shade of pale gold. It came down to her shoulders and was pushed back behind her ears. She had deep blue eyes and a lovely nose. She wore a strange dress, embroidered in odd places with fruit and flowers. Duncan was fascinated by the sight of an embroidered apple near her neck. She smiled and both Duncan and his aunt were positively startled by the beauty of her teeth.

His aunt might have been startled, but she was not for a moment daunted. She briskly began to describe her need in the way of an extravagant set of Trollope. Duncan said nothing. What a wonderful girl, he thought. How masterfully did she cope with his aunt! He laid deep plans. Terrific sets of Trollope took a long time to bind, or tool, or whatever it was. He would take this transaction out of his aunt's hands.

HE MANAGED the whole thing beautifully. The Trollope took a month: in two weeks he was taking Sigrid (for that was her appropriately romantic name) all over town. He was giving her the rush of her life. She lived, with another girl, in a big converted loft room in the Village. In fact, despite the absence of terraces and parquet, in the room of his dreams. She had a real talent for beautiful things. Her frocks were invariably exotic, if not always quite clean. She had two (no more) gold-flecked Venetian goblets; she wore a (second-hand) Fortuny tea gown; she was an artist at making fruit and vegetables do their utmost as decoration, and, under her hands, zinnias in a sugar bowl looked better than Duncan could remember Cleveland roses managing to look in silver vases. Duncan lost all his former visions of *poules-de-luxe*[2] and chic feminine members of hunt clubs. Sigrid was a woman of the world. She was mysterious. She had lived in the oddest places, for no apparent reason. Duncan had never before met a woman who had mixed in the highest artistic circles of Finnish, Austrian, and Peruvian society. In addition, she was calm, honest, and generous. Sometimes Duncan had a moment's suspicion that she laughed at him in her heart. He soon dismissed these qualms. She listened to his rendition of Brahms. He really fell in love with her.

In Cleveland, a taste for Venetian glass, Coromandel screens, carved scent bottles, cool wine, and amber jewelry presupposed money in the family for a generation or two. Yet here was Sigrid, without a penny to her name, living in an atmosphere of taste and of luxury. Duncan's rather cast-iron principles suffered a severe blow. His ideas of a suitable marriage turned completely around. He wanted to marry Sigrid. He couldn't see her in a Cleveland apartment, it was true. And as hostess to his mother's and sister's friends —well, that was also an odd picture. No matter. Something had to be done.

Late in July, he determined to take some action. He and Sigrid rode up the Avenue on a bus, after one of Sigrid's unmatchable luncheons of strange spiced fish, cold artichokes, and *coupe Jacques*.[3] He felt very cosmopolitan and knowing. They were going to the Museum. Sigrid looked especially striking in an enormous straw hat and one of her oddest fruit-and-flower dresses. Duncan couldn't imagine what his sister would think of that dress. He refused to trouble about that. He held Sigrid's hand and was deeply happy.

They went up the outside and inside Museum steps. Duncan adored mounting staircases. Slow progress up marble stairs made him feel like an historical figure. A cosmopolitan historical figure. They slowly and happily looked at Swedish glass, Greek and Chinese horses, Renaissance saltcellars,

Far Eastern textiles. Duncan planned to ask Sigrid to marry him. After they left these beautiful objects. While they were having tea. Not another day would he allow to go by without proposing marriage to Sigrid.

THEY WERE rather tired, but still happy, when they again reached the stairs. They descended the formal steps (this time Duncan pretended that he was leaving the Opéra in Paris) and went toward the cloakroom, where Duncan had left his stick. Just then a voice behind them said: "Why, Duncan! Fancy seeing you here!"

Duncan whirled around. Sigrid fell back a step. Duncan and the stranger began a rapid, disjointed, rather nasal dialogue. The stranger was a woman. She wore a stiff dark straw hat; around her neck were two baum martens nipping each other by the paws.

Duncan and the lady (for the stranger was indubitably a lady) went on and on. Sigrid sat down on a bench and looked at the woven toe of her sandal. Duncan didn't seem to miss her. He never once turned in her direction, and he was always between her and the lady. Now he was steering the lady toward the Museum door. Now he was telling her goodbye, with a wide smile and a dancing-school bow. Now the lady was out the door, and Duncan was turning toward Sigrid. So the thought of an introduction had never entered his mind. Sigrid swept her hair back under her hat with a rather cavalier gesture.

Duncan's face was set. He looked as though he were going to cry. Anyone would have felt sorry for, as well as ashamed of, him.

"Who was that?" asked Sigrid, in a peculiar voice.

"A friend of my sister's," said Duncan.

"You did not introduce me," Sigrid said, in a tone even more odd.

To this last Duncan said nothing.

"It doesn't matter," Sigrid said. "I shouldn't have liked her. She didn't wear a nice fur or a nice hat."

Duncan's head swam. His face became suffused. He looked a little as though he were about to burst. "She's an extremely nice girl," he heard himself saying, in the strangest tone that had ever issued from his lips.

"Perhaps," said Sigrid. "To me, she seemed closely to resemble your aunt."

Profoundly shocked, Duncan looked at her. My God, that hat, those shoes! My God, that hair! And under her amber necklace he noticed that her dress looked slightly dark, slightly soiled. Was not, in point of fact, exactly clean.

"She is much younger than my aunt" was all that, in his hatred, his fear, his disgust, his revulsion, his perturbation, he could manage to answer.

[1931]

1. ooze morocco: Moroccan goatskin tanned with sumac; moiré *doublures:* wave-patterned-taffeta end papers lining the inside covers of a book.

2. *poules de luxe:* tony fast women.

3. *coupe Jacques:* Fruit salad with ice cream, currants, and peppermint.

When It Is Over

WHEN IT is over, you say to yourself: "Never possibly can I feel that way again." It is like a wild beast in the heart, that turns its prey over slowly, seeking the soft places, the tender places between bone and bone, the yielding muscle and soft flesh, wherein the teeth may sink. It is at once the victim and the beast. Quietly they lie together, on fresh grass, and again enter the slow struggle, the torture beyond feeling. The dead yet living victim is turned; the eater seeks slowly, passionately, the next place in which to set its fang. The wounds are made but do not bleed.

Just afterward, a mood of pity descends on the freshly punished spirit. Everything in the world becomes piteous, and not a sound or sight can escape from the love wrapped in fog and obscurity: secret to itself. Those nearest the heart drain off the first pity. How lovely they are, and how vulnerable! Their flesh, their very being, draws out the misty love like a thread: over and over it wraps them round. Today they live; their hair seems exquisitely clean and lies bright on their foreheads. They are young. Their bodies and their wishes will come to nothing. It is our purpose to love them; yet the thread continues to wrap them round until they live inside a cocoon of this soft emotion which is part dread.

They cannot see nor hear nor feel the love that pours out to them. Soft and delicate as fright in the dark, over and around them it goes. They sink into it. The heart pulls them down. "Forgive me; forgive me," the heart says, "you are beautiful and you will die. You are not really young, happy, or beautiful. You are appearance; you change as I love you. This moment turns and changes, and you also change. Goodbye, goodbye," says the heart, taking its somber, its delicate, its tender leave. "I am all around you; you cannot really hear me, for I am one field, one wood, one acre too far away. The children toss the ball, but it is too dark to see it any longer. Farewell, farewell."

[Journal manuscript 1931]

Zest

WELL, SHE thought, as she closed the book, goodness knows that formula is simple enough. "Love someone or something, take interest in things outside yourself, and cultivate zest." The man was a philosopher after her own heart. No sharing of dubious confidences with a psychoanalyst who ate chocolates and smoked cigarettes behind and slightly to the left of your relaxed form; no expensive trip somewhere and back; no cooked-up love affair wasting time and, as often as not, energy. If she must get into a nervous state so that her hands and feet seemed too big and she couldn't be at all sure that the remarks of the people beside her in the theatre weren't directly concerned with her more obvious defects, here, perhaps, was the way out.

At this point a small shrill voice concealed somewhere inside the self she was so soon to reduce to minimum importance remarked rather clearly and with a 1920 accent: "There's nothing the matter with you that money couldn't cure."

That, of course, was nonsense. The psychoanalyst, between a caramel and a nougat, had cleared up all such foolishness for her years ago, in the days when ten dollars an hour seemed little enough to pay for fashionable peace of mind. "You could have all the money in the world," he had said, "and it wouldn't amount to that." She had heard his fingers snap masterfully behind her, to the left, and another delusion had been punctured forever.

Very well, then. She would now begin. She would first clear up this matter of love. How easy, in the privacy of the boudoir! The objective attitude and the zest might get her downstairs and out-of-doors, but the love could be managed without stirring from her chair. Whom, and what, did she love? Her eyes moved rapidly around the room, and her mind, entirely empty of any loved image, tagged after them. Her glance and her mind revolved wildly about for some time before the figure of her niece, Sally, suddenly appeared, as it were, from behind the chest of drawers. She really did love her niece, Sally. Sally was very cute. She also loved her new green evening sandals. She loved the slippers and Sally, and, it must be admitted, she also loved two rather decayed actors and a man she had seen once in the street. And she was pleased that Charles's wife was reported to have left him after having taken up with a mere boy. But whether pleasure in Charles's status of deceived and abandoned husband came under the head of love for Charles, she could not make out. When one was reduced to the state of emotional poverty wherein, although the heart were warm and ready, nieces and things to wear came first, it was hard to place old affections. The thought of Charles with a wife —he who from early childhood had kept everything under control—once had struck her as odd. Charles again reduced to a strong solitary existence was odder still. Somehow it served him right.

She had put in fifteen minutes on the first part of the formula, but she had to confess that it didn't work, right out of hand. She continued to look around the room, in a vague way, without discovering anything of interest, either directly or by inference. The next step was getting outside of herself and feeling zest. She got up, combed her hair, and powdered her face. The powder was too light. It showed up really gruesomely on her forehead and nose. Either she had been deceived into buying the wrong shade or she had become three shades darker in the last two weeks. That's what came of leaving zest out of one's considerations. She dressed and in no time stood gloved and hatted, ready for the street. Some women took three hours to dress, but, thank God, she had not yet reached that point of chic or decrepitude.

It was a fine day outside. Lots of birds and some boats were displayed on the calm of the river, she saw by peering out the corner window. She looked at the river with a poor imitation of zest. She stared at it with clenched jaws, with a kind of mean-spirited fixity. She recognized her failure. Things would be better when she got outside and worked up some healthy circulation.

IT WOULDN'T be fair to shop. That was getting inside, not outside, oneself. It would not be fair to call up Lucy, or in any way to fall back upon her usual habits. A taxi driver, one of the line beside the curb, stood, monkey wrench in hand, puzzling over the bowels of his machine. The hood was up. The English called it a bonnet. And a wrench a spanner. If he wasn't feeling zest, it was something very near it. His look, compounded of love, hatred, and intense interest, brought back to her her own look cast at the river, and she felt rather envious and ashamed.

"This floor will safely sustain a weight of 300 lbs. per sq. ft.," it said in black letters on the wall of the place where the trucks drove up, under the News Building. The floor was sustaining it at the moment. A huge truck surmounted by a tank was feeding something through a hose, down into the basement, or sub-cellar, or whatever it was. Oil, probably. The *News* needed a lot of oil. Those floors above her were full of machines. Machines lived on oil. "What will happen when the oil gives out?" her niece, Sally, had once asked her. Sally knew a lot about miscible oils. She took a course in them at school. But heavens, it wasn't oil. The hose and the great tank were full of ink. "Consolidated Ink Company," read the sign on the side of the truck. All that ink. Gallons of ink poured into the basement and piped, very probably, to all the presses. Think of it.

Really something to think about. Production on a large scale. Tons of paper, gallons of ink, thousands of reporters, water coolers by the hundreds, typewriters, linotype machines, telephones, stenographers, thousands of packages of cigarettes, ten thousand desks and chairs, all contained in the News Building, above her. It took the breath away. It startled the imagination. It awoke zest. She looked at the News Building, or as much of it as she could see, with zest. Understand the means and scope of anything and automatically the imagination widened. She was outside of herself, and inside the News Building. Her zest poured from her heart in much the same way that the ink poured out from the truck. The ink spurted to the presses; the presses roared . . .

She couldn't hear the presses. It was fairly quiet in the street. An elevated train made some noise in Third Avenue. All elevated trains came from the same place. There was a nest of them at the Battery. Side by side they stood, empty and ready, and you took your choice. You could soar all around the city on elevated trains. You could look out the windows straight into flats and factories, and go for miles, up through the Island and beyond the Island. Into a section where wooden houses and front yards still persisted. Or had persisted, ten years ago. Perhaps there were none of them left by now. But could the elevated be trusted? She, for one, had never seen anyone do a stroke of repairing on it. The stations shook when the trains came in.

A streetcar was much safer. She was fond of streetcars. For six solid years she had gone back and forth to and from school on pleasant, sane streetcars, or trolleys, as they then were called. The conductor used to hold out his hand in front of you and say "Fares, please." Sometimes the trolley proper became disengaged from the wire overhead, and a shower of blue sparks fell all around. The conductor leaned out the back window to fix it, which must have been hard on the spine, or in stubborn cases went outside the car and pulled and tugged at a great rate. And the conductor called out the names of the streets. That custom had gone into the discard years ago.

SHE GOT on a Lexington Avenue car and dropped her nickel in the box. No longer, naturally, could one expect trolleys to rush along, as in her youth. They stopped at every other corner and had to wait for the lights. The conductor stood guarding his box of nickels and never said a word.

There was one other woman on the car. Either women considered streetcars a low form of transit or they were, at this hour, engaged in doing something else. It was three o'clock in the afternoon. The car was passing through the quick-lunch district. The Brass Rail, its window studded with hams; the Automat, displaying illuminated and tastefully arranged plates of salads and cold cuts, like prize samples of culinary art; and two tearooms with candlesticks and checked curtains. A girl sat in the window of a tearoom, smoking a cigarette. All over town at this hour women were smoking cigarettes. They were tired. Tired of handing the French telephone, conveniently in one piece, to Mr. Haze, of almost pressing it against his ear with humility, with tenderness. Tired of "Essem Products outside; will you see him?" They were smoking cigarettes in the washroom at the office; in the Carnelian Room, the Powder Box, the Du Barry Room, at the movies; in chintz-covered chairs with ashtrays conveniently to hand in the shops, while the tired saleswoman used herself as an unwilling model, the hanger against her breast, her hand pressing the belt to her stomach. "Very smart."

Zest. Zest was needed. The car was now coming to the hat, sample-dress, and fine-shoe section. It had passed through the antique district, fortunately. Patchwork quilts and china dogs would never draw one tear from her. The hat-and-shoe district seemed to be experiencing a slump in trade.

It was practically giving things away. The lay figures in the windows stood dressed in silks and furs. Their flat silver heads leaned shyly to one side, with a fixed, thin grimace. Now that she remembered it, Charles had once lived over one of these very hat stores. He had gone in for bowls of mixed tulips and furniture that cried out for antimacassars.[1] He had never been over-burdened with sense.

Men improve with the years, as someone had said. Charles couldn't have improved to an appreciable degree if his wife had run off with that boy—or had she?

So far a depressing car ride. She knew what came next. Apartment build-ings, with their numbers on side streets, if possible; greeting-card stores, dairies purveying upper-class milk, and groceries selling grouse. Also cleaning-and-dyeing establishments. When the apartment-dwellers weren't buying greeting cards they were having their clothes dyed. A dull life at best.

Not a soul had left the car since she had entered it and perhaps the end of the line was miles away. Every so often, the doors opened and shut with a crash and someone got on, but no one got off. It was becoming crowded. The male faces opposite troubled her. They looked the type that would choose trolleys as a means of locomotion. Rather dopeless[2] and grim. She had for-gotten just why this trip had seemed a good idea. The world was going on without her. Millions of people were engaged in life and she and all these other misfits were taking a ride on a trolley.

It was then that the thought of lunch struck her forcibly. She had had no lunch. Strung up to a high pitch by a popular philosopher, she had forgotten to eat. The car stopped to let someone else on. She managed to get off first.

And there was a restaurant. You would never have expected it, but there it was, next to a store that sold greeting cards. A good restaurant, with tra-dition and branches all over town. Oysters, thick soup, a devilled crab . . .

Before she had her gloves off, and while the waiter was handing her the card, she saw the telephone. Straight across from her, beyond a glass door, was a most commodious compartment, furnished with a telephone and a chair. She gave her order and got up. Excitement, coming on top of an empty stomach, made her fumble in her purse for change. She felt happy and full of expectation and suspense. The car ride hadn't been so bad. She would take another after lunch. Away off to the limits of the Island, to unexplored districts, in search of zest. But she would telephone Lucy now, while she had the chance. All that about Charles's wife had been rather odd and unexpected, to say the least. She might as well get the details while she thought of it. Lucy would know.

[1931]

1. antimacassars: small cloths to protect the arms and headrests of upholstered furniture.
2. dopeless: clueless.

Journey Around My Room

THE MOST advantageous point from which to start this journey is the bed itself, wherein, at midnight or early in the morning, the adventurous traveler lies moored, the terrain spread out before him. The most fortunate weather is warm to cool, engendered by a westerly breeze, borne from the open window toward the ashes in the grate. At midnight, moonlight lies upon the floor, to guide the traveler's eye; in the early morning, the bleak opacity that serves the traveler in this region as sun brightens the brick wall of the house across the yard, and sheds a feeble reflected glow upon all the objects which I shall presently name.

This is a largish room, almost square in shape. It faces east and west, and is bounded on the north by the hall, which leads, after some hesitation, to the kitchen; on the south by someone's bedroom in the house next door; on the west, by back yards and the Empire State Building; on the east, by Lexington Avenue, up and down which electric cars roll with a noise like water running into a bottle. Its four walls are chastely papered with manila paper. Its floor is inadequately varnished. Its ceiling bears all the honors away: it is quite lofty in pitch, and it is clean, absolutely unspotted, in fact, save for a little damp over the fireplace, which, from some angles, looks like a fish. A fireplace, resembling a small black arch, occupies a middle position in the south wall. Above it, a plain deal mantelpiece of ordinary design supports a row of books, a photograph of the News Building taken from the

Chanin Building, four shells from a Maine beach, and a tin of Famous Cake Box Mixture. Above these objects hangs a Japanese print, depicting Russian sailors afflicted by an angry ocean, searchlights, a burning ship, and a boatload of raging Japanese.

THE INITIAL mystery that attends any journey is: how did the traveler reach his starting point in the first place? How did I reach the window, the walls, the fireplace, the room itself; how do I happen to be beneath this ceiling and above this floor? Oh, that is a matter for conjecture, for argument pro and con, for research, supposition, dialectic! I can hardly remember how. Unlike Livingstone, on the verge of darkest Africa, I have no maps to hand, no globe of the terrestrial or the celestial spheres, no chart of mountains, lakes, no sextant, no artificial horizon. If ever I possessed a compass, it has long since disappeared. There must be, however, some reasonable explanation for my presence here. Some step started me toward this point, as opposed to all other points on the habitable globe. I must consider; I must discover it.

And here it is. One morning in March, in the year 1909, my father opened the storm door leading from the kitchen to the back steps, on Chestnut Street, in Ballardvale, a small town in Massachusetts, on the Boston & Maine Railroad. A bare March sky with wind in it shed its light over the street; the gutters ran with melted snow under ice as thin as a watch crystal; last year's maple leaves lay matted on the lawn. My father and I walked down the hill toward the station, and said "Hello, how are you today" to Mr. Buck, to Mr. Kibbee, and to Stella Dailey. Old Jack Leonard had backed his horse up in front of Shattuck's store. A bag of potatoes, a ten-gallon kerosene can, and a black hound sat in the wagon, and a yellow cigar ribbon, tied to the whipstock, fluttered in the cold air. Across the tracks, the willows by the bridge let fall into the foaming water a mist of reddening boughs. The mill dam roared. The windows of the mill sparkled in the March sunlight falling without warmth. The station platform was empty. Above our heads the station master's wife shook her duster out the window, under the scalloped eaves. On this platform, for nine hundred mornings, I have said goodbye to my father, and each morning he has given me a kiss smelling of cigar, and a penny, and I have looked carefully at the Indian on the penny's head, and at the wreath on its tail, and have remarked the penny's date. But now I am older, no longer at the age when one looks at the dates on pennies. I am going away. I shan't ever see again old Leonard, or Shattuck's store, or the hydrangea bushes in front of Forrest Scott's house that in autumn spilled dusty-blue petals over the grass, or the mill dam, or the mill, or the swing in the Gardners' yard, or the maple tree in my own, or the hedge of arbor vitae around the Congregationalist church. Or hear, in the night, the express whistling for the crossing, or, in the daytime, the Boston train, and the train for Lawrence and Lowell, braking down for the stop, ringing its bell around the curve. Now, this morning, the Boston train is coming in from the fields beyond the river, and slows and brakes and stops. The steam shrieks out of the engine and smoke trails out, into the clear morning, from the smoke-stack, blotting out the willows and the mill dam. The conductor lifts me up to the step. That is the reason for my presence here. I took the Boston train in March, 1909.

GRANTED, THEN, that the traveler is here for an assigned, an established reason, the journey may proceed due west by slow degrees from the fire-place. Here I come upon two chairs that look worn to the bone, and a large, square green bureau, in execrable modern taste. The surface of this last is scattered over with objects of little real or artistic value. A sharp turn to the right brings me to the window, giving onto the brick wall before mentioned, and tastefully draped in dotted swiss. Then the entire west wall unrolls be-fore the eye. The window is flanked to the immediate northwest by two pictures: one of a thunderstorm, and the other of a small bunch of violets. I then come upon a hanging shelf whose well-proportioned but inadequate interior can house nothing larger than a 16mo.[1] So that here all the 16mos in the apartment lie down together, the lion and the lamb: La Madone des Sleepings, Apologia Pro Vita Sua, Whitehead's Introduction to Mathematics; the poems of Baudelaire, William Drummond of Hawthornden, Waller; the plays of Chekhov and Thomas Middleton; Walden; or, Life in the Woods; The Turn of the Screw, Montaigne's Essays, and Taras Bulba. Beneath this truly horrifying array of literature is situated a large and comparatively un-used desk, on which stand displayed pictures of myself and several other people, a pot of pencils, largely decayed, a cashbook that serves as a bill file, an inkstand that serves as a letter file, and a letter file that serves as a bill file. Also a lamp, an ashtray, a stamp box (empty), two postcards, a paper knife made out of a cartridge and bearing the arms of the city of Verdun, and a large quantity of blank paper.

The north wall contains nothing of interest save the bed and the traveler moored therein, a table, a lamp, and a picture of a water jug, a bowl, two lemons, and a pear (by Vlaminck). The east wall, on the other hand, is filled by an object of immense interest and charm, an object that combines service and beauty in unequal parts. It is an armoire; within its doors lie shirts, towels, pillowcases, and sheets, but the doors themselves—what serviceable quality could dare to compete in importance with this beauty! Vertically, along the edges of the doors, carved from wood, two garlands fall, composed of roses, rose leaves, pine cones, grapes, sunflowers, bursting figs, and lobster claws. The size, the stability of this piece (which has been lent to me by a friend until such time as she can find a purchaser for it), should hearten the traveler. On the contrary, it is at this point, precisely when the end is in sight, and the starting point almost gained, that the catastrophe of the journey invariably occurs.

For it is here, as I nearly complete the circle set, that at midnight and in the early morning I encounter the dream. I am set upon by sleep, and hear the rush of water, and hear the mill dam, fuming with water that weighs itself into foam against the air, and see the rapids at its foot that I must gauge and dare and swim. Give over, says this treacherous element, the fear and distress in your breast; and I pretend courage and brave it at last, among rocks along the bank, and plunge into the wave that mounts like glass to the level of my eye. O death, O fear! The universe swings up against my sight, the universe fallen into and bearing with the mill stream. I must in a moment die, but for a moment I breathe, upheld, and see all weight, all force, all water, compacted into the glassy wave, veined, marbled with foam, this moment caught raining over me. And into the wave sinks the armoire, the green bureau, the lamps, the shells from the beach in Maine. All these objects, provisional at best, now equally lost, rock down to translucent depths below fear, an Atlantis in little, under the mill stream (last seen through the steam from the Boston train in March, 1909).

[1933]

1. 16mo: sextodecimo, a small book made by folding large sheets of paper down to signatures of sixteen pages.

The Short Life of Emily

LET us follow Emily Hough out of the elevated train which she has heed-lessly taken to the wrong side of town; let us see her come onto the plat-form at Fulton Street, where, under the blistered and incredibly dirty peaked matchboard roof, a pigeon walks up and down and a man observes with great care the left side of his face in a slot-machine mirror.[1] Let us follow Emily and bear with her touching mistake, since, in a moment or two, she is to undergo a rare experience, an intense vision usually afforded only to those who are young and in love, to those who are rich and powerful and gay, or to those who, by some not quite normal mechanism, can imagine that they are all of these things and more.

Emily Hough is not young. She is forty, pretty poverty-stricken, and moderately mixed and sad. Mixed, because she has lived for five years in New York City without ever having disabused herself of the idea that all ave-nues down which elevated trains run are one and the same avenue. She uses the elevated rarely, to come downtown to see Mr. Doherty, who manages her small affairs (his office is on Vesey Street, overlooking a churchyard), or, on sunny days in the spring and fall, to take a walk along the Battery. The same train goes to both places; it was the train that led elsewhere that Emily almost invariably took.

So now, knowing that she is wrong, but understanding, from long prac-tice, exactly how wrong she is, she goes down the elevated steps, carefully clutching her skirt sideways and a trifle upward so that it misses the treads, holding the stair-rail with the other hand. Yes, the same mistake as always, and she must wait on the curb, in the narrow, gloomy street, until five trucks pass. She must see the street empty of trucks before she leisurely crosses to the opposite corner. She must mark a tall, bright building that rises ahead of her, six blocks away, her guide on all former occasions when she has had to approach Mr. Doherty's office from the most inconvenient angle, and her guide now. If she walks straight toward the tall building, she will, in time, reach Broadway, Vesey Street, the churchyard, and Mr. Doherty.

She goes up Fulton Street, the river, some river, the wrong river, glit-tering in a fresh breeze at her back. It is the early afternoon of a mild spring day. Chamois and Sponges, Twines and Netting, say the signs; electrical supply stores spill, into trays along the sidewalk, completely incomprehensible objects. Because she has come to know this wrong street better than the right one, she does not need to ask directions. She last walked up Fulton Street on a hot morning in August. Her errand was much the same then as now: she was on her way to Mr. Doherty's office to receive a sum of money, a large proportion of which she had already spent. But on that August morning she had been able to think of Aunt Clara as still alive, in New Paltz, knitting in her garden in the shade of a tree. Now, in early April, she must think of Aunt Clara under a glossy granite headstone in the New Paltz cemetery. Aunt Clara had died testate, and Emily is one of her legatees. Mr. Doherty has bidden her to his office, to apprise her of the amount of Aunt Clara's bequest. Emily suspects that the bequest is small and admits to herself, somewhat guiltily, that, last week, she very probably spent whatever sum it turns out to be. Time flies; bills mount up; she is no more clever at accounts than at the different sides of town.

She is now at Pine Street, and can cross quite easily, because there are no trucks, only people for the most part going in the same, or in the directly opposite, direction. Here is the stationery store full of account books, diaries, pencils, ink, and rubber bands; and here is the drugstore that specializes in panaceas: tonics for coughs, colds, rheumatism, asthma, lumbago, and other ills. Here is the bookstore exhibiting, as usual, in its window, a flayed and horrifying human torso, cut from cardboard, as large as life and far more brightly colored. Here is the picture and framing shop, displaying blindfold Hope with her lyre, General Washington with his aides, and the Isle of the Dead with its cypress trees. Small groups of men stand in front of all these windows, idly staring through the plate glass. Emily, in no great hurry to discover how little Aunt Clara has left her, would like to stand and stare, but shyness forbids her, and she goes on.

AND IT is now, just as she passes the really considerable crowd in front of the philatelist's, that she experiences, at first with some diffidence, and finally with something of a shock, that idea for the sake of which we have followed her thus far. Because it is sunny, because it is brisk and mild, because of her almost neighborly feeling for this street which, if she always kept her wits about her, she never might have seen at all, because of the quiet groups of people in front of the interesting windows, because she has a vivid sense of Aunt Clara's recent and untimely demise, suddenly, as she hesitates to cross

Nassau Street, she says to herself, half aloud and with a shy burst of conviction: "I am alive." She not only says it, but she feels it. She is extant; she is quick; she breathes; she is in motion; she lives.

As we can understand, such an idea, although it comes in a flash, takes some time to sink in. At first she feels herself logically unpersuaded. She hardly believes her ears; she is inclined to put the conviction down to some mistake. The fact of her solid existence in the only life she will ever have has never forcibly struck her before. This is an unprecedented experience for Emily Hough, as it would be for any one of us in her place: to know that she is in life this current instant. We can understand that we have been alive in the past—at breakfast, some hours before, or last week, when Cousin Emma was in town; and the expectation that we will be alive in the future, say this evening, when Caroline and Julius will come over for dinner—that, too, is a simple and comprehensible matter. We can readily see ourselves, vitally going on, a week from next Thursday, or even last year at this time. But alive at any given moment, whilst going on an errand, or eating lunch, or hesitating on the curb at Nassau and Fulton Streets at two-thirty on April sixth, between a philatelist's and a barbershop—no. If we are of a stubborn nature, we are likely to argue the improbability of the matter out at some length.

Emily Hough's nature is not stubborn. She eagerly accepts the unexpected knowledge of her existence and begins thoroughly to enjoy it. If she is alive, and she has definitely admitted that fact, then these other people must be alive as well. In fact, they are events in her life, and she in theirs. And this scene through which she is passing and has just passed is a scene in her life. The sunlight on the high buildings, the Panama 1901s and the envelopes decorated with pictures of Dewey fighting the Battle of Manila in the philatelist's, the man undergoing a haircut in the barbershop, the voice of the little boy shrilly crying "Papa, hallo !" —are a scene in her history as important, it might be, as Roncesvalles to Roland or Yorktown to General Washington and his aides. She feels elated and yet humble as she crosses Broadway with the help of a policeman and turns toward the churchyard. She is Emily Hough, partial legatee of Miss Clara Hough of New Paltz; she is now approaching her lawyer's office, from the most inconvenient angle; it is April sixth, 1933, and her heart is beating strong and sturdy, just as it has been beating for the past forty years, without a break, without a pause. She breathes air into her lungs; the sun is shining; she wears a hat, shoes, gloves, glasses; she has fur on her coat collar and a gold chain around her neck. This is Emily. This is herself. This is she.

IN THE elevator in Mr. Doherty's building, she says "Five" to the operator, and, on the card which assures the public that this particular elevator has been tested and is fit to carry passengers, she examines with care the signature of Joseph P. Callaghan. Joseph P. Callaghan is also, presumably, alive. She and J. P. Callaghan and the elevator operator and Mr. Doherty. All in the world at once. Contemporaries, as you might say. But when she gets out of the car at the fifth floor, something happens to her conviction of existence. The car door slams, and she is alone. Almost instantly, she forgets that she lives, that she breathes, that she has being—as is only natural, as we, too, in her place would forget. This is the fifth floor: that is all, suddenly, that she can really take in, or remember.

[1933]

1. slot-machine mirror: mirror on a machine dispensing candy or cigarettes.

The Last Tear

MRS. READ was heartbroken when she and Claire left Rome. It was late May; from the café where she went at five o'clock for large glasses of dark Trieste beer, she could look out at the evening sky where swallows whistled and hurled themselves about, excited by the late warm light. For two days before her departure, she walked about in a daze and would often come to herself in the Corso, in front of a plate-glass window full of knives or umbrellas. On the last afternoon she stayed at home, played patience, and drank all the Martell she had saved for the train. She had shed her last tear. Two years ago, on the night after she had seen Claire off for Madrid with one of Claire's groups of nice people, a tear had fallen into her glass of *vermouth cassis,* and she had named it her last. Claire had been away for two months that time and Mrs. Read took to *cachets*[1] that never really put her to sleep. But she had not wept since and she would not weep now.

Claire's one talent, from the age of seventeen to twenty-two, had been nice people. Mrs. Read knew that she had only herself to blame for this. Years ago, when she did not have her present good sense, she had determined that Claire's life was not to be spent arduously earning a living, as she had spent her own. Claire had attended a modern country day school for ten years. She had learned how to make pottery, weave textiles, design stage settings, write verse, sing part-songs, and paint imaginative landscapes. She could swim, ride, play tennis; she was an expert at bridge. She was always extremely popular with nice people. Mrs. Read often wished that Claire could make her own clothes and perhaps strum a little on the piano. Claire's school had left these two accomplishments out of its extensive curriculum. And after a time most of the other pursuits on the non-athletic, non-bridge-playing side faded away. Claire *knew* all about clothes and the finer kind of cosmetic. She had good manners and an amusing vocabulary. But, Mrs. Read had to admit, her general attitude toward life was one of profound lassitude. Between her groups of nice friends, she became so bored that she could hardly be urged to rise in the morning or go to bed at night. She spent her mornings shopping for hats she could not afford, and her late afternoons with some acquaintance in a good central position in a hotel bar. Recently, she had come to life somewhat. She wrote and received many letters from Continental centers. All winter she had heard from her friends while living with and sharing the slender income of her mother. And now the Stoats looked forward to seeing her in the early summer. Would she join them in Venice in June; they could go on to Salzburg together. So the Ballingers, the Gordons, the Hatchams, who had written warmly but projected no definite plans, received somewhat shorter letters from Claire. This summer it would be Salzburg and the Stoats.

Mrs. Read's attachment to Rome went deeper than Trieste beer. Although in winter the heating of her hotel was inadequate, in spite of the fact that none of the doors fitted their joints and the hot water ran cold, she loved the light, the air, the rude Romans, the bronze, the marble, the orange stucco, the fountains, and the gardens. On the coldest days she could eat herself warm, and sometimes, in the hotel, she met practical and businesslike women of her own age with whom she liked to talk. In Rome she was at peace with herself and proud of Claire. Claire's Italian was really excellent. She had worked very hard at it in Bellagio with the Worthingtons.

CLAIRE AND Mrs. Read left for Florence on the early train. That afternoon was quite jolly; they rode around in a *carrozza*[2] looking for cocktails. They had four apiece and drove to the *pension* in high spirits. Next morning, the sky was overcast and Mrs. Read knew again how much she hated this city. She thought the Duomo a fright; she could not bear the wide stretches of unrelieved gravel edged by small trees that the Florentines called *piazze,* or tolerate the tooled leather and silver knickknacks in the shops and the weatherbeaten English in the streets. Trams skirted the edges of cafés, missing the end chair by an inch; tourists hung with cameras, engaged in writing postcards, jammed the café tables. This was the city where she must spend the summer because it was cheap.

"I cannot," she said to herself that first morning. She said nothing to Claire. Claire really bought herself a hat and the dressmaker came to measure her for summer clothes. All that week, Claire bargained for gingham, chiffon, linen, and crêpe georgette.[3] For reasons of economy, Mrs. Read, in the intervals between shops, drank medicinal cognac and smoked Macedonian cigarettes. Sometimes in the evening, while Claire played her Spanish records for the younger *pensionnaires,*[4] she would go off by herself for coffee and rum at the corner café. The little trees were in full leaf. It was full spring —one could see that it was full spring, even though the Florentines did not provide gardens by which to gauge the season's progress. At these moments, just before eleven o'clock struck, Mrs. Read often heard a colloquy between the ghostly voices of Claire and Claire's friends.

"Your mother is a great darling!" the nice people always said. "Such an amusing woman!"

"Yes, isn't she?" the ghost of Claire's voice would answer brightly. "She knits all my sweaters. She is so clever!"

"And they are such lovely sweaters!" the nice voices would exclaim.

She wished, as the rum warmed her cold, tight throat, that she had always been alone, or that she never had allowed Claire to learn to read and write, let alone swim, ride, and weave. Then she might have had a happy life. She would not have needed Trieste beer or medicinal cognac or cigarettes or *cachets.* She would have needed nothing but the affection, the comfort, the companionship derived from a truly dutiful, uninstructed child. She and this other Claire could have led a quiet life somewhere under a fig tree and vine in a garden. She herself would have taught Claire to knit, to strum on the piano, to cook, to sing, to sew. And never, never would she have been at the mercy of the Ballingers, the Gordons, the Hatchams, the Worthingtons, the Stoats, all of whom, at one time or another, had thrust their nice claws into her heart.

She walked back to the *pension* and quietly let herself into her room. A thin layer of Spanish records covered her bed from top to bottom. She emptied the ashtrays, opened the window, and sat down to take off her shoes.

"Is that you, darling?" Claire called from the other room. "Where on earth have you been? It's so dreadfully late!"

"I've been looking at Florence," Mrs. Read said.

"*So* much lovelier than Rome," said Claire.

"And it's too late," said Mrs. Read, not exactly in answer.

[1933]

1. *cachets:* sleeping powders or capsules.
2. *carrozza:* a horsedrawn carriage.
3. crêpe georgette: transparent crinkled silk.
4. *pensionnaires:* patrons at an inexpensive hotel or *pension.*

Conversation Piece

MR. WILLIAMS received them. The dreadful heat outside stopped as soon as the hall door closed. Mr. Tracy knew Mr. Williams. Mrs. Tracy did not know either Mr. or Mrs. Williams. She had consented rather reluctantly to go to tea, on a hot New York afternoon, with two strangers who might bore her to death, for all she knew. However, here she and Robert were, and at least it was cool in the Williamses' front hall.

"Hello, Robert; how are you, Mrs. Tracy?" said Mr. Williams. They went into the room at the rear of the hall. The room was almost pitch-dark, owing to its situation at the back of the house with taller buildings on all sides. Two lamps were lit.

"Sybil will be here in a moment. And in a moment we'll have a cocktail. Will you have a cocktail, Mrs. Tracy?" Yes, she would have a cocktail. Mr. Williams seemed to be very nice. Then Mrs. Williams did come in as promised, and as if on cue, and greetings again went round.

"Isn't it hot?" Mrs. Williams said.

"Isn't it?" Mrs. Tracy answered. She couldn't see Mrs. Williams very clearly, the room was so dark. That sharp, appraising look invariably exchanged by two women who have never laid eyes on each other before didn't quite come off. Mrs. Tracy thought Mrs. Williams looked very nice. She had light hair and an extremely neat figure.

"What a lovely room!" exclaimed Mrs. Tracy.

"It's like living at the bottom of a well, really," said Mrs. Williams.

"That's a grand mirror," Robert remarked.

"Isn't it grand!" exclaimed Mrs. Williams. "It comes from Stunton Fyles —that is, we are almost *sure* it comes from Stunton Fyles." It was a large mirror that climbed the wall in scrolls almost to the ceiling. Robert and Mrs. Williams made off across the room to examine it more closely. Robert suddenly seemed to know all about Stunton Fyles. An enormous house in Somersetshire that had been cut up, after the war, and shipped to America in sections.

"Let's sit over here," said Mr. Williams to Mrs. Tracy. They sat down on a *fauteuil* upholstered in delicate mauve brocade. Its twin faced them from the other side of the room. That's where Robert and Mrs. Williams would sit, thought Mrs. Tracy. She and Robert sitting on opposite sides of the room with the host and hostess, respectively. Very pleasant, she thought. In her own house there was none of this charming balance. Everyone got pushed into corners. She recognized in Mrs. Williams, although she couldn't see her very clearly, a person who worked things out with nicety, to a degree.

"So you've just come back to town," said Mr. Williams, at her elbow. "Where were you?" She told him where they had been. Mr. Williams had once been there, too. Such a beautiful view of the mountains and the sea combined. But New Englanders did so few things with fish. Boiled, fried, or presented in a stew. The Scandinavians, on the other hand, had taken fish and subjected it to every culinary process known to man. Pickled, dried, preserved, fish soup, *timbales,*¹ pies . . . "Ah, here are the cocktails," Mr. Williams broke off to say. "Put them down here, Peter. Have one of these, Mrs. Tracy; they're very good."

Little ships in full sail stood perfectly still in a bulb in the stems of the cocktail glasses.

Robert and Mrs. Williams, across the room, were getting along beautifully. Mrs. Tracy turned her gaze back to Mr. Williams.

"My friend, Knud Swenson, the pianist, has told me all about Scandinavians and fish," Mr. Williams went on. "Do you know Knud?" No, she didn't know him. "Grand fellow; plays Mozart beautifully. Odd thing, for a Scandinavian to play Mozart so well, isn't it?" She agreed. "You'd think that there'd be too much of that heavy saga business in them, wouldn't you? Are you fond of Mozart?" Very fond. "Do you play the piano at all?" A little. Did Mr. Williams play the piano? Yes, Mr. Williams played. It was unusual to find a male American who played the piano well, Mrs. Tracy had found. That was true, Mr. Williams agreed. If he hadn't gone to school in Leipzig, *he* probably never would have played the piano. Did Mrs. Tracy know Leipzig? No, she didn't.

Mr. Williams poured everyone another drink. Robert was telling Mrs. Williams about the day they went deep-sea fishing.

Mrs. Tracy felt that Mr. Williams was carrying her through the conversation with great swiftness but not very much zeal. She felt rather dull and relaxed in this cool room, after having endured August heat for three days. Mr. Williams, returning, went on about Mozart at length. Such productiveness. No one would ever hear all of Mozart, he supposed, even if he sat for hours each day with his ear against a gramophone. But the delicacy, the purity, the subtlety, the form! "Of course," Mr. Williams said, "you will agree with me that all art must have form. The theatre has its proscenium arch—"

"Jim," said Mrs. Williams, addressing her husband from the opposite *fauteuil.* "Just think, Mr. Tracy knew Bill Nixon, and he hadn't heard that Elsa had married again!"

"They were friends of my brother's. I didn't know him well," Robert said.

Mr. Williams rose to pour another drink. He frowned and shook his head, with disapprobation and concern. "If ever a woman was responsible for a man's death, Elsa is that woman," he said.

"Dear, dear!" thought Mrs. Tracy. "So Mr. Williams has his disapproving side."

"Almost immediately, she married again," Mrs. Williams went on. "What happened to the three children I can't imagine. Left in Switzerland, probably. It all happened in Switzerland, you know. They found his body in a crevasse."

"Do you know Selina Force?" Mr. Williams asked Mrs. Tracy. Yes, she knew Selina. Mr. Williams's face lit up. "Fine woman, Selina, but pretty un-reliable. I used to know her when she was married to Allen Witters. Did you meet the boy she picked up last year in Tucson? I hear she wants a divorce. Do you think John will give it to her?"

"That Tucson boy is at least eight years younger than Selina," said Mrs. Williams, from across the room. "You would expect a little more sense from Selina even now, wouldn't you?" she added, in the pleasantest voice in the world.

Everyone expected more sense from Selina.

A whole shoal of mutual acquaintances, past and present, from whom one expected more sense now swam into the conversation. Cal Kimball was practically on the town; had they heard? Eunice Lynd had been making a spectacle of herself since early spring. Sara Goss (you know Sara) had taken up with a sailor or a steward or some such thing; and in the case of Malcolm Black, Mrs. Williams (and Mr. Williams and Mr. Tracy and Mrs. Tracy) were all certain it was suicide.

Mrs. Tracy, after the fourth cocktail, noticed the gloom in the room anew. It looked as though a thunderstorm were coming on. Perhaps it was just the tall buildings all about. She was talking in a much more animated way with Mr. Williams than at first. They were getting along famously. After the fifth cocktail she knew that she and Robert must go. It was getting late. Time had passed. Whenever her eyes became involved with details while her tongue sped merrily along under its own power, she knew that it was time to go. Her eyes went all around the room gathering up details. They followed the graceful curve of the Regency chair legs, of the gilt rococo mirror, of the precious and chaste *fauteuil* upon which she and Mr. Williams sat. They sailed purely and calmly along with the little ship imprisoned in the stem of the cocktail glass. As soon as Mr. Williams finished telling her every last item in the unfortunate case of Malcolm Black, she would rise; she would say "It has been delightful!"; they would go. Now she sat waiting, smiling a little because, scattered on the floor in the shadows, she seemed to see the fragments of a proscenium arch, cracked right in two, and Mozart's music, splintered into pieces and lying disject: there a trill, there a scale, and there a chord. Mr. Williams, now at the most grisly point in his story, would no doubt think it queer that she smiled. Ah, but she was perhaps providing him with a minor, a very minor, topic of conversation! He could say next week, to someone seated in this room: "Are you fond of Mozart's music? Do you know that odd, grinning Mrs. Tracy?"

[1933]

1. *timbales:* fish or meat in custard sauce, baked in bowls made of pastry.

Coming Out

GOING IN is like this: one morning you finally make up your mind that no one in the world, with the single and certain exception of yourself, has a problem, utters a groan, or sheds a tear. The entire habitable globe, to your distraught imagination, is peopled by human beings who eat three meals a day, surrounded by smiling faces, work with a will in offices, fields, factories, and mines, and sleep every hour of the night. All the young human beings are in love; all the middle-aged are either charmingly drunk or soberly busy; all the old are reading memoirs or knitting or whittling wood, completely jolly and resigned. The animal world, as well, gambols about in jungle and over llano and crag; happy bright-eyed sheep crop grass; the gay cow chews its cud; the laughing crow swoops over the cornfield. Fish and mussel, ant and peacock, woodchuck and mole, rabbit and cuttlefish go their several ways rejoicing. The cat on the hearth conceals no tattered heart beneath its fur, and the dog on the leash is ravaged by neither remorse nor despair.

You look back over history and it presents to your biased eye nothing but records of glamour and triumph. O happy, happy Aztecs; O splendid Punic Wars; O remarkably situated medieval serfs; O Renaissance figures, armed to the teeth and glowing with inward delight; O fortunate members of the

Children's Crusade; O jolly dwellers in the fifteenth, sixteenth, seventeenth, and eighteenth centuries! O Athenians, O Mongols, O Seljuk Turks, Semites, Visigoths, Manchus, Moors, and paleolithic woman and man! Happy, happy they!

As for you, the most miserable person in any age, you sob and clutch your breast and reject with a sneer all consolations of religion and philosophy. You kick, you snarl, you spit, and you scream. Outside your horrid home the peaceful world flows serenely by: traffic lights change, and the street-cars, instead of swerving off the tracks under the influence of a motorman in the throes of anguish, stop quietly at a lifted hand. People go from one place to another and seem equally pleased with either. Men and women, living their lives neatly and with hellish certainty and precision, rise in the morning, bathe, dress, eat breakfast, lunch, and dinner, smoke cigarettes, earn their livings, drink cocktails, brush their teeth, and, after a well-spent day, finally retire. Looms chatter, turbines whir, and automobiles consume gasoline (for, to your disordered mind, even the machines are happy). In the bowels of the earth miner does not attack miner with shovel and pick; sanely, and in an orderly fashion, all miners attack the coal, iron, or other mineral which they are expected to attack. The captains of ships do not furiously hurl their instruments of navigation clear across the bridge. No barricades are thrown up in the streets, and, in motion-picture and other theatres, the imperturbable patrons would never think of breaking into a howl and charging, in a body, the stage or screen.

Elsewhere, all is mild. But for you there is no hope. Your nervous system yawns before you like the entrance to the pit and you are going in.

The period of time over which you harbor these mistaken ideas about yourself and the rest of the world varies greatly. If your constitution is good, you may easily growl and snarl for the rest of your life. If you are of feeble stamina, you may sob and scratch for perhaps two months or two years. In order to give this article some point, let us assume that, after a reasonable lapse, you finally recover. A remnant of your life lies before you. You can choose several roads to happiness and a useful career. Let us examine these roads as briefly as possible.

You MAY, with great rapidity, start hating or loving. Your love may be of the Shelleyan or of the Christian variety: you may, on the one hand, sink infatuate on the breast of one individual (or, progressively, upon the breasts of several, in a series); on the other, you may figuratively embrace all mankind. Hate does not present many choices; if hate is your solution, you are fairly certain to hate all phenomena with equal joy and intensity, without troubling to drag into prominence any one feature from the loathsome whole. Or you may feel very noble or very powerful. Feeling noble or powerful also defies analysis; when one feels noble or powerful in any degree, one feels noble or powerful, and there's nothing more to say.

But no matter how rapidly you manage to go into your adjustment, no matter how eagerly you grab at the sops of love, hate, nobility, or the passion for personal dominance, you are certain to see, for one lucid moment, one clear flash of that world formerly thought so serene. For one split second you are upheld in a dead calm. You are no longer the world's lost child or the universe's changeling. You are a normal person, ready to join your fellows.

Standing on the latest point reached in the long and unbroken graph of lunacy that rises from the eoliths and culminates, for the time being, in the general situation at whatever day, hour, minute it happens to be, you may survey those fellows from whom you have long felt yourself estranged. You will survey them, I trust, with affection, or with malicious pity; it is not the part of a noble and newly normal soul to survey them with contempt. You will survey the intelligent unhinged, the unenlightened witless, and the plain cracked. And you will realize (only for a moment, you understand) that if you took to eating blotting paper, painting things green, living in trees, or indulging in frequent, piercing maniacal cries, you could not exceed the high average of oddity and derangement that you perceive all about you.

Having had your moment, you no longer have anything to fear. Crawl in and out of your nervous system as you will, you are an initiate. You are among friends. You are cured. You may again take your place as a normal person in a normal world.

[1933]

Dove and Serpent

ALTHOUGH THE houses stood securely fastened to the ground, as always, everything in the town went wild in autumn and blew about the streets. Smoke blew wildly from chimneys and torrents of leaves were pulled from the trees; they rushed across the sidewalks and blew against wagons and people and trains; they blew uphill and fell from great heights and small ones; they fell to the ground and into the river. Clouds rode high in the sky; the sun shone brilliantly everywhere. Or else half the town would lie in the shadow of a long cloud and half the town would stand shining bright, the weathervanes almost as still in a strong blast coming from one quarter as in no wind at all, the paint sparkling on the clapboards. Sometimes in the late afternoon the full sun came from two directions at once, from the west and reflected in a full blaze from the windows of houses looking westward.

The children were blown home from school, shouting and running, along with the leaves. They were blown up paths to side doors, or through orchards, or into back yards, where perhaps their mothers stood, taking the last clothes in off the line, apron strings flying out from their waists. The children rushed into kitchens that smelled of baking or of ironed clothes. The doors swung behind them; some of the wind came in, and some of the leaves.

On such days Jack Leonard would come out onto his veranda promptly every afternoon, at the first sound of a child's excited and breathless voice. Leonard had a stick in his hands; he leaned over the veranda railing and beat the stick hard against the resonant wood. The children yelled up at him "Old Jack, old Jack!" concealing their fright with derision. "Crazy old Jack!" they cried, and screamed and ran, while old Leonard's stick came down hard and curses came out of his mouth. In the house behind him, where he lived alone, the curtains hung in rags at the windows and a jumble of old crates and cans cluttered the doorsill.

The kitchen windows of our house overlooked old Leonard's garden and the long path leading up to Mrs. Parsons's door. Mrs. Parsons's path was the line separating our side yard from old Jack's slovenly rows of corn that were never cut down in the autumn, but were left to dry and later to freeze against frozen ground. Mrs. Parsons was a pillar of the Congregationalist church. Her son had gone to a military academy. Sometimes she took care of me when my mother went to the city. Her son's sword hung on the wall of the sitting room; a doll in a paper skirt, that held string, hung beside it. I used to look at these two objects for long unbroken periods; they possessed some significance that I could not pry out of them with my eyes or my mind. The doll and the sword were so pretty and so unexpected. The sword had a tasseled belt twisted around its handle. The doll's little feet under the paper skirt, the string appearing from the middle of a rosette in its sash, its bisque head and real hair and hard small mouth open in a smile—this was a problem I could not solve. As I remember my bewilderment, my judgment even now can do nothing to make things clear. The child has nothing to which it can compare the situation. And everything that then was strange is even stranger in retrospect. The sum has been added up wrong and written down wrong and this faulty conclusion has long ago been accepted and approved. There's nothing to be done about it now.

My mother's quick temper often estranged her from her neighbors. She was then a woman of forty, beginning to be stout. She carried herself well and could be extremely handsome when she troubled about her appearance. She went about her life with an air of great secrecy and she was very much alone. She would stand, early in the morning, when the kitchen was floating in sunlight, beside the sink, cleaning the lamps. She had large, beautiful, but clumsy hands; when she was tired or nervous she could not hold anything in them—everything she touched tumbled to the floor. She took up the scissors and cut the lamp wicks; she washed the lamp chimneys that were so prettily beaded around the top; she filled the base of the lamps with oil. After she had finished, she would stand by the window that looked toward old Leonard's house. The window had sash curtains over its lower half. My mother's gaze was directed through the upper, uncurtained panes. Sometimes she would stand there for a long time, perfectly still, one hand on the window jamb, one hand hanging by her side. When she stood like this, she was puzzling to me; I knew nothing whatever about her; she was a stranger; I couldn't understand what she was. "There's old Leonard again," she would say, "kicking the cornstalks."

The whole town, late in October, felt the cold coming on; in bleak afternoons the lights came out early in the frame houses; lights showed clearly across the river in the chill dusk in houses and in the mill. Everyone knew what he had to face. After the blaze of summer that had parched paint and shingle, winter was closing in to freeze wood and stone to the core. The whole house, in winter, turned as cold as a tomb. The upper rooms smelled of cold plaster and cold wood. The parlor was shut; the piano stood shut and freezing against the wall; the lace curtains fell in starched frigid folds down to the cold grain of the carpet. The little padded books on the table, the lace doilies under them, the painted china vases, and the big pictures hanging against the big pattern of the wallpaper all looked distant, desolate, and to no purpose when the door was opened into the room's icy air. The life of the house went on in the sitting room and in the kitchen, for in both these rooms there were stoves. If my mother happened to be on good terms with Mrs. Parsons or with Mrs. Gardner, who lived across the street, they would come to visit her in the early twilight, on those days when the lamps were lit at four o'clock. My mother made tea and the women sat talking in low secret voices beside the kitchen table. I sat in the sitting-room, and heard their voices and the sound of dry leaves blowing along the walk at the side of the house. The two windows of this room also looked out over old Leonard's garden; at this hour a lamp was lit in his back room, behind a window covered by a cracked and torn shade.

Still with a sinking of the heart, I remember the look of that room shut away between the closed door of the parlor, where no one could sit, and the closed door of the kitchen, where my mother sat with a neighbor. "You stay here," my mother would say, and step toward the kitchen door, and close it softly behind her. Secrecy was bound up in her nature. She could not go from one room to another without the intense purpose that must cover it-self with stealth. She closed the door as though she had said goodbye to me and to truth and to the lamp she had cleaned that morning and to the table soon to be laid for supper, as though she faced some romantic subterfuge, some pleasant deceit.

It was bitter weather, too cold for storms, too rigid and silent for the wind, when old Leonard first came to the kitchen door. Why he came I do not know. I heard his voice and my mother's voice answering, and I sat listen-ing, not able to make out the words, and was terribly afraid. I did not dare to move from my chair; I remembered his strong old body, his fierce old face with a nose like a bird's beak, his ragged beard, the sound of his stick beating against wood, the curses coming out of his mouth. I could not call my mother or go near the kitchen door. After he had gone, my mother said that perhaps he had come in to get warm. "He's an old man," she said, but these words explained nothing to me. "He likes to sit where it is warm and talk to someone. You mustn't be afraid of him. He can't do anything to hurt you."

Every time he came, my terror hurt me to such a degree that I thought I could not bear it. I could not understand why he should want to come, or why my mother should want to open the door to him. I should have slammed the door in his face, put out all the lights when I heard his footsteps on the path, drawn down the blinds, pretending that the house was empty. I could not see how my mother could bear to sit in the same room with such ugliness, such age. One evening my mother opened the kitchen door, and I saw him sitting in the rocking chair beside the window. He was peeling an apple; the peel hung down in one piece from the fruit, in a long curl; he turned the knife round and round. His hat was on his head, and he said nothing. My mother had made him a cup of tea and put a plate of bread and butter beside it.

He lifted his head and saw me and grinned down into his beard. If he had put out his hand to touch me, I could not have been more frightened; with half a room between us, I stood transfixed by that smile. "It's Mr. Leonard," my mother said, and lifted the stove lid, shifting the kettle to one side. "It's a cold night, and I'm giving him a nice hot cup of tea to warm him up."

The peel fell to the floor and old Leonard closed his knife with his thumb. Then I heard him speak the first words that were not curses. "We must be wise," he said to my mother. "We must be as wise as the serpent and as gentle as the dove. As the serpent, as the dove,"[1] he said, and picked up the cup of tea from its saucer. The peeled apple lay on the table beside him.

These words now lie in my memory as inexplicable as the doll and the sword. I did not know what they meant then, and I do not know what they mean now. It is such memories, compounded of bewilderment and ignorance and fear, that we must always keep in our hearts. We can never forget them because we cannot understand them, and because they are of no use.

[1934]

1. Matthew 10:16.

Letdown

IN ORDER that the reader may fully appreciate the full oddity of my association, at thirteen, with Miss Cooper, at sixty, I must outline briefly the oddity of the city which was the scene of our association. Miss Cooper lived in the Hotel Oxford, and I lived on Harold Street, and a whole world, a whole civilization, or, if you will, the lack of a whole world, of a whole civilization, lay between.

That city possessed a highly civilized nucleus composed of buildings built around a square. These buildings were copies of palaces in Italy, churches in England, and residences in Munich. The square's center was occupied by a triangular plot of grass, garnished at its three corners by large palms growing in tubs. The streetcars rattled by these. Perhaps, too, a bed of begonias and coleuses pleased the eye with some simple horticultural pattern. I can't remember clearly. It was the architecture which warmed my heart. The sight of imitation true Gothic, imitation true Italian Renaissance, and imitation false Gothic revival often gave me that sensation in the pit of the stomach which heralds both love and an intense aesthetic experience. And to this day I have never been able to extirpate from my taste a thorough affection for potted palms.

Harold Street, on the other hand, had not emerged from the brain of an architect of any period. It was a street not only in a suburb but on the edge of a suburb, and it was a carpenter's dull skill with pine planks and millwork in general that could be thanked for the houses' general design. Our house, built to accommodate three families, one to a floor, was perhaps two years old. Carpenters hammered new three-family houses together continually, on all sides of it. For several of my adolescent years, until the street was finally given up as completed, I watched and heard the construction of these houses. Even when finished, they had an extremely provisional look, as though a breath of wind could blow them away.

Sometimes I think that, between us, my mother and I must have invented Miss Cooper; this is impossible, however, because of our splendid ignorance of the materials of which Miss Cooper was composed. We both lighted upon her simultaneously through the commendation of the drawing teacher in my school, who thought I was Talented, and Should Have Further Instruction.

I was, it is true, thrown into a high state of nervous tension at the sight of a drawing board. This state passed for talent at the time. It must have been something else, since nothing ever came of it.

THE HOTEL Oxford stood a few yards up one street leading to the remarkable square. A fair-sized section of quarry had gone into its manufacture. And within it was heavily weighted down with good, solid woodwork, mahogany in color; with statues, large and small, of bronze and of marble, representing draped winged creatures which, although caught in attitudes of listening or looking or touching, gave the impression of deafness, blindness, and insensibility. (I thought these quite pretty at the time.) It was weighted with plush draperies, with gilt picture frames half a foot broad, with a heavy, well-fed, well-mustached staff of clerks. The little elevator, manned by a decrepit old boy in a toupee, sighed up through floors heavily carpeted in discreet magenta. Miss Cooper's studio was at the top of the building. It had no skylight and it looked out onto railway yards, but it was directly under the roof; it had that distinction.

The big room looked as though, at some time in the past, the great conflagration of art had passed over it, charring the walls, the floor, and the ceiling, together with the objects they contained. Everything looked burned and tarnished: the brown pongee[1] curtains; the dull bronze, brass, and copper; the black, twisted wrought iron; the cracked and carved wood of the Spanish chairs. Or perhaps it was the wave of art that had once washed briefly against it, leaving pale casts of the human hand and foot, life and death masks, a little replica of the Leaning Tower of Pisa, a tiny marble bowl surmounted by alabaster doves (the litter of art-form bric-a-brac) in its wake. In any case, there it was, and I had never seen anything like it before, and had it been Michelangelo's own workroom, it could not have been more remarkable to me.

Against this somber background, Miss Cooper stood out like porcelain. She was smaller at sixty than myself at thirteen. Her white hair, combed into a series of delicate loops over her forehead, resembled the round feathers that sometimes seep out of pillows. Her white teeth, solid and young, made her smile a delightful surprise. She dressed in the loose Liberty silks which constituted a uniform for the artistic women of the period; around her neck hung several chains of Florentine silver. Personal distinction, in those days, to me meant undoubted nobility of soul. Distinguished physical traits went right through to the back, as it were, indelibly staining mind and spirit. And Miss Cooper, being stamped all over with the color and designs of art as well as by the traits of gentility, made double claims upon my respect and imagination.

It is difficult to put down coldly the terrific excitement engendered in my breast by those Saturday afternoons. I would come in, unpin my hat, lay off my coat, and there was the still life, freshly fitted into chalk marks, on the low table, and there was the leather stool on which I sat, and there was the charcoal paper pinned to its board, and the array of wonderful materials: sticks of charcoal, beautifully black, slender, and brittle; pastels, running through shade after delicate shade in a shallow wooden box; the fixative; the kneaded rubber. And there was Miss Cooper, the adept at these mysteries. Sometimes in the autumn evenings, after the lesson was finished, she lighted candles and made me tea. That is, she brought in from a kitchen as big as a closet, off the hall, a tray on which sat two cups and two saucers of Italian pottery, and a plate of what I called cookies and she called biscuits. Many times, after a cup of this tea, I staggered out into a world in which everything seemed suspended in the twilight, floating in midair, as in a mirage. I waited for the trolley car which would take me back to Harold Street in a daze, full of enough romantic nonsense to poison ten lives at their root.

Sometimes I wondered about Miss Cooper's own work in the field of graphic art. Pictures produced by her hand—pastels and water colors, all very accurate and bright—hung on the walls. But there was never anything on drawing board or easel. Every summer she disappeared into that fabulous region known as "abroad"; she did not bring back portfolios full of sketches, but only another assortment of small objects: carved wood from Oberammergau, Tanagra² figurines, Florentine leather boxes, and strings of gold-flecked beads from Venice. These joined the artistic litter in the studio.

The enchantment worked for two years. In the autumn of the third, something had changed. In a pupil, the abstracted look in Miss Cooper's eye could have been put down to loss of interest; in a teacher, I could not account for it. Miss Cooper lived in my mind at a continual point of perfection; she was like a picture: she existed, but not in any degree did she live or change. She existed beyond simple human needs, beyond hunger and thirst, beyond loneliness, weariness, below the heights of joy and despair.

She could not quarrel and she could not sigh. I had assigned to her the words and the smile by which I first knew her, and I refused to believe her capable of any others. But now, behind my shoulder, those October afternoons, I often heard her sigh, and she spent more time in the closet-like kitchen, rattling china and spoons, than she spent in the studio itself. I knew that she was having a cup of tea alone, while I worked in the fading light. She was still gentle, still kind. But she was not wholly there. I had lost her.

It is always ourselves that we blame for such losses, when we are young. For weeks I went about inventing reasons for Miss Cooper's defection; I clung to some and rejected others. When we are young, we are proud; we say nothing; we are silent and we watch. My ears became sharpened to every tired tone in her voice, to every clink of china and spoon, to every long period of her silence. One afternoon she came out of the kitchen and stood behind me. She had something in her hand that crackled like paper, and when she spoke she mumbled as though her mouth were full. I turned and looked at her; she was standing with a greasy paper bag in one hand and a half-eaten doughnut in the other. Her hair was still beautifully arranged; she still wore the silver and fire-opal ring on the little finger of her right hand. But in that moment she died for me. She died and the room died and the still life died a second death. She had betrayed me. She had betrayed the Hotel Oxford and the replica of the Leaning Tower of Pisa and the whole world of romantic notions built up around her. She had let me down; she had appeared as she was: a tired old woman who fed herself for comfort. With perfect ruthlessness I rejected her utterly. And for weeks, at night, in the bedroom of the frame house in Harold Street, I shed tears that rose from anger as much as disappointment, from disillusion and from dismay. I can't remember that for one moment I entertained pity for her. It was for myself that I kept that tender and cleansing emotion. Yes, it was for myself and for dignity and gentility soiled and broken that I shed those tears. At fifteen and for a long time thereafter, it is a monstrous thing, the heart.

[1934]

1. pongee: soft Chinese silk, usually left in its natural light-brown color.
2. Oberammergau: a village in the Bavarian Alps, site of an annual Passion Play; Tanagra: Greek city known for tombs and excavation sites.

Not Love, but Ardor

"So THIS is where we are to draw our latest breath," she said.

"With some difficulty," he answered. "Why do they play the gramophone incessantly?"

"People must be lulled," she said. "Even reflected in black mirrors, a hundred feet below the street, people must be lulled."

They sat down on the silvered leather couch. In vaudeville, the team used to sit on a park bench, in one, the drop behind them representing an elegant street, or a lookout on Lake Como, with balustrades, urns, and purple cypresses.

"How are you?" he said.

"Splendid," she answered. "A little tired."

"People used to listen to band concerts," she said. "In dusty parks, full of dusty walks, dusty children, and dusty leaves."

"I know," he said. "Why don't you take off your hat so I can kiss you?"

The elevator opened and closed, by means of some obscure mechanical device. The doors slid to with silent ease; the pattern of silver lines on their halves met and was completed.

"So you thought I was irascible with the waiter," he said.

"Yes," she answered. "I thought so. You should guard against that tendency. It's a sign of the beginning of the end when one begins to send back food in restaurants."

"Your own philosophic calm can also be a little wearing," he said. "Your captious philosophic calm."

"It is far better for you to be irascible with me," she said. "I stand it because I think it is good for me. Salutary in its effect. I am giving myself, as you may have noticed, a short period in which I allow myself to be cowed."

"You don't miss a trick, do you?" he said. "You think you're on to it all, without a break."

"Part of my charm," she said. "My hat is off."

They kissed.

The squat copper-gold drum of the pillar in front of them gave off a light that should have touched the senses. It would have touched the senses of a Verlaine, say, or a Goethe.

"You are a handsome darling," he said.

"The configuration of my arms and breast is like a gentle landscape that should be further enhanced by groups of little sheep," she answered.

"Your remarkable memory shouldn't work in the daytime," he said. "I wonder if they time the sitters?"

The sitters, the gazers, the smokers.

Another elevator came down, opened, closed.

"This is advertised on posters, in every desolate and sunny railway station in Massachusetts and Vermont," she said. "Hither they all run, underground, for diversion, to be faced by an aluminum statue and a canned rubber tree. They go back to wooden floors and wallpaper."

"I, for one, never know why I come to this damned city," he said.

"To eat little brown chickens, to drink Calvet, to admire the views, to visit the places of amusement, to shun your acquaintances, and to kiss."

"Just because it's five o'clock in the afternoon, you needn't make me out a fool," he said.

"'Hold it all in contempt and then it will be true.' Chekov," she said. "Those elevators, for example. Soon we shall go upstairs and watch perfect figures on the screen move and display their carefully calculated passion and distress, and feel with everyone in the house that it is our own passion and grief which is enacted before our very eyes. Not that I have any passion or distress. Not that I have them or wish to have them."

"You talk so much about them that anyone would think you had," he said. "When I feel nothing I keep my mouth shut."

"Like the immortal gods," she said. "We sit here and feel nothing. Above the battle. In a hollow calm, without suffering. It is thus that the Olympian gods loved and moved, without suffering. To love without love, to suffer without suffering, like the immortal gods."

"You sound more than tired," he said.

"With divine ichor, and not blood, in the veins," she answered.

[Unpublished typescript, 1934]

To Take Leave

Now, look here, my fine pair, widely known as Sorrow and Romantic Attachment, I have entertained the thought of you over a long period of years. I have enjoyed you as a delight and endured you as a burden. I have summered and wintered you, and I have given you the unmistakable advantages of both penury and travel. Because of me you have been exposed to cities whose public splendor is equaled by their private squalor, and you have also experienced the close confines of suburbs whose scene and population have the unrewarding tone and texture of stale bread. I have had your good, not to say your education, at heart.

I have dragged you far south and quartered you in houses triply sealed against the sun, in a country of cracked church bells, oranges, lemons, mimosa, and cinerarias, where the honey has a bitter taste and the coffee smells of chloroform. Together we have taken refuge from the blinding streets in museums, where we were bored by small funerary objects, astounded by great sprays of coral rooted in bronze helmets, and pleased by various forms of painting and sculpture. We have listened to fountains in gardens. We have sat, long Sunday afternoons, in the parlors of third-class hotels, among the stopped clocks and the cracked ormolu.[1] With breast-high furniture all about us, we have heard the punctual after-dinner clatter of thick dishes echo against the steep, stained courts of *pensions;* in the morning we have stumbled over the slattern mop and pail; at night we have turned to sleep in rooms soaked through and through with the pattern of bad wallpaper. Together we have experienced the misery of things and the grandeur of nature (for volcanoes, oceans, and mountain passes have not been unknown to us).

Because of you, my horrid twain, and dogged by you every inch of the way, I have walked through hot or rainy streets and driven miles in various broken-down vehicles to post and telegraph offices; I have inquired daily for mail at little grilles that penned in surly natives of several countries; I have, each morning, met the old men and women, the old ashtrays, and the old newspapers in the waiting rooms of tourist bureaus. In all weathers, in all climates, in railway stations and on wharves, you have touched my sympathies and exacerbated my nerves. With the pair of you at my elbow, I have sat up all night writing letters and wept all day, waiting to receive them.

Faced with 1880 stucco façades, preserved in the white glare of Mediter-
ranean sunlight (which has many of the preservative qualities of formalde-
hyde), or surrounded by damp mountain airs and the huts and hay barns of
simple cowherds, things have been much the same between us.

Whether I ate off grass or bare boards or my lap or the hot or cold plates
on restaurant tables, I was invariably conscious of your presence. Standing
on bridges, leaning over balustrades, at the library, the work table, the hair-
dressers', I could not escape you. Bands played in the open square, piano
music fell down from high open windows, boats lowed at night on the river,
trains whistled half a township away, awaking the nostalgia and the yearning so dear to you. None of us heard these sounds alone.

It is your persistence, as well as your ubiquity, that has compelled me
to take my present stand. Landmarks disappeared and towers grew up out
of excavations, but nothing made any difference to you. Styles changed. The
human race acquired new habits, new means of transportation, new catch-
words, and new rulers. Walls that stood bare at our first meeting now rise
clothed in ivy; several new blights have wiped out several different varieties
of trees. Summers have increased in heat and winters in cold. What with birth
and death, since we three came together, a very nearly new set of people now
inhabit the globe.

We can't go on like this any longer, my friends and far-too-constant-
companions. I sometimes feel that you or I, or possibly the three of us in
combination, are obstructing the stream of progress. Our common advantages haven't done us much good. To continue to live with you would, in
my present opinion, dampen my enthusiasms and blunt my initiative to an
extent exceeding their present dampness and bluntness. I no longer wish
to spend another moment of time wondering, in the watches of the night,
whether the pair of you will be pleasant, accountable, and feasible tomorrow, as you were unfeasible, unpleasant, and unaccountable yesterday. The
intense pleasures of anxiety, as time passes, attract me less and less. Plans
for your liquidation occupy me more and more. This is a short speech to
take leave.

So goodbye, grief. Goodbye, love.

[1935]

1. ormolu: imitation gold leaf used for decorative moldings.

Saturday Night Minimum

WHEN THEY came in the lights had gone down; by the time they were set-tled at the table the spotlight had flooded the pillar behind the piano, and the girl standing against it. The girl wore a mauve dress and a little ermine cape, opened over her breast high around her neck. Her skin was a beautiful browned-peach color against the white and the blue. And her eyes, opened against the spot, in the face blanked out into a public smile, were the eyes of the prettiest little girl in the seventh grade of parochial school.

She began to sing. Her head turned from side to side and her lashes went up and down, shining and pretty, innocent, seductive, lively and mannered, against the blank openness of her smile.

"I'll stick to Monet tonight," he said. He had just discovered that he could keep talking, without getting into the screaming stage, on brandy.

"I'll have rye," she said.

Numerous pieces of pasteboard littered the table. He picked one up and began to read it, as if in defiance of the poor light, which made reading improbable. But he could read it, and he could read it aloud.

She heard whatever it said, and she kept on hearing the girl and seeing her, so invulnerable and so exposed, so parochial and so poised. The girl was happy. Back of the smile, back of the pretty eyes, she was thoroughly and competently happy.

The lights went on and they got their drinks. She hoped that his was Monet. Hers was certainly rye.

He settled back into the collar of his excellent suit and began to talk. Splendid. She liked to hear him talk. He always talked well, with logic and fluency. And a week ago she had begun not to notice that he talked for every-one within hearing, as well as for his immediate listener's ears. Those quick little licks his eyes gave, left and right, as his sentences formed their balance, led up to their verb, as each point came through, imbedded in its organized paragraph, didn't trouble her any more. His style was expository, so that she didn't have to egg him on, with questions and cracks, to urge him to ever higher flights of narration. She could agree with him from time to time: feed him "That's perfectly true's" or "You're quite right there's." That was all that was necessary.

"The whole concept falls to pieces if you attack it on another level," he said.

The spot came on, and a young man stood up to sing. He, too, looked pink and fresh and blunt. He was tall and blond and made very little play with his eyes. On occasion, when his voice got the better of him, he rolled them up, and closed them.

. . . He talked straight through the whole of what the young man had to offer and they had another brandy and another rye.

Elsewhere in the room talking must be going on, for the place was noisy. But the people at neighboring tables were sitting without saying a word. Entertainment was being provided, and they had drinks. They poured both down, without hardly a swallow. They were being it, seeing it, hearing it. They were the customers. They were being sold a bill of goods.

" . . . a much wider field of reference," he ended. "O, far wider," she agreed.

You can't be blamed for what another person winds around you, and builds you into. Another person, busily engaged in spinning round you their attention, their ideas of what would please them, their wishes, their efforts toward love, may finish the process, and begin to hate you, but that isn't your fault. You have been yourself all the time. You haven't noticed that any reeling and winding has been going on, and that you're halfway in and halfway out of a whole web emanating from another.

So that when the reverse process starts, you are safe from it, as well. You are just where you always were, attacking, it may be, a wider field of reference on different levels, surrounded by entire constellations of neatly related ideas.

With the third rye, the reverse process gained such momentum, that it was all over when she looked again at the spot-lighted girl. And this time, strangely enough, there had been no moment of hatred. The girl was exactly the same as she had been half an hour before and she now had her full attention. For her attention was again fully free; it had detached itself automatically; the cocoon had run its long thread back into her heart, where it belonged.

She sat intact, opposite him in the crowd, and felt the last filaments of her effort whip away from the face God had given him, the tie he had chosen himself, the voice that the Monet had made only slightly higher, the abstract ideas he had trained like seals. She now had him under control.

She rudely picked up one of the cards, and read it while he finished his peroration.

On Saturday nights there was a minimum charge attached to the drinks.

[Unpublished typescript, 1935]

Whatever It Is

" . . . I HAVE given up trying to understand why anyone acts in the way he or she does," she wrote to me. "After a winter of seeing several people too closely, I have come to the conclusion that the heart, as it was described to us in youth, went out with the horse, or, perhaps, that one set of human motives, so fully analyzed in literature and depicted in art, down the ages, became obsolete when central heating came in for the second time (the Romans had it first, didn't they?), and now everyone is puzzling to us, and we are puzzling to everyone, because of some obscure and rather mechanical interior renovation. The old fixtures have given out, and the new fixtures don't fit.

"Take the recent odd behavior of Horace Dewey, for example. You know what he is like: the kind that seems, at first glance, to have some quality, because his head is the right shape and he has the easy and rather outmoded air of never letting on. He always looked like a superior kind of traveling salesman, to me. This year, late in February, I began to see him again because he evidently had put some kind of hooks into Evelyn. He began showing up whenever she did, sometimes coincidentally, and other times a little before or after. There was never any outward sign of deep inner stirring on the part of either of them; Evelyn is too circuitous for that: she has Charlie to think of, and if Charlie is not exactly a marriage, he is a home, and that's where Evelyn thinks a woman's place should be. But she is so smart on one side that she's not quite clever enough on another. She put on a great calm toward Horace himself; what she couldn't do was to relax about other women. So if any female began to rustle toward Horace, even in the vaguest way, Evelyn would begin to study her as though she were a problem in geometry. Then, very quietly, she'd start opening and closing her own charm, somewhat in the manner of one of the more poisonous sea anemones. She'd open up her smile and her womanly affections, and then, when her victim made the mistake of advancing toward her one inch, she'd be all round her, closing in on all sides, and then there'd be that final venomous squeeze that finished her off. That's Evelyn, under the domination of love. Horace would be across the room, telling someone what had happened to him in Terre Haute, in 1923, and Charlie, as often as not, was at the office, finishing up a little work, so no one could really make a diagram of what was going on, unless she had had the misfortune of growing up with Evelyn.

"The only women Evelyn let alone were Margaret Trotter and myself. Margaret was too ridiculous to matter, I suppose, and Evelyn had heard me on the subject of Horace. It is an axiom that people who are most tiresome to others are perfectly delightful company for themselves, and Margaret, never caring what anyone else thought about her, would have shaken off Evelyn's tentacles without a quiver. Margaret, in her own estimation, is the most interesting woman, with the possible exception of Madame Curie's daughter, and a woman in her own line, somewhere in Scandinavia, in the world. Margaret has a science and God knows how many degrees, and, what is more, she has what she herself calls a "skill." She can measure something in the chemical line out of one retort into another without spilling a drop —a trick of that nature, I suppose. I have always thought of her as a kind of female pharmacist, because she has that semi-learned look, the nearest a woman can get to the really learned look found on male academic faces. As a matter of fact, I think it's fungi she's good at. I have often wondered whether it is the science that makes her sort of face the way it is, or whether such faces are inevitably attracted to the laboratory; she has, as you know, the competent, neat, blunt aspect that can only be described as a certain awkwardness of feature. But I have always been fond of her. She is simple and generous and never thinks of advancing or retreating or boring into, or striking back; you know where you are with her. It isn't much of a place to be, but you know where it is . . .

" . . . About a month ago I had the lot of them on my hands, one evening, including Charlie: it must have been a dull season at the office. He and Horace get along beautifully, as a matter of fact. They both like to expound situations, and they politely listen to each other alternately. Margaret, free of the fungi, for a time, came before dinner and brought her knitting and stayed on, merely because the suggestion was made that she might. Evelyn hadn't counted on Horace, for once, and I was one up on her there, and to say that she was beside herself would be to put it mildly. Her composure was so thorough and exact that it fitted every part of her except her eyes, and they weren't doing what you'd expect suffering eyes to do. They looked terribly small and bright; she couldn't manage the muscles around them, I suppose, since she had several other features to keep as normal as possible. She couldn't dart out at me, because when you've known someone since you were four there's a sort of no-go feeling attached to those tactics; Margaret she ignored and her public act with Charlie was ever the gentle wife. What she would have done to Horace, given the chance, I shudder to imagine.— It's enough to make you resign from personal relationships, to see a human being in such a state, I often think.

"Now, it was I who suggested the charades. I know, with those ingredients and all that. But I couldn't stand it any longer. I couldn't stand the usual Margaret phrases being produced effortlessly by Margaret, and, since I occasionally pity even the suffering venomous, I thought it might help to put Evelyn out of her agony. I thought she might get Horace aside and tear him to pieces in a nice way, and put it down to the exigencies of the third syllable, denoting frenzy. I didn't much care what happened to Horace. A handsome back of the neck had solved so many problems for him up to now, that it might be trusted to keep on doing its protective job.

"Well, we all had more Scotch, and Horace and I went out, and then Charlie and Evelyn, because Charlie remembered a special one they had done together for years, and then there was nothing for it but that Horace would have to go out with Margaret. I thought he could be spared from Evelyn until the last; the shambles should be put off as long as possible. Margaret said she couldn't act, but she put down her knitting and went. Immediately the door closed on them Evelyn and I had a quick drink apiece. We needed it.

"There was some mumbling and laughter in the other room (I will say that Margaret has one of the loveliest laughs I ever heard) and then there was a silence, and I thought they were going in for costume on a large scale, or something of that sort. I was in more or less of a daze, and would have waited forever, but Evelyn jumped up and said, in the best natured tone possible, "She's probably telling him about the fungi," and made for the door. I followed her, why, I cannot say. Perhaps I thought she might let herself go; she had spent such a long wearing evening being one part of her. We both went into the hall and toward the door of the other room, which was half open. Through it we could see Horace and Margaret clasped together in a passionate embrace.

"It wasn't a stage clasp. It was one of those embraces that one goes into, calmly and with delight, as into the sea on a sultry day, and it had in it, to the most casual eye, the timeless element of deep joy and perfect peace and satisfaction. And it was Horace's embrace. Margaret was in it, but it was his. And it was his kiss she was getting; he wasn't just sharing hers.

"I remember looking at Evelyn's side-face, in the instant before the whole thing broke up, and seeing a curl of her hair, beautifully placed over her ear—a curl that had been put there by a master hand, and I thought, in a flash, as one does in shipwreck, I have no doubt, of the beauty-shop I some-times go to, when out of funds. I saw the women sitting, without privacy, in a long row, under the metal hoods of the driers, looking supremely foolish and shorn, smoking cigarettes, with magazines on their knees. Evelyn, in more privacy, had sat under such a hood to get that curl, and I thought of the hours women pass in such pursuits, hoping for far more from the process than merely prettily curled hair. And I thought that there was a wrong track taken somewhere, and what good does it do? Are we all wrong on what con-stitutes what; why do we think these particular motions count? For, evi-dently, things go on not at all as we think they do, and we are idiots to follow a set of rules that have no relation to the game. And if human passion is going out, and is becoming ridiculous, like the motives in a Sardou play,[1] why didn't we make some effort to understand it, before it became so ridiculous, and stop this nonsense and find the clue to what feeds the illusory world that different people get into for different reasons,—whatever it is."

[Unpublished typescript 1936]

1. Sardou play: French dramatist Victorien Sardou (1831–1908), whose satire gave way to melodrama. Sarah Bernhardt acted in many of his plays, some of which (like *La Tosca*) were made into operas.

II

Journals and Memoir

On the Bogans

My knowledge of my branch does not go beyond my grandfather. His name was James Bogan; he was born in Ulster—Londonderry, I believe, was the town—in the 1830s. He was shipped out to sea when a young boy, and settled in Maine, where he was captain of sailing vessels out of Portland Harbor for many years. The one other branch of the Bogan family that I knew about before receiving your letter was a New England lot that went to Californa in '49.

You are quite right in saying that there are very few Bogans in this country, so perhaps the parent Irish stem may be the same. I have never been certain that it was a definitely Irish stem. I came across a form of the name in "The Battle of Otterburn," one of the ballads in Percy's *Reliques*.

The form given there is Bowghan, and a footnote credits the name to a corruption of the English *Buchan*. I have never really liked to believe that. I think *Bowghan* is a jolly forerunner of *Bogan,* or should be.

~

I never bothered to look up the Bogans, when in Ireland [in 1937]. I don't know if I ever mentioned it to you, but I never cared for the Bogans. My mother, who was a Murphy and a Dublin O'Neil, adopted by a Shields, always held them in a certain amount of scorn; and all my talent comes from my mother's side. The only Bogan I ever really cared about was my brother, Charles, who was killed, as you know, three weeks before the Armistice in the 1914–1918 War, and is buried in France.

[From letters to the poet Allen Tate, February 19, 1927, and March 4, 1941 (WTWL, 33–34).]

Self-Portrait, with Politics

MY WRITING reveals some "allegiances" (if this term means certain marks made upon it by circumstance). I was brought up in the Roman Catholic Church, and was exposed to real liturgy, instead of the dreary "services" and the dreadful hymnody of the Protestant churches. There was a Celtic gift for language, and talent in the form of a remarkable excess of energy, on the maternal side of my family. And I was handed out [. . .] a thorough secondary classical education, from the age of twelve through the age of seventeen, in the public schools of Boston. I did not know I was the member of a class until I was twenty-one; but I knew I was a member of a racial and religious minority, from an early age. One of the great shocks of my life came when I discovered that bigotry existed not only among the Catholics, but among the Protestants, whom I had thought would be tolerant and civilized (since their pretensions were always in that direction). It was borne in upon me, all during my adolescence, that I was a "Mick," no matter what my other faults or virtues might be. It took me a long time to take this fact easily, and to understand the situation which gave rise to the minor persecutions I endured at the hands of supposedly educated and humane people.—I came from the white-collar class and it was difficult to erase the dangerous tendencies—the impulse to "rise" and respect "nice people"—of this class. These tendencies I have wrung out of my spiritual constitution with a great deal of success, I am proud to say.

~

Because what education I received came from New England schools, before 1916, my usable past has more of a classic basis than it would have today, even in the same background. The courses in English literature which I encountered during my secondary education and one year of college, were not very nutritious. But my "classical" education was severe, and I read Latin prose and poetry and Xenophon and the *Iliad,* during my adolescence. Arthur Symons's *The Symbolist Movement,* and the French poets read at its suggestion, were strong influences experienced before I was twenty. The English Metaphysicals (disinterred after 1912 and a literary fashion during my twenties) provided another literary pattern, and Yeats influenced my writing from 1916, when I first read *Responsibilities.*—The American writers to whom I return are Poe (the tales), Thoreau, E. Dickinson, and Henry James. Whitman, read at sixteen, with much enthusiasm, I do not return to, and I never draw any refreshment from his "thought." Henry James I discovered late, and I read him for the first time with the usual prejudices against him, absorbed from the inadequate criticism he has generally received. It was not until I developed some independent critical judgment that I recognized him as a great and subtle artist. If civilization and great art mean complexity rather than simplification, and if the humane can be defined as the well understood because the well explored, James's work is certainly more relevant to American writing, present and future, than the naïve vigor and sentimental "thinking" of Whitman.

~

This is the place, perhaps, to state my belief that the true sincerity and compassion which humane detachment alone can give, are necessary before the writer can pass judgment upon the ills of his time. To sink oneself into a party is fatal, no matter how noble the tenets of that party may be. For all tenets tend to harden into dogma, and all dogma breeds hatred and bigotry, and is therefore stultifying. And the condescension of the political party toward the artist is always clear, however well disguised. The artist will be "given" his freedom: as though it were not the artist who "gives" freedom to the world, and not only "gives" it, but is the only person capable of enduring it, or of understanding what it costs. The artists who remain exemplars have often, it is true, become entangled in politics, but it is not their political work which we remember. [. . .] The true artist will instinctively reject "burning questions" and all "crude oppositions" which can cloud his vision or block his ability to deal with the world. All this has been fought through before now: Turgenev showed up the pretentions of the political critic Belinsky; Flaubert fought the battle against "usefulness" all his life; Yeats wrote the most superb anti-political poetry ever written. Flaubert wrote, in the midst of one bad political period: "Let us [as writers] remain the river and turn the mill."

[1939; a selection of Bogan's responses to a questionnaire in which the editors of the Partisan Review *asked about allegiances to groups and about a usable past particularly in literature, suggesting each writer choose between Henry James and Whitman as the more relevant to the future of American writing. LB also comments on the party politics of people like editor Philip Rahv and her friend Rolfe Humphries.]*

Unsent Questionnaire

MY DISLIKE of telling future research students anything about myself is intense and profound. If they know everything to begin with, how in hell can they go on eating up their tidy little fellowships researching? And I believe the less authentic records are, the more "interesting" they automatically become. Then, too, of course, I have many dark deeds in my past which I shall have to cover up, for posterity's sake. I remember very well, at the age of seven or so, making away with a couple of little gold baby-pins, fastened with a chain, a contraption which fascinated me, from the top of a bureau belong to a girl with long curls, who was older than I was, called Ethel Gardner, in Ballardvale, Massachusetts. I also have liked throwing things away and hiding them, ever since I can remember. I poked a small ring, decorated with a red stone resembling a ruby, down a crack in a staircase, in Bodwell's Hotel, in Milton, New Hampshire, around 1901, and I always used to bury my rag doll, Mag, and dig her up again. In the convent I fell in love with an altar boy, and wrote him a passionate letter, which was later found by a nun, and almost resulted in my getting expelled, then and there. Nothing came of this however, and I won a book, that year, for Catechism, and the Gold Cross for General Excellence, the next. (This cross was later pawned by my unfortunate brother, so I can't send it to you to prove my story.)

So you see, it's just as well if I don't delve into my past. I used to lie in confession regularly, I must warn you, from the time I first confessed, at the ripe moral age of about nine, through a harp draped with a dust-cover, in the convent parlor. (They must have been varnishing the confessionals.)

My great gifts of imagination always took the form of lies, in fact, up to my entrance into puberty, when I became a radical and a Fabian, and discovered Bernard Shaw, Aubrey Beardsley, Arthur Symons, Nietzsche, Wagner, Max Stirner, and Walter Pater. My first literary exercises were strongly influenced by William Morris and D. G. Rossetti and I wrote a long poem, or a sonnet sequence, every day, for about four years, after coming home from school. The effect of these labors, after about two years, was that I got conditioned, one June, in Greek, Latin, French, algebra—in everything, in fact, but English Composition. I was always rather good in physics and geometry, although my struggles, in the laboratory, with Bunsen burners and Gilley boilers, would have made the hair rise on the head of any competent physicist.—I used to weep, when under the influence of other people's poetry, and have a rush of blood to the head, resulting in violent nose-running and sneezes, when the muse descended on *me*. (This symptom passed, after about eighteen, and I don't suppose I have ever been authentically visited by Apollo, since.)

My passage from puberty into early maturity was swift, and I prefer to draw the veil over my experiences, sexual and otherwise, from the age of nineteen, when I married for the first time, to the present. [. . . E]xcept for ten years passed among the so-called bourgeoisie, my life at this time was lived among the lower-middle class, and they have short memories, owning to defective intellects and short memory spans. That I have no criminal records is entirely due to the kindness of several members of the legal and psychiatric professions, who, I am sure, put me down as nuts, and just let me go on, thinking that a stay in the booby hatch, now and again, would not run into as much money as a stay in a jail.

~

Birthplace: Livermore Falls, Maine, a town on the Androscoggin River, run by a paper mill. My father has often told me about the excellent hard cider made by Billy Bean, the proprietor of the town's combination brothel and saloon. B. Bean used to add all sorts of things to the original apple juice, including ground up sirloin steak, and the results of drinking this nectar, when it was ripe, were terrific. I often like to think that I bear traces of this firewater in the ichor which runs in my own veins . . .

Dates (what do you mean "Dates"?): August 11, 1897. Ten years before Auden, Isherwood, and L. MacNeice, and about two thousand after Sappho. This was quite a while to wait, wasn't it. It is my firm belief that I was Messalina, the Woman of Andros, a couple of nameless Alexandrians, Boadicea, Mary Queen of Scots, Lucrezia Borgia, the feminine side of Leonardo, Shakespeare's Sonnets, Madam Roland, Charlotte Corday, Saint Theresa (of Avila), and Felicia Hemans, before this. Born under Leo, you can readily see what the results would be (and have, I may add, been).

~

Influences: I think alcohol comes in here. I began to drink steadily after meeting one Raymond Holden, although I had been known to crook my arm, on two continents, before that. I like Mai-bowle with wild-strawberries in it, champagne, rye, and anything which happens to stay in a bottle, best.

Development: Slow and unsteady.

Literary and social preferences: In a world which makes Louis Bromfield a Chevalier of the Legion of Honor, A[rchibald] MacL[eish] an unofficial Laureate, and A[udrey] Wurdemann a Pulitzer Prize winner, I should give you my preferences! I should live so long!—My social preferences range from truck and taxi drivers who make me laugh, locomotive engineers, when they are good-looking and flirtatious, delivery boys, and touching old people and children [. . .] .

Political convictions: NONE.

Likes and dislikes: My God: what do you think this is: an encyclopedia? —I love food, music, beautiful and *beau/belle-laid-(e)* people of both sexes, babes in arms, flowers, clean rooms, aired sheets, oil-lamps, and books about bad taste. I also like love-making, when it is really well-informed, and some varieties of landscape. I dislike swimming, bathing in lakes or the sea, horseback riding, and dirty fingernails. Also: well-bred accents, loud talk, the professional literati of all ages, other women poets (jealousy!), other men poets, English accents, Yale graduates, and bad writing and bad writers.

Favorite Authors: [. . .] I like George Herbert, Shakespeare, Dante, Catullus, Lucretius [. . .] Swift, Stendhal, and Lewis Carroll. Also [. . .] Thomas à Kempis, Jesus Christ, and Rimbaud. Also Mallarmé and Yeats and whoever wrote Johnny I hardly knew yeh . . .

[1939; LB's prickly response to a request from the Wilson Library Bulletin, *then edited by the poet Stanley Kunitz, to provide data for a profile, which never appeared, and which LB may never have sent (WTWL, 187–91).]*

Self-Questionnaire

HAVE YOU ever sought God?
   No.
What is it that you have sought?
   I sought love.
And you sought love for what reason?
   Those about me, from childhood on, had sought love. I heard and saw them. I saw them rise and fall on that wave. I closely overheard and sharply overlooked their joy and grief. I worked from memory and example.
Have you ever been alone, before this? Can you remember?
   It is hard for me to remember anything by an act of will. It is my tendency to live critically, even hysterically, in the moment, without review or reference. But when I was not alone, I had a dream of nourishing loneliness.

I saw it all, including the time of day falling through the windows. I sat in a chair, a book upon my knees. There was no time of which I was the product or for which I waited. I looked upon this vision with joy. I can no longer.
Describe the configuration of the room, in the dream.

It was bare. Wide boards in the floor, a chair drawn up to the hearth, a tight bunch of flowers in a glass—
The insignia of luxury and leisure.

And of loneliness. The book opened upon the knees.
When were you ever alone?

When I was twenty-two and twenty-four, I lived alone in a native and a foreign city. In the native city I occupied a cubicle and wrote for three evenings a week three pages, now lost. I had a scorn for [word unclear] riches I never for a moment let myself desire. In the foreign city I lived in a large room, surrounded by a wide area of parquet floor and by walls bearing the images of the Empress Elizabeth and two men climbing a snowy hill. Beyond, the big Bechstein grinned in the deserted salon, full of curbed china and dusty tinsel lace. Frau W. dusted the chairs in the morning, peering at the woodwork and upholstery through her lorgnette. She was a widow with a beautiful voice. She loved an engineer in Baden bei Wien.
How did you occupy your energy and your leisure?

Mostly in suffering. I suffered mindlessly, without reference to events, to reality, to time, then as now.
You did not note architecture, or the weather?

Yes, I noted these always. I saw the afternoon shadows deeply strike through the baroque windows, as I had seen them fall, in my childhood, deeply slant and fall, drawing the eye inward into unimagined interiors, through the wooden joints and the wooden sashes that interrupted, in crass squares, the lines of clapboards (under which, at that hour, the shadow deepened). I noted the excesses of plaster and the beautiful horizontal reticences of wooden shutters. I saw the shadows lengthen to such a degree that the ground had no more place for them; they reached the walls, and spread upward, flat and definite, like unfruited espaliered trees.
You never sought God?

No.
What was it that you sought?

I sought love. Having been taught by memory and example.

By what means did you seek love?

I had no means. I was stupid, an exile in myself, sunk in a deep self-mirroring, self-effacing dream. I presented a still surface to the appearances around me, like a glass, stiffened into a polish capable of reflection by the same insane cohesion that keeps the particles of stone firmly within the stone.

You noticed? You observed?

The old man, on the spring mornings, swept together the fallen seed pods, sprayed out from themselves, along the cobbles of the street leading down to the theatre and the bronze statue, itself defined against the light new leaves. In my street there was a *Friseur,*[1] a dark hotel, and three cafés. It was a beautiful and a fallen city, smelling of mould, decorated with pediments on which bronze horses, their chariots, and their charioteers, leaped forward, in nineteenth-century arrogance; full of trees touchingly arranged along paths of beaten earth; full of cafés, courtyards, fountains, with broken pious statues wearing roses and crowns; the stone edge of their basins bore pots of geraniums; full of women's voices singing scales and the smell of fresh bread in the morning; full of the hungry and the dead.[2]

Through this you walked?

Through this I walked, wrapped in the deadening dream. Without memory, or reference. But one night I remembered oil lamps, in the Redoutensaal.[3]

About you the ordinary world revolved?

I had early been stamped by the exigent demands of a childish loyalty. The beauty and arrogance close to me often met sneers and rebuffs from the less endowed beings about her. Early I saw them jib and sneer. Early, early. From the beginning, I abjured the ordinary world.

Deliverance rose in your mind?

Not at first. Not in the days when I stared with fury upon printed words I could not read, that I could not unbraid into meaning. I remember such a day. I took the book down from the top of the bureau: I feel the grain of the binding under my hand; I see the marks upon the paper; I feel my fury rising. —It was from these words that the deliverance[4] later rose. But then they were closed to me.

How do you think that your apperceptions, your perceptions can be reproduced?

By chance, by indirection, by reference.

You are——?

The egotist who looks upon herself with joy. Like scales, cleanly, lightly played, myself rises up from myself.

Did you ever seek God?

No.

Describe the configuration of the dream.

It was bare. A small bunch of flowers in a glass.

And death and birth?

Sister Jerome died when I was ten. I gave birth to a daughter when I was twenty. My husband died when I was twenty-two.

Did you draw conclusions from this?

No.

What do you think of love and style?

They are both moving and ridiculous.

You were, perhaps, both a fool and a careerist?

Yes. In minor ways, I had the desire of surpassing the self through the self. But the pattern of self-abnegation was also strong. My sentiments, my sensitive, delicate, generous side made me a fool.

You had an ambition?

I wished to live without apology.

You suffer?

No: that has expensively been excised.

You wished——?

To live without apology . . .[5]

[1934]

1. *Friseur:* barber.

2. RL's reading, "the lumpy and the dead," appears in JAMR, 56.

3. Redoutensaal: Vienna's concert hall.

4. Although LB's handwriting suggests that she had written "delusions," both here, and in the previous question, RL's "deliverance" is more logical.

5. Elsewhere in the 1934 journal, but not as part of the questionnaire, LB notes the wish to live her life "at last delivered from ambition, from envy, from hatred, from frightened love; to live it until the end *without the need for philosophy;* that is all I ask. I fear the philosopher as I fear the ambitious, the seeker for God, the self-satisfied proud. In them lies evil."

Journals and Memoir

The Sudden Marigolds

WHAT WAS the matter with me, that daisies and buttercups made hardly any impression at all. [. . .] As a matter of fact, it was weeds that I felt closest to and happiest about; and there were more flowering weeds, in those days, than flowers in gardens—a sign, perhaps, of the whole rather depressed and run-down situation in the New England towns of the time, especially the semi-mill towns I grew up in. Yes: weeds: jill-over-the-ground and tansy and the exquisite chicory (in the *terrains vagues)* and a few wild flowers: lady's slipper and the arbutus my mother showed me how to find, under the snow, as far back as Norwich. Solomon's seal and Indian pipe. Ferns. Apple blossoms.

But the first time a flower really struck me as beautiful, strange, portentous, meaningful, and *mine,* was in the room in a private hospital where my mother underwent an operation. Was it the year I was kept out of school, *after* the convent, or the year before I went to the convent? After, I think, since that operation marked a kind of limit to my mother's *youthful* middle age, and brought in the worser hopes and the lessened energy of a distinct later period. The Dr. X (that she had loved for years) must have been involved in this setup (the Yankee hospital, for example); and must have faded out from the picture soon thereafter, with consequent tragic reverberation . . .

In any case, the room was quite grand, as I remember it; not at all like a hospital: dark brown woodwork, a fireplace with colored tiles and a mantelpiece, a sunny window and wicker chairs. My father, my brother, and myself came on a Sunday. My mother was lying in bed in a pretty lace-trimmed nightgown, her hair in two braids. She looked young and happy and was in one of her truly lovely moods, when affection rayed out from her like light. Someone had sent her a long box full of pink roses. Who could this have been? Not any of us.

I remember the roses, and disliking them: their long thorny stems, their innocuous color, and the asparagus fern in which they were packed. They seemed false, almost artificial, like wax or paper flowers: there was a touch of ill health about the curl and the veined color of their petals. The whole afternoon was rather frightening and forbidding; I sensed in the atmosphere that touch of "the other" world: of the conventional, Yankee world which I was on the verge of entering with real closeness, in which I would always have friends and allies, but also ill-wishers, if not enemies,—the world of school and church then alien to me; of accents not quite mine; of genteel manners; of the *right* side of things.—The roses rather struck a chill into me—was I eleven?—and I found myself moving away from my mother's bed toward the fireplace, on the opposite wall.

Here is what I saw. Someone had put, rather casually, certainly, into a small glass vase, a bunch of what I now know is a rather common garden flower called French marigold. The flowers were dark yellow, with blotches and speckles of brown, and they had, I think, a few rather carrot-like leaves mixed with them. The sight of these flowers gave me such a shock that I lost sight of the room for a moment. The dark yellow stood out against the brown woodwork, while the dark brown markings seemed to enrich the somber background. Suddenly I *recognized* something at once simple and full of the utmost richness of design and contrast that was *mine*. A whole world, in a moment, opened up: a world of design and simplicity; of a kind of rightness, a kind of taste and knowingness, that shot me forward, as it were, into an existence concerning which, up to that instant of recognition, I had had no knowledge or idea. *This* was the kind of flower, and the kind of arrangement and the sense of arrangement plus background, that, I at once realized, came out of impulses to which I could respond. I saw the hands arranging the flowers and leaves, the water poured into the vase, the vase lifted to the shelf on which it stood: they were my hands. A garden from which such flowers came I could not visualize: I had never seen such a garden. But the impulse of pleasure that existed *back* of the arrangement—with its clear, rather severe emotional coloring—I knew. And I knew the flowers—their striped and mottled elegance—forever and for all time, forward and back. They were mine, as though I had invented them.

The sudden marigolds. That they were indeed sacred flowers I did not learn until many years later.

[1954]

1. LB inserted a dividing colophon here.

The Gardner Family

PERHAPS ONE of the reasons why I hesitate to write of it is that, in writing it, I feel I shall lose it forever—and that I do not want to do. Not that moment, when I first stood in the door of Ethel's room, and saw what must, even at the age of seven, have struck me immediately and irrevocably: the order, the whiteness, the sunlight, the peace, the charm. It is at the door, looking in, that I always see myself, in memory: but I must have gone in more than once, and certainly the little objects which are the most precious part of my memory must have been observed close to, and taken up and handled many times. The dormer window looked out on the river, and had simple white curtains. The bed was under the slope of the roof. It, too, was white. I had never had a room of my own. This was Ethel's room.

Everything must have been white, even the furniture. It was a period when bedrooms had white painted bureaus, and the head and foot of beds (painted iron) were white, and little cane-seated chairs with prettily turned backs and legs stood about. [. . .] The bureau must have been low, perhaps with an oval mirror swung on two brackets above it; for I could see what lay on the top. Everything laid out with care, on the embroidered white linen cloth. A bolster pincushion, ruffled along its edge, stuck with pins, needles, and one or two brooches. The manicure things, laid in order to one side: scissors, file, orange sticks, and nail buffer—surely in the imitation ivory which was fashionable at the time. The china pin-tray, curbed and gilded at the edge, and painted with violets. The "hair-receiver," with a hole in its pretty cover, to match. The brush and comb, clean and set together. The buttonhook. The two tiny jars for paste and powder nail polish. The handkerchief box (I don't see this clearly, but I'm sure it was there). Then, last and most precious and beautiful, the ring tree.

Ethel had bracelets *and* a ring. I can't feel that she had more than one of each. The ring tree was made for several rings, but I can't remember any hanging on its minuscule branches. It was made of white china with a tiny green figure of delicate leaves on its saucer-base. The "tree" part was shaped like a leafless miniature tree, with at least three tiny branches—and a light scattering of gold, like powder, outlined its twig-like arms.

[1957]

WE HAD come to Ballardvale from Milton, with no house ready for us to live in, and began by boarding at the Gardners'. [. . .] I can only express my delight and happiness with the Gardners' way of living by saying that they had one of everything. Up to that time (except for a short period before Milton) I had lived in the Milton Hotel; I had seen normal households only on short visits; I had no idea of ordered living. Households, in the New England of that time, as I later came to know, were often haphazardly equipped. The old was made to do, and the new was coming into existence little by little. The front parlors would have pretty ornaments, gilt frames, carpets, and cushions; the front bedrooms would have white bedspreads and pillow shams; but the kitchen was often still the center of the house, and often a disorderly "sitting room" lay between parlor and kitchen. Many people, as my mother would say, did not "know how."

But with the Gardners it was different. Order ran through the house. There were no bare spaces, or improvised nooks and corners; the kitchen shone with paint and oilcloth; the parlor, although minuscule, was a parlor through and through. The dining room, with its round table always ready for a meal (the turning castor-set in the center, the white damask cloth), was used to eat in, three times a day, and the meals were always on time. There was a delightful little sitting room, off the front porch. And beyond the sitting room, in one of the ells (our bedroom was above it), ran Mrs. Gardner's workroom (she sewed), with a long bare table, a dress form, and a cabinet-like bureau where she kept her materials. This was the first workroom I had ever seen. I used to dream about it for years.

~

The piano [. . .] faced the sofa; and a large seashell served as a doorstop. On the mantelpiece sparkled a row of hand-painted china. The white curtains at the windows were of net, with a lace border, and the rug had a small flowered pattern. Mr. Gardner's flute lay on top of the piano, in a worn black leather case; and there was a music cabinet with a small marquetry design on its doors. It was delightful to play five-finger exercises in these surroundings. But when we first came to the house I could not read anything—neither letters nor musical notes. The house was my book.

One of everything and everything ordered and complete: napkins in napkin rings; plants in jardinieres; blankets at the foot of the beds, and an afghan on the sofa. Pills in little bottles in the sideboard drawer (the Gardners believed in homeopathic medicine). Doilies on the tables; platters and sauce boats and berry dishes and differently shaped glasses and crescent-shaped bone dishes and cups and saucers and cake plates in the dining-room china cabinet. A brightly polished silver card-receiver on the table in the hall. A hat rack. An umbrella stand. And, in the kitchen, black iron pans and black tin bread pans; a kettle; a double boiler; a roaster; a big yellow mixing bowl; custard cups; pie tins; a cookie jar. Mrs. Gardner often made, for midday dinner or for supper, *one* single large pie. I can see it on the kitchen table, with juices oozing from the pattern cut in its upper brown crust. And I can taste the food: pot roast with raisins in the sauce; hot biscuits; oatmeal with cream; sliced oranges; broiled fish with slices of lemon and cut-up parsley on top, with browned butter around it. Roast pork; fried potatoes; baked tomatoes . . .

Ethel's father worked in the railway office of a nearby junction, on a salary which was fairly small, even for the period. But every move of the family was planned. Extreme economy must have prevailed, even with Mrs. Gardner's dressmaking money added to their income. No sign of economic pressure was ever allowed to show. Things were kept up, and cared for, but they must have been renewed, as well. Disorder never was allowed. The complications of laundry and of the personal toilet—for there couldn't have been a bathroom—were managed with precision and almost invisibly. The washbowls with the big pitchers sitting in them, the lidded soap dish; the towel rack with its long-fringed linen towels; the toothbrush glass and the tin of tooth powder—these, too, neatly existed. The long slender vase for flowers. The rough bristled doormat outside the door . . .

Blessed order! Blessed thrift . . .

[1959]

Mary Shields Bogan

[. . .] I DO not at first see my mother. I see her clearly much later than I smell and feel her—long after I see those solid fractions of the houses and fields. She comes in frightfully clearly, all at once. But first I have learned the cracks in the sidewalk, the rain in the gutter, the mud and the sodden wayside leaves, the shape of every plant and weed and flower in the grass.

The incredibly ugly mill towns of my childhood, barely dissociated from the empty, haphazardly cultivated, half-wild, half-deserted countryside around them. Rough stony pastures, rugged woodlots, lit up and darkened by the clearly defined, pale, lonely light and shadow of weather that has in it the element of being newly descried—for a few hundred years only—by the eye of the white man. The light that falls incredibly down through a time-less universe to light up clapboard walls, old weathered shingles as well as newly painted, narrow-faced cottages, adorned with Victorian fretwork. In Ballardvale, the mill, warm, red brick, with small-paned windows (an ex-ample of good proportion, as I afterwards discovered); on side streets the almost entirely abandoned wooden tenements of the early mill town; on the main streets the big white or yellow houses with high, square parlors and bedrooms; the occasional mansard roof . . .

The grain in a plank sidewalk certainly came through more clearly to me at first than anything grownups, or even other children, did.

I must have experienced violence from birth. But I remember it, at first, as only bound up with *flight*. I was bundled up and carried away . . .

In the town of Milton violence first came through.

~

The flume cascaded down the rocks, with bright sun sparkling on the clear, foamy water. My mother was afraid of the flume. It had voices for her: it called her and beckoned her. So I, too, began to fear it.

~

The howl and whine of wind rose in the night. The high narrow houses on exposed hillsides, facing wide stretches of open country covered with trees, rocks, and bush, rocked in the wind. The weather changed unaccount-ably in the night.

The color of bare trees on the hills in March . . . The hillsides, once the snow had faded from them, had sunk into them, presented a color so bleached and so neutral that the color of massed twigs above them was warmed into purple—partly the color of distance, partly the color of bark.

How ugly some of the women were! And both men and women bore ugly scars—of skin ailments, of boils, of carbuncles—on their faces, their necks, behind their ears. Sometimes their boils suppurated. All this I marked down with a clinical eye. Then, their bodies were often scarecrow thin, or monstrously bloated. Mrs. X (one of my mother's "familiars") was a dried up, emaciated woman with a sharp nose and ferret eyes: a little horror. Later, I learned that she had carried on a clandestine love affair, for years, with the hotel's proprietor. I must put down his name: Bodwell. Like every other woman in these towns, at that time, she had a house full of veneered furniture, plush, and doilies; and she kept her sewing machine (again a custom) in the bay window of the dining room.

This was the town where I cut my thumb so badly, on a piece of bottle thrown out into the field. I ran to the brook and tried to wash off the blood. But it would not stop, so I put my hand against the front of my coat, and soon that was bloodstained all down the front. I was afraid to go home, but the blood frightened me more. I remember the doctor bandaging the thumb, beside a table, by lamplight.

And the town where the French and Yankee children—the girls—taught me their sexual games. Into these the boys were never allowed.

The secret family angers and secret disruptions passed over my head, it must have been for a year or so. But for two days, I went blind. I remember my sight coming back, by seeing the flat forked light of the gas flame, in its etched glass shade, suddenly appearing beside the bureau. What had I seen? I shall never know.

But one (and final) scene of violence comes through. It is in lamplight, with strong shadows, and an open trunk is the center of it. The curved lid of the trunk is thrown back, and my mother is bending over the trunk, and packing things into it. She is crying and she screams. My father, somewhere in the shadows, groans as though he has been hurt. It is a scene of the utmost terror. And then my mother sweeps me into her arms, and carries me out of the room. She is fleeing; she is running away. Then I remember no more, until a quite different scene comes before my eyes. It is morning—earliest morning. My mother and I and another woman are in a wooden summer-house on a lawn. The summerhouse is painted white and green, and it stands

Mary Shields Bogan

on a slight elevation, so that the cool pale light of a summer dawn pours around it on all sides. At some distance away the actual house stands, surrounded by ornamental shrubs which weep down upon the grass, or seem to crouch against it. The summerhouse itself casts a fanciful and distorted shadow. Then we are in the actual house, and I am putting my hands on a row of cold, smooth silk balls, which hang from the edge of a curtain. Then someone carries me upstairs. The woman goes ahead with a lamp . . .

Then I see her again. Now the late sun of early evening shoots long shadows like arrows, far beyond houses and trees: a low, late light, slanted across the field and river, throwing the shade of trees and thickets for a long distance before it, so that objects far distant from one another are bound together. I never truly feared her. Her tenderness was the other side of her terror. Perhaps, by this time, I had already become what I was for half my life: the semblance of a girl, in which some desires and illusions had been early assassinated: shot dead.

[1934 journal; revised 1959]

IN THE youth of a handsome woman, two currents and two demands run side by side in almost perfect accord: her own vanity's desire for praise and love, and the delight in the praise and love so easily given her. When these two currents lessen, a terrible loneliness and an hysterical dis-ease take their place. For the energy once expended on delight and conquest now has nothing on which it can be dissipated; it is continually meeting small defeats and rebuffs; it is like a river which has made a broad bed for itself but now has dwindled into a tiny stream that makes hardly any show among the wide sweep of pebbles that show the boundaries of its former strength.

~

My mother had true elegance of hand. She could cut an apple like no one else. Her large hands guided the knife; the peel fell in a long light curve down from the fruit. Then she cut a slice from the side. The apple lay on the saucer, beautifully fresh, white, dewed with faint juice. She gave it to me. She put the knife away.

(Or she would measure off, with one forefinger set across another, the width of some ribbon or lace which had run in rows around the skirt and sleeves of some dress she loved and remembered. "Narrow red velvet," she would say, or "white Val lace"; and the color and delicacy of the wide circles would be perfectly brought back into being. Or she would describe the buttons on some coat or winter dress: "cut steel" or "jet" or "big pearl." Suddenly all the elegance of her youth came back.)

Her hands were large and her fingers were padded under their tips. Their chief beauty lay in the way they moved. They moved clumsily from the wrist, but intelligently from the fingers. They were incapable of any cheap or vulgar gesture. The fingernails were clear and rather square at the tips. The palms of her hands were pink.

When she sewed, and that, in my childhood, was rarely, I could hear the rasp of the needle against the thimble (she had a silver one), and that meant peace. For the hands that peeled the apple and measured out the encircling ribbon and lace could also deal out disorder and destruction. They could tear things to bits; put all their soft strength into thrusts and blows; they could lift objects so that they became threats of missiles. But sometimes they made that lovely noise of thimble and needle. Or they lifted the scissors and cut thread with a little snip.

~

I remember a vignette of joy, one summer morning in the house in Ballardvale. I slept in the upstairs front room, in the big double bed, and I remember running from this room to the top of the stairs in the hall. I could see my mother, in a fresh cotton house dress, as she stood outside the front door, on the sloping lawn which ran across the front of the house. She was in one of her good moods. Was she singing, as she often sang, when these moods were upon her? What was it that gave that one moment, in that one morning, its distinction and delight? It must have been the first summer we lived in the house, for the next summer she went away, and I was sent to the convent in August . . . The summer I was eight . . . Still open to joy.

~

When she dressed to go to town, the fear came back. She could not dress without scattering things about the room. Bureau drawers hung open; powder was spilled on the floor. She was careless (except in her rare spells of thorough cleaning) about the order of a room, but carefully elegant about her own person. A round cake of Roger & Gallet soap in the pretty soap dish in the kitchen; orris root in the drawers with her starched petticoats; a chamois skin for her rice powder; and a bottle of Peau d'Espagne. How I hated this perfume! It meant going to the city; it meant her other world; it meant trouble . . .

She would bathe, in the kitchen. Then the crisp underwear went over her head; she pulled the strings of her corset and tied the ribbons in her corset cover. The long silk stockings, the patent-leather shoes, the shirt-waist of batiste or nun's veiling; the skirt, belled out around the bottom; the belt; the soft tie of lace at her throat. In those days, she still had her rings and earrings. One set was turquoise, surrounded by an edge of dia-mond chips. She put her earrings into her ears and the ring on her finger. She pinned a brooch at her throat. Her face, under its powder, was soft and mature; at the side of her cheeks, delicate down appeared when she turned her face to the light. Her lips moved over her teeth, when she spoke, in a way that warmed the heart.

She put on her hat and her veil, and lifted the veil down from the brim. She pulled the veil down over her face, and made a *moue* with her mouth, to adjust and loosen the veil (as though she kissed the air). How she loved herself! I have seen her come home from church and go straight to the mir-ror and there examine her face in the minutest detail, to see how she had looked in other people's eyes. Sometimes, when she was getting ready for church or for town, she would stand for long minutes, when she was al-ready late, becoming more and more angry, the line of anger deepening be-tween her eyes, while my brother or myself fastened her veil to her back hair, with a pin made of brilliants, shaped like an 8 lying on its side. She was always late. She blamed everyone but herself for her lateness. We had made her late. A dreadful chill came over our hearts.

A terrible, unhappy, lost, spoiled, bad-tempered child. A tender, con-trite woman, with, somewhere in her blood, the rake's recklessness, the baffled artist's despair . . .

[1931 journal; revised 1959]

My mother used to use the salt box as an index of time. "What will happen before it is used up?" What *did* happen—to her? I shall never know.[1]

[1961]

1. See also the portrait of LB's mother in "Dove and Serpent" in I: Fiction.

Childhood in Boston

PERHAPS THE beginning of my [recent] "depression" can be located at the occasion (a fall-winter morning and early afternoon) when I went back to the earliest neighborhood we lived in after coming to Boston. [. . . T]he whole area had slipped into true slumhood. The open field was gone; a large garage stood on its site: gray, metallic, forbidding. And the houses had crowded into the back scrubby field: a row of three-family structures, crowded as close to one another as possible. The air of a crowded necessitous place hit me like a breath of sickness—of hopelessness, of despair. The stores which had once existed in our block were gone: their windows cracked and broken. Only the old bakery, down the street, still persisted. [. . .]

A wave of despair seized me, after I had walked around the library (now bedizened with cheap signs and notices but still keeping its interesting curved walls). No book of mine was listed in the catalogue. (A slight paranoid shudder passed over me.)—I felt the consuming, destroying, deforming passage of time; and the spectacle of my family's complete helplessness, in the face of their difficulties, swept over me. With no weapons against what was already becoming an overwhelming series of disasters—no insight, no self-knowledge, no inherited wisdom—I saw my father and mother (and my brother) as helpless victims of ignorance, willfulness, and temperamental disabilities of a near-psychotic order—facing a period (after 1918) where even this small store of pathetic acquisitions would be swept away. The anguish which filled my spirit and mind may, perhaps, be said to have engendered (and reawakened) poisons long since dissipated, so that they gathered, like some noxious gas, at the v. center of my being.

~

The thing to remember, and "dwell on," is the extraordinary *courage* manifested by those two disparate, unawakened (if not actually *lost*) souls: my mother and father. I cannot bring myself to describe the horrors of the pre-1914 lower-middle-class life, in which they found themselves. My father had his job, which kept him in touch with reality; it was his life, always. My mother had nothing but her temperament, her fantasies, her despairs, her secrets, her subterfuges. The money—every cent of it earned by my father, over all the years—came through in a thin stream, often blocked or actually exhausted. Those dollar bills—so definitive! Those quarters and ten-cent pieces—so valuable. (I went to school on a quarter a day.) Those terrible splurges on her clothes, which kept my mother going! How did they manage to keep a roof over their heads! With absolutely no plans for the future— no foresight—no practical acumen of any kind.

Yet out of this exiguous financial situation came my music lessons—my music—my Saturday money (50¢, often) for movies and even the theatre; what clothes I had—that we all had—and food. Even a woman to help with the wash. Little excursions to the beach in the summer.

No books (the library supplied those). No social expenditures. Those two people, literally cut off from any social contacts, with the exception of one or two neighbors—often as eccentric as my parents themselves.—No invitations to classmates—or perhaps one or two—in all those years. Cut off. Isolated. Strung up with a hundred anxieties. And yet they survived— and I went through my entire adolescence—in this purgatory—with an open hell in close relation. A hell which tended to blow into full being on all holidays—when my mother's multiple guilts towards her treatment of her foster mother tended to shake loose.

I cannot describe or particularize. Surely all this agony has long since been absorbed into my work. Even then, it was beginning to be absorbed. For I began writing—at length, in prose—in 1909; and within a year (my last in elementary school) I had acquired the interest of one of those intelligent old maids who so often showed talented children their earliest talents —opened up their earliest efforts by the application of attention and sympathy. I went to the Girls' Latin School in the autumn of 1910, at the age of thirteen, for five most fruitful years. I began to write verse from about fourteen on. The life-saving process then began. By the age of eighteen I had a thick pile of manuscript, in a drawer in the dining room—and had learned every essential of my trade.

[1965]

The Repressed Narrative

THE POET represses the outright narrative of his life. He absorbs it, along with life itself. The repressed becomes the poem. Actually, I have written down my experience in the closest detail. But the rough and vulgar facts are not there.

[1961]

"AND ALL things are forgiven, and it would be strange not to forgive"—this Chekhov knew. Forgiveness and the eagerness *to protect:* these keep me from putting down the crudest shocks received from seven on. With my mother, my earliest instinct was to protect—to take care of, to endure. This, Dr. Wall once told me, is the instinct of a little boy . . . Well, there it is. I *did* manage to become a woman . . . Now, in my later years, I have no hatred or resentment left. But I still cannot describe some of the nightmares lived through, with love. So I shan't try to describe them at all. Finished. Over. The door is open, and I see the ringed hand on the pillow; I weep by the hotel window as she goes down the street, with *another;* I stare at the dots which make up the newspaper photograph (which makes me realize that I then had not yet learned to read). The chambermaid tells me to stop crying. How do we survive such things? But it is long over. And forgiven . . .

[1961]

THE CONTINUOUS turmoil in a disastrous childhood makes one so tired that "Rest" becomes the word forever said by the self to the self. The incidents are so vivid and so terrible that to remember them is inadequate: they must be *forgotten.*

[1932]

IT IS too late either to pour it out or to reconstruct it, bit by bit. What mattered got into the poems. Except for one or two *stories,* which I may be able to tell, it is all there. With the self-pity left out.

[1961]

AND THE poems depended on the *ability* to love. (Yeats kept saying this, to the end.) The *faculty* of loving. A talent. A gift. "We must always be a little in love," Elizabeth M[ayer] said to me (at seventy!) . . . Yes, but it becomes a difficult *task.* And one that must be dissembled . . .

[1961]

I KNOW R[1] to be a victim of Shelleyism and a person who can ultimately do me no good. But I also admit that I feel for him a kind of personal need: I have lived with him for so long that he has become almost like a fifth limb, like a member of my body. And I need even the imperfect love that he can give me. Along with the rest of the poor deracinated generation who in childhood saw the end of one sort of life and who in early maturity, by the turmoil of their lives, helped to form this new, childish, incomplete existence in which we are forced to live, I need some love, however imperfect.

My own insistence upon honor and maturity and decency may be merely a defense against the world.

[1933]

1. R: Raymond Holden, LB's second husband.

THE GREAT satisfaction of getting angry in public.

[1933]

I WAS fond of being a woman and often indulged in nervous battles. Those that I loved soon came to hate me. Those whom I loved I continued to love, sadly, bearing their faults; remembering them best by the boring walks, the long evening dazed with gin, the dead mornings, myself a dupe fed by mendacity.

[1934]

SAW MY real, half-withered, silly face in a shop mirror on the street, under the bald light of an evening shower, and shuddered. The woman who died without producing an *oeuvre*. The woman who ran away.

[1936]

The *Aperçu*

I WISH to live because I wish to set my brief, and lightly written, signature down upon the dreadful muddle of life presented to me.

[1934]

WHATEVER I do, apart from the short cry (lyric poetry) and the short remarks (journalism), must be in the form of notes. Mine is the talent of the cry or the *cahier*.[1]

[1935]

1. *cahier:* notebook. LB used the same *mot* in a letter to Theodore Roethke, November 6, 1935, in which she wrestles with her love/hate for the novel. "Someone like [Henry] James takes it and sweats over it for forty years and what thanks does he get, and who in hell cares what he's really doing, and after his death everything falls right back to where it was before. [. . .] I believe in the short story and the long short story: the novel, never. To hell with the novel. But I have such a wonderful idea for one. But my talent is for the cry or the cahier" (WTWL, 117).

Put me down as one to whom delicate *aperçus,* Swift's sentence structure, and Mozart's music, meant as much as the starry firmament and the moral law, and stood for proofs of life's inner cleanliness, tenderness, and order.

[1937]

My gift depended on the flash—on the *aperçu.* The fake reason, the surface detail, language only—these give no joy.

[1961]

But, I said, if I could put down part of a year, in periods of work, and in defiance of idleness [. . .], I could learn, perhaps, the run and complexity long envied in the styles that do not flag, even when faced by the necessity of long factual exposition. The styles as complex, as delicate as tackle made for some job requiring skill, patience, and strength: a tackle composed of blocks and rope, combining at once the principles of the lever, the inclined plane, and the wheel.

~

I shall work and make a book. Strong, because I still have strength; broken, because I never again shall feel that strength whole.

[1930]

Managing the Unconscious

To begin with:
>You must teach the Unconscious to flow into the channel of writing.
>Daydreaming by the writer and the reader. Projection of ideal situations etc.

Journalist's career does teach two lessons:

It is possible to write for long periods without fatigue.

If one pushes on past the first weariness one finds a reservoir of unsuspected energy . . .

If you are to have the full benefit of the richness of the Subconscious, you must learn to write easily and smoothly when the Unconscious is in the ascendant.

The best way to do this is to rise half an hour, or a full hour, earlier than you customarily rise. Just as soon as you can—and without talking, without reading the morning paper, without picking up the book you laid aside the night before, begin to write.

Write anything that comes into your head: last night's dream, if you are able to remember it, the activities of the day before; a conversation, real or imaginary; an examination of conscience. Write any sort of early morning revery, rapidly and uncritically.

Forget that you have any critical faculty at all. Realize that no one need ever see what you are writing, unless you choose to show it. You may, if you can, write in a notebook sitting up in bed. *Write as long as you have free time, or* until you feel that you have utterly written yourself out.

The next morning begin without reading what you have already done.

After a day or two you will find that there is a certain number of words that you can write easily and without strain. When you have found that limit, begin to push it ahead by a few sentences, then by a paragraph or two. A little later try to double it before you stop the morning's work.

Within a very short time you will find that the exercise has begun to bear fruit.

The actual labor of writing will no longer seem arduous or dull. You will have begun to feel that you can get as much (far more, really) from a written revery as from one that goes on almost wordlessly in the back of your mind.

When you can wake, reach out for your pencil, and begin to write almost on one impulse, you will be ready for the next step.

Watch yourself carefully: if at any time you find you have slipped back into inactive revery, exert pressure on yourself. Throughout your writing life, whenever you are in danger of the spiritual drought that comes to the most facile writer from time to time, put the pencil and paper back on your bedside table and awake to write in the morning.

At once, when you have put the above suggestion into operation, you will find that you are more truly a *writer* than ever before. You will discover that now you have a tendency to cast the day's experiences into words, to foresee the use that you will make of an anecdote or episode that has come your way, to transform the rough material of life into fictional shape, more consistently than when writing was a sporadic, capricious occupation which broke out from time to time unaccountably, or was undertaken only when you felt you had a piece firmly within your grasp.

Engaging to write. The next stage is: After you are dressed, look over the day before you and select some one section of it—fifteen minutes is enough—in which you will write.

Make this engagement a debt of honor.

You have given yourself your word and there is no retracting it. Leave people. If to get the solitude that is necessary you must go into a washroom, go there, lean against the wall and write. Write as you write in the morning, anything at all. Write sure or unsure, hurriedly or blank verse; write what you think of your employer or your secretary or your brother; write a short story synopsis or a fragment of dialogue or a description of someone you have recently noticed.

However halting and perfunctory the writing is, *WRITE*. If you must, you can write: "I am finding this exercise remarkably difficult," and say what you think are the reasons for the difficulty. Vary the complaint from day to day till it no longer represents the true state of affairs.

Do this from day to day, but each time you are to choose a different hour. Try 11 o'clock, or a moment or two before or after lunch. Another time begin before you dine. The important thing is that *at* the moment, *on the dot of the moment* you are to be writing, and that no excuse of any nature can be offered when the moment comes. There is a deep inner resistance to writing which is more likely to emerge at this point than in the earlier exercise. This will begin *to look like business* to the Unconscious, and the Unconscious does not like these rules and regulations until it is more broken in to them. It prefers to choose its own occasions and to emerge when it likes.

Can work done under the handicap of a headache be fit to do. And so on and on.

You must learn to disregard every loophole the wily Unconscious points out to you.

If you consistently, doggedly, refuse to be beguiled, you will have your reward. The Unconscious will suddenly give in charmingly, and begin to write gracefully and well.

If you fail repeatedly at this exercise, give up writing. Your resistance is actually greater than your desire to write, and you may as well find some other outlet for your energy early as later.

[1933]

Thumbnails

THE M[ABEL] Dodges of the world take everything they want, surround themselves with objects, people, and *movements* (analysis, thinking with the stomach or glands, Lawrence, Jeffers and the like).[1] [. . .] These women do not weep, or harden up in order to endure, or accuse endlessly, or become frightened. They want what they want from youth on. They take color only from what they have or where they live, or from the kind of fashionable idea that is current at some particular time or other. They work hard; they have no real sympathies (only "interests"); they early become unalterably set as themselves, so that other people have to attach themselves to them, like limpets, or revolve around them, like satellites—no real communion possible. When they are rich they have permanent secretaries.

[1932]

1. Mabel Dodge Luhan was an heiress who invited many writers and artists to her large "retreat" in Taos, New Mexico. Among them were the English novelist D. H. Lawrence and the American poet Robinson Jeffers.

SOMEONE SAID that Peggy Joyce[1] had been a great success with men because she smelled like leather.

[1932]

1. Peggy Joyce was a former Ziegfeld Follies dancer who married a series of millionaires. She played herself opposite W. C. Fields in the movie *International House* (1933).

THE LARGE ducks making love. The drake pushes and *pushes* the female's head under water with his beak. All this in a little mossy pool and fountain, where the water runs from a veritable shell, under vines, over the rocks.

[1933]

COMING OUT of an *idée fixe*. She sees creams and lotions on the toilet counter, lace jabots with which she might fix up an old dress: she thinks of hiring a sewing machine and buying a pair of pinking shears.

[1932]

THE LECHERY of men of middle age is as hard as a stone. They kiss as though they threw their faces against one; they do not wait and draw in passion as young men do; they strike out at a woman in a kind of frenzy, give embraces in a cold scuffle. They are afraid of being pitiful themselves, so they cannot give out that pity which a woman waits for in any embrace. They make love usually when they are drunk. They speak of golf, their sons and daughters, sometimes of their wives, in the intervals of throwing against a woman that hard face, those cold eyes, those hands tightened up like fists, that dreadful cold, half-open mouth with its licking tongue.

[1932]

DEATH IN the Afternoon turns out to be an elaborate rationalization of H[emingway]'s sadistic, masochistic emotional nature. The contest between a man and a bull is untenable on humanistic grounds, because based on grounds that should not yield up pleasure to the spectator. Were it a struggle between the untired bull and the man, the contest would take on the aspect of suicide or murder, in much the same way as a contest between a man and an oncoming locomotive.

Because the bull must be tired out, so that the man is able to face it at all, and because H.'s admiration goes to the man for classic gesture and courage against non-overwhelming odds, the admiration is decadent, stupid, and even a little obscene. The contest, too.

H. has been stopped emotionally at some point where sexual feeling and cruelty, either given or received, merged in his nature and absorbed each other. The thrill of pity always involves cruelty and this thrill is felt in the bowels and nerves in exactly the same way as sexual feeling.

The expository style in *Death in the Afternoon* is admirable; the emotions involved ignoble (both in themselves and because H. is not on to himself where they are concerned). His jibes at Faulkner and Waldo Frank are well taken; this envious hostility to other writers rises from the same source as the admiration for bullfighting. Quite clearly at bottom appears the senti-mental, sneering, bruising boy.

[1932]

PLATONISM SAUCED up with castles in Holland, splendid old squires who love their peasants, a library in a tower, a mystic young Englishman with high cheekbones, a lovely young wife separated from her high-caste Prussian hus-band. Scenes on the lakes, the sound of waterfalls, seasons described with great emotion (some of this stuff is really excellent). The writing, too, is good in its way: it owes a lot to Bloomsbury and V[irginia] Woolf; some effects are nevertheless delicate and moving. The young Englishman feels stillness within himself. The whole book rings with an attempt at stillness. What really takes place is, of course, adultery, the very dreariest adultery, glazed over with noble motives, described between paragraphs having to do with the center of the soul.

[Précis of The Fountain, *a novel by Charles Morgan, 1932]*

LET ME never forget [Henry] James's beautiful, understanding, touching articles on George Sand.[1] Even the earliest, 1897, is enchanting, and the lat-est one, written in 1914, carries over the same insight and sympathy. These pieces of criticism have endeared James to me as nothing else of his, and be-cause my sympathy was completely touched, I recognized some of James's excellences of style, never recognized so completely before: his success with large figures of comparison; his essentially literary, but nevertheless collo-quially lightened language—he had the true Yankee-Irish (more Irish than

Yankee, but an amalgam of both) gift for the use of the common word and the idiom of common speech. Toward the last, he tended to abjure these colloquialisms; he set them off, like bad or ill-dressed children, with quotation marks. They were absorbed into, and used rightly in, the earlier Jamesian style.

[1933]

1. For LB's comments on the French novelist and woman of letters George Sand (pen name of Amandine Aurore Lucile Dupin, 1804–76), see her letters to Edmund Wilson, July 10, 1925; Rolfe Humphries, September 5, 1935, and Theodore Roethke, December 1935.

IN THEIR cage, at evening in the zoo, one hippopotamus, with his great low hanging ponderous face, nuzzled the side of another. What if tenderness should be lost everywhere else, and left only in these creatures?

[1933]

I FELT that his soul was like a small rectangular piece of wood or bone: a domino: hard: one inch long and a half-inch wide, residing in the unmeasured depth of what we all possess.

[1933]

Out of All Moments Forever

"MY TIME will come," you say to yourself, but how can you know whether or not your time has not already come and gone? Perhaps one afternoon on the veranda in Panama, with the Barbadians whetting their sickles on the hill below, the Chinese garden green, the noise of breakers from beyond the hill, the crochet in your lap, and the cool room shuttered and the sheeted bed, perhaps that was your time. (But it was too early.) Or mornings in the sunny room in Boston, when the children cried loudly from the public school across the way, "A prairie is a *grassy* plain," and you sat on the low couch with your books and papers about you, happy and safe and calm: perhaps your time was then. (But you didn't see it at all.) Perhaps it has been spent, all spent, squandered out, in taking of streetcars, drinking gin, smoking cigarettes,—in connubial love, in thousands of books devoured by the eye, in eating, sewing, in suspicions, tears, jealousy, hatred, and fear. Perhaps it is now, on a dark day in October, in the bedroom where you sit with emptiness in your body and heart; beside the small fire, drying your hair,—older, more tired, desperately silent, unhappily alone, with faith and daydreams (perhaps luckily) broken and disappearing with the dreadful pain in your shoulder which presages dissolution, infection, and age. Perhaps this very instant is your time—pretty late—but still your own, your peculiar, your promised and presaged moment, out of all moments forever.

[1932]

It is not only the pianos that have vanished (the sound of the pianos along the streets on spring evenings when the windows were opened) but the world in which they sounded, and the young ears that they sounded for. I shall never forget how beautiful they were, or what they meant to me. And when I say that their world has vanished, I mean it poignantly: the slant of light over the shabby streets of that time. Totally shabby American streets with no shine or chic in them, only a few doorsteps, lampposts, carriage (wagon) wheels (and the sound that tired horses' feet used to make, when the horses shifted them), trees, and lighted windows—and the tireless scales, like grain pouring from the hand, or the bad pieces those children used to play.

[1933]

The Time of Day

Thoreau's journal: February 5th, 1855

"IN A journal it is important in a few words to describe the weather, or characters of the day, as it affects our feelings. That which was so important at the time cannot be unimportant to remember."

[copied down 1933]

Voyage autour de ma chambre.[1]
    The Xavier de Maistre journey is not so interesting as I expected it to be, such a voyage around every room one lives in would be of inestimable value to oneself, one's children: in a journal there's often too little of this kind of thing. The description should be detailed, pointed, and brisk. Times of day and the look of sunshine or firelight or early evening should be included.

[1932]

    1. *Voyage autour de ma chambre:* journey around my room. Title of witty sketch by Savoyard soldier Xavier de Maistre (1763–1852), on which LB modeled her own 1933 "Journey" (in I: Fiction).

THE MONTH, the time of day; children are coming indoors from roads bordered by orchards heavy with apples, into rooms with looped-back curtains, and old mirrors. Among the dahlias and asters of the lots gardens, their mothers pull the dried clothes from the line, reaching their arms above their heads so that their cotton dresses under the shawl thrown about their shoulders are pulled tightly upward from the thin apron string binding their waists. The wind rattles the lattice over the wellhead; the house smells of freshly baked bread. It is already dark; the month goes on; the apples will be gathered tomorrow.

    The age when one looks at the date on pennies, watches people's eyes and mouths, believes that something marvelous may go on in a shuttered house.

[1934]

WITHIN THE rooms of houses, seen as a child from the outside, I thought that something must be going on: that people must be achieving something to assail the dreadful monotony of day after day. I trusted them to be doing something. Whatever it was, was as yet closed to me, but these fronts of buildings, with afternoon light falling upon them with such terrible, dramatic effect—these certainly were important. Within them, life burned, a life in which I as yet had no part. I believed this; from my soul I believed it . . .

The wind blew; footsteps came to the side door; it was now late autumn: all the magnificent dahlias had wilted down from their props and the maple tree on the lawn was as bare as your hand . . . The sunlight was so strong, on bright days, that it cast strong shadows all through the house; you could tell the time of day and the season of the year from the way the shadow slanted back from table and chair legs, just as easily as from the shadows of objects out of doors . . .

[1959]

SHE DID not like books with no weather in them. Or paintings in which the objects cast no shadows . . .

[1961]

I SAW the clear afternoon, casting the shadows of chairs one way in the room, so that the season was as clear within a house as out of doors. The shadows had the time of day written into them, as well as the look of autumn.

[1930]

THE RIVER shows up every barge solidly and the light falls on the setbacks of the buildings strong and bright. October light has more time in it than any other. The day says "Late" with its light, as summer mornings say "Early" with theirs.

~

IT IS a day for everything. Smoke drifts from the chimneys of the tenements—not much smoke—as from a poor fire, but from the apartment buildings a steady blue stream goes out sideways with the air. Little figures of men on steelwork streets away sometimes come into view; the forms of derricks hold cables at clear angles, slender as threads. Light falls through the windows of empty apartments and lies on the floor marking the empty rooms with rectangles. The light falls against the leaves of plants, upright in the pots, and upon the lemon and tomato in the fruit dish and upon the faded and dusty chintz of a chair that has worn through a summer.

I am older now than in any October before.

[1930]

IN REALITY, how many clouds there are that blow over the city, that no one ever sees!

[1933]

THE EARLY darkness in September comes as the most blessed relief in the year. Pale green celery tops sprout out of bags in the delivery boys' carts and a mottled light falls over the shady side of the street, reflected from the windows in high buildings. Early morning in September.

[1932]

THE LONG late light, in childhood. Autumn desolation. The windy raw autumn afternoon, with light and dark alternating over the hills and fields, and great sweeps of gray cloud giving the light its silence, its feeling of tears, of sorrow, of desperation. The light that would return, over a lifetime of autumns . . . At a certain hour, a look of terrible mystery and silence . . .

[1961]

AND WHAT of that feeling of unearthly splendor, of great promise, terrible delight, at some seasons of the year? Or the excitement which came with early darkness, and cold; or with summer heat, letting down torrents of brilliant summer light, that had to be shut out of the houses? This look and sound of promise fled through the town with the trains, and with the ripples on the river. "Some day! Some day!" it said.

[1959]

IT IS only infrequently that I now feel that wave of mysterious joy go over me that I once felt in all meetings, partings, chance displays of natural or man-made beauty, accidental losses or gains . . .

[1961]

SANTAYANA'S CLASSIC world—the people of Chekhov "seen against the sky": this is what I knew in childhood and had no word for: this is "the light falling down through the universe," the look and feeling of which has haunted me for so long—

[1933]

THE LIGHT on leaves in the evening looked as though it did not come from the sun, but from space itself, or from some element in a universe so distant from our own that it must be felt, never seen, and never named.

[1932]

How Can I Break These Mornings?

I AM now taking two pills in the A.M.—one at 7:30 and one around 10:30. —This morning I thought that the first pill was going to see me through; a clear, untroubled interval would show up (take over) every so often— perhaps because I was moving around in the open air, having a *later* break-fast at the restaurant (dump!) and buying things at Sloane's. But soon that secondary sort of *yearning hunger* (which is not real hunger, but is in some way attached to the drug) began again. Heart bumps also slightly involved.

Of course I interpret everything in as black a way as possible.—(My left eye, incidentally, according to the eye man, is holding its own against the vascular difficulty—and the actual sight is not impaired. But, if left to my-self, my own diagnosis would have been exceedingly gloomy.)

I *must* get someone to look at my teeth!

And my business affairs must be elucidated—Some afternoon next week! . . .

A deep-seated masochism? Surely I have acted in a consistently *optimistic* fashion, ever since the 1933 breakdown.—I have surmounted one difficulty after another; I have *worked* for life and "creativity"; I have cast off all the anxieties and fears I could; I have helped others to work and hold on. Why this collapse of psychic energy? Granted that my demands upon both physi-cal and psychic endurance during those last spring weeks in Waltham and Cambridge were clearly excessive—why can't I refuel—recover?

Of course, I must have improved to some degree. My afternoons now (after lunch)—after a (usually) unplanned nap—are nearly normal. The evenings, too—especially after the two drinks I am allowed.—At the mo-ment (11:25) I am hoping to level off after the second pill. Yesterday, I took *three,* in the A.M., including one just after lunch. I nodded off at the eye-doctor's—waiting for him between 12:30 and 1:00. Thereafter I was v. nearly normal, with another pill at supper. (But I was with Ruth from 3:20 on—at a movie.)

How am I going to stand further isolation?

~

Journals and Memoir

The mere feel of the pen moving across the paper should be curative. That and *some* attempts to listen to music.—Who have I become? *What* has me in hand?

Deliver me!

Let me be strong and free once more.

Or at least *free*—and out of these waves of *malaise*.—For what am I berating myself? What am I afraid of?

Death—for one thing. Yes, that is part of it.—These deaths that are reported in the newspapers seem to be all my age—or younger.

But people keep hopeful and warm and *loving* right to the end—with much more to endure than I endure.—I see the old constantly, on these uptown streets—and they are not "depressed." Their eyes are bright; they have bought themselves groceries; they gossip and laugh—with, often, crippling handicaps evident among them.

Where has this power gone, in my case?

I weep—but there's little relief there.

How can I break these mornings?

[1965]

Final Questionnaire

Do you have the instructions clear?
      Yes.
Are you ready to answer truthfully?
      Yes.
Do you like to plan alone or with people?
      Alone.
Do you sometimes develop an unreasonable dislike for a person?
      Yes, but it's so slight that I can hide it.

Do you think ordinary people would be shocked if they knew your personal opinions?
    Yes.
When bossy people try to push you around——?
    I do the opposite of what they want.
Does it bother you if people think you're unconventional?
    Not at all.
If the odds are against something's being a success, would you still take the risk?
    Of course.
Do you feel the need to lean on someone in times of sadness?
    Yes.
Can you find the energy to face your difficulties?
    Seldom.
"Surprise" is to "strange" as "fear" is to——?
    "Terrible."

                                                                    [December 1969]

III

Letters

/ to Rolfe Humphries[1] /

July 24, 1924

Dear Rolfe:

You'll think me slightly crazed when I tell you I'm reading Goethe's biography now—on the advice, supposedly, that lives of g[reat] m[en] all remind us we can make our l. sublime. I never have read anything about anybody, really, so now, when the passion is on me, I might just as well wade through the *Dict. of Nat. Biog.* from beginning to end. There's such choice bits. Goethe had five love-affairs before he was twenty; at the age of seventy he fell in love again (when he should have been drawing up plans for a pleasant little steam-heated grave) and wrote the *Westöstlicher Diwan* (snappy title, that).[2] O, you great male poets! Think of the life ahead of you, Rolfe! No rest! No hope! I should think you'd shudder at the thought of being eighty-three, with no relief in sight. You'll fall for a girl of nineteen, at eighty-three (vide Goethe), whom you'll see one morning chasing the ducks, you will leap out of bed, write an immortal sonnet, clutch the grizzled throat, and breathe your last. Cicero, with all his talk of escaping from the tiger, didn't count on the capacities of octogenarian male poets.

My German is faulty, but the Goethe lyrics ring the bell.

Über allen Gipfeln
Ist Ruh,
In allen Wipfeln
Spürest du
Kaum einen Hauch;
Die Vögelein schweigen im Walde.
Warte nur, balde
Ruhest du auch.[3]

. . . that's from the *Wandrers Nachtlied*—the title is so beautiful, too. The stripped, still lyric moves me more, invariably, than any flummery ode ever written—although, of course, Keats and the Romantics were only partly flummery—but

Über allen Gipfeln
Ist Ruh

gives me such happiness that I want to cry.

Today I hope to finish my lightning passage.[4] I'll send it to you—since you're a brother in fright. Mine is more thunder than lightning, as I told you. The lightning startles me merely, the thunder would wring me with fright were I a mole underground.

What about that horse poem you did? May I see it?

O God, why were women born with ambition! I wish I could sit and tat, instead of wanting to go and write THE poem, or lie and kiss the ground.

If all this is mad blame the weather and an aftermath of Raymond's new Scotch.[5]

> Yours for the stripped and maddening earth,
> Louise

1. Rolfe Humphries: poet and translator (of Ovid's *Metamorphoses* as well as Lorca's *The Poet in New York*) and a lifelong friend of LB—despite her profound disapproval of his socialist phase.

2. *Diwan:* collection of short poems (on the model of the Persian poet Hafiz); *west-östlich:* combining western with eastern themes.

3. "On every peak / Lies peace, / You cannot feel / A trace of breath / In any tree; / In the wood the little birds are mute. / But patience. Soon / You too will sleep." Title: "The Wanderer's Night-Song."

4. In her long poem "The Flume" (see poetry appendix). The following month LB wrote Humphries she had "lost all interest in the woman in it, who used to rush around the house hoping she'd be betrayed. I'm sure she's been betrayed by this time and has taken to washing dishes and having babies [. . .] ."

5. Raymond Holden, poet, novelist, and managing editor of *The New Yorker* from 1929 to 1932, was LB's second husband. He died two years after she did, in 1972.

/ *to Edmund Wilson*[1] /

93 West Cedar Street
Boston, Massachusetts
July 10, 1925

Dear Edmund:

~

I have been reading Henry James very swiftly, so that I might, if such a thing were possible, get the color without too much of the sense. I am enchanted by the absolute sureness in method.—Even though he does the thing all wrong sometimes, he is always sure of how he wants to do it. The people that mirror the action never slip up, lose their outline, and become merely Tom, Dick, or Harriet. But I am not sure that they are invariably the right mirrors. Fleda Vetch is right in the first part of *The Spoils of Poynton:*— she is the last person in the world to reflect the second part—she is much too concerned. James realized this, and just left her out for a time, after the man married the other girl. I think that the scenes after Fleda and the mother find out about the marriage are pitifully inadequate. How can this calm contained creature, that takes a blow in the face without a word, be the same girl that rushed upstairs crying, "I should never give you up!" a little earlier? Some of the mercury gets rubbed off on the back of the mirror. James is impotent and afraid, suddenly. If Fleda made a fine dramatic row—took her shirtwaist off under the Poynton parlor windows, after the manner of George Sand—that would have been vulgar. So we are treated to a great peeled patch in the reflecting glass, with bright rich vision all around it.

That impotence crops up again and again. Even the earliest, gayest things have a touch of it in them. Someone could do an entire doctor's thesis on the Interrogatory Method in the Development of Conversation in the Novels of Henry James. [. . . text missing] has the weak-minded habit of repeating the last word uttered by the first voice. Echolalia is the clinical name for that. After this fashion:

Hic: "She was ill and we brought her some beef-broth."

Ille: "Ill?"

Hic: "Well, perhaps not ill, but having about her some sense of the shawl across the knees."

Ille: "Hardly knees."

Hic: "Shoulder would give the arrangement better. She drank the soup."

Ille: "Drank?"

Hic: "Sniffed it, rather."

That is not *echt* James, but there's very little reason why it shouldn't be. Lubbock says that there has only been one *Awkward Age*—one novel wherein all the action is expressed as action merely, wherein the characters acquit themselves like actors in a stage setting, wherein the setting itself, described as so much malleable stuff upon which these people make dents or cast shadows, suffices for all the "He thoughts" and "She felts" of less artful drama. The implications were terrific, the oblique conversational method immense, the *mise en scène* marvelous, but the book almost drove me mad. God knows what would have happened to the thing if the Duchess hadn't said a few plain words now and again. Someday when I am eighty and have a game leg, I'll make a list of the repetitions and variations of the "You are of a fineness" construction scattered through the book. It's like a little boy who has just learned that literal translations sound amusing, and who goes about doing his best for the ablative absolute. O, too much sharpening down of the fine cedar wood around the lead in the pencil, so that at last the lead itself is powdered away.

~

What was the matter with this man, Edmund? It wasn't exile merely. Part of him had been excised. The pity and terror were somehow misplaced. *The Other House* is such a failure, because the wires get crossed, the puppets go on talking after the play has run down; the voices go on like the horrid sound when the Victrola needle gets stuck in one groove of a record.

I think his sense that all sexual play is essentially evil is an extremely important detail. The array of innocent enough people who are made subtly monstrous because they have slept with someone outside the banns of holy matrimony—it's a child's sense of evil. I used to have it when I almost knew how babies were born, almost but not entirely. That's why *The Turn of the Screw* is so terrific. Miss Jessel died of an abortion, it is intimated, and it is made fearful—as though an abortion weren't a rather heartbreaking thing to die of. What Quint told the children was perhaps how babies were born. I think that James's greatest effects are built up out of that very horror, that outrageous mad fear. Whenever he is about to cave in under his own style, that sense of evil gets him through. Every one of his low sneaks is sexually irregular first. The rest, to him, followed in natural course.

I bore you, perhaps, dear Edmund, by all this. You have had it figured out for yourself years ago, no doubt. No one has really tried to get the clinical details on James, however. Why doesn't someone? [. . .] Rebecca [West] gets very mad at him because his young girls try to act as though they were suitable creatures for marriage, and had never heard of Mary Wollstonecraft. I get mad at him because is at once a great artist—such a sense of life, of differentiation, of light and movement!—and an old fool.

I have no one to talk to, you see, so you will let me steam at you occasionally, won't you? I'm reading Jacques Loeb on the physicochemical aspects of existence, in the midst of the stream of James. He rides his points somewhat. Thank heaven for art, that doesn't need to prove anything.

Write me more.

Ever with love,

Louise

P.S. Raymond's best, too.

1. Edmund Wilson is now best known as a critic (*Axel's Castle*, 1931; *The Wound and the Bow*, 1941), secondarily as a historian (author of *To the Finland Station*, 1940, on revolutions in Europe); but to LB he was a writer of poems, plays, and fiction, and the model of the artist who possessed broad learning.

432 East Manhattan Street
Santa Fe, New Mexico
February 1927

Dear Edmund: Don't, I beg you, think
That I have sunk my wits in drink
When you were sweet enough to send me
Your book,[1] as one who would befriend me.
I grabbed that book from out its cover   5
And cozened it as would a lover.
Out in the open sun I read it,
And did I like it? O you said it!
The long play I liked even better
Set out in paragraph and letter
Than on the Provincetown's rough boards.   10
The dialogues were sharp as swords.
In fact, I think it's not excessive
To say the whole thing's very impressive.
I much admire the way you tucked your
Sly points into your sentence structure.   15

The reason why I've been so tardy
To write you, is, like Thomas Hardy,
I've seen life show its seasoned fangs
These last weeks, in a lot of pangs.   20
A large tooth in my lower jaw
Has filled me with a kind of awe.
. . . .
Then Raymond's mother came to see   41
The great Southwest. We gave her tea [. . .] .
. . . .
We saw some Indians dance a wild
Greek comedy dance, at which you'd have smiled.
Not a calm rite to grey-eyed Pallas
But a lot of leaping with a phallus.   50
I told Mrs. Holden succinctly how
These things come out of *The Golden Bough*.
A nice short talk to distract her attention
From a lot of actions I really can't mention.

. . . .
And send me some poems, if you please.
Yours [highly?] for Life and Art—
Louise   90

1. *Discordant Encounters* (1926), a collection of Wilson's plays and dialogues.

                                                                      Hillsdale
                                                  Columbia County, New York
                                                                 Thanksgiving
                                                         November 22, 1928

Darling Edmund:
[. . .] Our fruit farm defies description. Wait until you see it. It is embow-
ered in lilacs and roses; plum trees circle it round, and vines fill up the in-
terstices. We are indebted to a friend for a fireplace and chimney; even at
this moment the mason and his helper are fitting brick to brick with im-
memorial gestures of the trowel. We'll never have a bathroom, so take several baths to last you over some little period of time, before you come up to
see us. Raymond has put in windows, and worked wonders with sheetrock
and miter box. I have scraped wallpaper, and planted an extensive bulb garden. We are to have some Blue Andalusian hens, and a small black goat, in
the spring, so that our friends will not lack fauna to observe when they come
to visit us.

                                         ~

There's been a big turnover in verse these last few months. I have written more and worse verse than at any other time in my career. I think it is all
wonderful, too, which makes it all the funnier. Does it rain—do I look out
the window and see a barn, or a cow, or a tree, or a horse and wagon, or a
stray dog—does it snow, or shine, or blow? Out comes the pencil, and down
go a few nature notes. How happy I feel! How easy art really is! Almost at
once I realize that the thing is just terrible.

                                         ~

                                                  Ever, with truest affection,
                                                  Louise
                                                  (The Hermit Crab)

/ to John Hall Wheelock[1] /

Hillsdale
Columbia County, New York
December 7, 1928

My dear Mr. Wheelock:

Thank you for your letter. Your decision on the manuscript has encouraged me more than I can say. [. . .] I realize that the poems you now have are really too few for a volume. However, I have a strong feeling that there should never be too many poems in a book of poetry. Thirty-five is, I think, the greatest number I should wish to publish at one time. I have as many poems again as the manuscript contains, that have been kept back, because I do not wholly trust them, and feel that by their inclusion the effect of the others might be blurred. You understand this feeling, I am sure. Perhaps, by the end of next summer, I may have ten new poems to add to the manuscript as it now stands—one of them a fairly long dramatic dialogue that I plan to do. With ten poems from *Body of This Death* [published in 1923], would that be enough?[2]

I should be very glad if I could send you, from time to time, new work as it comes. There are perhaps five more things that you could see immediately. I may not always be right, but it is, you will agree, a true instinct to wish to scant, rather than to fatten.

I am glad that you like "The Flume." I spent my childhood in mill towns, and was happy to be able to do something with that remembered noise of water.

Again thanking you for your thought and courtesy.

Sincerely yours,
Louise Bogan

1. The poet John Hall Wheelock had succeeded Maxwell Perkins as editor in chief of Charles Scribner's Sons.

2. LB's second volume, *Dark Summer,* would be published by Charles Scribner's Sons in September 1929.

/ to Ruth Benedict[1] /

Hillsdale

December 28, 1928

Dear Ruth:

The Blake filled me with joy as I wildly tore off the wrapper. Thank you for it, dear Ruth.——I did want it with real gluttony, and had no idea where to find it, even if I could have afforded it. [. . .]

Raymond and I have taken up chess and given up liquor—almost, that is. Chess, I find, is quite terrifying. That closing in on the king is like time and fate sitting in opposite quarters, and chuckling quietly, because their designs are not immediately apparent. It's no game for a person afflicted with claustrophobia. Somewhere at this moment, behind these pleasant hills, there is a great fat Bishop and a round ponderous Rook . . . O dear, O dear.

~

Ever with love—

Louise

1. According to the anthropologist Margaret Mead, her colleague Ruth Benedict, then an assistant to William Fielding Ogburn at Columbia, "filled his office with working poets—Louise Bogan, Léonie Adams, Louise Townsend Nicholl [. . .]" (WTWL, 5n2).

[March] 1929

Dear Ruth:

~

A great depth of snow has fallen here. A party of skiers with Yale voices have taken over the Inn for the holiday. I lie awake at night and shudder at the thought that they will inherit the earth. The sum of $10,000 was actually mentioned during the first evening, also the statement was made that money makes money. I never felt more like joining the Communist party. I have had the pleasure, during the month, of turning down an invitation to join the Poetry Society of America. So you can see that I have been warped from childhood, and will never learn the trick of mingling in a social way.

~

Sunday and Monday were quite soft; I heard a whole brook going very fast down a hillside,[1] and felt real full-bodied sunlight behind a haystack, on Sunday, and thought that spring was managing at least a hoarse whisper, and then this snow came. What will happen when it begins to thaw is beyond my imagination. The iris are nicely mulched, so that they, at least, cannot be washed from the ground. I think it would be amusing if the bulbs really did come up, don't you? Of course, I don't expect them to.

R[idgely] Torrence[2] is still off my works, no doubt rightly. I am sending you a sonnet [beginning "Dark, underground, is furnished with the bone"] that I thought quite good, at the time. Please be perfectly critical about it. Is all this bone business just funny? The other isn't right yet, and in any event, hasn't much importance, beyond some rather good phrases pointing to regression towards the infantile. Dear me. Pretty elusive, these talents.

~

Ever, with love,
Louise

1. An echo of LB's poem "Women," from *Body of This Death* (1923): "They do not hear / Snow water going down under culverts, / Shallow and clear."
2. Ridgely Torrence: a poet and playwright who had chosen poetry for *The New Republic* since 1922.

Hillsdale
Columbia County, N.Y.
April 16, 1929

Dear Ruth:

It has indeed been a wearing week: my daily trips to Hudson involved a train and a bus, and a station waiting room superficially like a scene in hell.[1] Then the weather—that was indeed beyond belief. Every morning the window presented a jolly snowy mid-winter scene. It has snowed since last Wednesday, off and on. Three days rain is enough to empty any sky, says the adage, and that's another adage disproved.

However, some of the house got painted, and a man cleaned up the orchard, so that the brush is piled on the vegetable garden to be burned, the grape trellis is mended, the outhouse cleaned out, and one thing and another. —I have painted the kitchen, the walls by choice and the floor by chance.

Tomorrow I start in on the living room and that will be indeed a blessed day. Literary works went by the board. I got down some notes on Philmont (that's where the station waiting room is; that waiting room where yesterday everything suddenly became insignificant and I had some sort of great mystic revelation—due purely to fatigue).—A little man in a lunchroom who served me delicious coffee and an immaculate sandwich, all set out on a tray spread with a pristine napkin, almost had me in tears, because he put such faith in a new electric sign that someone had sold him. When illuminated this sign goes through all the colors of the rainbow—they fade off— he told me about it with such hope and passion. Then he slyly started the popcorn machine, poor dear, and I bought a whole bushel with my remaining money. God keep me extroverted so that I can always see such saintly little men.

~

Ever with love,
Louise

1. Raymond Holden was in the Hudson, New York, hospital, having been operated on for appendicitis eight days earlier.

/ to Rolfe Humphries /

Hillsdale
December 16, 192[9][1]

Dear Rolfe:
Before we sink into the spell of literary coadjutation, let me express my own delight, nay, I might almost say, happiness, in receiving the *lovely* record of your voice, recorded by Speak-o-Phone Inc. on a nice metal disc. [. . .] The only drawback is that, due either to inordinate shyness, fear of the microphone, or of the attendant, or of the velvet curtains in the cubicle (it was a cubicle, wasn't it?) you forgot your early training in ventriloquism (speaking from or to the stomach, or voice issuing out from or in accordance with the stomach) and swallowed your vocables with such inconsiderate ease

that I could hardly make out, in the first sonnet, at least, what you were saying. Raymond says that your greeting is "Hello R and L, you big wheats,"
but I insist that you say "Hello, R and L, tweet-tweet." Please clear this up
for me. The second sonnet was rendered more clearly, but yet a little too
bas. However, we cannot say how pleased we were to have you thus canned,
on the music shelf in this, our little mountain cot, available at all times.
We'll make some for you and you can get one of those $4.98 toy phono-
graphs in Macy's to play them on. Wait until you hear me *throw* my voice!
What a pleasure that will be!

Now, for serious literary matters:

You are very sweet (my God, how long am I going to keep this up!) to
want to couple my name with yours, on the hind-end of the [Robinson]
Jeffers review. You are far too self-effacing, however. The ideas are really
yours, you just hadn't thought out a review for so long that they came hard,
and a conversation just cleared them up a little, that's all.

I think the review is excellent as it stands. The first paragraph is short
and snappy, and the writing in the second, third, and fourth beautifully ordered. My few suggestions are these (and if you want you can buy a couple
of tickets for *Fifty Million Frenchmen* for next Monday night in full payment).
[. . .]

The point should be *emphasized* that the figures in [Jeffers's poem] "Loving S[hepherdess]" have been seen *over* and *over* again—in *all* the volumes.
That the projection works automatically, like one of these machines that puts
records on by itself, by means of a mechanical arm. That if he'd written *Tamar*
(that book) alone and then shut up, he'd be extraordinary, but his fluency
has given the emotional mechanism away. No great dramatic writer could
possibly slip into such a groove—and this leads to:

2. Lyric poets can lack a sense of humor and still be great, but dramatic
poets, *never.* And there's not a drop of humor in one single poem. (Such nice
humor as "Well, let's go to bed!" or "Get the hell out of here, you cock-eyed
bastard!")

3. Our time (whatever it is) just loves poems about the internal organs
of the body, the mechanisms of sex, abortion, fecal processes, etc. It's like
looking inside the hood of an automobile, or watching the shafts and gears
and sprockets in a factory. (Don't you think that's a good point? I really think
it explains why people think J. has terrific profundity because he makes remarks about women menstruating.) (I'll take another quarter for that.)

4. (And this is the last.) The split-up lines make a hypnotic rhythm, so that he can be banal (as God knows he often is) right on top of being awfully good (and he has a grand ear for phrase and eye for detail, indubitably). All's one for that, when the reader gets all hopped up with the trick rhythm.

~

And how about four cheap seats for next Monday night at *Fifty Million Frenchmen?* Will you get them? Wouldn't that be fun? And you can take us to the Speak-o-Phone place and yell "Louder and funnier!" from behind the curtains.

Well, yours for intrauterine mechanics and the life of the soul.

Louise

1. LB misdates her letter 1928, for the Cole Porter musical *Fifty Million Frenchmen* (directed by Monty Woolley) did not open until November 27, 1929. While LB and Holden were in New York over Christmas 1929, their Hillside house burned to the ground.

/ to Harriet Monroe¹ /

5 Prospect Place
New York City
January 6, 1930

Dear Miss Monroe:
The day after Christmas, while we were away on a visit, our house in the country took fire through the carelessness of the man who was tending the furnace, and burned completely. All our things went, too—books, pictures, and almost all our manuscripts.—We are insured, both for the house and its contents, but insurance does not give back the things gathered over years, nor the books, never to be exactly replaced, and our work put into walls and rooms. We have recovered somewhat from the shock: after all, it is more important to be alive without possessions than dead either with or without them. We have come to New York to get work and start again.—[Lola Ridge's] *Firehead* came today, forwarded from Hillsdale, and I shall get it done this week. We have an apartment now, and as soon as we can get a few

pieces of furniture together, literary production can go on. I am sorry for the delay in getting the review to you, but it can be put down to an act of God, and most delays have worse reasons.

We are really quite well. Do not think us tragic figures. Our best greetings to you, as always, for this year, and all others.

Ever sincerely,
Louise Bogan

1. Harriet Monroe: founding editor of *Poetry* magazine (Chicago), the journal that opened American letters to modernism. She continued as editor until her death in 1936.

5 Prospect Place
January 17, 1930

Dear Miss Monroe:

I have read *Firehead* and begun a review, but I am puzzled by what may very well be my biased ideas concerning it. And since I know that Miss Ridge is ill, and no doubt puts much store by good reviews—especially a good review in *Poetry*—I do not feel that you should allow me to go on with my article, since my attitude must be a purely critical one. I can only say what I myself feel, and perhaps there is some lack in my nature that does not permit me to believe that Miss Ridge has been successful in this poem.

I have found from bitter experience that one woman poet is at a disadvantage in reviewing another, if the review be not laudatory. I do not feel capable, at the present moment, of taking upon myself Miss Ridge's hurt feelings, so would you allow me to send *Firehead* to you and to another reviewer? Were my own mind and heart more settled, I could more easily banish the idea of my inadequacy in this matter. Perhaps I put all this badly. You understand, I am sure. It is difficult for you to have to put up with this backing and filling on my part, but I must say what I feel and think. And in this case, it is my (perhaps mistaken) idea that Miss Ridge would take my remarks too much to heart.

With every good wish from us both—

Cordially yours,
Louise Bogan

October 24, 1930

Dear Miss Monroe:

I am enclosing the letter that lay on my desk ready to be mailed to you, when the news of *Poetry*'s 1930 prize awards reached me.[1] I cannot think of any recognition that has ever touched me so deeply. At the risk of seeming to air difficulties that are important to myself alone, I want you to know how successfully for the past year I have suppressed any impulse toward creative work. A set of unfortunate incidents brought this condition about. I can truthfully say that childish pique and even more childish pride had nothing to do with this creative despair. I should prefer to think that it was complete weariness with the continued reappearance of a personal legend that colored, in the minds of many people who might be expected to be without bias, opinion of my work.[2] For some years I had been out of touch with writers and cities and had forgotten the deadly persistence of rumor in a specialized group. At the second or third meeting with a kind of subtle and refined cruelty, I abjured poetry. I no longer wished to say myself.

I tell you these reasons because your award has not only made them clear in my mind, but to a great extent has nullified them. I am refreshed, and hope to get out of this fog a sane and balanced person.—That the prize was given to my work in general delights me, because I have never been able to compete, in contests, or to write to order or on terms.

Please do not think my frankness to you a breach of decorum. I hope you can feel that I do not say these things easily. But it is better to say them, and thereby work through to some kind of power over circumstance. I want you to know that your thought for me has had a broader influence than you could have planned.

Again take my gratitude, and the promise that when anything gets done, it will go to you.

Believe me to be,

Sincerely yours,
Louise Bogan

1. The John Reed Memorial Prize, given for LB's first two volumes and for poems published in *Poetry*.

2. LB had begun to worry that people remembered her friendship ten years earlier with John Coffey, the young Irishman who shoplifted (especially furs) in order, so he said, to call attention to urban poverty. Her apprehensiveness about gossip and undue attention would intensify whenever a breakdown was near.

/ to John Hall Wheelock /

The Neurological Institute
Fort Washington Avenue and West 168 Street, New York
April 11, 1931

Dear Jack:

I missed the Psychiatric Institute, or whatever it is, by a hair, so don't be too perturbed by the heading. I refused to fall apart, so I have been taken apart, like a watch. I can truthfully say that the fires of hell can hold no terrors for me now.

Whatever happens after this, I shall no longer sneer and fleer. One of my component parts, strangely enough, turned out to be the capacity to love. I still can love. Isn't that wonderful? I still can go into love humbly and take it, no matter to what end, and feel humble and [ashamed ?]: "Love comes in at the eyes"[1]—A pretty pass for one of my stiff-necked pride, don't you think? It comes in at the eyes and subdues the body. An army with banners.[2] My God, every poet in the world knew about it, except me.

Regularly, every day, I read *Uncle Vanya*. Do read it again. It is the lexicon of wisdom and pity.

Say a prayer for me, won't you? Thank you always for your friendship and kindness.

Yours—as ever

Louise

1. William Butler Yeats begins "A Drinking Song," "Wine comes in at the mouth / And love comes in at the eye."

2. an army with banners: "Who is she that looketh forth as the morning, fair as the moon, clear as the sun, and terrible as an army with banners?" *Song of Solomon* 6:10.

/ to Edmund Wilson /

The Lafayette
Portland, Maine
May 2, 1931

Dear Edmund:

Thank you for the left and right wing books. And of course you realize that
I'm not at the Hotel Lafayette, in Portland, Maine. I just put that in to make
it harder.[1] So much literature has flowed from my fertile brain, these last
few days, that the stationery has not been able to stand the gaff. Like sun in
April, to use a tried and true simile, it has disappeared.

~

My life here is one grand sweet song. I have aroused pain in at least three
hearts. Two of the hearts are nonagenarian, but what cares saucy Bogan?[2]
[. . .]

I'm glad you liked the Swift poem. The *Journal to Stella* wrung my heart.
The passion is so real, so imperfectly dissembled, and the wit is such a strange
mixture of roughness and elegance. I'm eager to have the poems. Thank you,
my dear, for getting them.

In addition to some love, I must add that I have stirred up a little enmity.
An old mussel called Miss Agnew sits outside my door and says, crustily,
"There seems to be a great deal of smoking around here!" Poor old thing!
How I love her. How I love everyone, even the worms in the worm-casts,
the snails in snail shells, the maggots in the cheese.

Well, my dear fellow, my charming old syringa, I must now close. Warn
men, women and children of my reappearance. Tell them to buy smoked
glasses. For, verily, yea, let it be said, that nothing or no one will be safe
from me from now on.

Yours with much love—

Rosily—

Louise

[P.S.] You didn't sound sententious. What an idea. *Anna Livia Plurabelle* got
me, too. Did you note that he [James Joyce] uses *Bogan* as a verb?

1. She was recuperating in a sanitarium in Connecticut, where the therapeutic regime included weaving, needle-spray showers, sunbaths, and "most simple-minded tasks." Describing it to Wilson in a poem appended to this letter, LB ended:

> My God, what was the crime. Did I deserve
> Therapy, out of possible punishments?
> What the betrayal, that the faded nerve
> Must bloom again by means not making sense?
> O, I shall mend! Even now I grow quite well,
> Knitting round washcloths on the paths of hell.

(WTWL, 59)

2. Cf. "What care I; what cares saucy Presto?" from Bogan's poem "Hypocrite Swift," also referred to in the next paragraph.

/ *to Allen Tate*[1] /

306 Lexington
New York City
April 1, 1932

Dear Allen:

I had feared that my review would distress you. I am sorry that you thought it full of personal bias, and even venom. I can only say that I was not estimating you as a person or as a friend. I was reviewing a book of poetry which aroused in me respect and irritation in about equal measure. If you objected to the tone of my review, I objected, straight down to a core beyond detachment, to the tone of some of the poems. I hesitated to accept the book [*Poems: 1928–1931*] for review because I suspected that a flavor of irritation would get through to the critical page.

When I did accept it, I tried in every way both to clarify and minimize the irritation. The review copies contained some misprints; I called up Scribner's and had them read me the passages as they should appear. Our copy of *Mr. Pope* had been burned; I got another from Balch in order not to pass upon it from memory. And I went to the Library and read a file of *The Fugitive* in order to get that background straight in my mind. You may not consider these efforts gestures toward detachment; I intended them to be. And I read every printed version of the "Ode to the Confederate Dead."

The first thing that annoyed me was the slightly pontifical air of the foreword. But perhaps this is stupid of me; I thought: Allen is merely serious, and that is commendable. When I sat down to the book, "Last Days of Alice," "The Paradigm" (in spite of its extraordinary insight), the eagle poem, "Ignis Fatuus," and some passages in "Causerie" disturbed me to such an extent that I simply did not know what to do. "Here," I said to myself, "is cold legerdemain, metaphysical arrogance (perhaps a phrase as meaningless as 'philosophic ambition,' but let it go——), deliberately conceived, put down without a qualm, managed to the last degree. These poems are sterile: Allen should not do this thing, and having done it, he should be brought to book therefor." As you know, Allen, in a poem, not only can the feeling be in excess to the matter, but devices, crotchets, and all skilled traps for the unwary, can exceed. In short, these poems struck me as elaborate ruses, as poetic sophistry (in the non-Protagorean sense of the term). They would have struck me as such in the work of my son, my father, my enemy, or the friend of my bosom. I should have tried to define them just as definitely in these hypothetical cases, as in yours. More especially if the writer had a talent such as yours concealed beneath them.

~

You were being a schoolmaster a little, weren't you?[2]

Yours—

Louise

1. Allen Tate: one of the poets who edited *The Fugitive* (1922–25), a little magazine whose contributors were associated with Vanderbilt University. Its poetry and criticism championed regionalism (in the form of anti-industrial Southern culture). Along with Tate, J. C. Ransom and R. P. Warren were its notable poet-critics.

2. Reviewing this letter in 1972, Allen Tate said that there *was* personal animosity, but that the review would probably have been much the same had there not been. ("My poems were never Louise's dish of tea.") Certainly their friendship was not broken by the disagreement here. As they parted for the last time, the year before her death, LB said to Tate: "Never a cross word these forty years." She had forgotten the review, and, as Tate recalled, "Well, so had I!" (WTWL, 64n1).

/ to Morton D. Zabel[1] /

April 29, 1932

LOUISE

306 Lexington Avenue
New York City
May 5, 1932

Dear Morton:

By now perhaps you have all the bulletins concerning Hart [Crane] from other sources.——Peggy [Mrs. Malcolm] Cowley had lunch with me yesterday. She said that Hart had begun to go to pieces in Havana. He ramped about the boat all Tuesday night and Wednesday morning. Wednesday noon he rushed into her cabin in pajamas, for a dramatic farewell to her and to life. (Peggy did not take this seriously: she had heard Hart's farewells before.) Then he made for the saloon, rushed through crowds of passengers to the afterdeck, and took a fifty-foot dive into the sea. The ship stopped; boats were lowered but nothing could be done. [. . .]——It is a great loss, but Hart could not have gone on, dashing himself against people, places, against night, morning, and midday. He could accept nothing simply; he had no defenses. Had he done much work on the Montezuma-Toltec theme, do you know?——The story went dead the day the boat arrived because all the ship's newsmen had been drawn off to meet Mrs. Hargreaves (Lewis Carroll's "Alice"). Hart would have appreciated that detail, don't you think?

~

A strange tea with Willa Cather, early in April. She is already an old woman, querulous and set in her ways. She bullies the waiter. She bewails the good old days when gentlefolk had the Metropolitan and Carnegie Hall all to themselves. [. . .] But she has a taste for high comedy; [Gogol's] *Dead Souls* seems the quintessential novel to her still hearty appreciation.

~

Yours ever—
Louise

1. Morton Dauwen Zabel, associate editor of *Poetry* at this time, was an academic who taught at Loyola, then at the University of Chicago. He edited work by and wrote books and articles on Conrad, E. A. Robinson, and Henry James; he also reviewed for *The Nation*.

306 Lexington Avenue
New York City
November 29, 1932

Dear Morton:

Yours of last month sometime has lain unanswered; all sorts of minor evils and near catastrophes have kept my nimble pen from letter paper, these four weeks back. The lady downstairs committed suicide by gas, for one thing, and, since the lethal chamber was situated directly under Maidie's[1] bedroom, Maidie got a good gassing, too, and was laid up for three days. This occurred the night of Harriet Monroe's visit to us. H. M. did not seem as well as formerly; we gave her one and a half glasses of Bacardi cum ginger ale: she said she liked it better than tea. I meant to get some flowers to her hotel before she left town but the suicide put a stop to my activities for that week. I'll write her soon.——The minor evils do not bear recounting— they're nothing much and leave hardly any mark on a spirit finally resigned, though quite unembittered, a mind open to joy, if any happens to be around, and refreshed, under the descending cloud of winter, more than I dared hope.

~

The letters [of D. H. Lawrence] are beautiful and terrible; Lawrence's lapse from being an artist into trying to be a prophet very well defined. "The conscience of our time," someone said to me the other day. Sure, and the poor, sad raggedy conscience, the self-tortured conscience it turned out to be. (I want to read T. E. Shaw's *Odyssey*.[2] *His* life I somewhat admire, under- cover agent or no. A ditty box, a motorbike, books, and the works of Mozart, a hard, pressed-upon existence with one or two necessities of the spirit squeezed out therefrom—far more admirable than D.H.'s globe-girdlings tied to a wife's apron strings.)

~

For Christmas I expect a warm dressing gown and a set of Thoreau's *Journals*. All I expect, and all I'll get. Enough.—Did you hear Stokowski's concert last Sunday, by radio? So beautiful: Handel, my lovely Gluck, the Leonora 3rd and Brahms's double concerto. [. . .] For five weeks now, I have done real work in piano technique with a severe friend, a girl who has carried over some of Leschetizky's method into her teaching, but not all. We do not *read* things together, we shred them out, note by note. Too much piano reading dulls the mind, destroys the fingers, and deadens the nerves. We're doing the C major Mozart sonata (No. 3): and I mean *doing!*

~

Yours for the contemplative life,
Louise

1. Maidie: Mathilde Alexander, daughter born to LB (at age twenty) and her first husband, Curt Alexander, in 1917, in the Canal Zone.
2. T. E. Lawrence (of Arabia) changed his name to Shaw in 1927.

/ to Katharine S. White[1] /

November 30, 1932

Dear Katharine:

Your note and the [*New Yorker*] check came this morning, and saved me from experiencing one of the most humiliating moments possible: that moment when one's last mossy vestment falls in rags at one's feet. Directly I sign my name to this note, I am going out and buy $145.00 worth of clothes, regardless, as my mother used to say, of cost or expense.

I feel guilty about the two missing pieces.—I can plead Thanksgiving (grisly festival!) and a fit of the sulks over the merits of work in progress.—Tomorrow, wearing four dresses, five pairs of shoes, and two hats, I'll begin a new one and get it to you by *noon on Tuesday*.

Yours in great haste!
Louise

/ *to Morton D. Zabel* /

306 Lexington Avenue
New York City
February 14, 1933

Dear Morton:

I began a letter to you on the 24th of January. How time has flown, that is, by what means, I can't correctly say. My review of [John] Masefield was hardly off the typewriter before I had to begin my winter's verse review for *The New Yorker*. That review (ten books polished off in 1100 words[1]) always disaffects me thoroughly, so that I have to take long ferry rides to Hoboken, long walks all over town, and long drinks of beer at four in the afternoon (alone, in Lüchow's, with the reflection of myself going up into infinity in the long funereal mirrors). [. . .] E[dmund] Wilson chided me for the flip tone taken in the *New Yorker* review. What else can one take? I take it for the good round sum of $75; I do not seek to justify this action, and if this piece of journalism cheapens me in the eyes of men and angels, I have no retort to make, save that I was paid $75 for the effort, and that I spoke my mind honestly, if glibly.

[. . .] We have seen a great deal of Mr. Wilson since Christmas. He comes in after supper and we play at the game whose name I have forgotten: you write a line of poetry and pass it on, and soon an entire poem is revealed, written by several hands. And very funny some of these efforts turn out to be. Edmund is a master at topical songs, too, written at high speed and sung to a tune that borrows [Jerome] Kern's rhythms and Gershwin's melodic line. [. . .]

There have been some very amusing parties in town of late. One was at Berenice Abbott's (the photographer),[2] last Friday. I went at six, expecting to get home in time for supper. I went with some qualms, having been

bored to death at a party in her studio last summer, where large androgynous females took up a lot of room and contributed little or nothing to the gaiety of life or the dignity of art. This party was quite different. The first person my eyes lit upon, as I entered the room, was Escudero in the flesh.[3] One of his little gypsy girl friends was with him—also his manager and interpreter. Also present were about a dozen charming Negroes from Harlem, all talented in the extreme, and a scattering of the less objectionable type of Lesbian. There was a bar; the drinks were excellent; the food was good; a blind pianist played for dancing; I looked well and danced continuously until far into the night, and Raymond engaged M. Escudero in conversation until early in the morning. It was the best party I have been to in years, and only goes to show that too many intellectuals in the same room have a negative and depressing effect, while a great many natural, happy, and unaffected Negroes liven things up masterfully. Escudero told R. that he could not read and write. "What is all that to me?" he exclaimed. I conveyed to E. that I thought him a great artist; we raised glasses to each other frequently. He would not dance or even make noises with his fingernails. I wish I could give such a good party. No M[atthew] Josephsons and K[enneth] Burkes and e. e. cummingses and M[alcolm] Cowleys. Just a happy crew of gentle voluptuaries.[4]
[. . .]

Yours, with admiration and esteem,

Louise

1. This review was published February 18, 1933, under the title "Snarling under the Sofa and Other Attitudes." It included the Masefield review as well as comments on several anthologies (one of them coedited by Theodore Roosevelt Jr.); books by Frances Frost, Wilbert Snow, and David Morton; and new poetry volumes by Edwin Arlington Robinson (*Nicodemus*) and William Rose Benet (*Rip Tide*).

2. Berenice Abbott, best known for her series of New York photographs in the 1930s, later took a series of photos of LB with a student named Emilie Buchwald for the short profile of the poet in the college edition of *Mademoiselle* (August 1956). LB is at the piano, on which stand sheets of music for Schubert and Clementi pieces.

3. Vicente Escudero (1887–1980) brought both fire and new rigor to flamenco dancing.

4. Although the notion of happy persons of color may sound condescending, LB clearly identified herself with the joy projected by flamenco performers and jazz artists, in preference to the dry affect of the mandarin intellectuals and coterie writers she mentions.

/ to Harriet Monroe /

306 Lexington Avenue
March 15, 1933

Dear Miss Monroe:

Mr. Moe wrote me on Saturday last that the trustees of the [Guggenheim] Foundation had awarded me a fellowship "for creative writing abroad"— for one year, beginning with April 1st.—I can't tell you the happiness and enthusiasm that this news has given my heart and mind. And for your good offices in the matter, I cannot express my gratitude. I am a little abnormal, because I fear so much and expect so little; help from outside has come so infrequently to me that I have taught myself never to expect it, and never, if possible, to ask for it. So that this fellowship gives me great confidence in myself and in the possibilities of future work that I may do. Nothing like it has ever happened to me before, I can assure you. I hope that some work will come through, and that it will be worth your faith in my abilities.

I plan to sail early in April for Genoa, and go down to Sicily before I visit Florence, the hill towns, and Venice. I'll write to you again before I sail.

Again, with all gratitude, affection, and esteem—

Louise

/ to Wolcott Gibbs¹ /

March 28, 1933

Dear Wolcott:

Here are the corrections. Thank you for saving me from "the opposite direction as herself"—(as one would say, from worse than death).—If Mr. Ross wants the house in "Conversation Piece" placed on the north side of 37th Street, and described in detail as a "large old-fashioned brownstone mansion, with a stoop," I'm afraid someone will have to write that in for me, because I certainly don't see any sense in writing it in, as myself. I've placed the house in New York (as opposed to Jersey City) and even the most bewildered person in the world, in the sense of the person most prone to bewilderment, ought to be able to read the rest in.

~

Yours—

Louise

1. The writer Wolcott Gibbs was substituting for Katharine White on this occasion when Harold Ross, the founder and editor of *The New Yorker,* asked Bogan for more detail in this short story, whose text appears in the fiction section.

/ to Morton D. Zabel /

The Bryant House
Provincetown, Mass.
July 27, 1934[1]

Dear Morton:

[. . .] Then E. Wilson invited me down here. In New York the one bright spot in my horrid early summer had been our German evening. We got together two nights a week and read Heine, aided by two dictionaries. E. W. plans to thread the morass of 19th century German thought and literature; Heine is his first step in the process of mastering the entire German language. We paid absolutely no attention to verb forms or case endings; we merely read the poems with the aid of TWO dictionaries. So that now we have Heine's early vocabulary (a pretty ghoulish one, as you no doubt realize) at our fingers' ends. We have fought through the early youth—native Jewish —early 19th cent.—moanings and broodings, the pure little lyrical intermezzi before us.—Edmund hopes to step into Goethe's *Faust* very soon. And from thence to Hegel, and from thence to Marx and Engels, I presume.— He is writing a long piece on the development of the science of history [*To the Finland Station*], beginning with Vico, continuing with Michelet, ending with Lenin. He has read every word Michelet ever wrote, including his letters: the eighty-six volumes (or so) are neatly piled along his study.—In case you thought that scholarship was dead, along these salty shores.

~

Ever, dear Morton—
Louise

1. Following her stay in Italy, France, and Germany from April to September 1933, LB's marriage and her equilibrium began to crumble. She was hospitalized, after a breakdown, from November 1933 to April 1934. After Labor Day 1934 she would hire a lawyer to proceed with a divorce from Holden, and in October move with Maidie to an apartment at 82 Washington Place.

/ *to Edmund Wilson* /

82 Washington Place
Manhattan
June 22, 1935

Edmund dear:

Your collection of Persian miniatures arrived this morning, and I was so happy to hear the tone of your humor again: you and your ladies swigging out of not one, but two decanters, and your dames with their stomachs only faintly veiled, tweaking dulcimers! I, myself, have been made to bloom like a Persian rosebush, by the enormous love-making of a cross between a Brandenburger and a Pomeranian, one Theodore Roethke by name.[1] He is very, very large (six feet two and weighing 218 lbs) and he writes very, very small lyrics. Twenty-six years old and a frightful tank. We have poured rivers of liquor down our throats, these last three days, and, in between, have indulged in such bearish and St. Bernardish antics as I have never before experienced. [. . .] Well! Such goings on! A woman of my age! He is amusing, when not too far gone in liquor; he once won a ΦBK and he has just been kicked out of Lafayette [College], from his position of instructor in English. He is just a ripple on time's stream, really, because he is soon going to Michigan to write a textbook on electrical fields. (How is the Dnieperstroi, by the way? I expect pictures of the Dnieperstroi, and get depraved

Persians instead! What would Marx and Engels say?)—I hope that one or two immortal lyrics will come out of all this tumbling about.

~

So they still give Tchaikovsky [in Russia], do they? Fancy that. I'll *bet* everything is gayer than you expected. How is the pink subway (why not a *red* subway)? Maidie has a whole act, depicting you in the pink subway: sort of a short operetta, with incidental songs. You must hear it sometime.

Well, my dear, we both love you very deeply, and Maidie is writing a separate note. God knows what's going to become of me. I feel so terribly happy, with or without Brandenburger: a form of incipient idiocy, no doubt. I wake each morning feeling younger and younger and I dance through each day with the abandon of at least an emu. I am also becoming quite pretty, so that, for the first time in years, gents try to make me on the streets.—Well, we'll all collapse like the one-horse shay, no doubt, during the next decade.

Send us more pretty pictures, my dove, my coney, and write, too. I DO miss you a lot.

Ever with love,
Louise

1. LB had met the young poet Theodore Roethke in late 1934. Their affair was short-lived, but their friendship continued until Roethke's death in 1963.

/ to John Hall Wheelock /

82 Washington Place
Manhattan
July 1, 1935

Dear Jack:

~

—I had the peculiar experience of falling mildly in love, about a week ago, with an enormous young man from Ann Arbor, Mich. He brought out all my Catherine the Great side, let me tell you, he being six feet two and weighing [fifteen] stone if he weighs a pebble. We had a magnificent week (he is aged twenty-six, by the way), and I found myself writing the most extraordinary Ella Wheeler Wilcoxism, as a consequence. This last will never be seen by human eye, I trust. Never shall I give the feminine sonneteers any competition. O, I'm a strange one, amen't I?

And I've just discovered Rilke. Why did you never tell me about Rilke? My God, the man's wonderful. Perhaps, sometime this summer, you will come down, in the late afternoon, and I'll provide some rye, and you can help me with some of the harder verses in the *Neue Gedichte*. My German is still so poor.

~

So let me hear from you, Jack.

Louise

P.S. (And this is the nasty part.)

In your current magazine, you blurb Raymond Holden as the author of a second book of poetry, *Landscape with Figures,* published in 1930. Now, I don't know whether you know it or not, but there was no such book. (I particularly loved the date, to give the whole thing some authority.)[1]

~

L.

1. LB follows with a list of fifteen "non-existent books" of her own, including such titles as *The Splendor Falls* (1918), *Up the Workers* (1925), and *Can We Forgive Her?* (1927).

/ *to Rolfe Humphries* /

82 Washington Place
Manhattan
July 2, 1935

Dear Rolfe:

It was nice of you, damned nice, to write me such a swell letter. You really are a great guy in many ways. I have moments when I'd like to kill you; on the other hand, there are moments when I'd like you to live forever.—At the present writing I feel that I shall live forever, and moreover, I feel that I want to live forever. Hangover. Why I should embark, in my present state, on a letter to you, I can't think. I really have been drinking far too much these last weeks, but I comfort myself with the thought that it's merely beer, as opposed to Jamaica rum and *fine champagne,* mixed. All that beer does to me is swell me up to hideous proportions; I'm rapidly getting a large corporation, and soon won't be able to see my feet. But to hell with it. I am so deliriously happy, most of the time, over nothing, over the fact of being able to breathe the daylight, of getting up in the morning, of eating, of sleeping. I hope that I haven't finally turned into a real manic depressive, and that this isn't the high state. I don't think so. Just a psychopathic personality with paranoid touches, as they say of people who cut other people up and mince them into the bathtub.

~ 1

I don't know what to do about "Roman Fountain." It's so sort of footless, as it is. *Clear* would be better before *gouts;* I'll change it. I wanted to get *thick* in, because the point about the fountains of Rome is, that there's so much water in them. None of your piddling little streams. Big gushes as thick as your arm, simply leaping up and scattering around; making a lovely big strong noise; rushing up like whole rivers. Great big bronze gents with great big bronze cornucopias or shells, or something, on their shoulders, and from that, great, enormous thick jumping water. To hell with that poem. It's minor, all save the first stanza. It doesn't do it. It should be all fountain, and no Louise looking at it.

And I'll change it to considered sacrifice.[2] Of course. Just sluttish writing on my part. The whole thing is rather meek and soft sounding, I think. There should be an *axe* or a *xylophone* in it somewhere, to edge the sound.

God help the man who has to edit our letters.

Write me again, and come to town soon.

Yours,
Louise

1. LB here discusses in detail two of Humphries's new poems, then recounts Holden's fib to Scribner's (see July 1, 1935, to Wheelock), enclosing her new poem, which she never published, "The Lie" (see appendix).
2. considered sacrifice: phrase from LB's poem "Baroque Comment."

July 6, 1935

Dear Rolfe:

~

[N]o matter what Eda Lou Walton has to say about dead boughs,[1] [. . . and]
in spite of all you had to say last winter on the subject of the elegiac quality
of lyric poetry, it should be written all the time, right now. [. . .] I believe
the great human change into a new world should be expressed, but I also
believe that when the Soviet arbiters say that Hamlet is foolish, they are talking nonsense, and destructive nonsense at that. And I hope the human race
will never be purged of those types, who, like Shakespeare, are victims all
their mature life of the most dreadful form of morbid jealousy, or of unconscious homosexuals like Hopkins and Housman, or of perfectly batty
people, who drive themselves into extreme fits over the fact that the land-
lady looked at them sideways, like Beethoven. God keep me from a world,
even without poverty and human degradation, in which there were no delicate sensibilities that could produce a remark like *Margaret, are you grieving;*
or *An expense of spirit in a waste of shame;*[2] that could not feel horror over mu-
tability and an excess of joy over the facts of perfectly physical passion, or
pity for the maladjusted or horror over the senseless cruel.

~

And if you do hear music, you can't say that Mozart will ever go out,
or that Beethoven's last quartets will ever need other values pinned onto
them but their very own. [. . .] I don't think that many things can ever be
done any better. Italian poetry and piano variations, for example (Dante
and Mozart). And my God, what about Bach?

[. . .] I am going to Boston early in August, and to Maine thereafter, to
see the Whites. [. . .] So do let's have the bay-crowning before that. Come
on, Rolfe, I shan't eat you. And we used to look so nice together in the street,
if you remember. I have a very pretty great big hat.

~

Do let me see you soon.
Louise

1. Eda Lou Walton, a critic and political activist, had called LB "a dead leaf on a dead
branch."
2. Title-lines of poems by Hopkins and Shakespeare.

/ to Theodore Roethke /

82 Washington Place
August 23, 1935

Dear Ted:

~

The difficulty with you now, as I see it, is that you are afraid to suffer, or to feel in any way, and that is what you'll have to get over, lamb pie, before you can toss off the masterpieces. And you will have to *look* at things until you don't know whether you are they or they are you. The lack of fundamental brain-work, so apparent in most lyrics, is not apparent in yours; you have a hell of a good mind, and real intelligence; real, natural, rich, full (in the best sense) intelligence. Your mind isn't a piece of ticker tape, going from left to right, like many minds, and it isn't full of gulfs and blank spots and arid areas. But it *is,* half the time, hiding from itself and its agonies, and until you let it do more than peek out, from time to time, you aren't going to get much done. "To My Sister" is a swell poem, because, as I said, you are right in it, mad as hell, and agonized as hell, and proud as hell . . .

Now in these Rilke poems (said she, ascending the podium) you get two things. You get a terrific patience and power of *looking,* in "The Blue Hortensia" one, and in the other[1] you get a magnificent single poetic concept carried through with perfect ease, because it is thoroughly informed by passion, in the first place. In the latter poem Rilke is terribly upset about his inability to get away from it all—you know that without my telling you, but let me maunder on. So he starts to write a poem, and he turns the lack of freedom into a perfectly frightful metaphor: he is unable to see any distance, any horizon (lovely word!), and he is so unable to see any that he feels himself *inside* a mountain, like a vein of ore. Everything is nearness, and all the nearness stone. Magnificent. And then what happens? Well, he can't stand it, so he turns to someone for help, and he drags the person into the metaphor. *I* am not adept at pain, he says, but if *you* are, make yourself heavy (isn't that *schwer* wonderful?) and break in, so that your whole hand may fall upon me and I on you with my whole cry . . . Now, a poem like that cannot be written by technique alone. It is carved out of agony, just as a statue is carved out of marble. And you must let yourself suffer, once in a while, lovey, in order that you may do same. Stay sober for a week. Anyone capable of writing "The veil long violated by Caresses of the hand and eye," [from Roethke's "Epidermal Macabre"] plus the "To My Sister" lyric, *might* come to the point of tearing off a lyric cry that would be, as someone I once knew used to say, heart-rendering . . .

"The Blue Hortensia" plumbs blue hortensia[s, or hydrangeas] to their depths. Here all sorts of comparisons are brought in, to aid the plumbing process. The color of the flowers is the color of old writing paper, faded into yellow and violet and gray, and it is like a child's many-times-washed apron —and by the time the reader gets to that, he is in a state of collapse, for Rilke has re-created the color in such a moving way that it's as though something new had been created in the universe. You see all that, I'm sure. Now, my duck, go and look at some of the flora, or even fauna of the electrical area, and do likewise.

~

I'd like to go off with you either to 1) Venice, or 2) Salzburg, or 3) a fold in the hills, for one week. After that period one or the other of us would come back on his or her shield, I have no doubt.

~

Now start in sobering and suffering, my fine boy-o.

Louise

1. The first poem in Rilke's 1903 suite *Das Buch von der Armut und vom Tode* (The Book of Poverty and of Death) begins: "*Vielleicht daß ich durch schwere Berge gehe / in harten Adern.*" LB paraphrases the poem's ten lines in her letter.

/ to Rolfe Humphries /

September 5, 1935

Dear Rolfe:

[. . . T]he mature soul rather enjoys the rain: clouded skies let you alone, and you don't have all that play and interplay of nerve-wracking light and shadow to cope with. I admit that everything is rather damp in my house at the moment, particularly as I seized upon yesterday or the day before to do a little laundry, and now I am surrounded by the lank form of towels that will not dry. Just a foretaste of my life in a cold-water flat, and I must recognize it and use it (I don't know what those *its* refer to, exactly) as such. Old philosophic Bogan, the weather sage.

But really, one thing I decided, after my sojourn in the madhouse, was that I should never let the weather get me down. I used to be at the mercy of clouds no bigger than a man's hand, and in that hour of twilight, when animals howl, I used to feel that all hell was rising up to oppress me, and frequently, I would weep. No more. I am serene from dawn to dark, and even the horrid watches of the night afford me no qualms. Grown-up. Mature.

~

I am reading the George Sand–Flaubert letters, and they are very rewarding. I am copying out the choice bits and will relay them to you. Flaubert was so sour and she was so full of love-love-love, that they make a fine pair. I admire her tremendously; she was not an artist, but she was a big woman, and there have been few enough of those in the world. She went through a life that would have killed ten men, and at the end, at seventy, she was wonderful: full of gumption and wisdom and good sense, and she loved children and the oppressed and fruit and flowers and wine and marionette plays and she worked like a tiger. I am going to put myself in training, these next ten years, to have such an old age, if I have an old age at all.

Flaubert said that most novels are written by disguised bourgeois, as distinguished from artists, and I think this very good. After the Commune, he said that what he feared was that the proletariat would rise into the stuffiness and the stupidity of the bourgeoisie, and there's something in that, too.

~

Louise

Hotel Albert
University Place, Tenth Street
New York
October 1, 1935

Dear Rolfe:

I was much surprised and pleased to see my fugitive verses, long hidden in your bureau drawer.[1] I think it's a shame I didn't do more rhymed reviews, but [Raymond] sort of had a sinecure on that, in those days, and he was so fluent and clever at it that I thought I was just a runner up and so stood back and watched. First chop or nothing, that's my unfortunate tendency.

~

I'm feeling wonderfully peaceful and rested, now that the roof has finally caved in, and if this typewriter behaves for a week or so, I intend to turn out work. *The Dog Beneath the Skin; or, Where is Francis?* is a wow. Of course all that knocking down of the straw men of the British gentility will get tiresome, if Auden sticks to it for the next fifty years, but he does write superbly, there's not the slightest doubt of that. Some of the choruses in this are unbeatable, and put against Eliot's present-day liturgy, they shine and resound. The comedy is very good, really Gilbertian, in spots, and he has learned a lot from Gilbert and from *Sweeney Agonistes* and even from Swift, or maybe he doesn't realize how much his line of stupid middle-class talk sounds like *Advice to Servants* and *Polite Conversation*. I must read those again. The long poetry review is due Oct. 28, and *The Dog,* for the *N. R.,* this week. I've sold most of the books to be included in the review; they went last summer, this summer, when I felt the need to eat. I had to sell the Yeats *Collected Plays,* even, and that made me sore, because the two Greek translations are included and one of them is unobtainable elsewhere. Ah well, there's nothing like eating, after all . . .

[. . .] Malcolm [Cowley, at *The New Republic*] seems very open to suggestion, these days. I can't imagine how he allowed himself to send me the Auden. In the old days it would have gone to Allen Tate, or Horace Gregory, and Horace would have begun his review, "I think that this is a very interesting play . . ." and Allen would have said, "In fusing the basis of the intellect out of the microscopic dualisms concurrent in the derivative dichotomies so uselessly prevalent, and notwithstanding the disuse fallen upon the gentility, destroyed by General Bragg . . ."

~

[. . .] I've had a sort of mild illumination about how important money is, since I saw the sheriff standing on my floor, and saw the furniture whisked out the door onto the sidewalk. I wanted to do nothing and see what would happen, but after they got about ten pieces out I ran for a moving van. [. . .] Yes; I understand now that all the spirited uppishness in the world wouldn't have stopped the Greenwood Cemetery (that was my landlord, I discovered, and a grisly one, too) from throwing me into the gutter, and I could have sat and quoted middle-class gush about the necessity for gracious living to them, and that would have been a laugh. I'm sorry I didn't kick the sheriff in the shins: I did stand up to him and tell him to get the hell out, and that was a good one. I really should have seen if he'd have drawn on me . . .

~

I'll be in the Lib. on Sat. A.M., and call me when you can. I'll send the manuscript poems back to you. You never have anything happen to you, in the way of fires in the hold or moth and rust . . .

Louise

1. The poems Humphries found were "To My Brother" and "Hidden." The latter, never collected, appears in the appendix to this volume.

/ to Theodore Roethke /

Hotel Albert
October 3, 1935

Dear Ted:

[. . .] This will be brief. I want you to look up my poem in the October *Scribner's*; it is incomplete as it stands in print, since someone, perhaps because of the exigencies of space, left out an entire line. The second stanza, as it came from my pen, read:

> Light, pure and round, without heat or shadow,
> Big in the cirrus sky at evening,
> Accompany what we do.[1]

The *cirrus* is important, because it echoes the *us*-es, or how do you make a plural of *us,* my sweet Master of Arts? I was very much touched when I saw this in print. Wheelock, as I wrote you, ravished it away from me, that night when we two plumbed the depths of German food and drink. I thought it a little album piece, and was keeping it in my bottom bureau drawer, for my literary executors to find, after my death. But I must say that it looks extraordinarily pure and defined as compared to the overstuffed effusions of Bernice Lesbia Kenyon (she's deleted the Lesbia, of late years: you should see her: she closely resembles a Swedish cook and she wears false furs (meow, meow) in profusion), and even of old False Face Jeffers. What an ass that man is! Him and his Pacific Ocean!

[. . .] I got $7.50 for my great "Baroque Comment" poem, and I spent it on soap (I love soap) and a new fountain pen and a bottle of very poor whiskey, and then I had $2.50 left over and I thought I might buy some highly expensive comestibles with that, but my deeper nature arose, and I called up Terence Holliday, who imports all the new English editions, and I asked him how much the Auden-Garrett anthology, *The Poet's Tongue,* was, and it was $2.40, so I rushed up to the highly refined Holliday Bookshop (he can't come it over me, for we worked in Brentano's together, just about the time you were getting that lovely set of second teeth), and I bought the damned thing, and it's marvelous: alphabetically arranged [by first lines] so that "Casey Jones" comes right before "Song for St. Cecilia's Day" practically, and it has nursery rhymes, and the wonderful nightmare song from *Iolanthe,* and God knows what else. I shall send it to you, if you send me a written certificate, in your fine Brandenburger hand, that you'll send it back, and not will it to your bastards. I'll send you *The Dog,* too, under the same conditions. I can't trust anything with a man after whom husbands (and a new lot of husbands, God help us) go gunning . . . [2]

It's a damned shame, since the number of my autumns are now numbered, that I can't laugh through this one with you, for you are the best laugher I know . . . the teeth and the mind combined have something to do with this. I have such an insane delight in beautiful teeth; the major disasters of my life have been based on them. Me and Poe . . .

~

Yours etc.,
Louise

1. When "Evening-Star" was collected in *The Sleeping Fury* (1937), LB had changed "big" to "held."

2. When Roethke called her on this, she replied: "No particular husbands. And you were the one who told me about the legend. *I* never thought you a sexual athlete. No indeed. Just a boy who was eight years old at the date of my first marriage . . ." (October 9, 1935; WTWL, 108n2).

/ *to Morton D. Zabel* /

Hotel Albert
New York City
October 7, 1935

Dear Morton:

I have been very much at peace, since the roof fell in; in fact, I haven't felt so peaceful in my life as now. Being evicted isn't really a tragedy, you know, if you are still youngish, and can scrape some money together, and have your work and a few friends. It's only tragic to the old, who have no money at all, and have to go to the workhouse. Yes; the entire lack of money makes it tragic. [. . .] I worked and fought for thirty-seven years, to gain serenity at thirty-eight. Now I have it. And it's not dependent upon the whim of any fallible human creature, or upon economic security or upon the weather. I don't know where it comes from. Jung states that such serenity is always a miracle, and I think the saints said that, too. Though there are certain ways, and a certain road that may bring it about, when it comes, it is always a miracle. I am so glad that the therapists of my maturity and the saints of my childhood agree on one score.

~

[. . . This morning I reread] the Blunden preface to Wilfred Owen's *Poems,* and the poems themselves. There was a real sensibility for you, and such a person is the only real realist, because he *feels* the horror, instead of merely recording it in a knowing and anthropological way. I suddenly knew, this morning, that such sensibility is so ennobling that, were it to come into contact with the group, it would ennoble even the Communist party of

America, and I knew, too, that until such a person, or such persons, became Communists, that the Revolution, if any, would be worthless and bleak slaughter, only. Perhaps Lenin was such a man. Everyone says he was; the Christ-mantle has descended on him so swiftly that we will never know. But certainly Wilfred Owen was a great poet, in all senses, and he might have been a great leader as well. I very nearly wept over him.

~

Ever with affection,
Louise

/to John Hall Wheelock/

65 University Place
New York City
October 29, 1935

Dear Jack:

I am sending you, this week, Viola Meynell's new novel, published in England by Cape, *Follow Thy Fair Sun*. Morton brought it back to me from England. He stayed at Wilfrid Meynell's, and met Viola. I have been, for a great many years, an intense admirer of her work, and, because she told Morton that she was looking for a new American publisher, he told her that I would speak to you. Putnam brought out several of her things, rather badly. You people, of course, published her memoir of her mother.

The present book is, I do not hesitate to tell you, in my judgment, the most remarkable study of the agony of love that I have ever read, whether by male or female pen. The course of frustration, disillusion, and despair is traced, as is usually not the case, with the author's bare nerves and sensibilities. It is not wrapped up in literature; it occurs on the page before us, as in the best drama and poetry. Colette is the only other woman I know who has looked so closely and felt so *accurately* that her words have the value of some major discovery about life. I am not, as you know, a great admirer of the novel; I even go so far as to deny that Henry James plumbed it or used it to any great purpose, and perhaps the reason is that it cannot be so used. But in this book, once the major theme starts developing, you get the real sound and the almost unbelievable—outside of poetry—evocation.

Do tell me what you think. [. . .]

Believe me to be, dear Jack

Sincerely yours,
Louise

[P.S.] Roethke says you took his poem. He has it, don't you think? Slight, but unmistakable.

/ *to Theodore Roethke* /

November 6, 1935

~

I take back a lot I said about James. I'm reading the letters, which I was unable to read, for years, and they are very fine, once you get used to his eccentricities. And now I can read the later manner like a shot, just as one can get going very fast and smooth with French, after a week of concentration and continued application to the text. It's really a beautiful manner, for anyone who likes periodic sentences. He says that the real test of a real feeling for writing is a passion for adverbs . . . "I'm glad you like adverbs—I adore them; they are the only qualifications I really much respect, and I agree with the fine author of your quotations in saying—or thinking—that the sense for them is *the* literary sense." That shows the difference between a prose-writer, even a great prose-writer, and a lyric poet. You can't be a lyric poet and love adverbs. Strange, isn't it. For James was a great prose-writer, there's no doubt about that. I am reading *The Bostonians,* which no one ever reads, and which Edmund has been trying to get me to read for years. It's magnificent. The first account in American of a Lesbian attraction. And so closely written, so accurately observed. Do read it. [. . .]

Think of being a novelist: always in your work, walking around in it, year after year, with never a break. Book after book, year after year. As I lay awake in bed last night I had a magnificent idea for a novel after James's own heart: perfect in form and shape: rather like an hourglass, as is *The Ambassadors,* but not quite. I must say, I get terribly sick of novels that go along, riding a hidden or ostensible *I,* in a straight line, with some bumps, from start to finish. Even Proust is tiresome in that respect.

~

Louise Sappho Bogan

[P.S.] Now relax and stop being badgered and stop worrying, for a while. You can't hear anything going on inside yourself, if you can't stay serene once in a while, my coney.

~

/ to *Morton D. Zabel* /

65 University Place
New York City
December 3, 1935

Dear Morton:

~

I went to the French exhibition at the Metropolitan, the day after I got back on my feet. I really went up to see the winter sunlight on the floor of the long room downstairs in the American Wing. I often do this, during the winter; the room is so gracious and beautiful, and the sunlight pours in, broken up into squares, onto the floor, and the whole thing gives *me* bunches inside, I can tell you. I stand on the stairway and look down, in a trance, for as long as I dare; I fear the Irish muggism of the attendants, to some extent, so I don't dare stand there too long. There's something about the fact that the room is *on ground level* that gets me; H. James could do a story about that, something about genteel atavism, and wanting to live in the 18th cent. Yes;

there's something in my blood that wants to look *down* into a long ground floor room with the sunlight in it. You can figure that out, if you can.

~

Ever, with appreciation,
Louise

/ *to Theodore Roethke* /

[December] 1935

Dear Ted:

I am so sorry that you are still under the weather, but I am glad that you're having good, sensible professional care. There's nothing like it, when one gets really down, and isn't able to make the motions by oneself.—Believe me, my dear, I've been through it all; not once, but many times (twice, to be exact). And after the first feelings of revolt and rage wear off, there's nothing like the peace that descends upon one with routine, lovely routine. At the Neurological Center, here in town, at one time I went through three weeks of high-class neurology myself. I had a room all done up in noncorrosive greens, and a day and a night nurse, and a private bath, and such food as you never ate, and hydrotherapy, including steam-cabinets, and a beautiful big blond doctor by the name of McKinney. I had a great triumph with McKinney: I made him shed a single tear and when you can make a neurologist shed a tear, you're doing well, as you probably know by now. You wouldn't be able to bring off that feat, because you've had a comparatively happy life, and because you haven't got the Irish gift for histrionics—not that I don't feel assured that you do pretty well in your Pomeranian way . . .

Well, there I was, and I got worse and worse, rather than better and better, because I hadn't come into myself as a person, and was still a puling child, on to people, and trying to make them tell me the truth. [. . .] You won't be THAT foolish. The good old normal world is really a lot of fun, once you give in to it, and stop fighting against it. Fight with your work, but let the world go on, bearing you and being borne by you: that's the trick. As old Rilke said:

Und wenn dich das Irdische vergaß,
Zu der stillen Erde sag: Ich rinne.
Zu dem raschenWasser sprich: Ich bin.[1]

~

Ever with love,

L.

1. "And should the mortal world forget you, / Say to the quiet earth, I flow like water. / To the rapid water say, I'm here." *The Sonnets to Orpheus* (1922), 29.

January 5, 1936

Dear Ted:

I am again sorry that I haven't written sooner. I hope you are feeling splendidly, in or out of the bath. I am feeling very well today, now that the fearsome holidays are over, which always tend to make everything and everybody tense and ugly, in this city: the contrast between carols being rung on church bells—aroundTwelfth Night, these become increasingly hard to bear —and Christmas trees and whooped-up wassail of all sorts—between these things and the New York streets in general, where, as usual, people flounder and rush, and run in and out of offices to earn things, and in and out of stores to buy things. Christmas and New Year's in Michigan are no doubt far less artificial and wearing.

Today has been dreary and full of slush, but I had a very good time, nevertheless, trying to plan a new set of rooms for Maidie and myself, in which we can have some sunlight and a piano. [. . .]

I have been reading Rilke's *Journal of My Other Self* [*The Notebooks of Malte Laurids Brigge,* 1910], and I recommend it to you, when you are all better: it has its depressing side, not to be sampled by invalids. I can heartily recommend to you James's *Notes on Novelists.* You have probably read this; I never tire of re-reading parts of it. The three articles on George Sand are superb. No one should ever take J. to task for lack of human sympathy, or for lack of understanding the erraticism of gifted women, or for narrow moral prejudices, after reading these. He loved G. Sand, and respected her throughout; his understanding of the mixed up de Musset–Italian doctor affair is complete, and he can even laugh at it: not a trace of old-maidish shock. In fact, I have had moments of cynicism over this business, even I, but not Henry. And the article on her worries with Chopin, and her tragic relationship with the daughter who betrayed her, is touching in the extreme. Do read these if they are in the library.

[. . .] The only human contact that I look forward to with any expectation is the visit of Janet Flanner (she does the Paris Letter in the *NYer*); she wrote that she is looking forward to meeting me this month, and she is quite a person, from all accounts, and writes, as you know, damned good prose.

As to Morton, my dear, he hasn't much—hardly any—intuition, you are right there, and his jesuitical kind of mind flattens out his convictions: his critical remarks are always rather on the fence, as though he must oblige all sides. He is, on the other hand, a true and real and generous friend; he has put up with my howls for years, and during the period when my howls were frequent and boring. And he is the true learned type; he is always fundamentally on the right side; he really knows, because his taste and intelligence are first-rate, even though his nerves are panicky (he is terribly afraid of some things, and runs to cover, poor boy) and his convictions, as I have said, tend to beat around the bush. I admire him more than almost anyone I know, and I should certainly go to him in any real crisis, and be sure of help. So don't write to him nastily.

~

Do write soon, my dear.

Ever with love—
Louise

/ *to Rolfe Humphries* /

January 24, 1936

Dear Rolfe:

I can't write any thumping prose on your two questions. I fought out my fight last summer, and, since I stopped being one kind of a neurotic, I don't keep on fighting the same fight over and over. I fight whatever it is out, and then leave it, and go on to something else. Sort of a personal new party line . . . That's the best way for it to be. I fought one fight—a crusade designed to make the man I loved tell the truth—for about five years, over and over again. Now I take about three months to get a thing laid out, so that I can see it all, and then I either accept it or get over it. That's health.

So you'll have to go back to my letters, if you want thumping prose, on that subject.

I can write you a quiet line or two, in answer. To the first question: I suppose any political regime that includes dictatorship is something for a writer anywhere to worry about. I don't think he should give as much worriment to the possible political set-up as he does to his writing. The less capacity for scattered worrying that a writer possesses, the better. Great artists in any field haven't been great worriers. Minor artists ought to worry about their work, for worry is only valuable when it goes toward making something hard, condensed, and durable. Minor art needs to be hard, condensed, and durable.

2) An organization of writers for the defense of culture seems to me to be a rather tendentious scheme. If culture is going to be overthrown, it will be, in any case. No puny organization of writers is going to stop it. Perhaps it is best for culture to get knocked on the ear from time to time. It always has been knocked on the ear, before now, and the disguised rubble built into the wall has gone down, and remained, rubble, and the beautiful incised stones and the headless statues and the partial stanzas and the bronze garlands and the pure speech and the rational thought have come through, in any case. Why worry? Why ask for the world without ruins? Why ask for a world in which art never changes or fails or is partially erased? The Fascists burn the books, and the Communists bar the heterodox, and what difference is there between the two? I must say I would just as soon die on the barricades for Mozart's music as not: if someone walked in this minute and said, Louise, if you don't go out and get shot, they'll take Mozart's music and throw it down the drain, I'd put my hat right on and go out and take it. But the thought of spending years moping along with a lot of other writers, defying anticultural forces: No. For culture isn't saved that way. Nothing is saved that way. And a lot of precious life is wasted that way. I'm an individualist, as you can easily see.

~

Write again soon.
Louise

/ to Morton D. Zabel /

Swampscott
August 10, 1936

Dear Morton:

~

Brief answer to your points on the Freudian discoveries, their use, value and applications:

1.) Of course artists and thinkers have known the real secret all along. And primitive people knew it too. (Myths: principally the high-point Greek ones.) No practitioner of the art of mental healing (yes, I know how invidious that sounds) ever omits, at some point in the cure, two great remarks made by two great men: "Know thyself," and "The Kingdom of God is within you." One or two doctors have said to me, as well, again quoting: "He who loseth his life shall find it . . ."

2.) No one wants to put all the burden on the Ego, i.e., the conscious will. No one but A. Tate and the Comrades. The thing to do, for happiness and sanity, is to lift the nagging burden of the Super-Ego, and to listen, as much as possible, to the stirrings of the Id, when stirrings are vouchsafed.—Responsibility is, as you say, the rock-bottom indispensable of sanity, but the courage to take responsibility must be trained into most of us—into people of our type. For responsibility is the mark of adulthood, and adulthood is based on "the conquest of fear," God save the mark.

3.) Therapy does not console; it cures, where it can. There is no cure for some people; just as a man cannot add a cubit to his stature, by taking thought; if you're born with certain things left out, you can't be cured; you can't be "born again."

—I had already noted the [Thomas] Mann essay, and copied out one of the same paragraphs that struck you: the one concerning the heightening which comes to the artist when he acquires the habit of regarding life as mythical and typical. That's only another way of saying that when one lets go, and *recognizes* the stream on which we move as the same stream which moves us

144   *Letters*

within—that it is time and the earth floating our blood and flesh, floating its own child—and stops fighting against the kinship, the light flows in; peace arrives. [. . .]

The class is dismissed for the day. Please pass the books to the front!

~

Ever with love,
Louise

/ to Theodore Roethke /

70 Morningside Drive
August 29, [1936]

Dear Ted:

So you were mad, were you? Well, H. M[onroe] turns us all down, from time to time, and I had a little poem rejected by the *Sat. Rev. of Lit.*, not so long ago. If one insists on being a lyric poet, those things happen. H. M. should have taken the poem, of course. Money should grow on trees, too. It's life, my poor young friend . . .

When you end up at Red Gap Normal College, I'll go and take your course, in my bonnet and shawl. With little velvet strings tied under my chin, and one of those jet plumes in front.

I'd love to see you helping with the wash. I'll bet you wet everything in sight and play with the soapsuds!

~

Write some and pray for me.

L.

/ to Rolfe Humphries /

Dear Rolfe:

My mother has pneumonia, and is, I think, dying. After a long struggle with her pride, I managed, this morning, to get her into St. Luke's.——How I feel, with my pride, I don't think you can imagine.

~

What we suffer, what we endure, what we muff, what we kill, what we miss, what we are guilty of, is done by us, as individuals, in private.——I wanted to kill a few interns this morning, and I shall want to kill some nurses tonight, and I know that it is a lousy system that keeps the poor, indigent old from dying as they should. But I still hate your way of doing things. To hell with the crowd. To hell with the meetings, and the public speeches. Life and death occur, as they must, but they are all bound up with love and hatred, in the individual bosom, and it is a sin and a shame to try to organize or dictate them.

Thank you for the poem. I shan't ever see you again, I suppose.

Louise

/ to Morton D. Zabel /

December 23, 1936

Dear Morton:

The [picture of the] Fury came intact, and it is so beautiful that I cried.[1]—— I would have written you before this, but my mother took sick the night before last, and today I managed to persuade her to go to the hospital, and it is pneumonia.

If you could have seen the fight she put up, right to the last. But now she is a poor dying woman. I wish I could stop remembering her in her pride and beauty—in her arrogance, that I had to fight so—and now I feel it would have been better if I hadn't fought at all. Because under it all was so much love, and I had to fight that too.

I'll write soon, after this is over—after I stop feeling that Lucifer should have won. *The damned, niggardly, carroty, begrudging world!*

Louise

1. Zabel had sent a photo of the "Medusa Morente," the copy of the sculpted head from the second century B.C., which she had seen in the Museo delle Terme in Rome in 1933. LB's next book, *The Sleeping Fury* (Charles Scribner's Sons, 1937), was already in press.

The Royal Hibernian Hotel
Dawson Street, Dublin, Ireland
April 14, 1937[1]

Morton, you can put me down as a Jungian. I swear to you (and you know I am incapable of faking an aesthetic reaction, or lying about one) that Cobh rushed at me like something out of my own Subconscious: the dream and the answer to the dream. All my life I have been stirred by the sort of houses that faced me along the quay: simple, blank-faced brick or stucco houses, with squarish small-paned windows.

~

From Cobh to Cork by bus.—It is all true: this is the loveliest country in the world. Where, anywhere else, terrible ugliness would stand, at the curve of the road, there is a long, low house in a garden, or a round tower, or a hedge with yellow gorse all over it. Never a mistake. It is as though all their feeling for *rightness* has been expended on the countryside itself, for they are terrible fumblers with all the delicacies and the amenities of living *inside* a house; you should see the hotel room, without *one* even feasible thing in it, not even a comfortable chair. But in the air, and under the sky, they don't make mistakes. Cork is a lovely, clean, spacious city; many bow-windows, and the whole affect pulled into harmony with broad streets and gray stone.

~

What is behind the façades [of Dublin houses], I hesitate to think. Irish clutter, probably.—I saw some, along with Irish poor taste, through some windows. O Morton, they can't clean a plate or a floor decently, or print a newspaper properly, and yet they have nobleness in their grain! I had a plate of ham served to me for lunch, with thumb-marks on it, by a slavey who might have been a duchess . . .

This morning I saw, for the first time in my life, a young boy, walking along the street, reading a book. And the beatific smile on his face, no one could believe.

It struck me, as I dressed this morning, that, not only was this the city where my grandmother was born and bred, but also that it is the city most displayed, dissected, hated, scorned, vilified, praised, wept over, distilled into literature, in modern time. It's like living in Troy, pretty near. For the modern Helen (M[aud] Gonne) has walked its walls, and the great successful modern war for freedom has been waged here, and as for dissection by masters, well—shall I name the works for you? Don't forget *Mr. Gilhooley,*[2] as you name them to yourself.

1. During the months of April and May 1937, LB traveled in Ireland on the unused portion of her 1933 Guggenheim fellowship.

2. *Mr. Gilhooley:* Liam O'Flaherty novel about 1920s Dublin.

The Royal Hibernian Hotel
Dawson Street, Dublin, Ireland
April 15, 1937

Morton:

Today the let-down of a week's tension began, and I wonder that I am alive at all to write you this, in one of the coldest, wettest, rainiest, filthiest twilights it has ever been my lot to endure. It has been a bad day all round. Instead of being interested and amused by the Joycean people who surround me on all sides, I have been appalled by them. Then this room is so terrible. What can you think of a nation that doesn't provide bedside lights for you, in a fairly civilized hotel? What can you think of a nation that seems to consist largely of women down on their knees scrubbing and rubbing, and yet whose restaurants cannot serve the simplest dish without a thumb-mark on, or a hair in it? And the set, unyielding Dublin face is hard to take: even after two days it begins to get on one's nerves. The whole town has a sort of stiff-backed neurosis.

~

Morton:

~

I haven't been faced by so many mirrors in months. God help me, I'm losing my looks! How long have I looked so old and homely? Why didn't you
tell me? [. . .] It's so sad to find oneself so superlatively ugly, as seen in Irish
mirrors. "An interesting face"—that's what mine will be in the future. And
believe me, I shall cultivate a moveless mask, from now on, for that's what
a face like mine (in its present condition) needs.

~

—On the train to Derry (after a bleak and freezing wait at Coleraine
Junction—it had begun to rain again), in the 3rd class carriage (I have taken
to 3rd class: it's very neat and clean) a strange, sick looking, rather tooth-
less young man (he looked forty but was perhaps twenty-six) was smoking
in the compartment as I entered it. I coughed, as I well might, after ¾ hour
on a bench on a station platform. He was reading a sad-looking, withered-
looking novel, and he looked terribly poor and sick. Was it his cigarette that
made me cough, he asked immediately, and I said no, of course not, and lit
one of mine. And then we talked. He, with a kind of learned reserve. An
Ulster accent. A suspicious look, until he knew I had Irish blood. And he
agreed, then, that Dublin is a strange, close-mouthed place, and he was all
for showing me the landscape. With pride. With reserve. And he summed
up the "troubles" (against England, and the Civil War of 1922–23, as well)
better than I could have hoped to hear them summed up. He carried my
bags to the hotel bus, and waited, in the rain, until I was in it. Poor, gallant,
sad, sick boy! In his cheap overcoat and his blue felt hat; with his pinched
face and frank, intelligent, homely eyes.

/ *to Edmund Wilson* /

The Northern Counties Hotel
Londonderry
April 21, 1937

Dear Edmund:

~

[Dublin is] perfectly beautiful. But it's cruel and shut-up and full of conspirators, believe me. James Stephens, in a review he wrote recently for the
London *Times,* of [Oliver St. John] Gogarty's book [his autobiography], admits this. Dublin, he said, is not a city; it is a conspiracy.—I had come to
the same conclusion, several days before I read the review.

You don't know what's up. The most moveless faces in the world con-
front you on all sides. I saw one woman, at a matinee, at the Gate Theatre,
who looked as though she had never moved her face, from birth. How she
managed to eat or speak, I can't imagine. Now I know where Yeats got his
idea, his obsession, of the mask. He had to take good looks, from time to
time, at Dubliners. And, after I had managed to get away, to Belfast (it
seemed, for a while, that I would be in Dublin for the rest of my life. I became
so petrified, physically and spiritually), I suddenly remembered the lines:

> What fanatics invent
> In this blind bitter town,
> Fantasy or incident . . .

[Yeats, "Quarrel in Old Age"]

Well, maybe a town has to be like that, in order that great literature be bred
in it. Florence, I'll bet, was much the same in Dante's time. Full of hidden
dissension. Hatred, *sub rosa* activities. Divided allegiance.—I hope the food
was better.

Bloated with tea, scones, cold meat, and little pink cakes, as I am, it's a
wonder I can put pen to paper at all. If my good sense hadn't scented the
reliability of "an egg and a rasher," I might not be alive to write these words.
—Whiskey is terribly expensive: 6/6 for a *half* pint. A double whiskey and
soda costs anywhere fom 1/10 to 2/6. Yesterday I bought a half pint of
Bushmills, since I was in the vicinity of that distillery. Very good, too. But

Letters

here in Londonderry the whiskey drinker, or buyer, is put down as a fallen person. You should see the liquor stores: they have black hell written all over them.

Londonderry is pretty awful, except for about three streets, and a lovely park. [. . .] From it you can see the whole town, for it is on the top of the hill, and all Co. Donegal, practically, and Co. Derry, lie below, with their lovely little hills cut up into fields. The light is so lovely. Yesterday I spent in Portrush, watching the Atlantic drive in from Iceland, between the dark cliffs. The clouded light makes the water look magical, and the whole country lives under that clouded light. It's incredibly beautiful, as a country, but terribly frightening. America set up, in the blood, some clarity and definiteness that is antipathetic to all this.——I never felt such a coward before. But here in the North, it is warmer-hearted than in Dublin. I didn't expect that.

~

> Ever, my old scuppernong,
> Your feeble friend,
> Louise

/ to Rufina McCarthy Helmer[1] /

August 5, 1937[2]

Dear Rufina:

Well, here I am in my ducky little apartment, as happy as a clam at high water (although just how happy that is, I have always had my doubts!). I have a table, a bed, a few chairs, and a few bibelots and books. Also some dishes and knives and forks and spoons. T. E. Lawrence never allowed more than four cups in his house, and I can understand, now, just how he felt. I have one cup, but a lot of old, superfluous, cupless saucers, and I'll give them to the Morgan Memorial soon. I potter around and clean and dust, and water the plant (yes, I have a plant, with which I soon will be in love: you remember [Auden's] "I had an aunt that loved a plant, but you're my cup of tea"). I also have a phonograph and a lot of records. This is the only way to live, I can tell you. I dread the fall, when, for shame's sake, I'll have to put up some curtains and down some rugs.——The fine view of the back piazza of the Psychiatric Institute, with its male and female patients, keeps me on an even keel, and in good humor. I always remember the three weeks I spent in its sister institution, the Neurological. I remember looking out, from the windows of hydrotherapy, over what must have been the very roof under which I now live, and seeing a woman hanging out clothes, and wishing that I, too, could be a normal resident of Washington Heights, and hang out clothes in a happy, normal way. Well, I've got my wish, and the mere mechanics of going to the grocer's now makes me happier than the present of pecks of diamonds. (All this is morbid euphoria, no doubt!)

~

Saturday is my birthday, and I'll be forty, and I never thought I'd live to see the day.——I am so glad you enjoyed *The Princess Casamassima*. It is superb. It settles the problem of the artist in modern society, for one thing. I think the final scene, when the hard-bitten revolutionary and the aristocrat (or at least the member of an upperest class) stand over Hyacinth's (the artist's) deathbed, and don't know what to say, either of them, is one of the finest in modern literature. In ancient literature, too, for that matter. Do read *The Bostonians*, if you haven't already. That is another masterpiece, and no one ever reads it. Everyone starts in, on James, at the wrong end: *The Golden Bowl*, etc. These works often bore and puzzle the beginner, and they drop James, and miss all the wonderful early works. *The Tragic Muse* is fine, too.

I knew *something* was going to be blown up, as I told you.[3] I have a new theory about the Irish: that they're really forest dwellers, with all the forest-dweller's instincts, and that since, or when, the Irish forests disappeared, they all developed a terrible neurosis, from being forced to be out in the open so much. I really think this is true. Just a lot of Druids at heart.

~

Louise

1. Rufina McCarthy (Mrs. William F. Helmer) taught high-school English in Boston.
2. From this time until the end of her life, LB lived at 709 W. 169th Street, New York City. An address block will be given only when she is traveling.
3. The IRA had exploded a bomb in Belfast on July 28, 1937, in a failed attempt to assassinate the English king, George VI.

/ to Morton D. Zabel /

Dear Morton:

It has been a little like equatorial Africa, here. Last night it began to rain, and has kept up ever since, and now there's that lovely cool-cold in the air, and everything smells a little like metal and farewell, and this is the smell I most love in the world: the first breath of autumn, smelled in late August. I have tried to figure out just why I love these days, and this light (best just after the rain just after heat) and I once decided that it was because I was born in August, and, maybe, first began to see and smell, and focus on days like this. That's a very good explanation, I think . . .

~

I saw *The Spanish Earth* this afternoon, along with two audiences: the Communist one, which came in before 1:00, and the regular, or bourgeois audience, which came in later and paid 20 cents more. The first audience cheered the Communist salute (described, by Hemingway, a little misleadingly, I thought, as the "salute of Republican Spain").——Hemingway was just *too* noble and humanitarian, and clipped-speech, throughout. You'd have thought that he'd never whooped up such a humanitarian spectacle as a bullfight, in his life, or never been passed bottles of beer by minions, while on safari. All full of the milk of human kindness, and the virtues of the dear *peasants* and the brave civilians. I don't see him doing any labor and union helping at home, however. I suppose an automobile strike isn't colorful enough for him.

~

There was certainly something awfully sentimental and fixed, about that picture. The whole tone of it bothered me, although, God knows, I'd like the Spanish Loyalists to get their country. But Hemingway was having such a hell of a good time, looking at a *War,* and being disgustingly noble about it.

~

What the Communist party needs is more jolly proletarian members, partly in liquor, most of the time, if possible. This God damned nobility of all and sundry is making me terribly ill. If the new world is going to consist of a lot of Communist stuffed shirts, you can count me out of it. I'll take to the roads, or the trees, or the crannies in the rocks.

~

Love,
Louise

/ to Theodore Roethke /

[September] 1937

Dear Ted:

The only homily I can send you is this: Stop forcing things. Stop trying to get a certain number of things taken, this year, just because you had a certain number taken, last year. Forget your score, and let yourself dam up a little, inside. Perhaps you're all sluiced out, for a while. Let whatever-it-is fill you up again, and don't write anything, or send out anything, for a couple of months.——That's the only way to get your weight back. A couple of years is better, of course, but I can't see you doing that, just now. But, for God's sake, forget the editors. Pretend you're in Siberia, and couldn't get anything printed if you tried.——I've had those "easy" periods happen to me; the one thing that saved me, after my first real lot of acceptances, was the fact that I went to Austria for six months, and couldn't get quick action from editors. Then I stopped writing like magazines, and went back to hard, painfully produced poems that sounded like myself.

~

And, as far as I'm concerned, you can have anyone who writes "odic poems." I'm going right back to pure music: the Christina Rossetti of our day, only not so good. My aim is to sound so pure and so liquid that travelers will take me across the desert with them, or to the North Pole, or wherever they are going. Up to Mt. Everest, for example.——This ambition has been brought on by my discovering the fact that Lawrence took the *O. Book of E. Verse* with him through Arabia. What more could poets ask than that? You never heard of anyone taking Karl Marx, Sidney Hook, or even Trotsky or Pareto, through Arabia with them. [. . .]

Louise

/ to Morton D. Zabel /

October 9, 1937

Morton dear:

~

Maidie and I, as bold as brass, walked into Wanamaker's, this noon, and asked if they would be good enough to show us their pianos. A very old guy, with eyelids like a turtle's, took us in hand (he was shadowed, throughout the proceeding, by another, even older guy, who probably wanted to trip up any sale, and get it for himself). We tried the "spinets," and they seemed O.K., until we tried the half-uprights, which weren't nearly so pretty, but had "normal hammers," or some such thing. We tried and tried, and the turtle kept playing beautiful arpeggios, not to mention "The Old Folks at Home" with variations, as against the only things Maidie and I can play, ad lib.: namely, on Maidie's part, a little Grieg number, and a few bars of a Mozart sonata (both of which keep to about an octave, and don't bring out the resonance of the bass or the brilliance of the treble), and on my part, the chords which presage, in P[elléas] and M[élisande], the downfall of M.'s hair. The turtle, I may say, was thoroughly unimpressed by both of these performances. —We tried and tried, and he led us to a horrid little instrument, which had been placed so near some steam-pipes that Maidie and I both caught on that it was made of matchwood and glue. The arpeggios kept ringing out. And then Maidie put her foot down for stiffness of action, and that led us to a darling black little "Federal" (American Empire, to you), half-upright, with "normal stringing/hammers," and gilt decorations here and there, and we took it, to the tune of $310. $25 down, and the rest in two years. But I *am* going to earn the two hundred in two months, and meanwhile we are to have a nice, commodious little piano.

How beautiful life is!—I have been waking up, these last few nights, and thinking how I used to waken at night, and toss and turn, worrying about what was going to happen, and rave (whenever there was an audience). But now I waken and stay awake for hours, and think that, after all, the worst has happened, and there's no more fear. [. . .]

Ever with love,
Louise

November 8, 1937

Dear Morton:

~

—I have just been reading, God help me, Yeats's complete works, and it stands out very clearly there that he was all shot to pieces when he first met Lady Gregory. He was thiry-four years old, and had had a hard, emotional youth, with lots of work and frustration in it. And, in spite of himself, in spite of all he could do, he fell to pieces. Maud Gonne had married someone else, and he had worn himself out on her, and on Irish politics and factions, etc. For a little while he could do nothing, but go around with Lady G. to the cottages and listen to the old peasants talk. He hated his work. He had come to a blank wall all round.

And then what happened? In a few years he is back on his feet again, starting an Irish theatre. He was acting in a new and even stronger way. He began learning how to write, all over again. He began to face reality even more. What do you suppose those later poems came out of? A break, a tragic break, which he lived through and got over, and mended from. *And he never repeated the thing again.* And how strong he became; what a fighter! As he says himself, if he had not gone through all that, in the late '90s, where would he have been when some real trouble started, and he had to fight for the plays of Synge, as well as for his own work? In 1905. Where indeed.

~

Everyone has to shift into maturity at your age, Morton. And most people of our calibre are just infants until they do . . . Think of Edmund out in the woods. Think of me, up in Wash. Heights. Think of Dante climbing the stranger's stair, and everyone else who were tested *to their full strength,* and came through.

And how about playing the piano, or doing some watercolors or wood carving?

Write soon.

Love—
Louise

/ to Rolfe Humphries /

July 8, 1938

Dear Rolfe:

~

—I particularly liked coming into New York by the ferry at Twenty-third Street. All that waterfront section is the dirty and clumsy and awkward and touching kind of thing I grew up with, and felt and loved. Mankind being kind of stupid. Not too smart. Bungling everything a little.—When the ferry-houses are full of chromium, and the funny corner restaurants are through, I'll be dead, I hope. Yes, I know it's sentiment. But I don't like the human race to get too smart and slick and clean and efficient. I don't know much, but I do know that's death, and it attracts bombs, too. [. . .]

Have just finished reading A. MacLeish's great speech, all about poets being challengers. It's the most awful tripe I ever read in my life, but I'll bet the League of American Writers feels set up by it.—From now on, I'm not going to pull my punches about that bird. Of all the tub-thumping perform-ances I ever read, it is the worst.

~

I STILL THINK THAT POETRY HAS SOMETHING TO DO WITH THE IMAGINATION; I STILL THINK IT OUGHT TO BE WELL-WRITTEN. I STILL THINK IT IS PRIVATE FEELING, NOT PUBLIC SPEECH.

You can easily see that I'm terribly mad, at the moment, about the C.P., and all its works. The girls at the subway entrance saying, in soft tones, "Stop the mad dogs of Fascism; help our boys dodging Franco's bombs," frankly make me sick. If the C.P. doesn't stop all this "mad-dogs" "depraved" stuff it will lose—well, I was going to say the respect of all intelligent people. But I take that back. There aren't, as far as I can see, any intelligent people left.

But by gosh, I'm one, and I mean to put up a lot more fight, to stand up for the abstract idea of warm-hearted and humorous detachment, than I have ever put up before. I have nothing to lose.

Your Fascist friend,
Louise

October 16, 1938

Dear Rolfe:

[. . .] —Your rooms sound wonderful; you will have them as ghosts in your dreams forever. The big room with the endless parquet floor, the enlarged portrait of the Empress Elizabeth, the photograph of two men going up hill in a snowstorm, the big handles on the doors, the wardrobe, the washstand and the ash tray on the desk, with which I lived in Vienna, will never leave me.[1]—You must bathe in it all, for it will mean something very nourishing to the Subconscious, in a few years. Not now.

And don't be too scornful of the baroque and churrigueresque, or whatever it is. Mexican baroque is the most beautiful in the world, in many ways. Not the simplest and purest, but the most fanciful: a real high point in the form. And if it annoys you in Mexico City, what are you to do in Rome which is almost entirely a baroque city, as it now stands. So study it and analyze it and appreciate it if you can. There must be some books you can get on the subject.

Here there is little new. I had a terrible time moving. The piano leg split from an old scar, and I never will get a chair to sit in, or be able to remove the bookcases from their bleak and soldier-like arrangement, side by side, around the room. The entrance room is rather nice: very empty, with a chest and a couch and a bookcase and two little chairs, and a lot of autumn leaves and some flowers. The front room, which has a really lovely view of the river, is the one which is stuck in semi-disorder. Chairs cost so damn much, and I have a phobia about buying furniture, since my unfortunate experiences with the hand of God, in the form of catastrophes, and the hand of landlords, in the form of evictions. Why make another effort, when all will be swept away by some terrible circumstance or other. My stars are against a settled abode, or always have been up to now, and, in my intuitive, superstitious and primitive way, I feel that it is flying in the face of fate for me to stay in the same house for two years.[2]—But enough of this.

~

Next time I may be funnier. Write soon.

Louise

1. See LB's sketches of Vienna in her 1934 questionnaire in the Journals and Memoir section.
2. LB had moved from one floor to another in the same building, at 709 West 169th Street, to the apartment where she would live for the rest of her life.

October 28, 1938

Dear Rolfe:

Just a short letter, to tell you that the Friends of Rolfe Humphries Society, Local No. 1, is bearing up, and hasn't lost its membership card yet.

~

I told you I thought Mexico was a bad idea to begin with. [. . .] —And do try to see something more than exploitation in those churches. The exploitation is certainly there, but the Catholic religion, in the stage when it threw them up, was an outgrowth of a human need. Simple people need superstition and prayer (so do complicated ones, for that matter), and no religion has ever been *imposed* on a people. The Indians don't dance just to get rain, or because their chiefs tell them to. The golden bough grew out of man's imagination. The Elysian Fields are underground and the Christian heaven is overhead for two deep psychological reasons. So I wish you'd look at the dust-catching architecture as a human being and a poet and child of the universe, once in a while. You might get some refreshment from it, then. And unless you get refreshment from your travels (along with loneliness and misery and a little heartbreak), how do you expect to get any poetry out of them?

You'll have to wait until it's over, in any case. I do know that. Only affected would-be's can write poems to the scenery right away. "Dawn: Taxco," or "Septuagesima Sunday in Girgenti," etc.

"Must close." More later.

Louise

St. Patrick's Day
March 17, 1939

Dear Rolfe:

[. . .] Hatred, suspicion, malice and madness seem to be reaching new highs everywhere. I heard, recently, of an attempted suicide, by a woman who has had everything, from youth on, to make her secure. She thought that the servants were poisoning her food. So what rule is there? Perhaps madness, like cancer, is a way of life trying to transcend itself. Last week, on a train at night—and how dreadful that experience still is, with one's face gloaming at you out of the glass!—I thought that whoever uprooted life, and set it walking around, equipped with brains and a heart, must have been a fiend rather than a god. We do not even know if it is better to have the heart partially erased—to be "normal" and at peace—or whether the mad and damned who "howl away their hearts" are not, after all, the highest manifestation of the life-force . . . I am sorry to be thinking so cosmically. I have been very tired. I went to Portland [Maine]—a symbolic return to the womb, I suppose—and now I am a little better.

~

There's a new song which enchants me. It goes:

"Jeepers, creepers! Where'd you get those peepers?"

Best luck. Love,
Louise

/ to Edmund Wilson /

Dear Edmund:

~

I was very much interested in reading an article on T. Mann by Erika Mann, in a recent *Vogue*. Thomas certainly has fallen on his feet, and the whole picture of him neatly wrapped up in an upper-middle class milieu, in Princeton, with a "couple" to wait on him, his Victrola, his grand piano, his writing desk with its "old coins" displayed on the top, and "the beautiful Empire bookcases from our ancestral home in Lübeck," gives me a pain.——I always said his eyes were too near together.

I made a visit to my own ancestral home, and am beginning to understand more and more what Yeats meant by "Paudeen,"[1] and why my mother was an admirable person, even if she nearly wrecked every ordinary life within sight.——She was against the penny-pinchers and the logic-choppers; she loved beauty and threw everything away, and, what is most important, she was filled with the strongest vitality I have ever seen.——And how the "Paudeens" (from which the other side of my nature unfortunately stems!) hated and feared her!

I'd like to see you, anytime. Best to Mary and the baby.

Louise

1. "Paudeen": the convention-bound Irish merchant class.

/ to William Maxwell[1] /

April 1, 1939

Dear Mr. Maxwell:

~

You know my pathological horror of public eating places. I just saw my doctor about it recently, and he said I should make a little effort, every so often,

1939   161 to face up to it, and try to throw it off. But it's a terribly hard fight. I don't want to sound too queer—but could you come up, some morning, or some noon, and we could take a walk, and really talk, and pick up a couple of hamburgers on the way? [. . .]

Your remark about the poem really moved me. There are only about three or four people from whom praise of that kind matters. They are, I may add, people who have hearts as well as other gifts.

Sincerely yours,
Louise Bogan

1. William Maxwell: the novelist and *New Yorker* editor with whom LB was to enjoy a long and complex friendship. He was eleven years younger than she.

/ to Allen Tate /

December 15, 1940

Dear Allen:

No, I don't think I was too hard on Blackmur.[1] Do you remember that wise remark of Hopkins's: A palace should at least be a house. It seemed to me (and to other people whose opinion I respect) that Blackmur's writing has too much self-indulgence in it. We all have been forced to learn how to write prose clearly, forcefully, and without fanciful and baroque curves, because we have written for an audience; and have had to sell our stuff. Blackmur has been coddled in this respect, it seemed to me. Arrow Editions is, after all, a sort of coddling publishing set-up. Blackmur has not learned that one proceeds step by step toward complexity: both of thought and expression. H. James *earned* his later style through process of long growth. He (James) knew how to write simply too.

After all these years, you still do not think that I work under *animus,* I hope.[2]

Ever cordially,
Louise

1. LB had reviewed R. P. Blackmur's essay collection *The Expense of Greatness* in the December 7 issue of *The Nation*. She found his views mercurial and his terminology heavy-handed. The review was called "Sensibility and Luggage."

2. See LB's letter to Tate above, dated April 1, 1932.

/ *to Edmund Wilson* /

January 27, 1941

Dear Edmund:

Thank you for your letter, with its interesting and valuable points about the rise and fall of conjuring.—I was about to set my hand to the pen, on this subject, when, last Thursday, Maidie came down with one of the worst throats I have seen in years. She was pretty bad for a few days—high temperature, and real agony of soreness—but today she is beginning to recover.—I will try to get you the poem, at the end of this month, but if I cannot, do not think I am being merely "fastidious." You know, as few others do, that I am a housewife, as well as a writer; I have no one to sweep floors or get meals, or get out the laundry, or, in the case of sickness, make egg-nogs and squeeze orange juice. All these tasks are very good for me, but they are tasks I never can allow to slip; and in the crisis of illness, I have no free time. Please bear all this in mind; and believe that the conjuring poem will be written sometime, if not now.[1] I know that the *N.R.* will not publish it, probably, after you leave, but that's their tough luck . . . Someone will, and I shall owe the whole idea to you . . .

~

With love to you all,
Louise

1. Possibly the unpublished "Fortune-Teller's Pack" (see appendix).

June 2, 1941

Dear Morton:

~

My pleasantest experience has been the renewal of a beginning friend-ship with Little [William] Maxwell. I have seen him several times this win-ter. One afternoon he came up, and we played records, and he is the most wonderful record-listener I have ever met. He really breaks right up, and is shattered, and is frank, and is disapproving, and is delighted, so that it seems another *you* is involved: another expression of one's own taste, only fresher. [Schubert's] *Gruppe aus dem Tartarus,* for example, actually laid him out. "That was a terrible experience," he said. And, of the final record of [Mahler's] *Lied v[on] d[er] Erde,* he remarked: "That is a perfect expression of the roman-tic's yearning for the Infinite . . ."—Maxwell is really an exquisite human being; and I wish there was something between love and friendship that I could tender him; and some gesture, not quite a caress, I could give him. A sort of smoothing. I may be able to work out something along these lines later! Seriously, I simply love him like a brother. He had me down to tea last week (Patchin Place), and such a lovely little apartment you never saw: plants on the windowsills, and pale furniture, and faultless bibelots, and a fireplace and books. He is all for the "light verse" you wish to exclude from the book. Something will have to be worked out, in that connection. The whole MS [of LB's *Poems and New Poems,* 1941] must be in Scribner's hands before July 1st. Have you any suggestions?

~

Ever with best love,
Louise

June 4, 1941

Dear Morton:
I feel like the Marschallin, if you must know;[1] but that is absurd, because there never has been, and never will be, of course, anything remotely re-

sembling that Overture, in the M[axwell] business. No foamings of lace out from the big baroque (rococo, rather) bed; no scampering of slender young male legs around the boudoir; no large-bosomed breathings and swellings and flutterings and burnings. I haven't any of the appurtenances pertaining to such a situation, from the rococo bed through the bosom; and my whole emotional set is also away from all these things: the cold stern light of the-response-with-insight having burned under the ribs for seven years. How-beit, I *should* feel like the Marschallin if I could! [. . .] We were speaking of how Rolfe's book was dedicated to me, and had been turned down by every publisher in New York. "You should have told him to put the dedication in after the book was accepted," said M. "O," said I, as quick as a flash, "so you admit I have enemies." Slight pause, and perfectly straight glance of the large brown eyes. "Of course you have enemies," he answered. Now WOULD YOU OR E. W. OR J. WHEELOCK OR ANYONE ever admit that, to my face. NO.

~

Sorry to have been so Abstract. I have been trying to get through *The New Criticism,* by John Crowe Ransom, for the past two weeks, and the col-oring has seeped into my own style, no doubt. What a true old bore that Ransom is! His greatest feats are his diagrams: the round one wherein the affect slides down from ten minutes past, to half-past, on the dial, when hit from the outside by the stimulus (the *attitude,* not the *affect:* excuse me!), is enough to make a cat laugh.

~

>Best love, though not of the Marschallin kind,
>after all these years; of a more distilled and
>brandied (spiritual) potency!
>Louise

1. the Marschallin: the middle-aged woman in love with a younger man in the Richard Strauss and Hugo von Hofmannsthal opera *Der Rosenkavalier.*

June 23, 1941

Dear M.:

~

[. . .] I'm glad you remembered the clothesline.[1] Clotheslines always stir my heart, and it is a pity that they have never really been touched by American art [. . .].

And it's fine about my first name. I simply *can't* first-name people until I've known them quite a while: a provincialism, no doubt. I have always shrunk up inside when casual acquaintances began Louising me, right away. —But if I start in calling you William, it will turn out that you have never been called William in your life. I started to call E. W[ilson], Edmund, way back in 1923; and I soon discovered that no one else called him that. But then I couldn't stop, and only this last year or so have I been able to call him Bunny. Edmund, by the way, is one of the few people who have ever gotten behind my masculine-protest side, far enough, to spring LULU on me, from time to time!

It has been horribly hot here, these last few days. But today there is a wind, and I can live again. That dreadful and truly vicious and insolent book by John Crowe Ransom is still to be finally reviewed. It is so awful that I did it in a snappish and counter-insolent way; but you can't do that. So I am spending some time cooling off, before I attack it again. *The New Criticism* indeed! It's plain Neo-Classicism over again, plus, as Stephen Potter calls it, some modern Surface Crawling. Variorum browsing. The whole attitude smells of snobbery and death.

~

This summer I am reading books on pianoforte technique, as a nice change from literature as such. (Last summer I read cookbooks.) Such books are wonderfully relaxing. They take nothing for granted. One says, for example, "[. . .] The trouble here is due to the conflict in stress between the two hands. The right hand has to stress the syncopated third beats, while the left hand has its normal stress resulting from the progression from the third beat crotchet to the first beat minim . . ." Isn't man a wonderful animal?

~

As ever, sincerely,
Louise

1. William Maxwell had described a visit to his hometown, Lincoln, Illinois. Later in her letter LB responds to Maxwell's tentative suggestion that he call her "Louise"; she had only reached the point of using the first initial of his last name, and explains her diffidence in the next paragraph.

October 5, 1943

Dear M.:

~

I must tell you, sometime, about how my poor father got lost, last Thursday, in the Grand Central Station; and how I and the stationmaster (who turned out to be a very brisk, intelligent, and humane man) finally found him. And you know what the G. C. S. is, in these days. Also, it was raining, and we couldn't get a cab; and Dad wouldn't part with his suitcase, which weighed a ton. That snub-nosed Reality that Mrs. Moore sensed in the caves[1] has certainly moved in upon me. I can hear it chuckling, in its flat-nosed way. [. . .] Meanwhile, I have the experience of what age is; and either God or Saturn or someone evidently didn't want me to miss that.—My father isn't senile; that isn't it exactly. It's age; and the smear it casts on life. Age without wisdom . . .

~

Ever,
Louise

1. Mrs. Moore, the main character in E. M. Forster's *A Passage to India,* has a revelation of vast emptiness on an outing to the echoing Marabar Caves.

/ to Morton D. Zabel /

May 24, 1944

Dear Morton:

[. . .] I saw Allen [Tate] and even Marianne [Moore]—rare vision!—at the big party given by the *P[artisan] Review,* about ten days ago. This was the first party I had attended—of this kind—in ten years; and the experience was interesting, if rather mild. Marianne appeared, in a very nice hat and grey get-up, with a sort of shawl and reticule; and it was a great lesson in Time, for me to look at her; for the last occasion when I had seen her had been in the run of work in the St. Mark's Place Branch Library, in 1922!—This was the winter before I went to Vienna; and I was in a dazed state of mind, and Marianne, as well as everyone else, came through to me rather foggily. But I remember very well, working with her in the winter afternoons, upstairs in that library with its dark-brown woodwork, its noisy children, and its general atmosphere of staleness and city dinginess.—Her hair was then a beautiful shade of red; she wore it in a thick braid. She was continually comparing the small objects with which we worked—mucilage brushes, and ink and stamping rubbers—to oddly analogous objects; and she smiled often and seemed happy. Mama kept running in and out as if she owned the place: I remember that, too. They lived across the street. She had no idea that I wrote poetry, and always treated me kindly, but rather like some assistant more or less invisible to her (as indeed I probably was, being, at that time, more or less invisible to myself, as well) . . .

~

Best love,
L.

Letters

/ to William Maxwell /

Dear W. M.:

I sat down and read the novel[1] all through, that very night; and, as I told you over the phone, I was much impressed by the new *largeness*. It has kept all its old poignancy. [. . .] The last chapter I liked; but I can see that you might want to give it more depth and sweep. And is it true that the boy actually gets rid of all his childhood, then?—Couldn't there be a loophole remark, in which it could be hinted that getting rid of one's childhood is almost a lifetime job; unless real steps are taken? Of course, Lymie has taken what would seem to be the ultimate step—attempted oblivion—but he has come back to life where everything is so partial that one has to renew the fight almost day by day.—I came upon a remark of Goethe's, famous to everyone but me, no doubt, from the last part of *Faust* II, in which he says that one must fight for one's spiritual freedom *every single day*. I had been wondering why I felt slack; and I hadn't really taken thought about these matters, consciously and conscientiously, for some years. I just thought that I was leading a good harmless life; and that grace would keep right on flowing in. This isn't the way it always works, it seems.

~

Ever,
Louise

1. See LB to William Maxwell September 28, 1944, note 1.

/ to Rufina McCarthy Helmer /

Dear Rufina:

[. . .] You have produced a book. Now you must stand outside it, tear it apart, and put it together again. I know how sacrosanct a first book is. One thinks: well, I've done it—all those words, all that time and effort and suffering—and I won't touch it; I won't change it; I will cling to it as it is, through hell and high water, and anyone who doesn't like it or understand it is wrong, terribly wrong. [. . .] Well, if you want to go through the difficult middle terrain, the Waste Land, the Valley of Doubt, that separates the *writer* from the amateur, you must take a firm grip on yourself, right AT THAT MOMENT OF DESPAIR AND CERTAINTY. You must put the book away, for about a month or so; and start writing something else; or start studying something else. You might start reading some Great Novels, and taking notes on them. You might read a few treatises on Dramatic Form, and how to get effects in plays, and in the theatre. You might start doing all of these things at once; and get so interested that you stop thinking of the already completed novel. *Madame Bovary* and *Sentimental Education* and *Crime and Punishment,* and one of the big Victorian set-pieces (anything but Thackeray!) and Jane Austen and more of E. M. Forster: those novels would keep you busy for quite a while. And you might read some well-made "mystery stories," too, and watch how they get their effects, build up their suspense and *get at the reader,* in general.—Then, and only then (after you have a few notebooks all full of perfectly realistic notes on FORM), you can go back to your book, and start re-writing it. Once you start working at it, in this *journeyman way,* you will have taken the *first step* toward getting on your own feet as a self-critic; and no matter what anyone says, you will be working as a conscious artist works, and not as someone who merely has written a FIRST NOVEL.

~

Love,
Louise

/ *to William Maxwell* /

September 28, 1944

Dear M.:

[. . .] I'm sorry I didn't snap right back, in approval or disapproval of your *Julius Caesar* title. I think it v. good.—But why don't you just sit around for a month or two, reading all sorts of snippets of things, in anthologies and elsewhere (in books opened by chance)—while your publisher is going through the manuscript; pray to St. Anthony (of Padua) and St. Theresa (of Avila)—and I'm sure the most beautiful and appropriate title possible will just fall in your lap.—Not that I have undergone a *conversion* in the last couple of weeks; but isn't it true that just waiting and praying (to whatever illustrious or charming character, now in the shades, that you will) is just as productive of Beautiful Accidents, as any other way you can think of?—Marianne Moore has a lovely new book [*Nevertheless*] (v. small, as books of poetry should be); and she has a lovely poem on patience in it and a lovely *aperçu:* namely, that skunks ("don't laugh," as she puts it) have sweet faces . . .

The prettiest title for a novel I have heard for some time, is being held in suspension for the book to be written to it, by a frail young man in the Library called Herbert Cahoon. He is rather given to surrealism, but the title comes from "The Last Rose of Summer," by Thomas Moore: *All the Lovely Are Sleeping.* I'm sure that there are numbers of other titles hidden under our very noses, in the most familiar poetry and prose possible.[1]

~

Ever,
Louise

1. In the end, Maxwell took the title of his novel from the Tennyson passage LB sent him a few days later (from "The Lotos-Eaters": "Lo! In the middle of the wood, / The folded leaf is woo'd from out the bud"). *The Folded Leaf* appeared in 1945, dedicated to Bogan.

October 22, 1944

Dear M.:

This week I am taking off for some minor personal duties (getting something to wear, for example). Then, I may go down to Swarthmore to visit Auden. He invited me down, and I quickly accepted. I think it will be fun: one of those eye-blink journeys, when everything shows up with remarkable clearness; for you are in a new place, everything seems sharp and fresh, you have no responsibility for anything; you can sit and talk and enjoy; and then —whisk—the next day you pick up and leave.—I think I'll take him a cheese, and an envelope full of your China tea . . .

/ to Morton D. Zabel /

July 6, 1945

Dear Morton:

[. . .]—I *don't* hate writing you letters. But this has been one of those years. A year unprecedented since I went into my "obscure period" in the spring of 1937—remember? When I renounced the world, and settled down to doing a lot of journalism to prove something, I can't remember just what. Well, anyway, I as suddenly decided to come off it, or come out of it, and accept all invitations to speak, read, teach, or turn handsprings, in public.

Not that I was overwhelmed by such offers. But they began to mount up, at that. One thing led to another and before I knew it, I was actually sharing a platform at the Young Men's Hebrew Association with none other than Dorothy Parker! [. . .] I rapidly worked out of my dismay at facing a totally Parker audience ([. . .] I had been wooed into the job by the promise of speaking alone, and then, who turns up but Dottie, all gotten up in a magenta turban and a coat lined with summer mink) and gave them the works.—O yes, I have learned a great deal since I saw you last. I am now an expert at judging the saturation point of any given audience to my works. I can now rise, as cool as a cucumber, and look them over, and shape the thing up. I can even cut and edit my own prose, *on my feet,* when I feel things are running overtime. [. . .]

The great and overwhelming surprise occurred last November; and I can't think why you have not heard about it. I think that the whole business really startled me so, that I thought it might startle you even more. Perhaps I have a psychic block about it. Perhaps I think that *you* will think that I have sold out! O dear! Yes; I have perhaps been keeping this from you. Well, let's get it over with. Let's face up to it.[1]

[. . .] It was v. good for me, because I had for so long indulged in tail-lashings about the good seed being passed by, etc., etc. I was becoming a little peculiar on the subject, and it did me good to face reality that was somewhat rosier in hue than usual.

~

Ever with best love,
your old friend and comrade-in-arms,
Louise

1. LB admits that she had been named consultant in poetry to the Library of Congress.

/ to Rolfe Humphries /

October 7, 1946

Dear Rolfe:

I am beginning to feel some of the backwash of my activities in September.
All seems rather stale, in spite of the fact that my bank account (God save
the mark!) is better than I ever can remember it having been; and in spite of
ruddy health, good expectations, etc., I don't seem to be able to *self-start,*
as I once did; and I am frequently stymied by writing jobs: I just don't write
things on time! This sultry, sullen Indian summer weather isn't helping any,
either. It condenses and reflects too many sultry (and sullen) feelings in my
own breast! O dangerous age of 49! O thoughts like dahlias and all late,
coarse summer flowers, that linger on till frost! If I could only write poetry,
all would be well, and all manner of things would be well. Or fall in love
with gusto, in a coarse, dahlia-like way! [. . .]

[. . .]—I have to do a piece on the surrealists, this week. And I think I'll
begin my memoir-in-the-form-of-a-horror-story—behind my consciousness' back, as it were: by writing a journal, and hiding it away from myself
—under the linen in the middle drawer of the chest.—No creative work in
five years! "No wonder you are calm," as you said to me once, " . . . the daemon has been silenced, and whatever silenced it is sitting pretty."

Well, it looks as though the calm were healing up. I don't really take
much pleasure in reading, any more. I get restless and guilty. So little time
left, before decay sets in! [. . .]

Your dahliaesque friend,
L.

/ to Katie Louchheim[1] /

February 25, 1948

Dear Katie:

~

I have been doing my best for you with the *liberal* papers. *The Nation*
seems to have fallen into some obscure kind of decline, so far as reviewing

of books is concerned; but I haven't lost hope. [. . .] Meanwhile, why don't you write a few sample reviews (on any book that interests you in any field) and send them on to me? Good practice, in any case; and valuable samples perhaps later. Make them crisp! Start with a short sentence, and keep your EAR on your nouns and verbs!

This "writing with the ear" (as it were) is really the best technical practice you can give yourself. Remember that the reader's attention span is usually v. short. I *cut* and *cut* my sentences, right up to the last version; always keeping the adjectives down to a minimum and the adverbs practically down to zero. The *verb* can do so much! I don't mean to make you write *completely* without color or sound; but try writing as barely as possible, at first. *Then* put in your connectives, etc. (Although I think that writing "at full spurt," and then paring down, is the best all-round way. Don't censor yourself in the beginning! Keep the feeling fresh, and be sure some *tension* is working at all times. But be severe, severe—at the end.)

~

Love to all,
Louise

1. Katie Louchheim, a deputy assistant secretary of state in the Kennedy and Johnson administrations, published her first book of verse, *With or Without Roses,* in 1966 (WTWL, 259n1).

/ to Katharine S. White /

October 14, 1948

Dear Katharine:

Thank you for the check, and for your thought and hopes directed toward *stories!* Just after my return to NYC in September,[1] I plunged into a piece of translation, with Elizabeth Mayer,[2] which fascinated but exhausted me. We were commissioned by a set of learned German professors to do a new translation of Goethe's *Werther;* and we managed to push the thing through in less than a month. W. H. Auden has just approved of the MS; and I hope the professors will do likewise.—I wrote the whole thing out long hand (in order to keep the tone flowing and natural) and I must say that a pile of MS, written in this way, is a v. satisfying object to contemplate. [. . .]

So now I go to bed at night, and lie awake in the morning, turning over the "stories" in my refreshed mind. They will be memories, and, since I am not the "confessing" type, it is hard to start them off. I tend to surround the facts with a certain amount of "philosophy," as well; and that is not good. I intend to throw the material onto paper v. soon, however; and then shape it afterward. Criticism, when practiced over years, makes the creative side rather timid.

~

Affectionately,
Louise

1. After spending part of the summer at the University of Washington, where Roethke had invited her to teach.

2. "She has lived about five or six lives, and is as full of intelligent curiosity and intellectual fire as she ever was, I am sure. She it was who took Benjamin Britten under her wing, when he was young and unknown here in New York, about ten or fifteen years ago. He lived at her house on Long Island for three years; and a year or so ago he invited her to his English summer festival; flew her over; and entertained her with all the grandeur possible. Elizabeth loved it. Wystan she has also befriended; he dedicated his *New Year Letter* to her. She lives at 1 Gramercy Park now, with her husband and a large black Bechstein that has come through all her difficulties in splendid shape . . ." (to May Sarton, February 12, 1954; WTWL, 262–63n2).

/ *to Morton D. Zabel* /

November 28, 1948

Dear Morton:

~

!As for Washington!

My Love is of a birth as rare
As 'tis for object strange and high:

It was begotten by Despair
Upon Impossibility. . . . [1]

I sat beside the Great Man [T. S. Eliot] at lunch; and I looked into his Golden Eye! How beautiful is the combination of physical beauty (even in slight decay), high qualities of mind and heart, and *perfect humility*. ("Humility is endless . . .") We talked, during the end of the entrée and *through* the coffee and ice cream! Of form, and Youth's fear of form; of rhythm (we got it back to the heartbeat and the breath); of the true novelist talent; of Henry Miller and little magazines; of Brancusi and modern architecture ("who wants to live in a machine?") and, finally, of the *cat* poems! I asked if he had enjoyed writing them; and he said that he had tried them out on "various young listeners." My favorite, I remarked, was the cat who taught the mice how to crochet. O yes, said he; that, among others, had "scandalized my adult readers."—One adult reader, namely, Allen Tate, was being visibly scandalized, just across the luncheon board.—Then, that evening, the lecture on E. A. Poe scandalized quite a few Southern diehards. [. . .]

Eliot had sat in on all our Fellows' [in American Letters] Meetings:[2] v. quiet, shy, reserved. He smokes incessantly, and at one point took time off to sharpen a pencil (with a pen-knife, in his lap). He looks quite frail, really; but what beauty! Well, it is all too late and too sad—but I must love him in a mild, distant sisterly way:

Therefore the Love which us doth bind,
But Fate so enviously debarrs,
Is the Conjunction of the Mind,
And Opposition of the Stars.

~

Ever, with remaining love,
L.

1. LB quotes this beginning stanza and later the last stanza of Andrew Marvell's "The Definition of Love," celebrating the elation she experienced on meeting T. S. Eliot. The occasion marked the end of a poetic dry spell that had begun in 1941 (EF, 344). When Eliot left for Stockholm (to receive the Nobel Prize), LB drafted "Song for the Last Act."
2. The Fellows awarded Ezra Pound the first Bollingen. Later, LB "regretted the prize," and said she should have voted with Karl Shapiro, the one dissenter (EF, 344).

/ to May Sarton[1] /

January 28, 1954

Dear May:

It was delightful to hear your voice, and to feel that you are working. Your letter this morning said many true things (and the poems, too). But what has never been explained thoroughly, by me to you, is the really dreadful emotional state I was trapped in for many years—a state which Raymond struggled manfully against, I will say, for a long time. In those days, my devotion came out all counterclockwise, as it were. I was a *demon,* of jealousy, for example; and a sort of *demon* of fidelity, too: "morbid fidelity," Dr. Wall came to call it. A slave-maker, really, while remaining a sort of slave. Dreadful! Thank God v. little of it got into the poems; but the general warp showed up in every detail of my life. Except for a certain saving *humor,* I should have indeed been a full monster.—During my illness, all this had to be relinquished, step by step. A new personality (that had been kept from coming into light and growth) slowly emerged; and it is this person that you now know. The successful love affair which began when I was thirty-nine and lasted for eight years was utterly different from anything that had gone before: perfect freedom, perfect detachment, no *jealousy* at all—an emphasis on *joy,* that is.[2] This is the only kind of relationship that is possible for me now: something given by me and received in an almost childish way. [. . .]

What you say about my own development is perfectly true. I am trying to break through certain blocks in the "long prose thing": that will be "memory," if not "desire." So far as desire is concerned, I must wait. If it comes again, with a strength which I cannot withstand, and a *benevolence* (that is not the word, but then) I can recognize: good! But if not, not.—As I said to you the other night, quoting (I think!) St. Paul: With a great price bought I this freedom.—You understand.

Bless you. Keep feeling and working. For the work is really, for us, the important thing. The channels must be kept open so that it may live and grow.

Love, dear May,
Louise

1. May Sarton, a novelist and poet, was then twenty-eight years old.

2. This lover, whom LB met at Southampton in 1937 en route back to the United States from Ireland, was an electrician from the Bronx whose family came from Sligo (EF, 286). On the back of the 1937 photo of the poet at her desk, "taken by the lover whom none of her friends ever met" (EF following 174, plate x), LB identifies the photographer as Tom Carr (Louise Bogan Papers, Amherst, Box 26 folder 46; see also the 1937 silhouette of Carr in Box 26 folder 94).

February 4, 1954

Dear May:

~

As for my eight-sided heart,[1] which you question, dear May, I can only say that the octagonal here is somehow symbolic of freedom. Love of things, I suppose, understood, more than love of human beings . . . The delight in objects, both natural and artifacts, which has grown in me ever since the *obsessive* person was left behind (or buried, if you like, in the lowest layer of the dream). The delight of the collector, which you sensed in my room; the delight of the naturalist (which I never had, when young, except in flashes, but which makes me scrutinize everything, from flowers to rocks on the shore, in these later years); the delight of the amateur in the arts (the piano and embroidery); the delight of the cook and the housewife . . . All these are substitutes, I know; but they keep me alive and not only happy but occasionally full of joy. I do not speak of the delight of the maker, for writing has never been anything (except v. rarely) but tough and artisan to me.

~

Love, dear May,
Louise

1. The reference is to a descriptive aside in LB's poem "After the Persian," part II, in which the ornamental pool "is eight-sided, like my heart."

February 16, 1954

Dear May:

[. . .]—I can't stand being in a *fog* about things. There is a rather sad joke between Maidie and myself concerning my mother, who had a rather terrifying way of picking out one detail which she presented as permanently baffling: the fact that she couldn't make soft custard, for example, because she didn't have the *right kind* of double boiler. This fact kept coming up; and, although I am sure that the *right kind* of d. b., in those days, probably cost fifty cents in the open market, she never bought one, and no one else ever did.——This is the sort of thing that I always try to put right immediately: if an *object,* or the lack of an *object,* seems to threaten my peace of mind, I either get rid of it or get it. In the realm of THINGS we can move fairly easily; and I refuse to make *things symbols* of bafflement. As for spiritual bafflements, or bafflements of situation, I want to get those out of the way quickly, too. To act *on* life; to be a *subject,* not an object . . .

~

Be happy, dear May, and remember that I proffer you all that I can proffer any human being. Which isn't, I suppose, v. much; but all of it is fresh and real and non-*patterned.*

Love,
Louise

March 17, 1955

Dear May:

[. . .]——I want to write you rather fully about the problem of argument in poetry, but cannot do it properly today. Of course, everything is material for poems—even the "passive suffering" (sometimes) that Yeats deplored; but argument should be dramatized, as Yeats learned to dramatize, rather than projected straight—the dramatic monologue helps. It is impossible really to argue, in lyric poetry, because too many abstractions tend to creep in—and abstract ideas must get a coating of sensuous feeling before they become true poetic material; unless one is a born satirist. Auden argues, it is true, but with much satire involved; his use of the rhymed [tetrameter] couplet in *N[ew] Y[ear] Letter* derives from Butler's *Hudibras* (a sturdy satirist) more than from the more waspish Pope. The element of wit has to be present; there is nothing duller or more unmalleable than serious conviction, seriously expressed. Even Eliot, in *Four Quartets,* keeps everything flexible, simple, and conversational, in the more argumentative sections.——Certainly "unadulterated life" must be transposed, although it need not be "depersonalized." Otherwise you get "self-expression" only; and that is only half of art. The other half is technical, as well as emotional, and the most poignant poems are those in which the technique takes up the burden of the feeling instantly; and that presupposes a practised technique.

~

Love on the day of all the Patricks!
Louise

/ to Robert Phelps[1] /

September 21, 1956

Dear Mr. Phelps:

~

I was moved, after reading your letter, to write you a long analysis of the factor (often hidden) of responsibility, in any writer's life. All human beings, of course, must face up to this factor, but with the artist it is often a baffling element, which seriously affects his work. I myself came into responsibility at the birth of my daughter, when I was twenty; and I have not been able to get away from it entirely, although the death of my father, five years ago, at the great age of ninety, eased it somewhat. Responsibility forms and teaches, of course; but it also keeps one from the complete grasshopper's way, for if one should slip into complete destitution, one takes others along. I hope I am not sounding smug, but please realize that I have taken many jobs (including filing cards at fifty cents an hour) in order to keep myself, and others, from full need. And I have several drops of maverick blood, I can assure you!

~

Sincerely yours,
Louise Bogan

1. Robert Phelps, a novelist and journalist, later coedited LB's criticism in *A Poet's Alphabet* (1970).

October 9, 1956

Dear Mr. Phelps:

I hasten to add the name of Simenon to your French list. The early and middle books, especially.—The one *famous* novelist I have known was Ford Madox Ford, in his rather loosened later years, around 1933. In those days he read Simenon continually, and called him the *finest* French novelist. Certainly there is something terribly close to the truth in this Belgian's passion for searching out "the tragic flaw" in the ordinary man and woman. One step divides ordinary life from the abyss; and Simenon's abysses are so terrifyingly squalid and everyday: the kitchen where the lodgers eat out of their tin boxes, in *Le Locataire* [the lodger], for example. And how good he is with those secret interior shifts of mood and emotion; with smells; with times of day, particularly daybreak, and "the hour between the dog and the wolf." And how satisfying it is to meet that crisp prose, which can accommodate violence and tenderness equally well. Do read him—the *romans policiers* along with the regular novels. His power of improvisation is extraordinary, too—and it is all *right* and at the center. His autobiographical *Pedigree* is extremely moving.

~

Sincerely,
Louise Bogan

October 19, 1957

Dear Robert Phelps:

I have read *Lolita* with a great deal of pleasure, and I am returning it to [you] by mail.—An account of a real *addiction* is v. rare, in any language, at any time—of a sexual addiction, all the more so. Part of the force here comes from the contrast between the *raffiné* protagonist and the crudity of the situation in which he finds himself; the concealed wildness and violence of the American "scene"; together with the *absolute* commitment. Nabokov has finally mastered the American idiom; it took him years, but now he has it. And such richness of perception! An end-product. I kept thinking of Chekhov's interiors and Turgenev's weather.

Thank you!
Write well. Lots of *pages*.
Louise B.

/ to William Maxwell /

October 20, 1957

Dear Bill:

How happy your word on the C[aitlin] Thomas piece made me! Put it all down to the three weeks of *absolute* seclusion I experienced at the Mac-Dowell Colony, in September—something I had never known during all my years as a "working writer."—I wish you would *apply* for "admission." The place is now open during the winter, and they like people to stay at least a month. Couldn't you? The first two weeks are rather odd: so much silence, and so many trees! Then the threshold of the grim Subconscious *lowers* . . . and things start. At least they did for me. Think about it.

Love,
Louise

/ to Morton D. Zabel /

December 29, 1957

Dear Morton:

[. . .] I gave the volume [*The Liveliest Art: A Panoramic History of the Movies*] to myself, as well, in a mad rush of sentiment and nostalgia . [. . . S]ome people and pictures and directors were either left out or underplayed: Murnau, for example, and that whole German school, with their camera angles and shadows and trapezes and fireworks. That *Joan of Arc,* too, with its great close-ups. And the early René Clair, etc. And Marlene, in that feather get-up; and later, always sitting on station platforms, or in *pigeon coops!* I don't think we wasted our time! What would my youth have been without the Bijou Dream, on Washington St., Boston—on Saturdays (10¢)? Or the Pastime (5¢)? Or later, the Modern and the Uptown (all Boston)? I couldn't spend all my time in the B[oston] P[ublic] L[ibrary]! And then later, in the '20s, when we all used to go and make up conversation, and laugh ourselves sick! (So *rude!*)—I actually saw Nazimova do *Salome* all *in white*! And *Mädchen in Uniform!* And *The Blue Angel!* No, the time was not entirely wasted, for people like ourselves, to whom the visual is so *relaxing*!

~

Love,

Louise

/ to Ruth Limmer[1] /

October 20, 1960

Dear Ruth:

~

The event of the week was my reading of John Updike's new novel, *Rabbit, Run* (Knopf). The boy is a genius. Every sentence counts. The story is rather contrived, but one believes every word of it. And the flashes of weather, and of the "American scene": drugstores, highways, main streets, factories, used car lots! And the passion and the *grief!* The sex gets out of hand, once in a while; but for the most part he uses the sexual aberrations to striking purpose. And he believes in God ("something there")! *Do* get it at once; it's worth buying—($4.00).

~

Love,

Louise

1. Ruth Limmer, an English professor first at Western College and then at Goucher College, was LB's first literary executor; she edited the letters, the criticism, and the journals.

April 24, 1961

Dear Ruth:

The most beautiful day of this unbeautiful spring—and I was trapped in a theatre seat, watching Martha Graham unfold her idea of what went on in the House of Atreus. A v. strange experience. I last saw Graham in the early thirties, as I remember: much lithe-er and leaping-er. I must confess that, yesterday, I thought her rather earthbound. Clytemnestra, to me, has always been a great tall woman of tremendous power and—efficiency, shall we say? A ruthless wielder of *will*. A semi-tribal goddess. A non-Mother . . . Graham made her into a sort of skulking middle-aged frump, in a bun-on-top hair-do and a damned black tea gown (damned in the sense that it might have been kicking around the closets of Hell, for about forty or fifty years, or millennia). One favorite posture: a sort of mobile *scooch,* by which she advanced to and from on *bent knees.* Also, a great deal of staggering, walking in circles, etc. Terrific emotion always accompanied by a great big kick, forward—involving the tea gown in a great big swirl.

[. . .] Also, some exceedingly bad poetic-prose issued from their vocal chords: "a mother's *curse*"(repeated on six or seven occasions); "flesh-mesh"; . . . "I am *Clytemnestra!*". . . etc. . . .)—Why must dancers attempt to be poets, as well? (Did you ever see Martha, in the E. Dickinson thing, lying on what seemed to be a park bench with one toe pointed to heaven?)

Well, everyone got everything possible out of their physical equipment, I will say. *Everything!* Crawling on the floor was usual; also the slant and the upside down. I could go on . . .

~

Love,
Louise

/ *to May Sarton* /

October 31, 1961

Dear May:

~

Now for the book [Sarton's *Cloud, Stone, Sun, Vine*] (*briefly*).

My objection to the sonnet sequence is in part a general objection: I don't think that such sequences can be written, nowadays, with any hope of effectiveness. They have received the kiss of death; not only in the 19th century, but in our own time—Millay's and Wylie's are, on the whole, pretty bad.—*Women* should not write them, any more! The linked formality makes [the] chance of discursiveness too great; and the sonnet, *as such,* is *never* discursive. It is dramatic; *the* dramatic lyric framework. Shakespeare, even, gets rather woolly, at times; although he continually keeps tightening up and slashing out: "the expense of spirit in a waste of shame," etc. The early sonnet sequences (Sidney's, for example) are based on a terrific concept of courtly (*demanding*) passion, and *morality.* They are pointed. They are channeled.— With D. G. Rossetti, etc., the whole thing begins to *dissolve.* One thing leads to another. Etc., etc.

I think, too, that it should be clear that your sonnets are written to a woman. This is not clear. (In 14 you mention a *father* and a *son,* where, I think, it should be a *mother* and a *daughter.*) These are the two main objections. One other small one: I feel that the sequence should end in a kind of unresolved positive *anger,* not in a questioning acceptance. "To hell with you."— But that's my Irish *vulgarity,* no doubt!

~

Now, take all this as the advice of one so *much older,* whose every second thought must be of death!

~

Love as always.
Louise

/ to Ruth Limmer /

March 4, 1962

Dear Ruth:

~

I saw *The Innocents*—did I tell you? With Deborah Kerr wandering around making a British face, and holding a candelabra and jumping at noises. Quint was properly fearsome, and Miss Jessell looked exactly like a Chas. Addams witch (the young kind). [. . .] The death of Miles really shocked the Coliseum audience. The two old ladies in front of me jerked about and showed distinct negative agitation.

Good old Henry J.! I came straight home and read the original story straight through. How wonderfully managed it is! and that "frame" bit—at the beginning! What the old boy knew—and was determined to express— was the hypocrisy of children, as well as the delusions of suppressed old maids. We get this duality in Maisie—although *she* is sort of a moral moron, rather than a little fiend.—*Maisie* [*What Maisie Knew*] I have always found hard to read.—I then went right through *The Aspern Papers,* and found new joys in it. That "lame" dressing table, and that "peevish" lock on the desk, or whatever it was! Such epithets! And such *ease* of language! [. . .] Come; why don't *you* take a dip in these wonderful waters! Read the preface to *Portrait* [*The Portrait of a Lady*]: see H. J. holed up in Venice, trying to get the book finished, but continually running to the window to watch the life and the color, outside. *Most* moving.

~

Love,
Louise

May 15, 1962

Dear Ruth:
Well, I have survived Mother's Day and am set for a spell of hardish work, in order to get rid of the one or two books which continue to plague me by sitting on top of the chest of drawers in a semi-annotated state. [. . .]

I went to a highly praised French movie, entitled *Jules and Jim*—and this turned out to be a strange production indeed: a sort of disguised homosexual fantasy, wherein a wife (that depraved looking Moreau woman) shuffles back and forth between her husband and a couple of lovers. The style is all 1912, to begin with, and this is charming, although strongly derivative from the early René Clair—*The Italian Straw Hat,* for example. The clothes, the furniture and the street scenes all have that now-so-appealing awkwardness— an awkwardness which was far from appealing *as I remember it!* Then the Great War turns up, in old movie shots, and then the triangle-quadrangle of lovers go to the country, into a darling little *châlet* filled with cunning *objects,* including a bent-wood rocking chair. (A rather depraved looking fat little girl turns up, at this point: the daughter.) Moreau really looks frightfully crazy and concupiscent; she finally drives off a bridge into a lake, along with Lover No. 1 —in an antediluvian closed coupé. A rather grisly funeral scene follows, and the husband is last seen walking downhill out of Père-Lachaise [Cemetery] —Several reviewers found all this *simply delightful.* You must see it, if it ever turns up again, merely for its undertone of fancy spiritual horror . . .

~

Love,
Louise

R. M. S. Queen Mary
At sea
May 24, 1963

Dear Ruth:

[. . .] Really, London was so *full* of handsome people. [. . . T]hose blonde male and female giantesses! And those noble faces, seen for a short span, on the underground—so full of intelligence and—insouciance (??).—And the scraps of well-balanced periodic sentences one heard, behind one, from time to time, full of long words and abstract concepts, and close reasoning! Really, what a people! Somehow they seem to be blooming nowadays. I never saw them so strong, fresh, and varied. Carrying (men and women) their market baskets, full of bread and fruit principally (it seemed); with a bunch of flowers in the other hand. Was it thus in Chelsea?

Of course, on the other hand, they *do* tend to *blither* somewhat, as you say; and a provincial upper class hotel (such as I struck in Bath), in the midst of a wedding, certainly resounds with the loud, certain, rather shrieking voices of the ex-Empire builders of both sexes. [. . .] How *flat* our native American sounds, in comparison! How low-pitched, how without accent or rise or fall: plain American, that the cats and dogs can speak, as Marianne M. remarks. [. . .]

Love,
Louise

Dear Ruth:

~

Well, I guess I'm over the worst of the fringe effects of the strange "medication" ("wonder drug") treatment. Believe me, it was rough, for about five nights: heart palpitation—the feeling of the center of the citadel being invaded. And blood pressure taken in all positions: sitting, standing, etc. And the semi-knowledge that the doctor was just as much at sea as you were. (This was nonsense, of course, as H. is tops in his field.) THEN— finally, the pill is changed, and the heart quiets down, and you say, "I'll never worry about *anything* again." One evening, with a gibbous moon hanging over the city (such *visions* we have!) like a piece of red cantaloupe, and automobiles showing red danger signals, as they receded down Ft. Wash. Ave— I thought I had reached the edge of eternity, and *wept* and *wept*. [. . .]—I'm now on a little white pill which makes me rather woozy, but is mild otherwise . . . (I'm writing *through* it, at the moment.)

~

Love,
Louise

March 10, 1966

Dear Ruth:

This is an add on the subject of Susan Sontag's remarkable book, *Against Interpretation.* I actually bought this volume, and I shall be glad to send it on to you, if you'd like.—The publishers say nothing whatever about her, and her work stands quite detached, from any stated education, origin, etc. She is extremely pretty, and smiles enigmatically on the back of the jacket, clothed in a semi-Beat get-up. (She has just led a protest of artists, in Los Angeles, of all places, against Vietnam, I see in the paper.)—The work shows that she has read *everything,* ancient and modern—in several languages; that she has formidable powers both of abstract thought and of *argument;* and that her knowledge of all sides of the modern situation—aesthetic, political, and philosophic—is extraordinarily full.—She is v. informed—and usually quite good—on the movies as well; in fact, the cinema comes through as slightly more important to her than any other "art-form." She even has hopes for the future of TV . . .

One strange characteristic struck me—and I don't think I'm being square to separate it out as a fault—a drawback—among Sontag's multiple gifts. She seems hung up on an eroticism so far out that it verges on what we must call—for lack of any decent word—pornography. She is particularly wild on the subject of blue movies—the artistic kind, of course. But sexual shock in general attracts her. She is on to herself in many ways—and she stands up for both *mystery* and *form,* in a kind of backhanded fashion; but give her a movie in which women are having an orgy, and she goes all out. —Is this Sontag, or is it post-Beat? Or what?—Shall I send the book on?

Love,
Louise

/ to Rufina McCarthy Helmer /

July 25, 1966

Dear Rufina:
[. . .] You should see the Village, these days! I went down recently to see an anti-Vietnam free-form play (written by an Irish girl from Seattle) [Megan Terry's *Viet Rock*] and it's really hard to make one's way around the streets. But all this is *ferment*—which should lead to something, someday.

My strange little (for it *must* be a child-ghost, embedded in the Subconscious) morning visitant is, I believe, yielding to work-exorcism, more than to medication. *It* vanished at 10:30 A.M. today, and hasn't been back. Work at the typewriter seems to bore it. For all it wants to do is *weep*.[1] O heavens, am I seeing the end of the tunnel, *at last?*

Love, and write,
Louise

1. LB's daughter, Maidie, named the child-ghost Little Lobelia, which LB took for the title of her metaphysical ballad about her weeping self.

/ to Sister M. Angela, I.B.V. M.¹ /

August 20, 1966

Dear [Sister] Angela:

~

"The Dream" is a later poem, written in my late thirties, after a complete change in my way of living, and in my general point of view about life (and the universe at large!). It is the actual transcript of "a nightmare," but there is reconciliation involved with the fright and horror. It is through the possibility of such reconciliations that we, I believe, manage to live.²

About form, I can say nothing. It comes, if one is lucky, and in a state of creative grace.

I hope these few remarks help. Thank you again.

Sincerely yours,
Louise Bogan

1. Sister Angela O'Reilly, I.B.V. M., who taught at the SS. Simon and Jude School in Arizona, was at this time working on her thesis (WTWL, 369n2).
2. "'The Dream,' by the way, is a poem of victory and of release. The terrible power, which may v. well be the psychic demon, is tamed and placated, but NOT destroyed; the halter and the bit were already there, and something was done about *control* and *understanding*" (to May Sarton, August 14, 1954; WTWL, 369n2).

/ to Ruth Limmer /

September 19, 1966

Dear Ruth:

[. . .]—It *is* difficult to see the world run by anything *but* a demon (the universe, too). The only hope is: that there must be an edge (a sort of *selvage*) of good, that holds and defines. And, of course, the very spectacle of crowding, hungry life, crowding into every crack and cranny of the material situation (cracking the *Manhattan schist* with an oak tree, as well as the spectacle of a piece of lichen accumulating in a crack of same) should continually excite, if not reassure us.—That new laboratory building of Columbia-Presbyterian just echoes with the barking of dogs; and I shudder every time I go by it, in the early morning.

~

A bunch of books went to the Phoenix [Book Shop], but I have been unable to find anything truly readable anywhere, although I actually bought, for $1, one of those maundering, tenuous late S. Sitwells, because the index was so fascinating—ranging from (to begin in the middle) *God* on to *Uganda,* Walruses, Waldteufel, Witches, Yoshowara (beauties of the), to Zumbo (Gaetano) and Zurbarán (Francisco).—Another purchase has been B. Britten's *Curlew River* (at Goody's, from the same decayed but smart old gentleman). One mono record. I sat down to listen to it, having plied myself with a mild Scotch and soda, and really enjoyed it. It's full of extraordinary detached noises, in the background, including a truly eerie gong; and P[eter] Pears, as the Madwoman, is suitably watery and wavering (I do get tired of that Britten waver-waver noise). The voice of the little ghost is also v. touching: just a little *needle* of sound, coming in as an echo to some monkish chanting, in both Latin and English. I wish you had been here to share this experience. I simply don't know one other person (with the exception of Maidie) in the company of whom I can listen to music. That is bad—and strange.

[. . .]—I'm typing out those last scattered poems, too.[1]—A new book by Anne Sexton has just arrived—with the compliments of the author, no less. O why can't I write psychotic verse! Neurotic verse pales into insignificance beside what those girls—Sexton and Plath—can (could) turn out.

Love, and write when you can.

Louise

1. LB was preparing the MS for *The Blue Estuaries* (1968), her last collection of poetry.

August 27, 1967
S.S. *Bremen*

Dear Ruth:

All is proceeding calmly and rather endearingly (for the flood of German which swirls around me, at table, and everywhere else, seems to be having a soporific effect). ANGST—possibly recognizing *its own* language—seems completely to have disappeared.—The sea is a millpond. The food is good. A brass band plays every morning, and "gaiety" goes on until 2:00 A.M.

~

NOTE: the library has v. odd books, bought about five years ago in a rummage sale. The unreadable, half-popular kind. So this is where they end up: riding the Atlantic.

~

Love—
L.

/ to Josephine O'Brien Schaefer[1] /

December 11, 1967

Dear Jo Schaefer:

Thank you for being so prompt with the V[irginia] W[oolf] notes.—I typed out the first set, and I plan to send *you* some comments later in the week. [...]

Everything you say is pertinent, I think—and fits into the pattern of my own insights. Her alternation of mood was, of course, a result of her illness; manic-depressives are swept from one extreme to the other. Her euphorias seem to have been fairly equally divided, as to timing, with her depressions. (This does not always occur. Ted Roethke, for example, was more manic than depressed in *his* cycle.) It is amazing that she was able to level off for considerable periods. She struggled v. hard indeed, constantly.—One point I made, in my [review of *The Captain's Death-Bed* . . .] was: that she was incapable of judging her contemporaries. Joyce was a low-bred fellow; Lawrence was a shocker. But she was v. good indeed at reconstructing an atmosphere of the past, and the color and motion of the genius of the admired dead— Jane Austen, for example.—Her feminism was bound up with her fears. Men were out to *get* women, etc.—and always had been.

We can keep these peripheral ideas floating around the *Diary* as a center, I think.

Don't worry about time or space! We can always cut and revise.

Best,

Louise

1. Scholar with whom LB coedited *A Writer's Diary*. LB had criticized Woolf's "skirting of evil" and pointed out that she was "frequently intellectually pretentious and always emotionally immature." When May Sarton objected, LB wrote: "I agree that my treatment of V. Woolf was rather partial; but I am so tired of people mooning over her. She had a v. inhuman side" (September 21, 1955; WTWL, 374n1).

/ *to Rolfe Humphries* /

May 18, 1968

Dear Rolfe:

I was v. sorry indeed to hear of your illness; but I feel sure that you must be on the mend, since you have just written such a fine poem, which I am happy to see.—I myself have had a rather mixed winter. By a series of events which no one could control, my circle of friends in N.Y.C. has rapidly dwindled. Betty Huling [on the staff at *The New Republic*] has been in a recurrent, and severe, depression, for a long time; the two old gals who live across the street from me have both become pretty senile; Peg Marshall[1] is in California, and so are you; and my closest woman friend—Ruth Limmer, who teaches at The Western College for Women—you have heard me speak of her—took herself off on a grand tour of Europe, including Russia and Prague. (She seems to have survived both locales.) I see Dave Mandel[2] for lunch, every once in a while, and there are other people I can talk to. Léonie is rather difficult, since she never *stops* talking . . . and is a fanatical Catholic Rightist, to boot. —Maidie I see about once a week; and I visit a literate youngish psychiatrist twice a month. But I get pretty lonely. This is a new feeling, for I have always been pretty vigorous and self-sufficient. A slight failure of nerve, no doubt . . . But I hate it, and wish it would go away.

Meanwhile, there are stories about this apartment. Columbia has bought the building; and that means ultimate razing. I plan to hold on. For Manhattan Island is evidently part of my destiny; I can't imagine living anywhere else. If I could live in the country, things would be simpler. But I can't envisage not being a townee . . .

[. . .] The books of verse that pour in are usually horrible, with titles like *The Lice* and *Body Rags*.[3] But this kind of downgrading will have to change sooner or later.——Have you read the new Norman Mailer [*Armies of the Night*]? He seems to be the king of the mountain, with the v. young, just at present.

The U. of Washington Press sent me Ted [Roethke's] *Selected Letters*. You and I figure in them, of course; but on the whole they are horribly dull— and exhibit Ted's worser, ambitious side far too clearly. And hasn't *The New Yorker* poetry been grim, recently? One poem, by Anne Sexton, made me positively ill. These ingrown and degenerate Yanks!

~

Love,
Louise

1. Margaret Marshall had been the literary editor of *The Nation* during LB's reviewing years.

2. David Mandel, author of *Changing Art, Changing Man,* who convinced LB to join in the Poets for Peace reading in November 1967 at Town Hall, where she read "To an Artist, to Take Heart" and, for the first time in public, "To My Brother" (WTWL, 375).

3. Titles of poetry volumes by W. S. Merwin and Galway Kinnell, respectively.

/ *to Ruth Limmer* /

March 10, 1969

Dear Ruth:

[. . .] I went into a small but severe slough of despond last week, when the news of Betty Huling's death reached me. We had been friends ever since 1930; and we had many a "good time," together: matinees and parties and this and that.——It was impossible for me to see her, in her last days, because of the general impact—and she wouldn't have known me, in any case. Her death was a mercy, of course; but I miss her.

~

The last pressure is concerned with the *NYer* books. They have appeared (again) in quantity.——I want to start off a piece with a mention of the *Id* rampant. But it's so hard to be definite about the *Id*. Impossible, in fact.—— But I have a picture of it snorting like a dragon, and lashing its tail, like demons . . . Say a prayer!

~

Love,
Louise

/ to William Maxwell /

June 30, 1969

Dear Bill:
The struggle with *silence* still goes on.——But I plan some secretarial help, after the holiday. If this doesn't help, I'll have another conference with you; and plan some strategy. Surely I can outwit this thing! I don't want to give up just yet.

As ever,
Louise

/ to Ruth Limmer /

Dear Ruth:

What a lovely letter!—And I am answering it, in my scrawl, to give you some *news*. Helped on by Dr. B. (who said, recently, that I had worked my-self into a *circular* situation, which would have to yield, at some point, by means of a *break* of some kind), I have *decided* to leave the magazine. After *thirty-eight* years; and seven years beyond normal retirement age.—I know that you are against such a move; but really, Ruth, I've *had* it. No more pro-nouncements on lousy verse. No more *hidden* competition. No more strug-gling *not* to be a square. Etc.

~

I am writing this at 10:00 A.M., at which time I am still a little *shaky*. So forgive.—Maxwell and I had lunch yesterday. He did not *press,* and I've given myself ten days—in which the damned books can be *sent back.*—Let's pray that J[ames] Dickey doesn't get the job. The [*Poet's Alphabet*] MS has reached McGraw-Hill. *This* I can work at. Also, at a new anthology with Bill Smith.[1]

~

Remember: this takes *courage*. But I'll come through!

Love, and happy journey!

Louise

1. There was no time for LB and William Jay Smith to complete this sequel to their 1965 coedited compilation, *The Golden Journey: Poems for Young People.* LB died on February 4, 1970.

IV

Criticism

Colette

CHÉRI AND *Mitsou* are the first of Colette's novels to be published in translations in America. From the long list of her books, written in the thirty years since 1900, one could choose other titles of perhaps equal brilliance. Her first literary period began in 1900, with the publication of the Claudine series; her mature literary career started with the appearance of *La Vagabonde* and *La Retraite sentimentale,* some ten years later. For twenty years Colette has been the most widely read and most sincerely respected woman writer in France. *Chéri* was published originally in 1920; *Mitsou,* published in 1917, was her first really objective novel. *Chéri* and its sequel, *La Fin de Chéri,* have already become contemporary classics. *Mitsou,* whose last pages drew tears from the eyes of Marcel Proust, is hardly more than a sketch for a novel of character, yet it stands unmatched in subtlety in the literature of our time.

The critical essays are ordered chronologically and grouped by topic. When Louise Bogan wrote more than one piece on the same artist or topic, the earliest commentary determines the placement of the group. Unless otherwise noted, all ellipses are LB's and all brackets the editor's.

Colette's excellence, long recognized by a European public that includes her fellow artists, is not easy to define by English-speaking standards. That she is a born writer and an exceptionally sensitive woman is evident. Her full-bodied gusto, her fresh senses and compassion unspoiled as a child's, are immediately clear to the running eye. She is not erudite. Her pages are singularly free from allusion and echoes of literature. She can be compared to little but herself because she has written her discoveries down just as she herself made them. She has lived her life—as a provincial girl, the wife of a Parisian man-about-town, a dancer in music halls, a woman of letters—and written of it concurrently. She has not checked the development of her talents by regrets for the past or yearnings into the future. The steps of her life, the ripening of her perceptions, appear as clearly in her novels as in the facts and dates of her biography.

The novelist, and particularly the novelist writing in English, works in a dangerously malleable form. His narrative, roughly, must adjust itself to a rising action, a knot, and a resolution; through this diagram, and because of it, characters must appear and change. In this loose texture, under these few demands it is difficult to detect maneuvers and sharp practices. Animus, stupidity, inaccuracy, and condescension, if disguised by a neat and fashionable manner and a long wind, can easily pass unnoticed. The good novelist is distinguished from the bad one chiefly by a gift of choice. Choice, itself a talent, as taste is a talent, is not, however, enough. Only extreme sanity and balance of selection can give to prose fiction the dignity and excitement inherent in more rigid forms of writing: drama, poetry, and the exposition of ideas.

Colette makes perfect choices. She writes with the naïve freedom of the amateur who has only himself for audience, and with the artist's unwavering adherence to form. Her simplicity of manner seems odd to the English reader, accustomed to the extremes of romantic rhetoric and to banal situations put down by writers hardened to their medium and not open to their material. The dated touch of nineteenth-century attitudes of mind still lies heavy upon modern fiction. In spite of loud assurances to the contrary, novels infected by their audience, warped by their authors' biases, bleached by literary form and custom, are the novels that, with few exceptions, come from the presses. Colette, backed by a tradition that includes [Stendhal's autobiographical] *La Vie de Henry Brulard,* puts down what she knows—what her sharp senses and hearty nature have told her as the truth. This, we can conclude, is her only secret.

The stories of Katherine Mansfield, so obviously influenced by Colette, illustrate the Frenchwoman's method of attack without giving a hint of her quality. For Katherine Mansfield's talent leaves off where Colette's begins. The Englishwoman's sensibilities could touch nostalgia, pity, and regret. They could not seek out the difficult human relationship, grasp it in essentials, reduce it to form. Where Colette struggles with the problem on its own terms, Katherine Mansfield shied away.

In *Chéri,* Colette chooses for her subject one of the most difficult situations in the rather limited gamut of relationships possible between men and women: the love of an aging woman for a young man; the dependence of a young man upon the passion and tenderness of an older woman. She makes her problem perfectly clear and does not slight its implications. Chéri is not a casual boy picked up by Léa late in her career. She has known him from childhood. She is the friend, contemporary, and confidante of his mother. Like his mother, she is a successful courtesan; unlike her, she is healthy, intelligent, and gay. Léa does not make the first move; it is the boy who chooses her. From the beginning, the psychological set is probable. And from the first kiss of these lovers, so ill assorted according to conventional standards, throughout the course of their love affair, Chéri's marriage, Léa's flight from unexpected sorrow, to Chéri's final rejection of her love and power, the mother-son basis of the bond between them is not for a moment forgotten. The last scene between Léa and Chéri is so complex and so moving that it stands beyond casual appraisal. These two, characters in a novel easily classed as scabrous, take on a tragic nobility; *"Léa,"* says a contemporary critic, *"se dompte comme une héroïne cornélienne."* [1] This seems improbable, but is nevertheless true.

Mitsou is so lightly blocked in, so delicately developed, that it barely merits the heavy title of novel. Mitsou, the little singer in a music hall, is the only character that has a name; the others are known by titles, like the people in an allegory or a harlequinade. Brief stage directions report the action for the most part; the scenes are perhaps five in number. Mitsou before the mirror of her dressing room, dressing, under the eyes of the young officers, "with a cheerless ease and an absent-minded immodesty which banished all coquetry"; Mitsou in the apartment furnished according to her own taste, and paid for by the Man of Means, an apartment "extraordinary, in spite of her good intentions"; Mitsou at her desk, writing serious little letters, full of grammatical errors and the newly awakened gentleness of first love—that is all we have, with the exception of Mitsou and her Lieutenant, in a strangers' embrace, seen against the ornate jumble of ornaments in her bedroom. What more could one do for this sober, well-meaning child, who does not miss her performance even though her lover goes away tomorrow? Colette does not attempt to do more. She defines her lightly, wakens her briefly, and lets her go.

Turning the light formality of French fiction to her own uses, Colette has colored French prose, for a long time rather grayed by reflections from Parisian streets, with the varied green of provincial gardens. Honest, sensuous, and witty, she has produced a solid body of work that owes little to masculine attitudes. Other translations of her books as excellent as these two should not be long deferred.

[1930]

1. *se dompte comme une héroïne cornélienne:* behaves like a heroine out of Corneille (seventeenth-century author of moral tragedies).

William Butler Yeats

CONTEMPORARY POETS are as incapable of wielding the barbed line as they are incapable, in the main, of feeling the high temper. William Butler Yeats stands as the distinguished exception to this general rule. His "Collected Poems," recently published, include the greatest political poems (although they denounce politics) of our time. Commentators yet unborn will break down their nervous tissues endeavoring to fit this last of the Romantics, the last (it may be) of the Contemplatives, strictly into the pattern of his age. Poets commonly dry up or peter out; Yeats grew from a singer of a few snatches of pure song into a master of technical subtlety and intellectual power. His native gifts—the extraordinary ear underlying his technical brilliance, his heritage of blood in which run wit, bitter intelligence, and a fund of beautiful common speech—always stood him in good stead. The later poems in his collection, written by an aging man (Yeats was born in 1865), stand as examples to the young who for some time past have made a brave show of maundering and the appreciation of maundering. This is great lyric poetry, the product of sensibility and intellect, conviction, stamina, and gall. If great political poems are to be written, it will be a poet similarly equipped who will write them.

[1934]

The Oxford Book of Modern Verse

IT IS no small task to gather into one anthology, and to reconcile critically, the schools of English poetry which have flourished since the death of Tennyson. William Butler Yeats, the editor of *The Oxford Book of Modern Verse* (1892–1935), has attempted it. The book opens with Pater's lines on the "Mona Lisa," printed as *vers libre,* because Pater, according to Yeats, was the one writer who had the entire uncritical admiration of the post-Victorian generation. It proceeds through Victorian holdovers (Bridges, Blunt), through the smoky lyrical flames at the end of the nineteenth century (Wilde, Dowson), into the comparatively airy and open years at the beginning of the twentieth. The Georgians take up the tune on their oaten pipes; the Imperialists, the seafarers, the Imagists arrive along with a few Hindus and Irish; Pound brings in echoes from Provence, Alexandria, and China; Eliot (the other American included) changes and distills. Sitwellian fireworks begin to fizz and whir, and war breaks up the game. Twenty years after the war a new school appears; young men who were children in 1914 begin to write at white heat, disabused with a wrecked and disordered world.

Yeats, who all his life has suspected politics, will not admit that it is political passion alone which now moves the young. "Suffering has compelled them to seek beyond the flux . . . Here stands not this or that man but man's naked mind." His preface closes on a note of belief in the sincerity and intellectual passion of these young men. He does not assign the influence of his own sincerity and intellectual passion to them, although there is more Yeats in all of them than many of them would care to admit.

Yeats's preface is simple in tone, catholic in appreciation, profound in judgment. Hurrahs for his side and contempt for the side of others do not occur in it. Some poetry, because he cannot read it without pain, he omits. (Wilfred Owen's work, which Yeats rejects because "passive suffering is not a theme for poetry," is the one real omission from the book.) Some poetry (Hopkins's) he reads with great difficulty, but includes at length. He has several rather peculiar enthusiasms (for W. J. Turner, Herbert Read, Dorothy Wellesley, and C. Day Lewis). On the other hand, he singles out poets whose gifts have been somewhat overlooked: Sturge Moore and Oliver Gogarty. He includes one discovery, Margot Ruddock, whose poems remind him of Emily Brontë's. And he appreciates Tagore along with Auden and MacNeice, Edith Sitwell at her emotional best, Pound at the high point of his style, D. H. Lawrence at the most intense of his sensibilities. He neither overemphasizes nor underestimates the stream of Irish song let into the stream of English by Synge and by the later translations of Lady Gregory and Frank O'Connor. His selection from his own work is superb.

"I think England had more good poets from 1900 to the present day than during any period of the same length since the early seventeenth century," Yeats says, in closing his argument and findings. A clear, heartening statement to hear after the many hollow groans often emitted concerning our time. On the evidence here presented, the reader is inclined to agree with one of the good poets of all time.

[1936]

The Greatest Poet Writing in English Today

William Butler Yeats, at the age of seventy-three, stands well within the company of the great poets. He is still writing, and the poems which now appear, usually embedded in short plays or set into the commentary and prefaces which have been another preoccupation of his later years, are, in many instances, as vigorous and subtle as the poems written by him during the years ordinarily considered to be the period of a poet's maturity.

Yeats has advanced into age with his art strengthened by a long battle which had as its object a literature written by Irishmen fit to take its place among the noble literatures of the world. The spectacle of a poet's work invigorated by his lifelong struggle against the artistic inertia of his nation is one that would shed strong light into any era.

The phenomenon of a poet who enjoys continued development into the beginning of old age is in itself rare. Goethe, Sophocles, and, in a lesser degree, Milton come to mind as men whose last works burned with the gathered fuel of their lives. More often development, in a poet, comes to a full stop; and it is frequently a negation of the ideals of his youth, as well as a declination of his powers, that throws a shadow across his final pages.

Yeats in his middle years began to concern himself with the problem of the poet in age. He wrote in 1917, when he was fifty-two:

A poet when he is growing old, will ask himself if he cannot keep his mask and his vision without new bitterness, new disappointment. Could he, if he would . . . copy Landor who lived loving and hating, ridiculous and unconquered, into extreme old age, all lost but the favour of his muses . . . Surely, he may think, now that I have found vision and mask I need not suffer any longer . . . Then he will remember Wordsworth withering into eighty years, honoured and empty-witted, and climb to some waste room, and find, forgotten there by youth, some bitter crust.[1]

We can trace, in Yeats, the continually enriched and undeviating course of an inspired man, from earliest youth to age. We can trace the rectitude of the spiritual line in his prose and poetry alike. And there is not a great deal of difference between the "lank, long-coated figure . . . who came and went as he pleased," dramatizing himself and his dreams in the streets of Dublin (the youth who had known William Morris and was to know Dowson and Wilde), and the man who, full of honors in our day, impresses us with his detachment and subtle modernity. Yeats, the fiery young Nationalist, rolling up with his own hands the red carpet spread on a Dublin sidewalk "by some elderly Nationalist softened or weakened by time, to welcome Vice-royalty," is recognizable in the poet of advanced years who does not hesitate to satirize certain leaders of the new Ireland.

Yeats's faith in the development of his own powers never failed. He wrote, in 1923, after receiving from the King of Sweden the medal symbolizing the Nobel Prize:

It shows a young man listening to a Muse, who stands young and beautiful with a great lyre in her hand, and I think as I examine it, 'I was good-looking once like that young man, but my unpractised verse was full of infirmity, my Muse old as it were, and now I am old and rheumatic and nothing to look at, but my Muse is young.' I am even persuaded that she is like those Angels in Swedenborg's vision, and moves perpetually "towards the dayspring of her youth."

2

The Irish literary and dramatic movement, in general belief, rose, late in the nineteenth century, in some vague manner from the temperament of the Irish people. As a matter of fact, Ireland in Yeats's young manhood was as ungrateful a soil for art as any that could be found, in a particularly materialistic time. The native Celtic genius that Arnold had felt to be so open to the influence of a "natural magic" had been, for over a century, drawn off into politics. The Anglo-Irish tradition, having produced in the eighteenth century Swift, Congreve, Edgeworth, Goldsmith, Berkeley, and Burke, flowered no longer.

The Land Agitation (the struggle of the peasantry against their landlords) and the Young Ireland and Fenian Movements (the struggle of the Irish people against English rule) from the forties on had absorbed the energies and the eloquence of talented young Irishmen. Irish writers, as Stephen Gwynn has said, having been taught by Swift that written English could be used as a weapon against their oppressors, never forgot their lesson. The Catholic Emancipation Bill, by the efforts of Daniel O'Connell, was passed in 1829. In 1842 the Young Ireland Movement was given a newspaper by Thomas Davis: the *Nation,* whose motto was "to create and foster public opinion in Ireland and make it racy of the soil."[2] The *Nation* also fostered a school of Irish poets. Their audience was eager for stirring and heartening words; the verse which spoke to it most clearly was the rhetorical and sentimental ballad, celebrating the Irish race and inciting it to action and solidarity. This verse, when it was not written in the sentimental and insipid vein made famous by Tom Moore, was filled, as has been pointed out, with the hortatory gusto of Lord Macaulay. Versifiers used its forms with skill, and one or two—Clarence Mangan and Sir Samuel Ferguson—touched them with real color and depth of feeling. But there is no doubt that Irish litera-ture, in the years between 1848 and 1891, had fallen upon barren times.

The year 1891 brought Parnell's death. The tragic end of a leader in-tensely hated and loved, and the loss of much political hope thereby, threw the national consciousness violently back on itself. Yeats has described the situation (he was twenty-six at the time). "Nationalist Ireland was torn with every kind of passion and prejudice, wanting, so far as it wanted any litera-ture at all, Nationalist propaganda disguised as literature. All the past had been turned into a melodrama with Ireland the blameless hero, and poet, novelist, and historian had but one object, to hiss the villain, and only the minority doubted the greater the talent the greater the hiss. It was all the harder to substitute for that melodrama a nobler form of art, because there had been, however different in their form, villain and victim."

At the breakup of the Catholic State in the wars of the seventeenth cen-tury, "Irish laws and customs, the whole framework of the Gaelic civilization, had been annihilated." Music, literature, and classical learning, loved by even the poorest of the Irish, had been driven into hiding, with only "hedge-schoolmasters" and wandering bards to keep them from oblivion. During the years when the *Nation* was coming to be the literary force behind Irish Nationalism, traditional Gaelic survived in the minds of Gaelic-speaking peasants. Elsewhere it had disappeared, and from these minds and memo-ries it was rapidly fading. After generations of poverty and oppression, the orally transmitted songs and histories had become fragmentary. Few edu-cated Irishmen knew them, since no educated Irishman knew Gaelic. The Irish language was forbidden in the national schools, and the sons of Anglo-Irish landlords and rectors who passed through Trinity College in Dublin learned English culture and English literature. Standish James O'Grady had published his *Bardic History* in 1880, but, since O'Grady was a champion of the aristocracy, the book made little impression on the partisan-minded country as a whole. When, in 1894, an Irish landlord with some literary am-bitions, Edward Martyn, said to another of the same class, George Moore, "I wish I knew enough Irish to write my plays in Irish." Moore replied, "I thought nobody did anything in Irish but bring turf from the bog and say prayers." And Yeats has testified in an essay on the Irish Dramatic Movement: "When we began our work we tried to get a play in Gaelic. We could not even get a condensed version of the dialogue of Oisin and St. Patrick."

3

Where so much of the spirit of art had to be revivified, so many of its forms repaired, and so tight a mold of fanaticism broken, a man was needed who had in himself some of the qualities of the fanatic—a man who was, above all else, an artist, capable of making an occasional compromise with a human being, but incapable of making one with the informing essence of his art. New light and air had to be let into the closed minds and imaginations of a people made suspicious and hysterically provincial through persecution and disaster. It was impossible to weld the opinions of factions, but all could be drawn into "one net of feeling." A man of sensibility, however, was not enough. Not only insight and imagination, but ruthlessness, fervor, disinterestedness, and a capacity for decision and action, were required.

William Butler Yeats first appears, in the memories of his contemporaries, as a rarefied human being: a tall, dark-visaged young man who walked the streets of Dublin and London in a poetic hat, cloak, and flowing tie, intoning verses. The young man's more solid qualities were not then apparent to the casual observer. But it was during these early years that Yeats was building himself, step by step, into a person who could not only cope with reality but bend it to his will. He tells, in one of his autobiographies, of his determination to overcome his young diffidence. Realizing that he was "only self-possessed with people he knew intimately," he would go to a strange house "for a wretched hour for schooling's sake." And because he wished "to be able to play with hostile minds," he trained out of himself, in the midst of harsh discussion, the sensitive tendency "to become silent at rudeness."

The result of this training began to be apparent before Yeats was thirty. George Moore has recorded how, on meeting him in London (having been badly impressed by his "excessive" getup at a casual meeting some years before), he thought to worst Yeats easily in argument. The real mettle of his opponent soon came into view. "Yeats parried a blow on which I had counted, and he did this so quickly and with so much ease that he threw me on the defensive in a moment. 'A dialectician,' I muttered, 'of the very first order'; one of a different kind from any I had met before."

This intellectual energy, this "whirling" yet deeply intuitive and ordered mind, with its balancing streak of common sense, had come to Yeats through a mixed inheritance. The Yeats blood, perhaps Norman, had been Anglo-Irish for centuries, and it is notorious that English families transplanted to Ireland often become more Irish than the native stock. Yeats's paternal grandfather and great-grandfather had been Protestant rectors, in County Down and County Sligo respectively, and there had been eighteenth-century soldiers and government officials on this side of the family. Yeats's mother was a Pollexfen; her stock was Cornish—that is to say, English-Celtic. Her father, William Pollexfen, a lonely strong man whom Yeats as a child loved and feared ("I wonder if the delight in passionate men in my plays and poetry is more than his memory"), had settled in Sligo as a shipowner, after a career as master of ships. Yeats spent several of his childhood years and many of his adolescent summers near the town of Sligo, and from that Western country-side, so full of the beauties of lake, mountain, and sea, and from its people, who still had Gaelic in their speech and legends in their memory, he drew the material of his early poetry.

Yeats has told of the deep emotional reserves in his Sligo-born mother, "whose actions were unreasoning and habitual like the seasons." From his father, John Butler Yeats, a man of original mind who had been trained in the law but turned to painting and to the pre-Raphaelite enthusiasms current in the seventies and eighties, Yeats early heard that "intensity was important above all things." The father's passion for Blake, Morris, and Rossetti soon was shared by the son. Yeats had some English schooling; he later was an art student in Dublin. During this period he became a Nationalist. The elder Yeats had friends among Unionists and Nationalists alike, and, well acquainted with the liberal English thought of his time, enthusiastically espoused the cause of Home Rule. His son's Nationalism was both intellectual and emotional. He became the friend of John O'Leary, an old Fenian who had returned to Dublin after imprisonment and exile for youthful conspiracies; and Maud Gonne, a great beauty and successful agitator, was also an influence helping to channel his youthful ardor toward the more heroic and mystic side of the Nationalist movement. In both of these people Yeats felt imaginative and courageous character which transcended political bigotry and dogma. At no time, from the beginning of his career onward, did he for a moment yield to the hard letter of Irish politics. It was the spirit in those politics he wished to strengthen and make serviceable. His ends, and the means to bring about his ends, were always clear in his mind. "We cannot move the peasants and the educated classes in Ireland by writing about politics or about Gaelic, but we may move them by becoming men of letters and expressing primary truths in ways appropriate to this country."

His art was poetry, and, almost from the first, he used that art as a tool, his avowed purpose being to rid the literature of his country from the insincere, provincial, and hampering forms of "the election rhyme and the pamphlet."

~

6

"We should write out our thoughts," Yeats has said, "in as nearly as possible the language we thought them in, as though in a letter to an intimate friend." And again: "If I can be sincere and make my language natural, and without becoming discursive, like a novelist, and so indiscreet and prosaic, I shall, if good or bad luck make my life interesting, be a great poet; for it will no longer be a question of literature at all."

If we grant naturalness, sincerity, and vigor to Yeats's late style, we still have not approached its secret. Technical simplicity may produce, instead of effects of tension and power, effects of bleakness and poorness. What impresses us most strongly in Yeats's late work is that here a whole personality is involved. A complex temperament (capable of anger and harshness, as well as of tenderness), and a powerful intellect, come through; and every part of the nature is released, developed, and rounded in the later books. The early Yeats was, in many ways, a youth of his time: a romantic exile seeking, away from reality, the landscape of his dreams. By degrees—for the development took place over a long period of years—this partial personality was absorbed into a man whose power to act in the real world and endure the results of action (responsibility the romantic hesitates to assume) was immense. Yeats advanced into the world he once shunned, but in dealing with it he did not yield to its standards. That difficult balance, almost impossible to strike, between the artist's austerity and "the reveries of the common heart" —between the proud passions, the proud intellect, and consuming action— Yeats finally attained and held to. It is this balance which gives the poems written from (roughly) 1914 on (from *Responsibilities,* published in that year, to poems published at present) their noble resonance. "I have had to learn how hard is that purification from insincerity, vanity, malignance, arrogance, which is the discovery of style."

Technically, the later style is almost lacking in adverbs—built on the noun, verb, and adjective. Its structure is kept clear and level, so that emotionally weighted words, when they appear, stand out with poignant emphasis. "The Wild Swans at Coole" (1919) opens:

> The trees are in their autumn beauty,
> The woodland paths are dry,
> Under the October twilight the water
> Mirrors a still sky;
> Upon the brimming water among the stones
> Are nine-and-fifty swans.

Equipped with this instrument, Yeats could put down, with full scorn, his irritation with the middle-class ideals he had hated from youth:

> What need you, being come to sense,
> But fumble in a greasy till
> And add the halfpence to the pence
> And prayer to shivering prayer, until
> You have dried the marrow from the bone;
> For men were born to pray and save:
> Romantic Ireland's dead and gone,
> It's with O'Leary in the grave.
> . . . .
> Was it for this the wild geese spread
> The grey wing upon every tide;
> For this that all that blood was shed,
> For this Edward Fitzgerald died,
> And Robert Emmet and Wolfe Tone,
> All that delirium of the brave?
> Romantic Ireland's dead and gone,
> It's with O'Leary in the grave.

["September 1913"]

On the other hand he could celebrate Irish *salus, virtus* [soundness, valor], as in the poem "An Irish Airman Foresees His Death" and in the fine elegies on the leaders of the 1916 Easter Rebellion.

And Yeats came to be expert at the dramatic presentation of thoughts concerning love, death, the transience and hidden meaning of all things, not only in the form of a philosopher's speculation, a mystic's speech, or a scholar's lonely brooding, but also (and this has come to be a major Yeatsian effect) in the cracked and rowdy measures of a fool's, an old man's, an old woman's song. *The Tower* (1928) and *The Winding Stair* (1929) contain long meditations—some "in time of civil war"—upon his life, his times, his ancestors, his descendants; upon the friends and enemies of his youth.

The short plays, composed on the pattern of the Japanese Noh drama, which Ezra Pound had brought to Yeats's attention—*Four Plays for Dancers* (1921), *Wheels and Butterflies* (1934), *The King of the Great Clock Tower* (1935) —Yeats made the vehicle for the loveliest of his later songs, for all his later development of pure music:

> Come to me, human faces,
> Familiar memories;
> I have found hateful eyes
> Among the desolate places,
> Unfaltering, unmoistened eyes.
>
> Folly alone I cherish,
> I choose it for my share;
> Being but a mouthful of air,
> I am content to perish;
> I am but a mouthful of sweet air.

> [*At the Hawk's Well*]

The opening song in the play *The Only Jealousy of Emer* illustrates the variety of stress, the subtlety of meaning, of which Yeats became a master:

> A woman's beauty is like a white
> Frail bird, like a white sea-bird alone
> At daybreak after stormy night
> Between two furrows upon the ploughed land:
> A sudden storm, and it was thrown
> Between dark furrows upon the ploughed land.
> How many centuries spent

The sedentary soul
In toil of measurement
Beyond eagle or mole,
Beyond hearing or seeing,
Or Archimedes' guess,
To raise into being
That loveliness?

A strange, unserviceable thing,
A fragile, exquisite, pale shell,
That the vast troubled waters bring
To the loud sands before day has broken.
The storm arose and suddenly fell
Amid the dark before day had broken.
What death? what discipline?
What bonds no man could unbind,
Being imagined within
The labyrinth of the mind,
What pursuing or fleeing,
What wounds, what bloody press,
Dragged into being
This loveliness?

7

From youth on, Yeats has thought to build a religion for himself. Early "bored with an Irish Protestant point of view that suggested, by its blank abstraction, chlorate of lime," he eagerly welcomed any teaching which attested supersensual experience, or gave him a background for those thoughts which came to him "from beyond the mind." "Yeats likes parlor magic," George Moore maliciously remarked, in the nineties. At that time, when religious belief and man's awe before natural mysteries were rapidly breaking up, the wreckage of the supernatural had been swept into mediums' shabby parlors and into the hands of quacks of all kinds. Many men of Yeats's generation took refuge in the Catholic Church. But Yeats kept to his own researches. He had experimented, when an adolescent, with telepathy and clairvoyance, in

William Butler Yeats

the company of his uncle, George Pollexfen, a student of the occult. He later studied the Christian Cabala and gradually built up, from his own findings and from the works of Blake, Swedenborg, and Boehme, his theories of visionary and spiritual truth. But he was never, as Edmund Wilson has pointed out, a gullible pupil. He invariably tried to verify phenomena. And today, when we know more than we once knew concerning the meaning of man-made symbols, the needs of the psyche, and the workings of the Subconscious, Yeats's theories sound remarkably instructed and modernly relevant. His *Anima Mundi* closely resembles Jung's universal or racial Unconscious, and even his conceptions of Image and Anti-Image, the Mask and its opposite, are closely related to psychological truth.

Of late years, after a lifetime spent in efforts to break up the deadening surface of middle-class complacency, Yeats has drawn nourishment from the thought of the relation of eighteenth-century Anglo-Irish writers to their society. These men—Swift, Berkeley, Grattan—had behind them, he believes, a social structure capable of being an aid to works of imagination and intellect. The ideal of the artist built into his background, sustaining it and sustained by it, Yeats has termed "Unity of Being." He has striven all his life to give Ireland a sense of what such a society can be, and to make himself an artist worthy of the energy which built "the beautiful humane cities."

In age, he shows no impoverishment of spirit or weakening of intention. He answers current dogmatists with words edged with the same contempt for "the rigid world" of materialism that he used in youth. He is now content to throw out suggestions that are not, perhaps, for our age to complete, as it is not for our age fully to appreciate a man who reiterates: "If we have not the desire of artistic perfection for an art, the deluge of incoherence, vulgarity, and triviality will pass over our heads." But adherence to that creed, and that creed alone, has given us the greatest poet writing in English today, and Ireland the greatest it has ever known.

> Move upon Newton's town,
> The town of Hobbes and of Locke,
> Pine, spruce, come down
> Cliff, ravine, rock:
> What can disturb the corn?
> What makes it shudder and bend?

The rose brings her thorn,
The Absolute walks behind.

[Introduction to "Fighting the Waves," *The Dublin Magazine*, April–June 1932]

[1938]

1. From Yeat's essay "Per Amica Silentia Lunae" (By the Friendly Stillness of the Moon).
2. racy of the soil: having the original tang of the national spirit.

On the Death of Yeats

I have been busy with a single art, that of . . . a small unpopular theatre; and this art may well seem to practical men, busy with some program of industrial or political regeneration, of no more account than the shaping of an agate; and yet in the shaping of an agate, whether in the cutting or the making of the design, one discovers, if one have a speculative mind, thoughts that seem important and principles that may be applied to life itself, and certainly if one does not believe so, one is but a poor cutter of so hard a stone.

August, 1912

YEATS'S BREAK with his early style and subject matter—though the break never was, and never needed to be, complete—dates from 1909 or a year or two earlier. It has been said that this break was the result of his entrance into practical affairs. This statement is only partially true. Yeats's youthful ambition was to be a man of action, and he was more active in organization —in the Nationalist movement and literary societies—in his twenties than at any later time. It was only when he broke with the popular theatre, which had interested him for ten years, and refused to make any further attempt to satisfy middle-class ideals of art that the resonant tone characteristic of the later poems sounded for the first time.

Synge died in 1909. Two years earlier the *Playboy* riots[1] had occurred. And it was in this same period that Yeats witnessed the scandal raised by popular opinion and the Irish newspapers over the question of whether the city of Dublin should build a gallery to house Sir Hugh Lane's gift of Impressionist paintings. He witnessed, that is, in an acute form, the hostility of the middle class toward disinterested artistic expression, as it had been witnessed a generation earlier in France. The bourgeois mind demanded that art be moral or useful, and not only discredited the artist's function but outlawed the artist. Flaubert and Baudelaire were summoned before courts of law, and in Ireland the citizens of Dublin attacked Synge with outright violence.

Ireland, because of its ambiguous political status, threw up bourgeois culture late. And it was there produced in such a clear form that the transformation of the countryman's economy into that of the town dweller is an easily visible process. Yeats wished to give his country not only a sense of its former greatness but also a feeling for the nobility of the arts in general. After the bigotry aroused by *The Playboy,* he began to see that his ideal was antipathetic to his audience.

> I believed . . . that a new intellectual life would begin, like that of young Ireland, but more profound and personal. . . . I could not foresee that a new class . . . would change the nature of the Irish movement . . . Power passed to small shopkeepers, to men who had risen above the traditions of the countryman without learning those of cultivated life . . . and who, because of their poverty, ignorance, and superstitious piety, are much subject to all kinds of fear. Immediate victory, immediate utility, became everything, and we artists, who are servants not of any cause but of mere naked life . . . became as elsewhere in Europe protesting individual voices.

This was written in 1907. In 1909 Yeats begins to speak of "the mask," and to write those direct poems filled with scorn for "Paudeen" [the Irish shopkeeper] and Paudeen's wealthy "betters." *Responsibilities* (1914) developed this phase fully. The role of action was finally refused, and the artist's role finally accepted.

The common admonition administered to a writer when he refuses to express the opinions and ideals current in his lifetime, choosing instead his own subjects and symbols, is that he thus risks preciosity and final sterility. Yeats, in refusing to cater to the middle, had two fields open to him—"aristocratic" and "vulgar" expression. These ends of the scale are equally rejected by the bourgeoisie: subtlety puzzles and coarseness shocks them. Yeats wrote his new plays in a form derived from the aristocratic Noh drama of Japan. He interested himself in the most "unserviceable" subjects—the Cabala, spiritualism, Hindu philosophy, Byzantine civilization. In *A Vision* he built up a whole mystical system and applied it to historic facts. The later plays are so wrapped in symbol that they approach sheer incantation, and Yeats steadily refused to make their intention clear. He said to a musician who was to write music for these plays: "Lose my words in patterns of sound as the name of God is lost in Arabian arabesques. They are a secret between the singers, myself, and yourself."

The revolt against the idea of art's usefulness could hardly be pushed farther than Yeats in this manner extended it. Did the poems, then, written in this vein, in the last thirty years of his life, from the age of forty-four to the time of his death at nearly seventy-three, suffer?

On the contrary, they went on to ever greater degrees of power and suggestiveness; they touched the borders where poetry becomes ultimate evocation, and the regions where religion rises from universal mystery.

> These lovers, purified by tragedy,
> Hurry into each other's arms; those eyes
> By water, herb, and solitary prayer
> Made aquiline, are open to that light.
> Though somewhat broken by the leaves, that light
> Lies in a circle on the grass; therein
> I turn the pages of my holy book.
>
> ["Ribh at the Tomb of Baile and Aillinn"]

For two years, between the ages of sixty-seven and sixty-nine, Yeats wrote no poetry. "I had never been so long barren." Then began a new period of creation, to which we owe the great poems which have been appearing in English and American magazines during the last few years. In these poems "aristocratic" and "vulgar" forms unite. The songs and meditations are often "coarse" and written in as simple a form as street ballads or broadsheets. Yeats never abandoned the ballad forms first learned from Sligo peasants in his childhood: one or two appear in every volume, and the "Crazy Jane" songs in *The Winding Stair* (1933) are late and intense examples of the type. The

last ballads go beyond even these; there is nothing quite like them in literature. The last lyrics of Goethe, written in age, seem literary in comparison.
These poems are unstained by any breath of false resignation or "ennobling"
feeling. They express the sane bawdiness of healthy old age, in phrases written, nonetheless, with every distinction, every knowledge of effect, every
delicate sympathy native to a sensitive nature. Meditation and speculation
are there, but behind them, to the last, still exist "naked life" and the vivid
sensual world.

Any artist old or young can take courage from these poems. And he can
discover in Yeats's prose writing—which developed, like the poetry, from
elaboration into simplicity, and documents fully the struggle of a long life
—old evils again to be combatted, however new and disguised their modern
forms. A battle has been fought against them up to the very last days of a
man recently dead, who emerged the victor.

[1939]

1. Demonstrations against the perceived distortion of Irish culture in John Synge's play
The Playboy of the Western World (produced at Yeats's Abbey Theatre in 1907).

Last Poems and Plays

OLD MEN mad about painting are more fortunate than old poets. With a
brush strapped to their wrist, if necessary, old painters can go on with their
work. But poets use words, and with words, thoughts and opinions are apt
to leak in. And if they are childish opinions, or if the thoughts have stiffened,
are mawkish or reactionary, the last poems become ridiculous and unreadable in a later period. Aging Wordsworth and Browning did not do the concept of the old poet as sage any good turn, but Hardy and Yeats have again
proved that the old poet need not be the old fogey or the old fool.

The poems in Yeats's *Last Poems and Plays* have no "noble" or "wise" (in
the Victorian sense) wrappings upon them. They are, on the contrary, the
most naked and terrible he ever wrote. They call up terror; they do not

soothe; they shed cold and ruthless light on man, his motives, and his works; and they keep repeating the unpalatable truth that life is horror and failure as well as joy and accomplishment, that patterns superimposed on man cannot reach his devious and cruel heart. They are concerned with lust, betrayal, wildness, and rage, and they are written in the randy measures of street ballads as often as in the purer metres of literature. At the same time, they are concerned with "beautiful lofty things"—with all that mankind knows of love, courage, and the gall that fights against stupidity, half-truths, and injustice. Sometimes, even, they are the love poems of an old poet still capable of love, as witness one of the tenderest poems in English, "John Kinsella's Lament for Mrs. Mary Moore."

Yeats, as an old man, came to reject with complete scorn all middle grounds. It was to the simplest or to the most complex he turned: to peasant songs, or to the most disinterested, useless, and gallant of man's actions and art. He has been accused of writing Fascist marching songs; it is impossible to read this last book of poems and not know that to be a slander, even if Yeats's own answer to this lie did not already exist in print. Yeats's frequent bitterness on the subject of politics is based on the political history of Ireland since the death of Parnell. It is necessary to know that history in order to understand Yeats's anger against the present situation in his native land. It is necessary only to have an ear, a heart, and some experience of living, however, in order to appreciate the power and beauty of the poems in general. The Irish poets whom Yeats exhorts to "learn their trade" have here an example of what kind of spirit poetry demands. And future generations, of whatever nationality or belief, are not likely to be stirred to pity or contempt by Yeats's stoic epitaph:

> Cast a cold eye
> On life, on death.
> Horseman, pass by!

[1940]

Collected Poems

THE FIRST edition of the *Collected Poems* (1933) broke off with the volume *The Winding Stair,* published in the same year. The final collected edition adds to the earlier work the poetry written by Yeats from about 1935 to 1939, the year of his death. This additional material embodies, therefore, the last preoccupations, as well as the last stylistic development, of the great Anglo-Irishman, born in 1865, whose first book appeared in 1889. The record is thus closed of a long career spent almost exclusively in furthering the ideals of disinterested art in a period marked by triumphs of rationalism and of the machine; the cause of the individual in a time of human depersonalization; and the cause of a small nation in a period given over to various forms of imperialism. The means that Yeats chose to achieve his ends have often been derided; and it is true that his "magician" side often brought about curious shifts in his conduct and thinking. His life, moreover, does not follow any conventional pattern of peace found after conflict, of humility following after pride, of spiritual reconciliation in age. But if the last poems often present the picture of a pride-ridden old man who clings to his crankiness with an almost insane zeal, they also present an old poet continuing to explore his complicated nature and his complicated times up to the last—while extending the limits of his art with unflagging ingenuity, subtlety, and daring.

Yeats never "adjusted" to the conditions of his age or of his society. He not only constructed a religion for himself, but he spent many years "docketing the universe": building a picture of time, space, and causality which fitted the needs (and no doubt quieted the fears) of his own peculiar temperament. His ideals were both spiritual and aristocratic; he gave his allegiance to peasant and aristocrat; and he wasted neither time nor sympathy on "passive suffering" or ideas of human progress. In his universe, built in the form of a Great Wheel, man's soul went through successive incarnations—bound to an impersonal fate, but rescued by the possibility of a personal destiny. This destiny left man freedom to act and to create—to oppose the work of the spirit to the mechanisms of nature.

It was the failure of mankind in general—and of Irishmen in particular—to grasp and forward this destiny that provoked in Yeats, as time passed, an increasing bitterness and irritability. He himself had taken on discipline early; he had put off his youthful indolence and had spent years working in the more practical side of the drama, at the Abbey Theatre. But in the field of art an Irish middle class, newly come into power, let him down; and Irish politics took a turn of which he did not approve. Because of these struggles against opposition, Yeats's wit, shrewdness, and powers of intellect began, in his middle years, to develop and come into view. He began to write with ease concerning the contemporary scene, and to display his prejudices without fear. His mind became infinitely restless and ceaselessly inquisitive. He also developed, along with growing powers of invective, a kind of magnanimity—a magnanimity, it is true, which worked best in retrospect. In the poems written many years after the Easter Rebellion of 1916, he was able to celebrate the heroism of his enemies as well as of his friends; and his later work is filled with praise of human nobility, wherever found.

Around 1935, after a period spent in efforts to compromise with the Irish Free State government, under which he had served as a Senator, he came perilously near adopting ideas of undemocratic coercion and force. He quickly withdrew from this position; and the only trace of his passing belief in "marching men" comes through in the extravagant marching songs. In the years from 1936 to 1939 he experienced a tremendous renewal of power. This renewal expressed itself in two definite, and opposed, poetic manners. On the one hand, he began to elaborate poems of the "Crazy Jane" variety, in which, to old broadsheet rhythms, unstinted praise of coarse human vitality is set against the powers of church, state, and, indeed, every ordinary form of orderly life. At the same time he continued to produce, in his more "lofty" style, celebrations of human greatness, usually in the form of elegies to the past glories of his own generation. He flaunted "an old man's frenzy" and an old man's pride; but if he often pushed intensity toward harshness, he instinctively kept to intensity, knowing that without passion no art can live. Even in the midst of his die-hard show—which at moments verged on the theatrical—he slipped in passages of self-mockery bred of self-knowledge; and beneath his praise of crude human vitality a new note of pathos can be detected. Something stiff, divided, and hieratic drops away from the personality. The wiles of the old magician are transcended; and the final impression is one of a self-fulfilled artist using, up to the end, for selfless purposes, the unbroken spirit of an indomitable man.

[1951]

William Butler Yeats

W. H. Auden

FOR THE benefit of those serious students of poetry who must exist somewhere in a collapsing society, I here mention the name of W. H. Auden, an
extremely gifted young English disciple of discontinuity, who does not spurn
the current spectacle as poetic material. He has set the Isis and the Cam on
fire; there is always the chance that the conflagration may extend to the
Hudson and the Thames.

[1934]

The Dog Beneath the Skin

W. H. AUDEN has emerged rapidly from the soliloquy darkened by private
associations, a form that might have hampered him for a longer time. His
first dramatic efforts, *Paid on Both Sides* and *The Dance of Death,* were founded
on the feeblest possible dramatic framework: the charade. He has written,
in *The Dog Beneath the Skin, or, Where Is Francis?,* with the competent aid of
Christopher Isherwood, a long, highly amusing revue, whose satire is so deft
that it may stand, without cutting a sorry figure, beside the early Gilbert.[1]
Along with the satirist's wit, the imagination of a poet and the broad humor
of a sane young man are also involved.

   Auden's play is closer to the original music-hall entertainment so admired, in the nineties, as a refuge from the torpid, affected art and literature current at that time, than Eliot's "Sweeney Agonistes" or Cocteau's
Orphée, derived from the same source. It is less dependent on pure oddity
than Cocteau's play, and it is not heavily symbolic, like Eliot's. It is a light-
hearted yet fundamentally grave parable of the noble youth who descends
from his class to give humanity in general a hard and unprejudiced stare.

   The hero, Alan, accompanied by a comic dog called, after its quarry,
Francis, sets out from the ideal English village in search of the lost noble

heir. The two make their progress through the symptomatic institutions of a debased and lunatic society in the leisurely but erratic manner of all innocent pilgrims steered by an author's moral indignation, from [Bunyan's] Christian and [Swift's] Gulliver on. They are accompanied on certain stages of their journey by the press in the person of two journalists who comment, aid, abet, prod, rescue, sympathize, and interpret. They take boat and train journeys; they invade a tottering monarchy, a night-town, a Fascist insane asylum, a rest cure for self-poisoned egotists, an operating theatre, and a de luxe hotel. The Dog, in spite of a lamentable taste for double whiskies, served in a bowl, shows remarkable cleverness and devotion throughout. He proves his true valor when the simple-hearted Alan falls into the clutches of a night-club entertainer; he casts his skin and stands up from it revealed as Sir Francis Crewe, the object of Alan's search. The two, in their roles of the seeker and the found, return to the village as comrades. Alan sees all in a new light and the one-time Dog sums up, in public, his general feelings about the world seen from below:

> As a dog, I learnt with what a mixture of fear, bullying and condescending kindness you treat those whom you consider your inferiors, but on whom you depend for your pleasures. It's an awful shock to start seeing people from underneath . . . You are units in an immense army: most of you will die without ever knowing what your leaders are fighting for or even that you are fighting at all. Well, I am going to be a unit in the army of the other side.

Auden and Isherwood are by no means the first young members of the English upper class who have pilloried their caste. Even the rather unsettled Sitwells have put down, in terms far from uncertain, the grotesque antics of members of the three estates. The most noticeable ingredient in Auden's attitude is his lack of hatred; he has much pity and strong anger, but he is not bloodthirsty and he does not blame. He surveys the scene from above and below; he gives it elevation, section, and plan, but he does not rant against it. The hysterical, the gloomy, the portentously righteous and solemn note is missing, yet the power of his indictment is not diminished because of its absence. And there is a hint given from time to time that it is man's present (and perhaps future) partial capacity for sense and for good, his defective and divided nature, that helps to distort the scene.

W. H. Auden

To men of action, pity is sentimental and insight into the human heart unnecessary. To a poet, pity and insight may also kindle the fire of action and sharpen the pen in the hand. Auden fearlessly incites to action, after he has shown that what must be fought are not only the outer horrors but also the flesh on the bones and the stupidity in the veins:

You have wonderful hospitals and a few good schools:
Repent.
The precision of your instruments and the skill of your designers is unparalleled:
Unite.
Your knowledge and your power are capable of infinite extension:
Act.

[1935]

1. Sir William Schwenck Gilbert (1836–1913), a poet and satirist, who later composed comic opera librettos, the most famous of which were produced by Richard D'Oyley Carte at the Savoy Theatre. Gilbert's collaborator was Sir Arthur Sullivan (1842–1900), who wrote the music to his words for thirteen enormously popular musical comedies produced in London between 1875 and 1896. *Iolanthe or the Peer and the Peri* (1882), which LB mentions in a letter to Roethke (October 3, 1935), praising Auden and Garrett's two-volume anthology *The Poet's Tongue*, was one of Auden's favorite Gilbert and Sullivan operas.

Letters from Iceland

THOSE PEOPLE who wish young poets to be deadly serious and all of a piece will be annoyed and baffled by Auden's travel book, *Letters from Iceland*, written with Louis MacNeice, a new collaborator. These letters, rhymed and unrhymed, are consistently amusing and frequently brilliant, but they do not repeat the tone of books written by emotional travelers, philosophical travelers, trippers, or escapists. Both Auden and MacNeice are on to the kinds of attitude which can be struck by the English, whether poets or not, in strange landscapes. They have chosen to stick to an amateur and detached standing; as travelers they have kept outside the ranks of explorers, old Etonians of the Peter Fleming tradition, and Wordsworthian nature lovers.

When, in the northern wilds, they came upon a real professional English traveler, "handsome, sunburnt, reserved, speaking fluent Icelandic," they were more amused than abashed. Auden, having contracted to do a travel book on Iceland (he was drawn to that country because of his Icelandic name and a childhood interest in the sagas), spent the summer of 1936 on the island, at first alone and later in the company of MacNeice and other friends. Rejecting from the first the idea of the necessity to brood and moon over *ultima Thule* [mythic northern zone], or to indulge in Romantic *poésie des départs* [poetry of parting], he was rather at a loss how to begin. Iceland had been visited by other men of letters and had produced some great native prose. It offered to the view glaciers, waterfalls, geysers, a volcano, and many rocks coated with sphagnum moss. One traveled through it by bus (in which conveyance Icelanders are always sick, Englishmen never) or on horseback. Auden learned to ride, stayed at inns and farmhouses, and struggled to be offhand about the scenery. ("One waterfall is very much like another.") He soon succumbed to a certain "effect of travel, which is to make one reflect on one's past and one's culture from the outside." He had brought along a volume of Byron, and he began to cast into a variation of the *Don Juan* stanza, with light-verse freedom, the thoughts and part of the life-history of an English poet of twenty-nine, then isolated at the top of Europe, where modern roars and squawks penetrated but faintly. The "Letter to Lord Byron," which makes up five chapters of the book, is always a remarkable technical *tour de force,* and in spite of its tendency to slip into rather self-preening triviality, has its moments of insight. Through this disused Byronic stanza form, Auden once more helps to break up the limiting measures which have hardened around modern poetic expression, and which force poets into stock attitudes, usually of pomposity or gloom. This stanza can accommodate the casual mention of everyday experience, as an example written after Auden's return to England shows:

> Autumn is here. The beech leaves strew the lawn:
> > The power stations take up heavier loads;
> The massive lorries shake from dusk till dawn
> > The houses on the residential roads;
> > The shops are full of coming winter modes.
> Dances have started at the Baths next door;
> Stray scraps of MS strew my bedroom floor.[1]

Louis MacNeice, a poet of Auden's time at Oxford, who has brought a special kind of North-of-Ireland talent into the younger English group, joined the amateur expedition. Things went on much the same. The friends played rummy in the evening and traveled through the severe and ungrateful countryside by day. MacNeice's serious contributions to the book—three poems—do not suffer by comparison with Auden's fine introductory poem, "Journey to Iceland." His lighter contributions are extravagantly funny. The two noticed different things. The spectacle of a whale being torn to pieces by winches gave Auden "an extraordinary vision of the cold controlled ferocity of the human species." MacNeice was impressed by children singing "The Music Goes Round and Round" in their native tongue.

The authors have not shirked the factual side of their job. The book has maps, charts, and guidebook information on food, transportation, money, etc., as well as quoted accounts of historic events, a bibliography of books on Iceland, and a set of Icelandic proverbs. Nor have Icelandic arts and letters, or the character and habits of modern Icelanders, been neglected. The photographic illustrations are excellent.

A good many readers must still exist who hope that bleak landscapes have an elevating influence on the human spirit, who believe that the uplift element in glaciers must be considerable. To them this book will be a disappointment. It will also disappoint those who, in their secret heart of hearts, expect portentous statements from serious and gifted young poets. Auden and MacNeice often sound, it is true, a tiresome schoolboy note. Their continual determination not to be taken in by cant makes them sheer away from emotion. The "Last Will and Testament" at the end of the book, for example, spirals up through sheer brilliance into a region where only *Coterie-sprache* [the inside joke] can breathe. On the other hand, it is a sign of health that both young men are capable not only of humor but of hilarity. And they never project individual fear and frustration out into current blanket hatreds. Their will and testament ends:

> We leave our age the quite considerable spark
> Of private love and goodness which never leaves
> An age, however awful, in the utter dark . . .
> And to the good who know how wide the gulf, how deep
> Between Ideal and Real, who being good have felt

The final temptation to withdraw, sit down and weep,
We pray the power to take upon themselves the guilt
Of human action, though still as ready to confess
The imperfection of what can and must be built,
The wish and power to act, forgive and bless.

[1937]

1. Auden's stanza form in "Letter to Lord Byron," yet more unusual than Byron's eight-line *Don Juan* stanza, is narrative rhyme royal.

The Oxford Book of Light Verse

SOME YEARS ago, W. H. Auden, with a collaborator, produced an anthology designed to lure English schoolboys toward the forbidding subject of "poetry."[1] Now, in the preface to *The Oxford Book of Light Verse,* which he has edited, he has set himself the task of proving why poetry has lost, in great measure, its power to express ordinary life and delight the general ear. The fault, he says, lies with the results of the Industrial Revolution, which broke up an agricultural society, moved people from their bases, made the division between classes sharper, and drove the poet into gloomy Romanticism and into specialized groups of his own kind: "introspective, obscure, and highbrow." A good society, Auden concludes, is the only society which can survive, and a poet in such a society will be able to "write poetry which is simple, clear and gay; light and adult."

Long ago, from an entirely different point of view—that of the "pure artist"—Yeats gave much the same reasons for poetry's muddle and decline. Poetry, he said, flourished in "the hut and the castle." It is the middle classes, bred in strength by the Industrial Revolution, that have no appreciation of poetry's impact. From simple working people come folk songs, gay snatches of all sorts, chanteys, proverbs, and nursery rhymes. From levels of society where leisure allows a cultivated taste to flourish comes verse written with high skill: epigrams and various forms of verbal play. The middle classes, with skimpy standards and frightened, insecure taste, produce nothing but a great dislike for "vulgarity" and a passion for verse reeking of sentiment or sounding, in some vague way, uplifting and "noble."

Auden takes light verse to include verse "which is neither emotional nor obscure, but . . . casual in content, popular and unpretentious in form, and easily understood." Light verse, he adds, can be serious. (Eliot proves this with his early *Poems,* although Auden does not mention the fact.) But light verse, primarily, is to be enjoyed. To quote Yeats again: "Only that which does not teach, does not cry out, does not persuade, does not condescend, does not explain, is irresistible."

There is no doubt whatever that the poems in Auden's collections are irresistible. From Chaucer through Skelton and the anonymous writers of lovely little carols, ballads, and rhymes (how nice to see "Hey, diddle, diddle" appreciated!); from Shakespeare's and Ben Jonson's songs to Herrick and *Hudibras;* from Marvell to Dryden ("London Bridge" comes in around here); from Swift's verses on his death, that masterful combination of cultivated form and ordinary speech, to Gay, Pope, Burns, and Blake; from a fine collection of rough Irish ballads on to Lamb, Landor, Tom Moore, Byron, Barham, Hood, and Praed (who is said to have influenced Pushkin), the lightness, the fancy, and the realism flow. Then, after an anonymous alphabetical song on the Corn Laws, we are treated to the full nonsensical talents of Lear, Carroll, and W. S. Gilbert. Auden has long been enthusiastic about American folk songs; he includes unhackneyed Negro spirituals along with "Casey Jones," "The Man on the Flying Trapeze," and "Frankie and Johnny" ("orally collected"). We get light verse from unexpected people: Hardy, Lawrence, Housman, V[achel] Lindsay are printed near Yeats. The more professional modern writers of gay rhyme have been omitted. The whole anthology is so completely clear of the musty, the pompous, the would-be, and the hateful sides of mankind that it makes confidence in the human breed mount. It would be fine to have a New Society to match it.

[1938]

1. W. H. Auden and John Garrett, eds., *The Poet's Tongue,* in two volumes (G. Bell, 1935).

The Double Man

NEW LIFE can come into an art only when that art becomes more casual in tone. A shift in emphasis or a change in subject matter does no good. A stuffy state of mind and a bigwig style will stifle a poem about sharecroppers as quickly as a poem about peacocks in the twilight. Once rigidity or efflorescence has set in, it is useless to try to escape the effects. Something else, completely different, must be done. Change must be sharp; the whole encumbered ground must be cleared, and this clearing can only be the direct result of an examination of conscience which brings humility.

Obscured as modern poetry has been by every kind of rhetorical curlicue, intellectual pretension, and spiritual gloom, the reaction had to be fundamental. W. H. Auden, in his new book, *The Double Man,* has cleared a lot away, including much of his former self. He returns to the nice, crisp, open beat of four-stress iambic lines and to the couplets of the letter in rhyme, and he has reduced modern wisdom (of which there is some) to the simple proposition that man is not perfect, or perhaps even perfectible; he must, however, keep going and try to do the best he can. Expecting the impossible of himself, and failing to achieve it, leads to dangerous self-contempt, panic, and despair.

In a rhymed letter to a trusted friend one can tell the truth, bring in many things not accessible otherwise to poetry, make a running comment upon the world and one's own soul without becoming pompous, examine the surroundings without pedantry. Auden does all these things in the "New Year Letter (1940)," of some seventeen hundred lines, addressed to Elizabeth Mayer. The poem is followed by a series of notes taking up more pages than the poem itself. These notes will undoubtedly irritate readers eager for a smooth flow of poetry as such, especially since some of the notes are irreverent. Believers in man's sublimity and the social optimists alike are in for a few jolts here. Auden ranges over embryology, psychiatry, anthropology, history, metaphysics, sociology, and modern views on the nature of the universe. He quotes Chekhov, Henry James, Margaret Mead, the authors of *Middletown,* Søren Kierkegaard, Kafka, Rilke, Wolfgang Köhler, Thucydides, and Carl Jung, among others. That it is a real enjoyment to read these notes and relate them to Auden's text will not count, perhaps, to outraged specialists in the various fields. Other people will not care for the thought of the poet as student, notebook in hand, and not wrapped in a prophetic garment.

Quite apart from its sources and philosophy, "New Year Letter" is a pleasure to read. It is full of the aphorisms proper to, and charming in, the rhymed couplet. It runs to straight, unadorned nouns and verbs, so that the occasional epithet comes as an accent and surprise. The poem has two climaxes of real power. One of these is a lyric burst, an actual emotional passage of a kind Auden has not up to now been given to.

A group, chiefly of sonnets, "The Quest," follows. It is in Auden's former manner and sounds a little composed. A short epilogue and prologue to the volume continue the cool, reticent sincerity into which Auden seems steadily to be working.

[1941]

For the Time Being

EVEN BEFORE *The Double Man,* Auden had changed from a closed dogmatic materialist belief toward an open moral faith. The general effect of the two long poems in his new book—*The Sea and the Mirror: A Commentary on Shakespeare's "The Tempest,"* and the title poem, written in the form of a Christmas oratorio—is one of restlessness under control, of talent steadied and enlarged. The two poems, taken together, constitute the most minute dissection of the spiritual illness of our day that any modern poet, not excluding Eliot, has given us.

We are unfortunately used to writers who repeat their pattern, from youth to age, without deviation. They begin as young sheep or young goats and end up as old sheep or old goats. Americans are suspicious of "conversions." In a country where the strongest religious coloring is that of romantic Evangelicalism, we associate conversion with revivalism and expect a spiritual change to be an emotional reaction, slightly hysterical in character. Auden's change occurred on a non-romantic level, in a region where the beliefs of Christianity and the proofs of modern psychological knowledge meet. Auden has taken less time than Eliot, indulged in fewer gestures, put less emphasis on ritual, in his search for a religious attitude. A streak of York-shire common sense, underneath his complexity, has kept the younger man on the side of simple feeling and away from elaborate orthodoxy.

The Sea and the Mirror deals with Shakespeare's *Tempest* characters after the ending of their play. Each character finds himself, but only according to his original capacity. Nothing whatever happens to the truly evil or silly people. As it turns out, the thoughts of the reformed intriguer, Alonso, King of Naples, are more interesting and more poignantly expressed than the thoughts of the reformed magician, Prospero. Alonso's letter to Ferdinand, on the delights and dangers of power, is one of the high points in Auden. The speeches are a little museum of form: one in *terza rima* is followed by a ses-tina, a sonnet, and a ballade. The long concluding speech of Caliban to the audience, written in a prose which combines certain characteristics of the later Henry James with baroque periods comparable to the prose of Donne and Bossuet, has an eloquence that one would have supposed a modern poet incapable of producing; and the analysis, in this speech, of the modern spiri-tual *malaise* restores to literature a subject long neglected under the present-day pressure of "rational" thought. The lengthy, exact, intricate, and many times terrifying recital is a perfect answer to those advocates of "useful" poetry who would reduce all expression to a mechanical base. There appear to be qualities in the human spirit, even now, that require a full rhetorical diapason for complete expression.

The oratorio, *For the Time Being,* deals in a different way with the problem of modern spiritual estrangement and offers a way out through faith and suf-fering. Auden here has undertaken a technical problem of large proportions. He is trying to get formal poetry working on a larger than usual scale and to link it to music and the human voice, from both of which it has been long alienated. He has gone back to the one big musical form where English poetry has been successfully employed. The oratorio, under Handel, suc-ceeded in enlarging the English song into choral magnificence. Auden gets much variety and dramatic contrast into his own work. Its lyric passages are moving, its satire (as in the Herod speech) sharp, its philosophic passages (the Simeon meditation) articulate, its humor sometimes lively and some-times appropriately horrifying. We again realize how limited and barren the field of modern poetry has become when we are presented with such a num-ber of human thoughts and emotions, boldly designed and arranged to set one another off. This elaborate work has an interest, an intellectual validity, an emotional range so rare that it should be read with the seriousness and attention it deserves. That it has been seriously composed, as opposed to being thrown together for effect, is as evident after a tenth reading as after a first.

[1944]

The Collected Poetry of W. H. Auden

A MOMENT OCCURS (or should occur) when the growing artist is able to bequeath his tricks to his imitators. The mature writer rejects the treasured "originality" and the darling virtuosities of his apprenticeship in art, as well as the showy sorrows and joys of his apprenticeship to life, often just in time. "How they live at home in their cozy poems and make long stays in narrow comparisons!" Rilke once said, speaking of the run of versifiers who never change or grow. Once youth's embroidered coat is cast aside, what is left? Only imagination, ripened insight, experience, and the trained sense of language, which are usually enough.

The Collected Poetry of W. H. Auden is a sizable volume for a poet born in 1907 to have credited to him in 1945. Auden, it has for some time been apparent, has succeeded Eliot as the strongest influence in American and British poetry. And he has managed, in this collection, by skillful arrangement and deletion, to present himself to the reader as he exists at this moment. He does not draw attention to his growing pains or take us step by step through stage after stage of his development. He begins the book with one of those poems ("Musée des Beaux Arts") which announced, a few years ago, the beginnings of his maturity—a poem that seems as simply composed as a passage in conversation. It is not filled with Anglo-Saxon compression, or clogged with modern apparatuses and machines, or trimmed with off-rhymes. Earlier poems on his favorite subjects and in the special manner of his youth are included in the book. But they never leap out at us. The general tone is one of composure and simplicity, of that ease wherein, for a time, a young master can rest.

The collection gathers up, fortunately, poems that have so far been scattered in plays or books of prose. The sonnet to E. M. Forster once served as the dedication for *Journey to a War*, written in collaboration with Christopher Isherwood. Other sonnets and a verse commentary come from the same volume. The fine "Journey to Iceland" is out of *Letters from Iceland*, written in collaboration with Louis MacNeice. Some choruses from plays turn up as separate poems, now with titles. The volume also contains two prose passages —the early "Letter to a Wound" and a "sermon" (from *The Dog Beneath the Skin*) entitled "Depravity." *For the Time Being* is reprinted complete, and there are several new poems.

What is the particular thread that runs through this collection, the clue to Auden's importance and power? In what way is his great gift different from Eliot's, and in what way is it of importance to Auden's contemporaries? Auden shares with Eliot a sense of his time. He is, however, much more exuberant, restless, sanguine, and unself-conscious than the older poet. And he is a natural dramatist in a degree surpassing Eliot. Eliot can dramatize his lyrics but rarely projects dramatic action with force. Auden dramatizes everything he touches. He is wonderfully effective with that most dramatic of lyric forms, the ballad. At the same time, his purely lyrical endowment is so deep and so natural that many of his songs sound as though they had been worked up at a moment's notice as improvisations. He can sing about as many things as the Elizabethans, and with the same disregard for the demands of the high literary line and the "refined" literary tone.

Eliot's importance is based on the fact that he had the sensitiveness and the melancholy foreboding to sense the general tragedy of his period when that tragedy had not yet impressed other observers. Auden, nearly twenty years Eliot's junior, stands farther from the shadow of the nineteenth and early twentieth centuries; he is more able, therefore, to deal with particulars. He is conscious of his physical surroundings down to the last contraption of "light alloys and glass"; conscious of his spiritual scene down to the last sob of modern self-pity, down to modern brutality's last threat. He has smashed the "taboo against tenderness," as someone has said; he is not afraid or ashamed either to laugh or weep. (How gloomy everyone was, after Eliot!) He knows what Rilke felt and foresaw, what Kierkegaard rebelled against, what modern psychiatry has plumbed. He is not ignorant of facts or clumsy in dealing with them. He is able to absorb and speak of any item in the extraordinary crowd of objects and techniques he finds on all sides. He is able to define and present a range of ideas, passions, compulsions, manias, anxieties, fears, and intuitions that at present float about, only half-perceived by many people and most poets, in our intellectual and emotional climate. He is at once able to act and to imagine, to formulate and interpret.

Behind him stand exemplars he acknowledges—Rilke and Henry James, Freud, the Symbolists and post-Symbolists, and Surrealism at its most effective. Part of the excitement in reading the volume through derives from the fact that we are dealing with a poet one of whose inner urges will always be to transcend himself, that we are reading the work of one who is still a young man, so that there will be more to come.

[1945]

The Age of Anxiety

A HEALTHY AND civilized poetry should be able to express anything. It should be varied, comprehensive, and flexible. Experiments in the larger poetic forms have in our period lagged far behind experiments in poetic texture—experiments, that is, in language as such. Modern poets have been haunted by the now completely outdated formal poetic play. Shakespearean drama has cast a particularly strong spell over poets writing in English. The nagging belief that somehow the poetic drama could be restored to its former immense prestige has hampered the most gifted of contemporaries. Even Eliot and Auden have succumbed to the temptation to tinker with decrepit dramatic machines. Recently, however, Auden has given up these attempts and has applied himself, singlehanded, to the task of creating new semi-dramatic structures. He has already written an oratorio. His new work, *The Age of Anxiety,* bears the subtitle "A Baroque Eclogue." In this long poem, a series of conversations, dramatic monologues, and occasional songs, he tries to crystallize to some degree the fluidity and complexity of modern character, and at the same time, as a dramatic poet should, to stylize the commonplace, everyday scene and event.

The dilemmas of the Romantic hero, fighting it out against Fate, are no longer fully satisfying or evocative to a modern audience. In a period when values are uneven, when motives are warped and masked, when the citizenry does not know exactly who it is or where it is, a poetic form is called for that combines short surveys of the situation at large with detailed inquiries into individual human types. An eclogue, as any professor will tell you, is a pastoral poem in the form of a conversation—pastoral and primitive in the time of Theocritus, and highly sophisticated during the eighteenth century. Auden's adjective "baroque" suggests the fanciful. His eclogue, far from being pastoral, starts with a conversation in a city bar, goes off into a dream sequence, proceeds (with dialogue, monologue, and song) to the apartment of the single female character, and finally frays out in the subway and the city streets. Practically nothing happens, yet a good many matters are analyzed by means of that poetic "reason" in which the happy guesses of the imagination, as well as the oddest suggestions of fancy, play a part. While his characters occupy themselves in giving various answers to their own questions (Why do I feel so queer? Is it the general situation or is it I? Who are all these other people, and are they baffled in the same way that I am baffled?), Auden takes on a subsidiary task—to point up and freshen the language with which they communicate with one another. Avoiding the more threadbare English metres, he works in a closely stressed line reminiscent of Anglo-Saxon prosody. He also uses alliteration with great vigor and freedom, exploring its more elegant as well as its massive and powerful possibilities. Again, he makes use, when the occasion requires, of archaic and obsolete words, not as a casual affectation but in order to weight, diversify, and amuse, and he deals easily with the American vernacular: witness his superb stylization of the radio commercial. Here experimental language, rescued from the useless doldrums into which the Surrealists have forced it, is restored as a useful tool in the serious poet's equipment.

This modern eclogue is clearly transitional, but by intention, not by chance. And the characters never lapse into the dullness of allegory. They are symbols, but with enough admixture of human reality to make them interesting and plausible. The general tone of the poem is that of high comedy. Auden is not attempting to plumb the deepest labyrinths of the heart and mind. He is making a survey of contemporary manners and morals on the basis of what he considers the highest sort of ideal—the Christian. But he allows crosslights from other ideals to fall upon his scene: see Rosetta's speech on Israel, for example.

Auden has now reached a middle period, in which it is difficult for any poet not to indulge in self-repetition or self-parody. He has largely managed to dodge both these traps. His inventive powers, both in language and form, are still enormous, and it is delightful to watch him go about the task of re-vivifying old rules. Assonance, consonance, alliteration, an ancient, closely stressed rhythm—all these poetic procedures he frees from the books of rhetoric, so that they again function in living poetry.

[1947]

Poets of the English Language

THE STUDY of English literature as a respectable branch of learning is comparatively new. It came into being in a faltering fashion, making its appearance at Oxford as late as 1893, after having been put into practice at the new University of London and in Scotland. Once accepted, the new subject had to fight free from one hampering method after another. First it had to escape from the dry procedures of German philology, then from an equally arid habit among English professors of erecting barriers between "literary periods" and of implacably tracking down influences and sources. This methodology was abandoned, under Professors Saintsbury and Raleigh, only to be succeeded by teaching habits that substituted charm for insight, so that the central qualities of English poetry and prose were more or less obscured by masses of anecdotes and chitchat about the lives, domestic problems, wives, friends, and dogs and cats of this author and that. During the twenties of this century, the emphasis shifted to the texts themselves—a shift all to the good, except that such direct analysis soon became extreme. In the case of verse, the poem was removed so far from any contact or contamination (even from the poet who had written it) that it became a sort of laboratory specimen, and its dissection, in some scholarly quarters at least, was pursued with the relentless fervor usually allotted to a delicate, purely manual operation, like the boning of a shad.

The critical and scholarly need that has gradually become pressing and obvious, as psychology, anthropology, and a freshly ventilated sense of history have begun to crowd in upon the study of literature from every side, is one of relation and comparison. Although the subject of comparative literature has grown in importance, the relationship between literatures of different cultures and languages, between literature and the changes of history and opinion, of morals and manners, and between literature and its sister arts does not show up in many commentaries or textbooks. *Poets of the English Language* in five volumes, edited by W. H. Auden and Norman Holmes Pearson, is a pioneer effort to place poetry in the midst of history and life, and to connect it to other arts with which it shares a common creative source. The two editors, both scholars and teachers and one of them a major poet, are uniquely fitted for a task that involves revaluation as well as valuation. The selections range from the Middle Ages through modern times, but the editors have wisely sidestepped controversy by not touching upon the work of living contemporaries. The first volume, "Langland to Spenser," brings English poetry through Middle English (which, as the editors remark, was close to being the language of a tribe) to the beginning of the "Shakespearean poetic temper," when English became the language of a nation. Volume II, "Marlowe to Marvell," deals with the poetic situation throughout the English Renaissance into the Baroque era; Volume III traces the story through a century of tremendous upheaval and change, from Milton to Goldsmith; Volume IV, "Blake to Poe," covers the early and great Romantics; and Volume V, "Tennyson to Yeats," copes with the Victorians and their successors, down to the year 1914. The introductions to the volumes describe, often with great originality, not only the central emotional, intellectual, and power drives of succeeding eras but take into account the more subtle climates of opinion, feeling, and taste that pervaded this or that period. These prefaces, moreover, emphasize the fact that while literature is produced by human beings, it is also touched by the mystery of the Muse—frequently breaking into new life and form just as history has, as it were, stopped happening; or at a moment when a culture seems so exhausted that nothing in the circumstances hints at the possibility of a renewal of imaginative life.

The editors' important achievement of relating poetry in English to European, British, and American history at large, over six centuries, has been accomplished with a minimum of machinery. Each volume opens with a calendar, one side of which lists poetry, work by work, while a neighboring column establishes the general background, event by event. This calendar, although it often bears out certain Spenglerian hypotheses, lacks any Spenglerian concealed pressures. To study its exposition of coincidences, time lags, and unexpected linkages is a delightful occupation. Here is French Impressionist painting showing up in the same year (1863) as Taine's "determinist" history of English literature and a year after Meredith's *Modern Love*. Here is Frazer's *The Golden Bough,* published in 1890, along with the first series of Emily Dickinson's *Poems*. Nobel invents dynamite in 1867, the year of *Peer Gynt* and Mark Twain's *The Jumping Frog;*[1] and Freud's *Die Traumdeutung* [interpretation of dreams] announces a new century, in 1900, contemporaneously with *Sister Carrie* and Stedman's *An American Anthology.* The tragic year 1914 has Joyce's *Dubliners,* Stein's *Tender Buttons* and Frost's *North of Boston* to its credit.

As many long works as possible are given in their entirety—*Antony and Cleopatra* and *Samson Agonistes,* for example. And the editors have not turned away from poems bristling with difficulty, such as Hopkins's "The Wreck of the *Deutschland.*" The unexpected and the neglected (for instance, the hymns of the Methodist Revival, and the light and nonsense verse with which the Victorians worked off some of their unconscious conflicts) appear beside the "standard" pieces of the English poetic repertoire, while the poetry of two great "mad" poets, John Clare and Christopher Smart, brilliantly set off the works of their more reasonable contemporaries. Neglected Americans —Thoreau, Melville, and Longfellow as a translator—are given their just due. E. Talbot Donaldson has been called in to write a note on Middle English, and Auden contributes a short survey of English prosody that is certainly as valuable to the lover of poetry in English as a knowledge of musical form is to an amateur of music. *Poets of the English Language* is a peculiarly modern achievement. It could have been produced only in our time, and it is a work for which we should be grateful and of which we should be proud.

[1951]

1. Mark Twain, *The Celebrated Jumping Frog of Calaveras County, and Other Sketches* (1867), a collection of twenty-six stories and journalistic sketches.

The Shield of Achilles

IN THE fall of 1935, Auden and Spender, along with C. Day Lewis, formed (in spite of basic differences) a triad in the minds of British and American readers, because of a shared Oxford background and an awareness of poetry's "social" obligation. In troubled times, they had taken to heart Wilfred Owen's dictum that the duty of a poet is to "warn." The refreshment brought into the poetry of the thirties by these gifted and serious young men was strongly apparent from the beginning; this new "poetry of conviction" immediately began to influence contemporaries young and old. And at the very start it was evident that Auden was the versatile satirist and Spender the "Romantic" of the group. These two were, in fact, so much each other's opposite that they acted as mutual foils, and their roles have not altered with the years.

Auden, in his latest volume, *The Shield of Achilles,* continues to treat his material with the incisive wit that is capable of serving the most serious ends. He is ceaselessly restless and inquisitive, inexhaustibly inventive, full of curious ancient and modern erudition, filled with strong likes and dislikes, and still profoundly involved with modern dilemmas, although his emphasis has shifted from political to moral and spiritual areas. He has a sense of evil as well as a sense of history, and has developed what could be called a sort of modern "occasional" poem that becomes a commodious carrier not only for his general ideas, predilections, and frankly expressed prejudices but for some genuine, though often wryly revealed, feeling. His "Bucolics," included in the volume, are examples of this delightful form, which should become valuable to poets at large as a great change and relief from the rather hampering dramatic monologue and the verbal showpiece composed on the subject of nothing. Always a master of the vernacular, Auden, an American citizen since 1946, has recently managed to shift his diction and conceits close to the main stream of American humor—a supremely difficult feat for a native Briton. It is as though he had been able to tap some common source of wild and irrepressible comedy. Purists bothered by Auden's "unserious" side should be impressed by the sense of measure and the religious intuitions (humane and without a trace of gloom) in the sequence "Horae Canonicae." Auden, at forty-eight, not only has fulfilled promises but keeps on renewing them.

[1955]

The Criterion Book of Modern American Verse

AUDEN, AS editor, wisely casts a wide net into American poetry of the last fifty years—a net, moreover, in which the meshes are not too coarse and not too fine. He does not draw back from talents that are small but pure, and the inclusion of such talents gives the book a density that is interesting and valuable. For Auden, it is a poet's sincerity and intensity that count. The poets are arranged chronologically, and the list, because it begins with Edwin Arlington Robinson (1869–1935), to whom fame came late, can include two pre-moderns, Stephen Crane and Trumbull Stickney, who died young. From Gertrude Stein, happily considered as the poet she was, through Anthony Hecht (b. 1922), Auden marshals material that in one way or another deserves mention, but there is nothing routine or formal about his choice. The experimentalists appear along with poets working in conventional form; the writers of light verse complement their more serious kin; many neglected figures are given their due, while a few inflated reputations are gently cut down to size. Auden leaves out Eliot and himself, and while we understand the underlying tact involved (since, in the broader sense, both men can be considered American), both omissions constitute a major loss.

In his introduction, Auden points out several differences that, he has found, distinguish American poets from their European counterparts. In the first place, Americans tend to think of themselves as unique individuals and not as members of a professional class or brotherhood; secondly, since Americans are more loosely related to tradition, they can more easily break free from it. As a result, American poets differ greatly from one another even within a single generation or "school." The danger of this sense of individuality, Auden goes on to say, shows up occasionally in strain and overearnestness; the danger is not of writing like everybody else but of crankiness and a final parody of one's own manner. In a footnote Auden speaks of "the undeniable appearance in the States during the last fifteen years or so of a certain literary conformity, of a proper and authorized way to write poetry," but he refuses to link this tendency to any one cause, such as the role of patron to poet, which American colleges and universities began to take on during those years. He realizes that several factors have joined to produce poetic conformity at mid-century. "The modern" has now reached the officially accepted stage in every art, and with official acceptance a noticeable slowing down of impetus and stiffening of method is sure to take place. Poetry, in America as elsewhere, has not escaped this process.

[1957]

Homage to Clio

W. H. AUDEN's latest collection of poems proves his continuing power as an international poetic force. Auden assumed the position of leader of a poetic movement early in the thirties, while he was still a student at Oxford, and in 1939 he finally chose America as his permanent base of operation, where he became, at thirty-nine, an American citizen. The *chef d'école*,[1] a usual phenomenon on the Continent, is rare in England and even rarer here. Our literary community has been, and continues to be, so loosely organized that a poetic forerunner or innovator may either fall into sudden neglect (Whitman) or take to such eccentric ways that he sacrifices prestige (Pound). The poet as leader must have convictions as well as originality, and he must have the ability to pass on a fair proportion of what he knows or has invented. And so his audience narrows, for his students and disciples will for the most part be workers in his own field. Nowadays he does not have to be physically accessible, as Mallarmé made himself during his evenings in the Rue de Rome, but he must be fluent and industrious enough to display his ideas regularly in print, in prose as well as verse, so that any alteration in his method or change in his point of view can be freely indicated. It is a position that can be extremely wearing. At present, in a free, literate society, a teaching poet's followers, by the weight of their numbers and the intensity of their attention, can exhaust the very powers they admire. Their poet is in constant peril of being battered, psychically and spiritually, into unrecognizable shape or of being egged on to performances that are not natural to his gifts.

Auden, now fifty-three, has withstood these pressures for many years. His new book shows no corruption of subject, distortion of aim, or souring of emotion. The bravura of his early work has to a great extent disappeared, but the technical dexterity remains unfailing, and his new poems, often written in the simplest and most seemingly artless of forms, continue to advance from point to point with satisfying skill. Auden has not suffered, moreover, from that constriction of interest that often afflicts poets, like other human beings, as they move from youth to age. He has kept in touch with what is going on, and he has remained cool, sensible, and good-tempered without losing hold of his talent for diagnosis and interpretation. He credits Clio, the Muse of History, with secrecy and silence, but he is more aware than many of his contemporaries of what she has already said and what she is at the moment preparing to say. He has always been conscious that he is living in the midst of a historical and cultural situation quite unlike any other, and he has kept on as a student of the facts from which this situation stems. He is not afraid of being light (it would be an unnaturally severe reader who could bring a charge of frivolity against the series of clerihews[2] at the end of this volume) or official (he can write occasional verse that exceeds, in weight and meaning, its ostensible function). But it is in his mastery of the dark and difficult theme that he continues to show his full authority. The poems "Dame Kind," "An Island Cemetery," and "Goodbye to the Mezzogiorno," and the prose notes on personal love—shocking, profound, complex, and warmly satiric, in turn—are new works from which the general reader, as well as the student, can derive nourishment now and for a long time to come.

[1960]

1. "*chef d'école*": head of the movement or school.
2. clerihews: epigrammatic biographies in comic couplets.

Henry James

The Princess Casamassima

FOR ALL the varied critical attention given, in the last twenty years, to the novels of Henry James, those of his middle period are seldom read. When they are read, their real intention is often missed or is interpreted in some peculiar, special way. F. R. Leavis has recently pointed out several flagrant misinterpretations of James (including the classic mistake made by the critic who thought Isabel Archer divorced her husband and married an American businessman at the end of *The Portrait of a Lady*) and has explained the neglect of the early and middle James by the fact that readers, steered toward the works of the late, "difficult" period, and baffled by these, make no further investigation. The three books which, appearing in the center of James's career, fully exemplify the virtues of his early manner—*The Bostonians, The Princess Casamassima,* and *The Tragic Muse*—are those most completely ignored.

The Princess Casamassima, it is true, has recently come in for some attention, since critics interested in novels concerned with revolutionary activities have discovered that in this book James deals with revolutionaries in the financially depressed London of the eighties. Although I cannot claim to have unearthed every scrap of material written about this book, I have read a fair amount and can say that not one commentator has shown signs of understanding the design James has so clearly presented in it. Usually *The Princess* has been put down as a melodramatic and rather fumbling attempt at a novel dealing with a revolutionary theme.

Several good reasons exist for these critical misconceptions, but before we deal with them, it would be well to get clear in our minds, since one of the charges against the book is that its material has not been thoroughly grasped, exactly what degree of mastery over his material, of insight into his characters, James had reached when he wrote it. *The Princess* was probably written concurrently with *The Bostonians.* Both novels were complete failures when they appeared (in 1886). James believed in both books, although for reasons that remain obscure he did not include *The Bostonians* in the definitive New York Edition. But *The Princess* was included, with a preface which delicately but firmly pointed up the book's intention.

During the seventies James had produced no completely successful long work. And certainly *Watch and Ward* (1878) and *Confidence* (1880) are not only the most clumsy novels ever signed by James but the most clumsy pieces of fiction ever signed by a man of genius. They display the unsure approach of the writer who is doing it all from the outside—from the notebook, the stiff plan, the bad guess. Through some spurt of development James, in 1881, wrote the finely balanced, deeply observed *Washington Square* and *The Portrait of a Lady*. He was now able to base his books upon his characters, as opposed to supporting the action with some artificial diagram of conduct. Each character now casts light and shadow and is in turn accented or illuminated by the darkness or brilliance of the others. James had not finished profiting from Balzac, but he was now Turgenev's intelligent pupil as well. The realistic method was becoming more effortless at the same time that the technique of suggestion took in more territory with greater ease—so that the chance of James's fumbling, at this period, any problem he put his hand to is small.

The Princess Casamassima, it is true, opens with a block of Balzacian realism mixed with Dickensian melodrama that is extremely hard for modern readers to accept. In the later chapters of the book detail and suspense are to be brought in with sureness and ease; every part of the situation is to be elucidated by that sure technical skill so characteristic of the pre-theatre James. The first three chapters, however, are thick with underlining and filled with a kind of cardboard darkness. The characters are so overloaded with reasons that they closely approach the line dividing drama from burlesque. The delicate little boy called Hyacinth, the son of a French working girl who is also a murderess, and an earl, her victim; Miss Pynsent, the tender old maid who has raised the child; Mr. Vetch, the battered fiddler with leanings toward anarchism—at first glance these appear cut out of whole cloth. And in spite of a few flashes of insight, the scene in which Hyacinth witnesses his mother's death in prison is dated and overcharged. Thus balked at the outset, it is little wonder that the reader expects to find a measure of falseness everywhere in the story.

Given the remarkable figure of Hyacinth and the remarkable fact of his sharply divided inheritance, what use does James make of them? It may be best to give the story in bare outline. Hyacinth, grown to young manhood, is apprenticed to M. Poupin, an exiled veteran both of '48 and the Commune. (Hyacinth's own maternal grandfather, James tells us at an early point, died on the Paris barricades.) Poupin teaches him revolutionary principles along with the trade (James considers it a minor art) of bookbinding. The youth then meets the two people who are to bring about the crisis in his life. The Princess Casamassima, separated from her husband and foot-loose in London on her husband's money, first dazzles Hyacinth with her interest in revolutionary plots and then with her interest in himself. And Paul Muniment, son of a north-country miner, an active, realistic, and inscrutable worker deep in revolutionary activities, attracts the ardent boy. Hyacinth actually gives over his life to Muniment, promising in a moment of enthusiasm that he will be the instrument for an act of violence whenever the need arises. Muniment accepts his pledge and binds Hyacinth fully, by a vow taken before witnesses. Hyacinth tells the Princess, after she has given him some minor glimpses of the great world, of his origin and dedication. Miss Pynsent dies; her small legacy enables Hyacinth to go to the Continent. He comes back changed. What he has seen has convinced him that certain objects, of which he had no former notion, should be preserved, not destroyed. The Princess has meanwhile met Muniment. She brings her charm to bear on him, with the secondary purpose of extricating Hyacinth from his vow; but primarily to get herself deeper into true conspiratorial circles. Hyacinth, whose determination to do what he can to further the cause of the people remains unchanged in spite of his secret change of heart, thinks that the pair have cast him off. Then the call comes: a duke is to be assassinated and Hyacinth is picked by the mysterious instigator of these affairs to be the assassin. The revolutionary group, at this news, splits into two factions: those who wish to save Hyacinth and those who are willing to let matters take their course. Muniment, although he professes sympathy for Hyacinth and says that he is free to choose, does nothing. The Princess rushes to save the boy and to offer herself in his stead. She and a kind, methodical German conspirator meet at Hyacinth's lodgings. But the boy has already shot himself, with the revolver meant for the assassination.

Critics have construed this story according to the set of their own convictions. Van Wyck Brooks, for example, although appreciative of James's success with Poupin, Vetch, Miss Pynsent, and others, considers Hyacinth an insufferable little snob. And Hyacinth is, according to Brooks, an embodiment of James's own yearning after the glories of the British upper classes.

> This unfortunate but remarkably organized youth . . . is conscious of
> nothing but the paradise of which he has been dispossessed. . . . In real

life the last thing that would have occurred to a young man of Hyacinth's position would have been to "roam and wander and yearn" about the gates of that lost paradise: he would have gone to Australia, or vanished into the slums, or continued *with the utmost indifference* at his *trade* of binding books. But this attitude represents the feeling of Hyacinth's creator. [Italics LB's]

C. Hartley Grattan believes that Hyacinth's "sense of deprivation" vitiates the worth of his radical impulses:

> The conviction that it is senseless to do anything, no matter how small the act, to destroy the upper classes leads to the climax of the novel in Hyacinth's suicide.

But Grattan admits James's insight into his material.

When the social-minded young English disinterred the book some years ago because of its theme, Stephen Spender wrote in *The Destructive Element:*

> The observation of political types in this book is really remarkable and curiously undated. . . . Paul Muniment . . . is a true revolutionary type. He has the egoism, the sense of self-preservation, the cynicism of a person who identifies himself so completely with a cause that he goes through life objectively guarding himself from all approach, as one might preserve for the supreme eventuality a very intricate and valuable torpedo.

Spender's evaluation of Hyacinth is this:

> Hyacinth, with his strong leaning toward the upper classes and yet feeling that he is somehow committed to the cause of the workers, might today have become a Socialist Prime Minister: a Ramsay MacDonald who . . . would dismay his followers by going over to the other side and becoming the most frequent visitor at large country houses and of dinners at Buckingham Palace.

Now Hyacinth, in the very essence of his character as James with great care and at considerable length presents it, could never become what Spender thinks he could become, any more than what Brooks thinks James should have made him become. Before turning to Hyacinth, let us examine the character of the Princess. Who is she? What is she? What has she been, and what is she likely to be? The development of her character must have meant a good deal to James since she is the only figure he ever "revived" and carried from one book to another.

She was Christina Light in *Roderick Hudson,* the character in that early work who evokes the mixed feelings of admiration and exasperation that James was later to call up through many of his women. She is the daughter of an Anglo-American shrew and adventuress who forces her, by a threat of scandal, into a marriage with the highest bidder. James managed to bring out, even at a time when his art was still imperfect, Christina's marred idealism and ignorant pride, so that they freshen every page on which she appears. The coarser and weaker people, in contrast with her straightforwardness, show up in a sorry way. Roderick Hudson, with whom she falls in love and whom she tries to galvanize into some kind of manhood, crumbles, after losing her, in much the same way, James makes us feel, as he would have crumbled had he won her. Brought up to deadening shifts, she has one flaw. She is not truly courageous. She marries the Prince at once after receiving the shock of her mother's revelations.

In the later book she is the single person who is continuously presented from the outside. James never "goes behind" her. We are never told what she thinks or how she feels; we merely see her act. James clearly presupposes a knowledge in the reader of her early tragedy. To watch her casting her charm and enthusiasm about; to see her reacting more and more violently against her money and position; to see her—after Muniment has told her that it is her money alone which interests his circle, and has prophesied her certain return to her husband now that the Prince has stopped the flow of that money—rushing in desperation to offer herself as a substitute in the affair of the duke's assassination—all this can puzzle us if we know nothing of the beautiful girl who moved through the scenes of *Roderick Hudson.*

Now "the cleverest woman in Europe," she bears a grudge against society strong enough to force her into repudiation of everything her trained taste fully values. When Hyacinth bares his own tragedy to her, the relation of the two is lifted out of a stupid contrast between a revolutionary-minded woman of the world and a talented pauper. For what the Princess knows, as she listens to him, and what the reader should also know, is that she is herself illegitimate. James, far from being taken in by it, deeply realizes that the life she represents is as undermined by the results of cruelty and passion, for all its beautiful veneer, as Hyacinth's own. Having failed in her youth to face a crisis and see it through, she knows in her heart that when she thinks of herself as "one of the numerous class who could be put on a tolerable footing only by a revolution," she is thinking dishonestly. It is her despair and her defects which push her toward extreme revolutionary enthusiasm, as much as her generosity of spirit. But in Hyacinth she recognizes—after she has emerged from her first sentimental ideas concerning him—complete devotion, consistency, and fineness. This boy "never makes mistakes," and is incapable of going back on a given promise. She shows him specimens of English county families, toward whom her own reaction is: "You know, people oughtn't to be both corrupt and dreary." But what Hyacinth tenders them, as he tenders her, beneath his devotion, is a kind of gentle pity.

For this son of a criminal and an aristocrat is not, as he has been made out to be, a little snob, an affected artisan with a divided nature and ambitions beyond his station. James with every subtle device of his mature art, from the first sentence describing him to the last, shows the boy as an artist, a clear, sensitive intelligence, filled with the imagination "which will always give him the clue about everything." James has endowed him, indeed, with the finest qualities of his own talent; and this is what is meant when James says that Hyacinth had watched London "very much as I had watched it." Hyacinth is, like James, "a person on whom nothing is lost." If the character has a fault, it is that James has distilled too purely into his creature the sharp insight, the capacity for selfless devotion, the sense of proportion, the talent for self-mockery and gentle irony which seldom exist in genius without an admixture of cruder ingredients. But James wanted a cool and undistorting mirror to shine between the dark and violent world of the disinherited on the one hand and the preposterous world of privilege on the other. Such a clear lens (Maisie, Nanda[1]) James was later to place in the center of psychological situations. He was never again to place it, and with the final polish of genius added, between social classes. For that matter it has never been placed there, up to the present, by anyone else, although Conrad, in *Under Western Eyes,* a book almost certainly modeled on *The Princess,* examined the revolutionary side of the picture through the clear spirit of Razumov. We are used, in fiction dealing with social problems, to the spectacle of the artist absorbed or deflected into one class or another. James kept Hyacinth detached to the end. And though the solution for the artist, in the insoluble situation James has constructed, is death, as the symbols of the two extremes he has instinctively rejected (after he knows that his own life must exist independently, apart from either) stand by his deathbed, we feel that what they both have been left to is not exactly life.

The book is full of wonderful moments. Short mention should be made of the ultimate opacity and brutality of Muniment, as he is shown in contrast not only to Hyacinth but to the more humane members of the revolutionary circle; of James's masterly analysis of Hyacinth's spiritual coming of age, resulting, on his return from abroad, in increased self-sufficiency and a more complete grasp of his work; of the complex rendering of Hyacinth's rejection of the thought of violence when his mother's murderous hands come before him; of the superb portraits of the solidly disillusioned Madame Grandoni, the morbidly jealous Prince, and those true fools and snobs— Captain Sholto and Muniment's horrible invalid sister. The scenes of submerged London have been praised. What is even more astonishing than these is James's knowledge of the relentless mechanisms of poverty—poverty's *minutiae.*

It is interesting to trace down the source of James's understanding of Muniment. We remember that the elder James was surrounded by socialists of the Fourier school, and that he "agreed with Fourier that vice and crime were the consequences of our present social order, and would not survive them." The younger James had, no doubt, seen Muniment's counterpart multiplied about him, in Fourier's more fanatical followers, in his childhood.

"Very likely . . . all my buried prose will kick off its tombstones at once," James wrote to Howells in 1888. After, it would seem, Stendhal's hundred years.[2]

[1936]

1. Characters at the center of *What Maisie Knew* (1889) and *The Awkward Age* (1899), respectively.

2. Stendhal (pen name of Marie-Henri Beyle, 1782–1842) spoke of entering his stylistically clipped novels like *The Red and the Black* in a lottery; the grand prize was "to be read in 1935," or a hundred years in the future.

The Later Phase

F. O. MATTHIESSEN's intelligent study of James's later period, *Henry James: The Later Phase,* appearing one year after the rather neglected James centenary, presages, it is to be hoped, other criticism directed toward the Works and produced by critics who do not hate James or misprise good writing. Matthiessen mentions at one point the present interest in the international scene as having some relation to a new interest in James. It would be one more queer twist of circumstance if Americans now come to an interest in their great compatriot because of reasons quite separate from the central values in James. What James really was—a great "poet" and a profound psychologist—and what he actually accomplished, is beyond any interest of a "timely" kind, no matter how pressing and serious such an interest may seem to be.

James's reputation has been affected by the turns of fashion before this. He has been earlier than his time, later than his time, and his work has fallen into neglect between "periods." He has been thought outmoded, when his modernity was notable; genteel, when he had become the sharpest critic of "gentility"; a dull expatriate, when his books flashed with incisive American wit; "fine drawn," when, at the end of his life, his writing was loaded with almost an excessive weight of insight and experience. He lost one audience at the end of the eighties. He gained a younger one in 1918, only to have it almost completely fall away during the experimental and eclectic decade of the twenties. The Parrington–Van Wyck Brooks sort of attack appealed to exactly the type of reader who, by nature and training, would decry James in any case: the middle-class mind dead set against anything it cannot "use" or "understand." James, being a shining mark, drew to himself all the concentrated vituperation such minds are capable of producing. Every dictum of Flaubert's—and there are many—concerning the hatred of the artist felt by the rank and file of the bourgeoisie was proved as a deadly truth by the attacks made, and the misinterpretations thought up, by such critics, on the subject of James.

Matthiessen has made a choice among the works, and deals at length with the three last novels—*The Ambassadors, The Wings of the Dove,* and *The Golden Bowl*—published during James's lifetime; together with, in passing, *The American Scene* and the two posthumous and unfinished novels, *The Ivory*

Tower and *The Sense of the Past*. This phase Matthiessen calls "major." It might better be called the "past-master" period, for James had been "major" for twenty years or more before he entered into his last and greatest powers of thought and expression. A period of mature experimentation—with the theatre, with the strict dramatic form as applied to the novel, and with various special viewpoints (notably those of the child and the neurotic)— intervened, in the nineties, between the middle and late James. The later novels have often been singled out for special praise—or blame; they have never, however, been analyzed with the thoroughness they deserve, and we must be grateful to Matthiessen for the attention he has paid to their sub- tleties, and the care he has taken not to split their form and content into two unnatural divisions. He is out to shed light, and direct attention not only toward the master's "pattern" but also toward the magician's enchantment surrounding that pattern and the fine mind's relentless insight into it. This is the James, Matthiessen with tacit irony reminds the reader, who has been accused of identifying himself with his characters. This is the "snob" who was taken in by the European scene. This is the dim-witted old man drawing out a tangle of conclusions from desperately small premises. We see, instead, the deliberate, immensely skillful artist in his sixties adding to his effects; the clear-eyed man who can penetrate, to the point of clairvoyance, almost every human obscurity. We see James writing these last novels with a speed incommensurate with their complexity. During the three years of their com- position James also produced the life of William Wetmore Story, the Ameri- can sculptor, and several short pieces. The delightful Story biography, revealing James's perfect grasp of the American artist's problems during the period with which he deals, is a Jamesian success too little known. It is a pity that Matthiessen does not include a detailed estimate of it in his treatment of the last phase, where it belongs. Matthiessen has access to eight working notebooks, running from 1878 to 1914. Not a great deal of clarification of James's intentions is, however, drawn from this source.

One or two matters not accented by Matthiessen come to mind, to- gether with what seems to me a real underestimation, based on imperfect analysis, of *The Golden Bowl*. Matthiessen believes that James's twenty years' absence from America, during a period of crucial American social change, made him uneasy with the "multimillionaire" Adam Verver. Do we not see, instead, in Mr. Verver, as well as in Maggie, James's recognition of a new American type? Surely some kind of maiming and distorting force, as well as increased powers of specialization acting upon basic American romanticism, aggressiveness, and naïveté, reverberate through *The Golden Bowl*. Mr. Verver and Maggie are at first grotesques. They are at once far too powerful and far too infantile. Maggie must learn that love and "help" cannot be bought, or called in, and later neglected; that these things turn out to be dangers to face up to. Matthiessen states that the dynamics of the book are provided entirely by Maggie. The exact opposite is true. Maggie is reduced to impotence and fear when she tries to go it alone; to run everyone. It is only when Charlotte steps out on the terrace with her silent offer to help that Maggie is deflected from her crass, childish, and neurotic course. And behind Charlotte is the Prince's "humility" and delicate sense of balance and form. In this book it is the Europeans who "save" the Americans; it is the Americans who have become corrupted by power, and "taste" pushed too far. Note should be made of Mrs. Assingham's extraordinary analysis, at the end of the novel's first part, of the relation between the four principal characters —an analysis securely based on the truth of modern psychology, and all done without benefit of Freud or Jung. James, in *The Golden Bowl,* had come to the point where he could hear aright, in spite of "stock" pretenses, the whole hidden story of the human heart, including its minor "intermittences." The reader is led, through small truths, toward stern, prodigious human facts. He experiences, not minor interpretation, but comprehensive wisdom.

From one point of view, *The Golden Bowl,* written in the same year (1905) as Debussy's *La Mer,* is one of Impressionism's triumphs. Both works are formal accomplishments "of magnificent scope" of that school. And the later James must be approached in the same way as one approaches music. Soon any surface stylistic oddity disappears. The center continually shifts, but the development of theme never stops for a moment and never errs. As in great music and in tragic life, the shifts are always toward the larger and unsuspected capacity, modulation, event; and toward a final major resolution.

James knew that democracy was diversity. To step into his world of Americans, Europeans, and every international combination of the two, is to find oneself in developing diversity. To read James we must follow "the silver clue . . . to the whole labyrinth of the artist's consciousness: his active sense of life." To understand James we must be the opposite of his "awful Mona Brigstock, who is *all* will, without the smallest leak of force into taste or tenderness or vision, into any sense of shades or relations or proportions —the thriftily constructed Mona, able at any moment to bear the whole of her dead weight at once on any given inch of resisting surface."[1] The Mona Brigstocks, American or "international," should leave James alone. The non-Monas should go toward him without fear, if they have not already found him.

[1944]

1. James's own comment on this crass character from his 1896 novel *The Spoils of Poynton;* it appears in the introduction he wrote for the novel in volume 10 of the New York Edition of his works (1907–9).

The Bostonians

THE BOSTONIANS, evidently written sometime between James's fortieth and forty-second years, serialized in the *Century Magazine* in 1885, published in both England and America in 1886, has never until now been reprinted in an American edition. Its non-appearance in the *Collected Edition* (1907–9) has raised various questions, chiefly concerned with James's apparent later squeamishness toward the frank insight of his early work. Whatever the reason, James never rewrote the book, as he did some others. It stands, therefore, as perfect "early James." That it has not become, and will never become, a "period piece"—a novel irremediably of its time, an outmoded lump of costume drama—can be put down to the fact that James, even in his early forties, "knew the world." *The Bostonians* is shot through with the lights of humor, with the satire of a detached, experienced, civilized intelligence. Far away from the milieu he presented, James drew the picture of Boston in the seventies with the greatest variety of detail, the utmost vivacity of presentation. He is grinding no ax, shedding no tears, driving through points without fanaticism. His separation from his material gives him a freedom that is almost the freedom of an expert in some sport; James often, here, plays a wide, high, and handsome kind of game. The underlying tone of the book is gay—the tone of high comedy.

The title is not to be applied to the inhabitants of Boston in the large. James makes it clear that his "Bostonians" are two young women—Olive

Henry James

251

Chancellor, of a certain position and means, "a spinster, as Shelley was a lyric poet or as the month of August is sultry," living on the water side of Charles Street; and Verena Tarrant, the daughter of a mesmerist and all-round charlatan, who lives in a wooden cottage "with a little naked piazza," on an unpaved "place" in Cambridge. Verena has a "gift"—the gift of eloquence. She is able to move audiences, speaking inanities in a voice that James compares to both silver and gold. She is a kind of *reductio ad absurdum* of that influential American figure, the platform orator. Gotten up in a costume resembling that of a circus rider, she opens her pretty mouth and exerts her fresh and genuine charm upon a variety of audiences in the cause of women's rights. Olive is, by contrast, a far more complicated character. A woman of distinction (James insists on this throughout), no fool, completely in earnest in her desire to establish some contact with "the toilers"—the workers who, she senses, touch reality beyond and "beneath" the layer of middle-class vulgarians she despises—Olive is yet sterilized by an aridity of spirit, baffled by genteel prejudices, and warped by a nervous constitution. Set against James's portrait of a woman reformer of an earlier period—the warmhearted, eccentric, but touching Miss Birdseye—Olive Chancellor is a rather terrifying resultant of Puritanism gone to seed, a female organism driven by a masculine will, without the saving graces of masculine intelligence or feminine tenderness and insight.

These two young women move in a tepid atmosphere of post-Abolition idealism. It is an atmosphere still peopled by the cranks, faddists, cultists, evangelists, revolutionaries, and dogmatists so usual in America in the forties and fifties—the intellectual and emotional débris of the breakdown of faith, the beginning of the "scientific view," of the general ethos of still crude industrial and moral revolutions. James knew these visionaries, of all shades of sincerity and sanity, well; his father's New York home had been a sort of clearinghouse for them. It is James's background of plain experience and accurate youthful observation which makes the revolutionaries in *The Princess Casamassima* so modernly recognizable and the cranks of *The Bostonians* so sharply alive. In these two books, written almost concurrently, James pays these characters his clear-sighted and ironic *devoirs* [compliments], and leaves them for good.

The "outside observer" in *The Bostonians* is, insolently and cleverly enough, a young man from the recently "conquered" South. Of first-rate intelligence, completely "unreconstructed," holding "unprogressive" ideals of manliness, courage, and chivalry, Basil Ransom, introduced into the midst of these, to him, vaporous ideas expressed by these decaying, except for Verena, personalities, has a civilized set of principles to fall back upon— principles that seem "medieval" to his cousin Olive and her "set." James's artistic and moral courage in contrasting, at the time, Ransom's "prejudices," Ransom's humorous and "feeling" nature, Ransom's underlying flexibility of outlook with the eerie and run-down New England prophets of "progress" and "change," cannot be underestimated. James had, it is true, Turgenev's example. Turgenev, earlier, had bent an artist's eye on the follies committed in the name of "progress" by the romantic Russian reformers and their allies in the middle class (he invented the term "nihilist"). *The Bostonians* loses nothing by being read along with *On the Eve* and *Rudin,* and Verena Tarrant often resembles a Turgenev heroine. But James, in describing her surroundings and giving her motives, is solidly on his own ground.

Ransom's pinpoint sharpness of eye results in a sort of continual sparkle in the first part of the book. The young Mississippian does not hesitate to put a name to things; he sorts out the real from the artificial instantly. He spots the self-sufficient sincerity of the little woman doctor with the same swiftness with which he puts down Verena's father as a "carpetbagger" and a "varlet." He sees through the pretentiousness of Mrs. Luna; and he does not fail to see true discrimination and actual passion for justice in Olive, in spite of his quick recognition of her manias. James succeeds in keeping Ransom free from a romantic emphasis. As Philip Rahv, in his preface to this edition, says, "In the figure of Ransom [James] created with remarkable prescience a type of intellectual who has only in the last few decades come to the fore in the English-speaking world . . . a type, exemplified in writers like T. S. Eliot or the school of Southern agrarians, whose criticism of modern civilization is rooted in traditionalist principles. Thus James anticipated . . . one of the major tendencies in twentieth-century thinking" [insertion LB's].

Behind the central figures—and how masterly is the introduction and first grouping of these—James has painted in with complete verisimilitude, combined with his own peculiar kind of poetic light and coloring, the New England social, spiritual, and physical scene as it has never been rendered before or since. Anyone who has grown up in New England during the last fifty years can vouch for the truth of these delineations of New England social and spiritual tremors. Here is the top layer shot through and through with the humanitarian feeling which must, rather guiltily, accompany utilitarian push and compromise—seeking for "roots" and reality. Here is the entire middle class yearning upward, toward "the fragrance of Beacon Street." James bares the many thin layers of provincial snobbery with scalpel nicety. Turns of both vulgar and affected speech; wrong entrances regretted; all sorts of little affronts taken as "liberties"; shabby genteel uneasiness; upper-class *idées fixes* and brutalities of placement ("it is as though [I] had struck up an intimacy with the daughter of [my] chiropodist" [insertions LB's]); the beginning of newspaper curiosity into private lives; the pushing tactics of the vigorous outsider—the whole brittle, energetic, shifting scene, filled with cruelty, uncertainty, nervousness, and "nerve"; here it stands in James as in our memory.

Nor does he scamp the scene's *décor* and backdrop. Note the poignant description of the period's American bleakness, seen in "the red sunsets of winter" from Olive's drawing-room windows. Remark the details of another Boston dusk, as Ransom walks the Boston streets before Verena's "big" lecture. Consider the exquisite description of the Cape—the background James puts behind the bitter struggle between Ransom and Olive for the "possession" of Verena. One sentence, beginning, "There were certain afternoons in August, long, beautiful, and terrible, when one felt that the summer was rounding its curve," can be set, for sheer power of evocation, against anything in Emily Dickinson.

I have always associated the little "Square," Union Park, in Boston, with *The Bostonians*. Set between two busy and now run-down avenues, it takes the form of a flattened oval—that shape dear to the nineteenth century. Great trees shade it, around a grass plot running its length, decorated by two small cast-iron fountains. The red brick houses, with their "salient" bulging fronts running from top to bottom of the façades, exemplify the first Boston architecture purely American-nineteenth-century in character. The naïve assumption, usual at the beginning of a period of technological and political triumphs, that anything sufficiently bold and powerful must last forever, is built into these "fronts" along with their brick and mortar. It was in such a house that Miss Birdseye lived, and that Ransom first saw Verena. But things change. Today—and for the last forty years or so—these houses have been shabby boardinghouses or "light-housekeeping" rooms. The roomers, armed with their paper bags of food and their milk bottles, return to them at night under the shadow of the gracious trees, mount the steps beside the flourish of scrolled iron railings, and enter the big doors under obsolete, elaborate "gasoliers." The materialist spirit that thought to build enduring mansions built, instead, the most solid and dismal furnished lodgings.

In *The Bostonians* James fixes the crudities and misapprehensions of that spirit. Far from identifying himself with Ransom, he uses this character to throw uncompromising light on a humanitarianism itself grown harsh, proud, and aggressive, cut off from the humility and the realism which must be charity's true base. He shows us perfectionists blind to their own imperfections, liberals neutralized by their "liberality," radicals bound by unyielding dogma to callousness; as well as the "moist, emotional" yearners and the hysterics of both sexes, unconsciously seeking a ritual and a master that they consciously reject. *The Bostonians* is happily again available to those who have overlooked one of the greatest of American novels, which has existed, as it were, in the shadow of the very culture upon which it sheds light, since 1886.

[1945]

T. S. Eliot

Collected Poems

THE LATER poems of T. S. Eliot, for years fugitive and hard to come by, are at last joined to his early work in the recently published *Collected Poems.* So the record, up to now, of the poet who has changed the accent of poetry written in our period is at last completely available to us. We can trace Eliot's "horror of a life without faith" from its first complete statement in "Gerontion," through its elaboration in *The Waste Land,* to its logical conclusion in "Sweeney Agonistes." "Sweeney Agonistes," still a fragment and likely to remain one, twitching to music-hall rhythms, reduced men and women to gargoyles who gibbered in a world where even the comparative nobility of despair was not possible. Faith began to stammer in "The Hollow Men," and from that point on, Eliot's belief mounts beyond his irony and pessimism, not in an unbroken line, but in a line renewed when broken. It is now possible to read the beautiful poems of the transition period ("Journey of the Magi" through "Difficulties of a Statesman") in their proper order, as well as the latest brief lyrics, the nonsense rhymes, and the fine "Choruses from 'The Rock.'" The last poem in the collection, "Burnt Norton," rather long and, compared to the crisp early poems, rather vaporous, brings the later phase to conclusion that resolves on a note of balanced calm and even a mild sort of joy.

Of the quality of the poetry there is little need to speak. Eliot, the self-styled "minor poet," brought back into English poetry the salt and the range of which it had long been deprived. From Dante through the Symbolists, he took what he needed from the varied stream of poetic resources; he swung the balance over from whimpering Georgian bucolics to forms wherein contemporary complexity could find expression. The *Collected Poems* are more than a work of poetic creation; they are a work of poetic regeneration.

[1936]

The Family Reunion

ELIOT'S PLAYS and poems, subsequent to his espousal of the Anglican faith, have not been entirely joyful. They have been well streaked, in fact, with his early defeatism and despairs, and the social-satirical note has seemed to be vanishing from them by degrees. *The Family Reunion,* a verse play with a contemporary setting, will appear to the reader waiting for pure spiritual joy to sound, after the fanfares attendant upon conversion, almost too good to be true. The new play presents an integrated Eliot, completely in control of himself and so filled with insight that the old Eliot comes in for some pretty close dissection, if not caricature. It is no small feat to bring off a Christian (a Jungian, a Sophoclean) theme of reconciliation with the conscience (the unconscious sense of guilt, the Eumenides) and at the same time to expose, down to the last set phrase, the hollow conventions of an upper (in this case, English) class. It is no small feat to surround and examine an early phase of the self by means of a later one.

The play is divided into two parts of three scenes each. In the first scene of Part I, it is the social irony which first attracts the attention. The two non-ironic characters—Harry, the eldest son, who returns to his mother's house ridden by real or imagined guilt—and his aunt, Agatha, who is addicted to clipped sibylline speech and an occasional piece of late-Eliot incantation—sound definitely suspect. There has been just about enough sensitive foreboding in Eliot. Cellars and attics, "the noxious smell untraceable in the drains," "the attraction of the dark passage, the paw under the door" sound so like parody that one is put on guard. A new element, however, soon appears to exorcise the old horror. Downing, Harry's "man," who has "looked after his Lordship for over ten years," is sheer practical common sense, and this Figaro-like conception is reassuring. Eliot, one feels, cannot be planning to recede once more into neurotic terrors while Downing, offstage, cleans up the car. And a complete recession does not, in fact, occur. We are drawn, it is true, with the struggling Harry, right down to childhood and back, straight through the necessary confrontation of the Eumenides. Eliot probes from the outside into the neurotic's tendencies toward cruelty and suffering in a manner one would not have thought possible. Harry, able at last to face his pursuers and accept them, liberates himself. He is then free to escape the deathly house, his mother's relentless will, and the stupidity of his relatives. His sibylline aunt bids him Godspeed. Downing goes with him, and the spectacle of master and man riding off to spiritual liberty in a well-kept car is the play's one faintly ridiculous effect.

Eliot of late years has talked at great length about the value of religious experience. *The Family Reunion* is the first incontrovertible evidence that he has thoroughly experienced the phenomenon. It is interesting to note that other than traditional Church of England symbols have contributed to this play.

Any person who has ever experienced the smallest success in the struggle for spiritual reconciliation will recognize that Eliot here demonstrates in detail the uncheatable nature of the combat. And Henry James never flayed the upper-class English with more delicate skill.

[1939]

Four Quartets

FOUR QUARTETS is the first T. S. Eliot volume of serious poetry to appear in America since his *Collected Poems,* published in 1936. The first three poems included have been in print for some time, however. "Burnt Norton," with which the book opens, is familiar as the final piece in *Collected Poems,* and "East Coker" and "The Dry Salvages" were published in the *Partisan Review* in 1940 and 1941 respectively. Taken together, the four rather long works —"Little Gidding" is the other one—show Eliot experimenting in his tireless way. They also show a crucial turn in his thinking, and in his general approach toward the Anglican religion, which he embraced, along with British citizenship, in 1927.

The four poems are linked together by two devices. First, the basic construction of "Burnt Norton" sets the form of the others. Each has five sections. Each has a lyric in its second section, followed without pause by a meditation—development of theme, as it were. A second lyric stands alone in each fourth section as a detached melody. These lyrics and reflections, falling in their allotted places, are supposed, no doubt, to have the effect of the changes in the sonata form. This intended effect comes through, although not, of course, as definitely as in music. The second device is the use of place names as titles to all the poems. Eliot being the subtle inheritor of the Symbolist tradition, these specific localities afford him points from which to range or on which to brood. Burnt Norton is an English country house with a rose garden. East Coker is the town in Somersetshire from which Eliot's forebears emigrated to America in the seventeenth century. The Dry Salvages, according to the author's note, are "a small group of rocks, with a beacon, off the N.E. coast of Cape Ann, Massachusetts." And Little Gidding is the site in Huntingdonshire where, in 1625 or so, Nicholas Ferrar set up an Anglican religious community, which flourished in a quiet way until its destruction by the Puritans about twenty years later. Eliot, therefore, weaves back and forth between his native America and his adopted Britain. He has touched his own presumably Puritan sources and also celebrated, as a convert to the Anglican communion, a shrine belonging to what has been called the golden age of the Church of England.

The form and background once straight in our minds—Eliot gives no explanation of either beyond the note quoted above—we can read the poems for mere enjoyment, for they are certainly as beautiful as anything he ever wrote. The lyrics, especially the second in "East Coker" and the two in "Little Gidding," show what the poet can do in the province of pure emotion when all irony has been eliminated.

It has been said that some of Eliot's utterances about religion have been suspiciously melodramatic. Eliot, in making religious tradition a frame for his art, chose—the artist's inevitable choice—cohesion and integrity. But a choice of form was evidently not enough. It is interesting to trace Eliot's shift from formal interest in his religion (its history, rituals, and so on) toward a far from formal interest in his own post-conversion spiritual development. The four poems in this book, together with his play, *The Family Reunion* (1939), are records of that development, wrung out of him despite all obstacles of reserve. Eliot's conversion was accompanied by a certain amount of pride and arrogance. In "Burnt Norton," however, the classic procedure of spiritual death and rebirth begins and "the dark night of the soul" is heralded. The poem bears all the marks of deep depression. It is faint and minor in tone, circular and repetitive in thought. A flight back to childhood is considered, and the way out, through darkness and mental suffering, is recognized to be necessary only in an academic way. Here, human sympathy is also academic, if not actually lacking. This is the middle Eliot manner fading out and running down.

But in "East Coker" the suffering has been faced, lived through, understood, and the poet is back on his feet. The old lamenting and beseeching have completely disappeared. This is a terribly bitter poem, but the bitterness has some of the early Eliot edge, and it is directed outward, toward reality. The passage on renunciation at the end of section three; the "wounded surgeon" lyric, in a wonderfully effective stanza form; the surprising and unexpected direct personal comment on self and career with which the poem ends—all these are new and fine. The key becomes major, the effects broader. The broadening persists throughout "The Dry Salvages," and in "Little Gidding" many of Eliot's themes—one could almost say fetishes—are brought together in a real feat of reconciliation.

Eliot here stands at a distant remove from the "aged eagle" role in which he presented himself, with considerable affectation, in *Ash-Wednesday* thirteen years ago. He has learned lessons in patience and sympathy, a firm basis for renewed poetic strength.

[1943]

Federico García Lorca

FEDERICO GARCÍA Lorca, Spain's greatest modern poet, who was shot at the age of thirty-seven in Granada in the early weeks of the Spanish war, was, like Yeats, fortunate in having direct access to a living folk tradition. Again like Yeats, Lorca was open to the avant-garde movements of his time. Yeats came under the influence of French Symbolism; Lorca had his Surrealist period. The poems in the first section of his *The Poet in New York* (well translated by Rolfe Humphries from the poet's perhaps incomplete typescript) are thoroughly Surrealist. They were written in 1929 and 1930, when Lorca, already famous in Spain for his songs and ballads, lived in New York as a student at Columbia and traveled as far north as Vermont.

Lorca had a right to Surrealism as non-Spanish poets have not; his native literary tradition stems from Góngora. And the modern Spaniard has cut loose from the idea of a religious hell so recently that the private hell of the Subconscious floats closer to the surface in both Dalí and Lorca than, nowadays, in artists of other nationalities. These facts must be borne in mind by the reader who, like myself, distrusts Surrealism's worth and pretensions and the worth of any poet who adheres too rigorously to its tenets. In the case of Lorca, we have proof of his poetic worth in his non-Surrealist work. The brilliant and popularly inspired *Gypsy Ballads* were published in 1928, and we have examples of them in the latter part of this book. His Surrealist period in America and Cuba followed. Later, Lorca published his "Lament for Ignacio Sánchez Mejías" (already translated into English by A. L. Lloyd as "Lament for the Death of a Bullfighter"), and in that late and superb poem we can see what the poet finally did with Surrealism. He used it as Baudelaire used "Gothic": he made it humane and the vehicle of emotion.

His ballads get at the nerve centers directly. Their oral tradition comes through at all points; we understand why this poetry is sung by illiterate people all over Spain. Objects in them move, glitter, give off heat, cold, and odor; expand and contract, glow and resound, and the heart of the reader goes through corresponding processes, is made to feel. They are grown out of the heart as wheat or grapes are grown out of the ground.

[1937, 1940][1]

1. This version of LB's 1937 review of Lloyd's Lorca translation, conflated with her 1940 review of the Lorca translations by Rolfe Humphries, appeared in PA.

Elizabeth Bowen

MODERN FICTION of the subtler kind when written by women is likely to depict at length the trouble resulting from unsuitable and complicated people falling in love. The stays and obstacles once provided by difference in social position, family feuds, missent letters, and trumped-up misunderstandings have narrowed into drama arising from the fact that the lovers have neuroses that do not match, are in love for the wrong reasons, in love too late or too soon, or are incapable of love at all. Elizabeth Bowen in her previous novels has described such combinations, and Colette has worked with them for years. Miss Bowen has also probed with great thoroughness into the reaction of sensitive children, sometimes the offspring of mismatings, thrown into situations of which they hold only one or two clues. *The House in Paris* successfully brought off an atmosphere of emotional tension, resulting when the past, present, and future converged on such a child, who was caught, between journeys, in rooms full of the tragedy to which he owed his being. *The Death of the Heart* turns on a girl of sixteen, the product of a misalliance, who, when introduced into the "edited life" of her half-brother's smart London household, throws upon it the full glare of her innocence, breaks through its surface, and shows the lack of human feeling on which it is based.

Miss Bowen's young Portia Quayne is the daughter of a late second marriage, following an impulsive liaison, between a middle-aged conservative Englishman and a silly but warm-hearted widow. The first Mrs. Quayne with rather mean nobility divorces her husband and casts him off. Mr. Quayne, cut loose from his pleasant country moorings, is forced to live shabbily on the Riviera with his new family. After his death and that of Portia's mother, his son Thomas takes the child into his home, knowing that his father wanted some settled, decorous English experience for her. Portia, still feeling grief for her mother, enters a household built up with great taste and care by Anna, Thomas's wife. Everything in the exquisite house overlooking the park—the aquamarine curtains, the furniture rubbed "so that you can see ten feet into the polish," the ritual of beautiful food, the series of delightful effects—depends upon Anna. Even the family friend—called St. Quentin and a novelist—is choice and seems picked to match the wallpaper. Portia's brother, sunk in the depths of passionate cravings which marriage has not solved, is Anna's. And Eddie, the neurotic, charming young hanger-on, to whom Portia gives the full weight of her innocent affection, is Anna's—not her lover, but her amusement and her foil. It is Anna who at once instinctively ridicules the child, as she ridicules anyone of awkward human worth. Portia, learning of an ultimate betrayal, runs first to Eddie, who of course, although he has worked off some of his warped tenderness on her, rejects her; then to Major Brutt, another misfit in Anna's *décor*. Major Brutt telephones the house and tells Thomas that Portia demands that they come to some decision about her. In a masterfully done scene the three disabused adults—Anna, Thomas, and St. Quentin—thrash the matter out at the dinner table. ("This evening the pure in heart have simply got us on toast.") They come to a decision. They send a servant, Mrs. Matchett, Portia's only confidante in the household, to fetch Portia back in a taxi, as one would send for a lost parcel.

Miss Bowen has elsewhere spoken of "the limitations of English narrative prose, with its *longueurs* and conventions dangerous to truth." In her novels she has taken every precaution to reduce these conventions to a minimum. The strokes come close, and every stroke tells. Miss Bowen is particularly good at reflecting one character in another, always making it clear that some people see things partially while others take in every detail. Matchett, the self-contained upper servant, with her toughened sympathy and snobbery and her pride of the good artisan, sees everything. Eddie sees everything—in his way—and himself, "at once coy and insolent," only too well. Matchett can sum people up. Of the "sacrificing" first Mrs. Quayne she says: "I couldn't care for her; she had no nature"; of Anna: "Oh, she has her taste and dearly loves to use it. Past that she'll never go." Eddie says of Anna: "She loves to make a tart out of another person. She'd never dare to be a proper tart herself." Thomas has an occasional moment of insight into the society about him: "self-interest, given a pretty gloss." But Portia, not yet absorbed into "the guilty plausibility of the world," sees more than everything. She detects the impossibility of a natural human relationship between these people who write letters, go to dinner parties, talk at tea—always "stalking each other." She watches "thoroughly"; she tries to shake some human response out of Eddie; she importunes; she nags with the implacable fury of first love. At the end she gives the show away to simple, kind Major Brutt. "Anna's always laughing at you. She says you are quite pathetic. . . . And Thomas thinks you must be after something. They groan at each other when you have gone away. You and I are the same."

Miss Bowen's talent is so rich and so searching, and this novel stands so far outside the class of novels which resemble packaged goods put up for the trade, that one is tempted to give her nothing but praise. She sees deeply, but not widely enough. Corruption has not lately entered the class of which she writes; the heart is not dying in these people: it never lived in them. And her tone, too keyed up, never lets down for a moment; the *longueurs* are deleted to such an extent that they are missed. Beautifully done descriptions of times of day and the weather edge the action—to a tiresome degree. The backgrounds for emotions are chosen with care; one, an empty seaside boardinghouse on a Sunday morning, is almost unbearably appropriate. Miss Bowen can cook the vulgar English to the same crispness to which she treats their betters. But *The Death of the Heart* is too packed, too brilliant, for its own good. What Miss Bowen lacks is a kind of humility. She has forgotten more than many novelists ever knew, but what Turgenev, for example, knew, and was chary of expressing, she cannot quite deal with. Once in a while the reader hears the accent of self-satisfaction, if not display, in the novelist. But for all that, *The Death of the Heart* deepens our view of the horrors experienced by open innocence up against a closed world.

[1939]

Elizabeth Bowen

James Joyce

Proteus, or Vico's Road

JOYCE HAS been writing *Finnegans Wake* for seventeen years. In 1922 *Ulysses* was published in Paris; this book was begun the same year. *Transition* has brought out about half of it, intermittently, under the title "Work in Progress"; and a number of fragments have appeared now and again in pamphlet form. A whole school of imitators has clustered around its linguistic and philosophical example, and its influence has been so strong that critics have been led to write of it in, as it were, its own terms. Something unheard-of and extraordinary was happening to language, history, time, space, and causality in Joyce's new novel, and the jaw-dropping and hat-waving of the front-line appreciators were remarkable in themselves. Because this subjective, or rolling-along-in-great-delight-with-a-great-work-of-art, school of criticism has had its innings with Joyce's books, the plain reviewer might do well to approach the work at first with a certain amount of leaden-footed objectivity, remaining outside the structure and examining it from as many sides as possible.

Joyce himself, as we shall see, has given a good many clues to what the book is about. The first thing that strikes the reader, however, is the further proof of Joyce's miraculous virtuosity with language. *Finnegans Wake* takes up this technical skill as it existed at the end of *Ulysses* and further elaborates it. Then Joyce's mastery of structure and his musician's feeling for form and rhythmic subtlety are here in a more advanced—as well as a more deliquescent—state of development. The chief reason for the book's opacity is the fact that it is written in a special language. But this language is not gibberish—unless it wants to be. It has rules and conventions. Before one starts hating or loving or floating off upon it, the attention might be bent toward discovering what it is, and how it works.

This private tongue is related to what Panurge called the "puzlatory,"[1] and it is cousin to the language of E[dward] Lear, L. Carroll, and the writers of nonsense verse in general. It is based on the pun and is defined, by Fowler, as: "Paronomasia (Rhet.) 'wordshunting.' Puns, plays on words, making jocular or suggestive use of similarity between different words or of a word's different senses." Upon this rhetorical device *Finnegans Wake* is borne, no matter what limits of intelligibility or impenetrability it touches. Two examples may illustrate it:

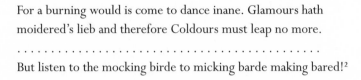

> For a burning would is come to dance inane. Glamours hath moidered's lieb and therefore Coldours must leap no more.
> . . . .
> But listen to the mocking birde to micking barde making bared![2]

Now let us examine the texture of the writing. This, as one would expect, is firm. Moving for the most part in a private idiom, Joyce keeps unerringly to style's economy, precision, and weight. Through a thousand variations, through a confusion of tongues, the fundamental sinew of the writing persists; the book can be opened anywhere, and a page read at random, in proof of this. The remark of Richard Strauss to a young musician comes to mind: "Why do you write atonally? You have talent." Joyce is not writing as he is writing to cover up inexpertness. Prosodically, he is a master, as can readily be seen if he is compared with his apprentices.

He is a master-musician and a master-parodist. Here, even more clearly than in *Ulysses,* Joyce brings over into literature not only music's structural forms—as exemplified by the fugue, the sonata, the theme with variations—but the harmonic modulations, the suspensions and solutions, of music: effects in words which parallel a composer's effects obtained by working with relative or non-relative keys. Phrases and whole passages are transposed from a given style, mood, tempo, signature into a more contrasting one. Certain proper names—Finnegan, Earwicker, Anna Livia, Dublin, Phoenix, Howth, James and John, Lucan and Chapelizod—reappear in truncated, anagrammatically distorted, or portmanteau forms. The night-river leitmotif reads, at its most normal: "Beside the rivering waters of, hitherandthithering waters of. Night!" Its variants are numerous and remarkable. Joyce, the parodist, in *Ulysses* always effectively colored matter with manner. The number of styles parodied in *Finnegans Wake* is prodigious. But these present parodies differ somewhat from their predecessors; they are actually more limited. The punning language in which they are framed gives them all a mocking or burlesque edge (the prose poems, only, excepted). This limitation and defeat of purpose—for an immense book written in two main modes only is sure to grow monotonous—is the first symptom to strike the reader of the malady, to be later defined, which cripples *Finnegans Wake.*

Thus equipped, then, with his private vernacular, Joyce proceeds to attack what certainly seems to be every written or oral style known to man. A list of these styles would fill pages. The range and variety can only be indicated here. All forms of religious liturgy (Bible, prayer book, sermon, mass, catechism, litany); conversation; letters informal, formal, and illiterate; the fable, the examination paper, the chronicle; fashion notes and soapbox speeches; the hair-splitting argument and the sentimental narrative. And here are dialects and jargons—"every known *patois* of the English language." Slang, journalese, and specialized vocabularies: of heraldry, the race track, the courtroom, the nursery. Also uncounted foreign tongues, from Sanskrit through Anglo-Saxon to modern European, back to pidgin English, baby talk, and the sounds children make before speech. There are also just plain noises, onomatopoetically expressed, from bangs and howls to twitters and whimpers.

The "auditive faculty" of Stephen Dedalus has been expanded so that the functions of the other senses become subsidiary to it. Joyce has put down everything he has heard for the last seventeen years. We now can examine some evidence from Eugene Jolas, the editor of *Transition,* as to Joyce's method of work. Jolas says: "It was necessary [in compiling a complete MS for publication] to go through a number of notebooks, each of which had esoteric symbols indicating the reference to a given character, locality, event, or mood. Then the words accumulated over the years had to be placed in the segment for which they were intended." And what Joyce was up to in general—the underlying theme and philosophical purpose of the book— has been partially elucidated by Joyce to Jolas and others. Jolas says:

> We know that Mr. Joyce's ambition has been to write a book dealing with the night-mind of man. . . . We have tried to keep in mind that the dramatic dynamic is based on the Bruno theory of knowledge through opposites, and on the Vico theory of cyclic recurrence. . . . History being, in his earlier words "a nightmare," Mr. Joyce presents his phantasmagoric figures as passing back and forth from a mentality saturated with archetypal memories to a vision of future construction.

Another of Joyce's favorite exegetes sheds a little more light (and it can be definitely stated that light is needed, since the one actual fact which is clear to the reader, without exegesis, is that the action takes place in one night or one aeon of time, and is concerned with a man—a giant, an earth-force—asleep). Stuart Gilbert says:

> Joyce's new work is partly based on the historical speculations of Vico. . . . Vico held that there is a recurrent cycle in human "progress," as in the movement of the stars. Societies begin, continue, and have an end, according to universal laws. . . . Every nation passes through three stages, the divine, the heroic, the human. The prelude and aftermath of each cycle is complete disintegration. . . . Vico contemplated the writing of an "ideal and timeless history" in which all the actual histories of all nations should be embodied. . . . "Work in Progress" is, in many aspects, a realization of Vico's project. . . . It is interesting to note that an exceptionally intricate passage in Mr. Joyce's book is, in effect, a fantasia on the quinary scale. . . . Even the difficult passages of the "Anna Livia Plurabelle" fragment become lucid when read aloud in the appropriate rhythm and intonation by the author. In fact, rhythm is one of the clues to the meaning . . . for each of the polymorphous personages of the work has his appropriate rhythm, and many "references" can be located by reference to the rhythm of the prose.

With these few "clues" well in mind, the reader can only open the book, without further explanation, and battle his way into it. Life is too short to read all the glosses which have already multiplied around it and will continue to multiply. Some of its themes are perfectly clear. The pedestrian reviewer can add a few scattered notes, put down during her own two weeks' life with the literary monument.

There is every reason to believe that a *complete explanation* of the whole thing will come, after a longish lapse of time, from Joyce himself. This happened, it will be remembered, in the case of *Ulysses* after about nine years. . . . There is nothing whatever to indicate that Joyce has any real knowledge of the workings of the Subconscious, in sleep or otherwise. Carroll has far more intuition than Joyce into the real structure of the dream. There are no sustained passages which give, for example, the feeling of nightmare. The punning style, as a matter of fact, precludes this. It is as though Joyce wished to be superior to the Unconscious. . . . At one point he brings in a long apologia for his own method and language. The effect of this interpolation is very queer. . . . Some sections start off with indicated time, but these indications seem to be afterthoughts. . . . The later versions of the fragments already published seem to be changed out of sheer perversity: a clause is omitted leaving nothing but a vestigial preposition; a singular noun is shifted to the plural, and the meaning is thereby successfully clouded. . . . The most frightening thing about the book is the feeling, which steadily grows in the reader, that Joyce himself does not know what he is doing; and how, in spite of all his efforts, he is giving himself away. Full control is being exercised over the minor details and the main structure, but the compulsion toward a private universe is very strong. . . . Joyce's delight in reducing man's learning, passion, and religion to a hash is also disturbing. . . . After the first week what one longs for is the sound of speech, or the sight of a sentence in its natural human context. . . . The book cannot rise into the region of true evocation—the region where Molly Bloom's soliloquy exists immortally—because it has no human base. Emotion is deleted, or burlesqued, throughout. The vicious atmosphere of a closed world, whose creator can manage and distort all that is humanly valuable and profound (cunningly, with Godlike slyness), becomes stifling. . . . *Ulysses* was based on a verifiable theme: the search for the father. The theme, or themes, of *Finnegans Wake* are retrogressive, as the language is retrogressive. The style retrogresses back to the conundrum. To read the book over a long period of time gives one the impression of watching intemperance become addiction, become debauch.

The book's great beauties, its wonderful passages of wit, its variety, its marks of genius and immense learning, are undeniable. It has another virtue: in the future "writers will not need to search for a compromise."[3] But whatever it says of man's past, it has nothing to do with man's future, which, we can only hope, will lie in the direction of more humanity rather than less. And there are better gods than Proteus.

[1939]

1. "puzlatory": the term used by Panurge, "everyman" companion of sixteenth-century French author Rabelais' giant Pantagruel, for his inscrutable and falsely erudite made-up language.

2. In the first two of these three lines from *Finnegans Wake,* part 2, episode 8, Joyce is parodying, or encrypting, *Macbeth.*

3. Albert Thibaudet's comment on the effects of poet Stéphane Mallarmé on French writers, which LB refers to in a letter of April 18, 1939, written to Morton Dauwen Zabel as she was composing this essay on *Finnegans Wake.* She notes the Joyce work's "prosodic texture," "wonderfully varied and firm. No Cummingsish adverb-avalanches. [. . .]—But is it a true picture of what goes on in sleep?" By April of the following year, LB turns against the

"repulsive book": "The *tone,* even through the jargon, is so *little,* so meachin', so infantile, so smarty pants, so SMALL. [. . .] The cunning got him, boy, the cunning got him" (To Zabel, April 14, 1940; WTWL, 187).

Approaching Ur

A SKELETON KEY to Finnegans Wake, by Joseph Campbell and Henry Morton Robinson, is the first full and painstaking attempt to translate, page by page, the dream-language of Joyce's last work into English. The authors have attempted to trace, furthermore, "in thin lines" the skeletal structure of the enormous and baffling book. They have provided a synopsis of the whole, given indicative names to the four large sections and to the chapters. They have identified and translated many of Joyce's quotations—those in identifiable human tongues. They have tried to keep his alternately looming and dissolving characters straight; listed references and cross-references in footnotes; have labored, that is, to give the reader some intelligible ground to stand on and some recognizable space to move around in. Like archaeologists, whose tasks theirs of necessity so much resemble, they have uncovered one more layer of Joyce's extraordinary verbal buried city. They also supply, in an introduction and conclusion, another fairly impassioned defense of the book as a work of art, and of Joyce as a great conscious artist.

The quality of being *closed* becomes more and more evident as expert attention is directed toward *Finnegans Wake.* The book does not seem, like certain structures of great literature, to be a tower or high place, built on earth and open at the top and on all sides to the Nature about it. Into a limited locale (at its largest, Dublin, on the island of Ireland) are brought all ages of man and some of nature. In one narrow room and one sleeping mind, the developing human faculties, from the brute upward, grow and dissolve and reform. The circle of Vico's history is superimposed upon the circle of Dublin. Macrocosm and microcosm, symbol and reality, inextricably mix.

The present "translation" proceeds page by page; but the translators have of necessity chosen certain passages, and what has seemed to them the core of these passages, for detailed comment. It is interesting to notice what portions of a knotty (or merely repetitive) passage the elucidators have separated out, and what portions—sometimes containing matter which another

James Joyce

observer might consider interesting or crucial—they omit. The footnotes, too, while generally filled with the most helpful kind of information, have moments of complete blankness as to what the text seems to present in the most forcible way. The use of this "key" is therefore stimulating to the thoughtful student in more ways than one. It brings up new problems with every step of ground it clears.

Time must pass, and thorough research be made, before certain fundamental questions concerning *Finnegans Wake* can be answered. One question that comes to mind is: are we dealing with a work (always granting that it is a work of incontestable genius) essentially small in inner meaning and even in essential design, a work that has nevertheless exfoliated into a semblance of growth and complexity? Are we dealing, that is, with a work, the product of a man and artist who has never come into maturity? Or are we dealing with an essentially great work, the product of a man and artist who has suffered life and transcended his suffering; who is no longer the victim of his talent, his circumstances, or the tensions within his own character, but has become master of them all? Are we getting from this fantastically distorted and interwoven speech, these amazingly contrapuntalized themes, illumination and truth; or are we being led into the mystery of a childish individual's dreaming game, with the rigmaroles and jokes and tricks of the child (or immature man) presented to us neat?

Joyce's lyric gifts, his full equipment as a trained realist, his ingenuity as a fabulist, his skill as a parodist, his sharp wit and Jesuit-trained learning, his innate musician's ear—these attributes are as clearly evident in *Finnegans Wake* as they are in any piece of writing he ever produced. What difference does it make if we are listening to the operations of sleep; we have heard such operations in great pieces of literature before this. Even if Joyce was a sick man, we are listening to a writer who was in many ways a martyr to his genius and to his age. But we want to penetrate the disguises he has had to throw about himself; or the symptoms he has been forced to assume. We have this desire not out of niggling curiosity, but out of real interest: that we may receive the help and refreshment that any true artist's struggle with his material gives us, particularly when we are caught with him into the same deforming time.

The poet and the "comic fabulist" are equipped with uncommon gifts by which they are able to get around interior "censorship." They have tricks, as it were, to get the information through. They transpose the dangerous and (actually) untellable truths of the Subconscious into imaginative terms, not easy to bring, otherwise, into the light of day. What strikes the more detached observer when faced with the extreme opacities of certain portions of *Finnegans Wake* is the certainty that concealed beneath his very eyes is a submerged fable having to do directly with Joyce, with Joyce's relations to the world, with Joyce's attitude to his time. Is not the whole book a masked attempt at the fullest *apologia pro vita sua* that Joyce has yet given us? And this last confession and apology certainly must be more revealing (consciously or unconsciously) than anything written in his earlier career. Under the ostensible action, under H. C. Earwicker and Anna Livia Plurabelle, and Shem and Shaun, and the multitude of other clear or ambiguous figures, from time to time another drama shows: the drama of Joyce's own life, up to the writing of the book, and during the writing of the book. It is a drama terrifically malicious in expression; it flays one contemporary after another; it brings down all façades of learning and worship in one mass of mocked-at débris. Joyce is doing more than returning compulsively to the Dublin from which he is an exile. He is razing more than Dublin structures with the fires of his love and hatred.

What exterior situation, then, brought Joyce to the pass where, to get his secret across, he had to resort to a kind of desperate cunning? To resort, as well, to the often monotonous, often trivial, often brutal, ruses of the accomplished *farceur?* Or to the insistent sobbing minor lyric passage? (It seems at times that these two "tones" are the only ones in the book.) Does this work stand like a terrible half-buried monument, both to the recent past and the near future: outlining a deforming epoch when a work of art must become oblique expression—a joking show, a wry song, a cockeyed cinema-mythology—in order to exist at all?

"The price of virtuosity is abject slavery to a complaisant tool; that of creative artistry is wilful dominance over a recalcitrant tool." What do we finally see in Joyce: virtuoso or artist; compulsive neurotic or a writer with himself entirely in hand? This question requires a deeper analysis than has yet been dared by Joyce students and disciples. It is not a skeleton key we need, so much as eyes to see in spiritual (was it?) darkness; and ears with which to separate cunning (are they?) confusions.

[1944]

Ezra Pound

Cantos LII–LXXI

TEN YEARS ago it was the custom for avant-garde critics to call those people who were puzzled by Ezra Pound's *Cantos* imbeciles. Such people then
were beneath both explanation and contempt. Now it is different. Pound's
publishers have gone to the trouble, as they publish his new volume, *Cantos
LII–LXXI,* to provide a neat little explanatory brochure, which slips into a
neat pocket pasted on the inside back cover of the book. This brochure, entitled "Notes on Ezra Pound's Cantos: Structure and Metric," contains two
well and clearly written essays, one on Pound's matter and one on his manner. A photograph of Pound, making him look even more scowling than he
frequently sounds, embellishes its cover.

Pound's moral ideas are based, we are told, on the discipline of Confucius; his economic ideas, on those of "certain of the Canonist writers on
economics," "certain of the economic theories of the corporate state,"
Major Douglas,[1] and the obscurer economist Silvio Gesell. Pound believes
that everything in the modern mess could be fixed up if "the democracies"
would "finance their war and defence with statal economy"—this in spite of
the fact that Pound is against war. Pound is no Fascist at heart, we are told,
although he likes to live in Italy; and the Chinese have taught him the use of
"extreme ellipsis." Also, the *Cantos* actually are not based on the fugue form
but may have been strongly influenced by the structure of Dante's *Comme-
dia*. Pound has already given us an *Inferno* in the early *Cantos;* in the present
"American Colonial and Chinese cantos," we are in the midst of his *Purgato-
rio*. At any moment, as his apologist puts it, Pound may "plunge into the
Empyrean." On the metrical side, we are assured, Pound is breaking up the
iambic metres, usual and often monotonous in English poetry, with trochees
and spondees.

After Pound's long and rather insolent cultivation of opacity and ambi-
guity, it would be easy to become hilarious at all this blueprinting. And it
would be easy to poke fun at Pound himself, since he seems to be almost to-

tally without humor. But one must realize that he is [in] many ways a great figure. He did an extraordinary job thirty years ago of bringing life to English verse, and his influence has not yet petered out. He has written beautiful poetry. That he now sounds less like a poet than like a case history is tragic rather than comic. Faced with these new *Cantos,* one's warmest charity is certainly called into play. The dullness and brutishness of the Ming and the Manchu rulers, described in the first section, are equalled only by the fustiness and mustiness of John Adams's notations on life and business conditions with which Pound deals in the second. We are given, in this latter part, not "the idea and ideal of democracy as it was conceived in the mind of one of the founding fathers," which the publishers rather sentimentally promise us, but the atmosphere of American Colonial laundry bills and old promissory notes. Pound's early ability to open up gaps in his narration, through which we saw tranquil sea- and landscapes and lovely, cool forms of antique beauty, has totally disappeared. The only asides are scatological ones, of an extremely childish and petulant kind, and a few yelps of pure race hatred. As for the metrics, they often are those of prose (which is a mixture of iambs, trochees, and spondees).

Perhaps this is Purgatory. If so, we can only hope it is to be brief. For if Pound plans to make "plunges" into Paradise, he must be able to put aside his hatred, as Dante managed to do. If one hates anything too long, one not only begins to resemble what is hated but one forgets, one becomes incapable even of imagining any longer, what it is that one could love. What Pound would do in a paradise unencumbered by old bills of lading and growls about usury, it is becoming difficult to think. Moral indignation is one thing; *l'amor,* which Dante said moved the sun and other stars, is something even more difficult.

The ideograms occurring here and there in the text are certainly beautiful, and it is a great pleasure just to look at them.

[1940]

1. C. H. Douglas, an English mining engineer who, in the 1920s, identified a disparity between society's control of goods produced to meet its needs ("social credit") and the private control of "financial credit" by the banks.

The Pisan Cantos

OFFICIAL JUSTICE has now dealt with Ezra Pound, and this autumn New Directions has again taken up the task of publishing his works. Two volumes announce the beginning of this program: *The Pisan Cantos*, twenty poems written by Pound while he was a prisoner in the Italian city awaiting trial as a traitor, and *The Cantos*, which includes not only the Pisan section but all of his "epic" (in Pound's view, any poem that contains history is an epic) that he has written to date. The initial sixteen cantos first appeared in book form in 1925, when Pound's reputation was at its height. At the start, this "epic" exhibited in full the range of Pound's genius. It is a late work, begun when he was nearly forty and firmly in command of his difficult style. T. S. Eliot's *The Waste Land* (1922), dedicated to Pound, had given the modern world its first major poem in English. It was time for Pound to commence gathering together the fruits of his already long career: his scholarship in medieval romance literature (chiefly the literature of Provence), and his interest in the culture of the Italian and French Renaissance, in Greek literature from Homer to Callimachus, and in Chinese poetry and ideogram. His episodic and disjunct style suggested cinema technique, or so critics have decided, for it involved the flashback, breaking up the sequence of time and of place. Each item made sense but had no apparent connection with any other. And from the first Pound employed his most obvious trick: the use of classical tags, often in languages, such as Greek and Chinese, that need transliteration, or in dead tongues, such as *langue d'oc* [medieval Provençal]. As we look back with time's perspective, we realize that his various devices, if often used legitimately, were frequently the result of his mystifying, or sorcerer, side. The not clearly understood creates wonderment and awe, but bafflement and irritation as well. There is something hypnotizing, even for the initiate, in being confronted with a language one can barely pronounce, and the uninitiate are likely to be bowled over by words as simple as "to agathon" when they come at them in large black Greek capitals. But it was the Chinese ideogram which really offered Pound the chance to become a master magician. The ideogram is lovely beyond belief, yet it thwarts almost any attack made upon it by non-Chinese reason. There it is; one is impressed; the spell takes hold, and Pound has the reader in his image's power. These Poundian procedures had their good aspect, however. The poet was breaking down prejudice against forgotten or neglected cultures. He was striking across the lines of specialist scholars, so strict and so snobbish in our day. He was presenting the past as though it were all simultaneous and were still going on; he was making the point that in art this synchronization and timelessness actually exist.

Pound's streak of charlatanry, in *The Cantos* as a whole, was so interwoven with valuable insight that it was fairly negligible. What became really annoying was his growing tendency toward obsession. The obsessed always lack that final ingredient of greatness, humility. They are also invariably bad-tempered and vituperative. They hammer and they scold. Finally they stop making sense, and end up ranting in an exasperated gibberish. Pound never reached the gibberish stage, but at his worst he presented a picture of a fanatic who must always be in the right, who cannot turn a hairsbreadth from the small and concrete toward the large generality, who bores by quoting from documentation, and who sets up a pattern that gradually hardens, until we get nothing but deadly repetition. In the cantos written just before the war, Pound seemed to have lost his ability to control his manias, and his increasingly vulgar presentation of them often made him sound less like a lover of the highest cultures and more like a rude inheritor of none. But he could, at his best, revive, in lines of the most exquisite weight and the purest flow, the classic world, the crystal beginnings of men and gods.

Pound's imprisonment in Pisa seems to have brought him back to art and to life. *The Pisan Cantos* shows a new sense of proportion. He begins to feel pity and gratitude, and he begins to smile wryly, even at himself. I cannot think of any other record by an artist or a man of letters, in or out of prison, so filled with a combination of sharp day-to-day observation, erudition, and humorous insight. The diatribes against usury (Pound's King Charles's head[1]) occur, but they are now a minor theme. The gibes at enemies continue, but they are now mixed with the memories of friends—and what great and brilliant friends! And Pound cannot give enough gratitude to the Negro soldier who secretly made him a desk out of a packing box, to get him "offen th' ground" (he was living in a tent). He speaks with tenderness of a visiting lizard, and he jots down reminiscences of his art and life, beginning with the moment when, as a young poet, he thought of dumping the entire edition of his first book into a Venetian canal. All this may help us to understand the stresses that beset this American poet, whose art time will in the end surely honor, and without whose influence and energy we should not have modern poetry in English as we know it today.

[1948]

1. King Charles's head: whimsical obsession (Dickens).

Section: Rock-Drill 85–95 de Los Cantares

SECTION: ROCK-Drill 85–95 de Los Cantares is the title Ezra Pound, now in his seventieth year, has given to a group of eleven new Cantos, the first to appear in book form since The Pisan Cantos, of 1948. New Directions has printed the text with meticulous care, and certainly care was necessary because of the presence not only of many Chinese ideograms and a great scattering of Greek but of words, phrases, and sentences from almost every living European language, as well as from one or two dead ones. The Cantos, Pound long ago remarked, are "a poem containing history." Notoriously, he has never been content to present history cold; he has made his hot and frequently obsessive insistences perfectly clear as the work has progressed over the years. Now "the truth must be hammered home by reiteration, with the insistence of a rock drill." (I quote from the book's jacket.) If this motive had been developed to its full implications, the present section would have been unreadable. Fortunately, it has been only partly carried through. Pound, even in his later years and in his continuing tragic situation, has kept one part of his work free from the rigidity of dogma; the fluidity of poetry keeps breaking into the fixed design.

The new Cantos show some surface changes. They are shorter and more compressed, and a visual dimension has been added to mere words-in-print not only by the now familiar ideograms but also by a few Egyptian hieroglyphs, a stave of medieval musical notation, and even, on one occasion, the signs of the four playing-card suits—heart, diamond, club, and spade. These symbols often serve as a sort of shock and refreshment to the eye rather than as an aid to meaning, for although the Chinese written characters are frequently transliterated, we are given, almost always, their sound and not their sense. Because of this new concision of language, however, which amounts to a verbal shorthand, the shifts between Pound's themes are at least quite easy to follow.

These themes tend to overlap, but we can separate out three major ones. First, there is the repeated statement of large principles of sound human law and effective human action; second, the celebration of art and life at its purest and rarest (always in examples taken from a real or legendary past); and third, the theme—if it can be called such—of small, idiosyncratic obsession (the evils of usury and debased currency). This third one is peppered, as always, with Pound's malice and bad temper. These three areas of the poem dissolve into one another as do patterns in a natural element, like water or cloud, instead of proceeding in straight lines according to logical degrees of argument. The first theme opens the new work, and the disciplinary adages on which, according to Pound (and Confucius), high historic periods are built alternate with praise of *paideuma,* a favorite Poundian concept, which involves a living tradition leading into a living culture—teaching, training, discipline, correction, letters, knowledge, science. At the beginning of Canto 90, the exploration of *paideuma* disappears for a time, along with every sign of personal pique, and we find ourselves in one of Pound's magic circles, with an antique landscape of extreme loveliness unfolding before us. Praise of poetry at its source (the Castalian spring), of the sea and moon, groves and altars, fauns, nymphs, and sirens, of leopards and carved stone, of pines and birds, brings into view the poet who has every effect of evocative language under perfect control. This innocent natural beauty (a kind of lost *Paradiso)* washes over into Canto 91, but soon not only history but Pound's most shocking interpretation of modern history are upon us again; the old bad words reappear, the thought and emotion become darker and more turbulent. From this point on, Pound's power of exquisite imagery is evident only in single lines or even in single phrases, but there are still moments of passionate tension, and the quotations—chiefly from Greek poetry—are always, although fragmentary, pertinent to their context. In spite of everything, the main impression of these *Cantos* is far from that of a rock drill. At the end, a Homeric motif briefly reappears—a breath of loneliness felt by a man far from home, with a long journey still ahead. Pound now presents to us the shadow, as it were, of a personality, but one from which every layer of self-interest and self-pity has been burned away. It is sad that traces of small and bitter vindictiveness still remain. "A man of no fortune and with a name to come."

At present, Pound has no direct imitators. The contemporary generation writing in English has learned from him, it is true; the rules he formulated for the Imagists, more than forty years ago—directness, naturalness, precision—still hold. The actual form of the *Cantos,* however, now seems slightly fossilized—worthy of note as origin and as process but with no truly invigorating aspects.

[1956]

Gustave Flaubert

THE MOST important novel to be published in English in 1941 was the first intelligent translation into English of Flaubert's *L'Education sentimentale.* This novel, first published in 1869, was written after *Salammbô* and just before the final version of *La Tentation de Saint Antoine.* It is now generally acknowledged to be Flaubert's masterpiece. A profound and sardonic comment on Flaubert's own generation and the France of his youth, it is in every way pertinent to the human and social dilemmas of our own day.

The novel was viciously attacked by the critics and neglected by the general public, at its appearance. Only a few friends—Banville, the Goncourts,[1] George Sand—understood Flaubert's intentions or appreciated his success in putting them through. Sand realized that Flaubert's readers were still too close to the events described, and too involved in the Second Empire point of view, to wish to appreciate the book's ruthless analysis of social change and human motives. They recognized themselves too easily. And Sand complained that Flaubert gave no overt clue to where his sympathies lay. She wanted "an expression of blame . . . to condemn the evil. People do not understand that you wanted precisely to depict a deplorable state of society which encourages bad instincts." Flaubert had run into this sort of obtuseness in the French public and government before this. It had brought about the suit against the morals of *Madame Bovary*. He was incapable of agreeing with Sand's rather sentimental moralistic demands. His idea of the relation between the individual and society was far more complicated than hers. Society warped the individual but was it not individuals who had created, and blown up to enormous proportions, the governments which symbolized this hampering agency? Perhaps the basic evil lay deeper, in the constitution of the human heart.

Flaubert was depressed by the book's failure. He wrote in 1874 to Turgenev that he was still astonished that this work had never been understood. He finally decided that the book lacked "the falseness of perspective." "Every work of art," he said, "ought to have a point, a summit, make a pyramid . . . or better, the light should strike some point of the sphere. Now, there is nothing of that sort in life. But Art is not nature!" Here Flaubert partially understands that in this novel he has created a new genre. Critics, including Henry James, have misunderstood the book's conclusions because they were in no way dealing, here, with another *Madame Bovary:* not with "realism" or "romance," but with satire of a high but hidden order.

There is no doubt that *Sentimental Education*[1] is a difficult book to get the hang of, at a first reading. The reader must have a fair working knowledge of reaction and revolution in nineteenth-century France. To use a figure of Lowes Dickinson's, France was, throughout the century, politically in a state as though tracked by the Furies. It was a century of nervous unrest and of new and untried theory. And all theories, once applied, backfired in the most appalling way. The revolt against the Orléans line brought in the July monarchy (1830) and Louis Philippe's deadweight bourgeois rule. Universal suffrage, granted after 1848 and thought to be the instrument to establish the kingdom of God on earth, resulted only in Louis Bonaparte and, after three years of the Second Republic, the Second Empire. Paris fought for freedom; the provinces, fighting for the still unlaid ghosts of the old régime and Napoleon, finally voted away the newly granted franchise itself. Added to the political melee was the social one. The Industrial Revolution struck France in the thirties, in the factories of Lyons. All political parties were thrown into the rise of money, and the new concept of the right to work. The resulting confusion was severe. It is precisely this confusion, and its results, mirrored in the characters of the men and women who were at once its creators and its victims, that Flaubert here describes.

The book, written under the Second Empire, covers the period from 1840 to Louis Napoleon's *coup d'état* of December, 1851—save for the last two chapters, which form a coda to the whole. The action, excepting a few short passages, is seen through the eyes of Frédéric Moreau, of the provincial landed middle class, newly come to Paris, as the book begins, to pass his law examinations. A new spirit is in the air. The tradition of Romanticism and of the bohemian painter, writer, and poet had worn almost completely threadbare. The period of the career based on money deals of one sort or another (*Enrichissez-vous* [grow rich] was said to be the counsel of Louis Philippe to his subjects) had begun. Art and industry, art and journalism, stood opposed, in spite of naïve efforts to reconcile their purposes. (*Industrial Art* is the name of the magazine run by Arnoux, the husband of the woman Frédéric comes to adore; the paper of the unprincipled Hussonet begins under the name *Art* and ends up entitled *The Man About Town.*) Stock-jobbing, loans, investments, and mortgages were the preoccupation of deputies and ministers. Borrowing a little money and making more, getting in with "influential" people, occupied the minds of law students, writers, painters, and hangers-on. The movement of opportunism elaborates and expands into a mounting frenzy. Notes fall due; debts pile up; the fate of men and women depends on the worth or worthlessness of shares. Bankruptcies, auctions, bailiffs finish the hopes of guilty and innocent alike. Underneath runs the theme of personal treachery. Friends betray one another; old men revenge themselves in their wills; women take it out on rivals by holding over them old debts and promissory notes.

The revolts of Republicans and the new Socialists against bourgeois rule form the book's secondary theme. The theorists make plans and hold to rigid formulas. Spontaneous outbreaks of the people link up with the planned action of the revolutionaries. Barricades go up; arms are requisitioned from the citizens. The crowd swarms into the Tuileries; grand pianos and clocks are flung out of windows. One of the book's great set-pieces describes the Paris street fighting in 1848. And the book closes with Paris again under arms; the dragoons, aided by the police, galloping against the citizens under the gaslight with sabers drawn—and the Second Empire has begun.

Senecal, the democratic dogmatist who develops by degrees into a tyrant and member of the police, is the character which has astonished modern readers by its deadly accuracy and contemporary pertinence. "Where are the labor poets?" Senecal asks, when shown a library. He wants, in literature,

280   *Criticism*

content and not form. He thinks *tableaux vivants*[2] corrupting for the daughters of the proletariat. As a factory overseer, he extracts fines ruthlessly. "Democracy," he remarks, "does not mean license for the individual. It means a common level under the law, the division of labor—order!" "You've left out humanity," Frédéric answers. It is Senecal who kills Dussardier, "the good fellow," the honest believer in Socialist virtue "who attributed all the evil on earth to authority."

And Flaubert traces down "an insane desire for authority, of whatever kind if only it be authority," in all these people who have lost so many natural links to life. "France, feeling herself without a master [after '48], began to cry out in terror, like a blind man without a stick, or a child that has lost its nurse" [insertion LB's]. And the reader continues to recognize these characters. There is something startlingly familiar in Hussonet, the journalist who prints gossip and slander as news, who "extols the fifth-rate and disparages the first-class minds." Arnoux, the intermediate type between bohemian and businessman, infected with the failings of both—"his mind was not elevated enough to attain to art nor ordinary enough to think solely of profit, so that he was ruining himself without satisfying anyone"—is closely akin to Frédéric, who feels the resemblance. Arnoux is a gourmet and gives little dinners "with ten kinds of mustard." Deslauriers, Frédéric's friend, in the words of the Goncourts, is "with his fond envy, his intermittences of perfidy and friendship, his solicitor's temperament, a perfectly drawn type of the most widespread kind of scurvy humanity." Mlle Vatnaz, the emancipated woman, venomous, the dupe of her passions, a literary hack and go-between with a business head, is still not a complete grotesque.

Then there is the gallery of "conservative humbugs," male and female, whom Flaubert does not spare. "Bigotry of the rich rivaled the frenzy of the starving. . . . Property began to be confused with God, and attacks on it . . . almost resembled cannibalism." But Flaubert was out to show up "the bourgeois in [working-class] blouses as well as the bourgeois in coats." He examines with the same detachment social theorists, the hysterics, terrorists, and fakes on the fringes of the Socialist movement, and the conservative money and power jugglers and their "distinguished" circle, ready to grease the palm of any government that came into power. The stupidity of the workers' meeting and the complicated spite of the dinner party are both analyzed. Flaubert wished to clear the reader's mind of all "accepted ideas" concerning the supposed nobility of either group. Suddenly, at the end of the book, we look back and see how each category has received its touch of clear-sightedness: these liberals who are at bottom neurotic reactionaries; these members of a new middle class who not only "have no interest in the things of the mind," who do not act according to motives of patience, pity, duty, love, or generosity, but actually do not know that such qualities exist. And has Flaubert spared from his satiric justice of treatment the supposed prototype of a lifelong love of his, Mme Arnoux? She has been thought to stand in the book as an unclouded exponent of womanly sweetness and virtue. Is she not, rather, a sort of Madame Bovary in reverse—a woman who rejects passion because she pietistically fears God's punishment, whose virtue brings her to the pass of offering herself, in age, to a man who suddenly recognizes the true incestuous nature of his devotion to her?

The profound psychological truth of the book's two final chapters is unequaled in modern literature. For in these two scenes Flaubert's uncanny knowledge of the pathology of modern life becomes startlingly evident. The nostalgic reminiscence of Frédéric and Deslauriers, casting back to their youthful frightened visit to the prostitute's house, reveals the continuing infantilism of these two grown-up children who have never been able to lift themselves over the threshold of maturity, who cannot learn, who can only, in spite of some native decency and generosity, repeat, and flee life's consequences. The modern split between emotion and reason stands revealed. Flaubert elsewhere remarks: "You do not possess Christianity any more. What do you possess? Railroads, factories, chemists, mathematicians. Yes, the body fares better, the flesh does not suffer so much, but the heart continues to bleed. Material questions are resolved. Are the others? . . . And as you have not filled that eternal yawning gulf which every man carries in himself, I mock at your efforts, and laugh at your miserable sciences which are not worth a straw." *Sentimental Education* is a handbook to the present because the gulf of which Flaubert speaks, after seventy years, has not been filled but only widened and deepened. The thirst for some saving authority has grown stronger, the childish bigotries more complete. Let us examine our theorists, Flaubert says, and throw out their false premises. Let us enlarge the provable human data. Have these nervous insurrections accomplished anything; are we following the "advanced notions" of a parcel of "buffoons"? Should "the government of a country be a section of the Institute, and the last section of all"?

Some partial answers lie in this novel, panoramic and profound, written in the "ivory tower" of Croisset and published one year before the inauspicious events of 1870 which ushered in the Third Republic.

[1942]

1. Edmond Goncourt (1822–96) and his brother Jules (1830–70) coauthored social histories, art criticism, and naturalistic novels.
2. *L'Education sentimentale* might better be translated *The Education of Feeling.* The French noun *sentiment* can also mean sensibility or consciousness or even opinion. A clear moral irony underlies Flaubert's title-phrase.
3. *tableaux vivants:* parlor-game enactments of scenes from art and literature.

Folk Art

WILL FOLK art save us from creative and moral aridity if we can find and use it? The reiterated insinuation that formal art is fraudulent because it is difficult to understand and makes no effort to appeal to the majority—that it is, in fact, somehow treasonable to mankind's higher purposes and aims—is a typical bourgeois notion that has been around for a long time. That formal art cannot be put to any immediate use also lays it open to materialist denigration. The conviction that the simple is straight and pure and true, while the complex is concocted and double-dealing, is a partially moral one. It is a conviction which shares room, in the minds and emotions of many people, with an unconscious yearning for a lost rural world. In America, just enough time has elapsed since real urbanization set in for this yearning to roll up to its present proportions and to have acquired its present rationalizations. In spite of these desires and beliefs of the middle-class Subconscious, the fact remains that no civilization has ever produced a literature out of folk (either current or revived) alone. The formal artist cannot be outlawed. The whole question is muddled in the extreme. Let us examine it with as much detachment as possible.

It is true that the formal artist, at least twice within living memory, has succeeded in getting past modern barriers to a real folk tradition, and that remarkable literature has resulted in both cases from the intersection of the formal with the folk line. Lorca's genius was ignited in the most brilliant way by Flamenco tradition, and Yeats was fortified and refreshed from the beginning by his close knowledge of the Irish peasant. Both these poets received the experience of poetry still attached to music, at the improvisatory stage; and of an audience creatively involved (actually listeners, as distinguished from mere readers) in what they as poets produced.

But the fact is that only the most abnormal situations, political or otherwise, kept these two folk traditions alive so late in an industrial and urbanized Europe. The turning toward the folk, at the end of the eighteenth century, was not only preindustrial but prerevolutionary; and the same sort of ferments were present in Yeats's Ireland and Lorca's Spain. The current attempts in America to get back to primitive material are natural enough, but they are different. They are the desire of a far from revolutionary population to get back to some earlier fun, as well as some earlier integrity. Certainly the material is there. We can trace the line of the American folk song through the ballads of English, Irish, and Scotch origin (broken away from their original scene and transformed) through the work songs of all kinds (sea chanteys, songs of the plantation and the cattle-range), the hymns and spirituals, up to the beginning of town life. Then the culmination of the American folk song appears. Stephen Foster, the untrained and greatly gifted writer of "popular songs," managed to express fully the emotions common during this period of transition. On the one hand, through him the loneliness as well as the rough gaiety of a primitive society found its voice. On the other, Foster gave expression to something quite new: an emotion which was to become increasingly persistent in the American spirit—the sense of profound nostalgia for an already disappearing non-urban way of life. The strong sentimentalization of Foster by his modern audience proceeds from the holdover of this crucial though hidden nostalgia into our own time. Clearly, he was the end of one kind of American folk, the point beyond which no unadulterated development of his kind of material was possible.

We begin to get the production of the urbanized folk after the hymns and marching songs of the Civil War. The railroads building and having been built, we get the railroad songs. The cities once made, we get the hybrid genteel, and the barbershop ballads, and what is more vivid and interesting, the songs of the "underworld": brothel, saloon, dope joint, and prison. The earlier tradition fell into neglect as the way back to the farm became more and more closed. It was rediscovered and refurbished, along with hooked rugs and pine blanket chests, when the 1914 war broke up American Victorian and aroused, in some not quite understandable fashion, the middle-class enthusiasm for the American antique. The folk tradition, as a result, has become thoroughly "bourgeoizified." At present there is no way for the artist to get at it, for it has been dragged into a region where nothing living or nutritious for his purposes exists. It can be looked at and listened to, admired and imitated; but it cannot at the present time be called upon to do any truly important task. Only a writer thoroughly immersed in middle-class values, and soaked through and through with the sentimentality of the middle, could for a moment believe that this mummified and genteelized folk could contribute any spark of life to his purposes.

The English and French tradition of town-folk (with a head start of some forty or fifty years of true industrialism over the United States) channeled itself into the music hall. "The supreme embodiment of the surviving character of the English working people," writes one chronicler of the English nineteenth-century scene, "was the music hall. . . . Springing spontaneously out of the sing-song of the upper tavern room and the old out-of-door gardens of the artisans of the pastoral past, it became for a space of time a British institution. Its morality was to make the best of a bad job; its purpose to make everyone free and easy. . . ." The authenticity of this institution, created by the first articulate development of urban folk for its own enjoyment, soon impressed itself on the artists and writers of the time. Through it, they were able to skirt the middle, find excitement and restorative energy, and make a point of contact with "life." But the music hall decayed. It was based on that period of "proletarian" existence when the workers were stiffly encased in the tradition of knowing their place and imitating their betters. This tradition exploded in 1918; and we hear Eliot making a final tribute to Marie Lloyd, with added gloomy prognostications for the future:

> It was her capacity for expressing the soul of a people that made her unique. . . . It was her understanding of the people and sympathy with them, and the people's recognition of the fact that she embodied the virtues that they most genuinely respected in private life, that raised her to the position she occupied at her death. I have called her the expressive

figure of the lower classes. There is no such expressive figure for any other classes. The middle classes have no such idol: the middle classes are morally corrupt. . . .

Eliot then goes on to express his fear that, with the disappearance of the music hall, and "the encroachment of the cheap and rapid-breeding cinema, the lower classes will drop to the same state of protoplasm as the bourgeoisie," and, moreover, when this state has overcome them, that they may die off from sheer boredom! This essay, written in 1923, closes with words of deep dismay as to the possibility of the hastening of this general disintegration by the development of another mechanical device for transmitting entertainment—the radio.

Eliot underestimated his "lower classes." The music hall disappeared only after it had reached a high point of breadth and elegance. Folk expression continually runs toward this elegance, contrary to the *idée reçue* of its being by necessity clumsy and "vulgar." (And this elegance is not to be confused with the empty slickness of the revue kind.) But as a rather stuffy set of prewar conventions broke, the urban crowd shifted toward a freer, less imitative and reverent habit of mind and manner. Something new began immediately; persistent energy released itself into new forms and new media.

The energy is now at a more primitive level than formerly; these shifts go back and forth, as this current of urban life or that is released and breaks; many reasons requiring specialized attention are here involved. But the fact remains that American folk has never been more vigorous than at this moment. In "hot jazz," words are attached to music, as in all primitive states of poetry and music. Improvisation (the "lick") is in every talented performer's power. The rhythm is the important matter; the music has all the harmonic tricks under control with which to surround and embellish the beat. The various mechanical devices which Eliot feared and deplored have served, as a matter of fact, to aid the development and dissemination of this folk art. The folk now gets exactly what it wants to listen to. If the radio does not give it what it needs in sufficient quantity, people have their records and juke boxes, and, of course, the live performers. The vigor of folk at present is shown by its tendency to raid over into "classical" and bring back whatever tunes please it. The juke-box repertoire is a thing in itself: there the hymn tune (disguised) shares popularity with the crooned ballad and with certain holdovers from the open spaces of the past. Compared to the songs of the upright piano and sheet music era, even the most naïve songs are less awkward and saccharine, more vitalized. And the imitation "folk song," such as the really remarkable "Blues in the Night," has taken on a finish which always characterizes folk in a good creative period *of its own*.

It is interesting to note that at this particular stage, "popular" interest in accident, sudden death, and the morbid in general (unlike American songs of an earlier day) has very nearly disappeared, along with the "topical song," that sister to the broadsheet.

A proposition could be drawn up:

Folk crosses formal art:

1. When folk has reached a moment of comparative breadth and elegance (when it can express anything, from the grotesque through emotion and satire, well).
2. When formal art has become easy and secular enough to recognize just where folk lies; and, having located folk, understands what is happening there.

A long period of time must elapse before, in America, the demands of this proposition can be fulfilled. But Eliot's fears were unjustified; just as the present middle-class hope that L. Stokowski can be crossed with Disney,[1] or some genteel poet with the songs of pioneering backwoodsmen, is at once previous and misplaced.

LET us now take a brief glance at the American intellectual. The intellectual is a middle-class product; if he is not born into the class he must soon insert himself into it, in order to exist. He is the fine nervous flower of the bourgeoisie. His task, ideally, would be the close critical observation of the field in which he stands, while keeping his attention alert for new movement in the landscape as a whole. That the intellectual fails in this job is one reason for the wholesale mixture of genres, the unrebuked mistakes of prize committees, publishers, etc., the general insolence of entrepreneurs—in fact the general failure to understand what is going on which marks the small remaining section of American life still interested in literature.

The intellectual, being nervous, is subject to all the floating airs of modern religion (present in quantity, no matter how fogged and misted into the semblance of something else). One must not forget that religious enthusiasm (and intolerance) has always been inextricably mixed with every materialist idea; has been a concomitant of all material push since Calvin. Intellectuals range through the finest gradations of kind and quality: from those who are merely educated neurotics, usually with strong hidden reactionary tendencies, through mediocrities of all kinds, to men of real brains and sensibility, more or less stiffened into various respectabilities or substitutes for respectability. The number of Ignorant Specialists is large. The number of hysterics and compulsives is also large. It is natural that the truly sensitive intellectual should have spiritual needs; for such a person the necessity for those moments in life when one is forced to see reality without wraps and unrationalized is strong. This necessity leads to a real breakthrough into maturity on the part of some individuals. For the less sensitive, the spiritual necessity hardly exists; they require not steadying insight but emotional outlet. It is in this class that we find the hot-gospellers, the morally pretentious, the reformers, and the seekers of closed systems of salvation. These men and women are not entirely the products of an imperfect culture (for the type appeared in quantity in France in the nineteenth century) but of a culture somehow blocked and mixed; and of the impact of this curious situation upon natures more simply constituted than they themselves suppose. Flaubert wrote down an approximation of the type in *Bouvard et Pécuchet*. He gave the two simple-minded copyists a set of manias which is still complete for the dislocated middle-class mind of our time; manias ranging from the collecting of antiques to an absorption in various forms of science and politics. These two prototypes of the middle-class yearner with a few retouches could represent not only the modern lecture-listening audience, but many of "the experts who tend the complicated machinery of modern civilization."

One characteristic of the Bouvard-Pécuchet sort of enthusiasm is the violent repudiation after violent interest of one craze after another when the satiation point is reached. The revulsion shown by the intellectual toward the artist, during recent years, resembles this sort of compensating tendency. The too-great emphasis of emotion and hope placed upon the artist in the preceding period is lifted and placed at an opposite point. The D. H. Lawrence, Proust, Hart Crane kind of semi-worship went over, for a time, to Malraux;[2] and then became transformed into something else. The very complexity of the artist's equipment became as much a target for the subsequent badgering and denigration as the non-material quality of his aims. It is moral blame of the most childish kind that we find most frequently expressed; and real puzzlement, also at a childish level. The atmosphere of former religious paroxysms and squabblings returns; the old fights between established religion and the sects and between the sects themselves; the old tiresome yet dangerous extremes of the persecutory centuries.

Now, one would think that the unstable intellectual should stand out against all these moral acrobatics and tergiversations: if not as judge, at least as arbiter. If he cannot remain firm, he should at least be in another part of the field, out of the melee and ahead of it. But as things turn out, he is either squarely in the mix-up, name-calling with the best or making motions of advancing, the while he has managed rapidly to retreat into something truly comforting in the way of pre-Copernican scholasticism, or has made a full flight back to Aristotle. And if he is of no real use in reconciling embattled sects, perhaps he could do a little simple journeyman's work in keeping entrepreneurism in its place. But here he rather fails us, too.

At this point it is necessary to remember that the middle class has produced, at the expense of much time and effort, a whole literature of its own. Its own writers, bred out of its own bone and flesh, educated in its own schools and amenable to its own scheme of manners and custom, have fanned out into the middle region; adapted in every way to express the middle intellect, temperament, grasp of reality, powers of analysis and emotion. Some of these poets, novelists, critics, biographers, and belletrists were born middle; some either rose or sank to where they at length find themselves. The complicated but smoothly oiled machinery of the publishing business, the general run of reviewers, the committees giving out literary awards, the more benumbed mass of academics: all these agents function, for the most part (and changing the figure), inside the same structure. During certain short periods, certain wild individuals stay outside and throw rocks, but since these intransigents tend to disappear for long intervals, the easiest supposition is that they are absorbed. And the periods of almost complete absorption present a very amusing spectacle indeed. These are the times when the book sections produce, week after week, month after month, serious judgments on books, but when everything judged and the judges themselves are cut out of the same piece of medium material. The commodity books are being dealt with by the commodity critics—a spectacle which would be purely funny if there were not elements of rather tragic irony in it.

The intellectual should at least know the difference between kinds, and have the courage to speak up when matters get really out of hand. He should make some admonishing gesture when a particularly startling piece of mutual aid comes through. He should know how the literary mechanism works: the way blurb-writing and prize-giving, journalists and literary impresarios engage with each other. He should be able to sense, watching the open pulls and twitches given reputations, all the subterranean maneuvering which must go on so that certain effects are produced at eye-level. What about the distinguished specialists who write blurbs for dust-jackets? Is this a harmless bit of fun, or a plan to get around the subsequent remarks of the book reviewer? What about the American prize committee (situated rather disadvantageously, one might suppose, for anyone not a journalist, in a school of journalism) which, having ignored brilliant talent, young and old, falls back ever again upon old standbys? What about the extra-literary influences which manage, from time to time, to bring to laudatory view a book of gibberish? What about certain anthologists who teeter on the verge of being members of the vanity press: are all their contributors paid? Who is to deal with these matters but the intellectual?

Meanwhile, the cry rises that poetry has disappeared. This plaint often comes from the dead center, say from the core of the Sunday book section. It rises with particular sharpness during times of cataclysm. The middle wishes poetry to throb, as it were, under the historic processes without a break; to light up ambiguous terrain with continual succeeding flashes of "inspiration." But poetry cannot be counted upon to act as a sort of combination faith-healing and artificial thunder and lightning. Poetry of the lyric order disappears for a century at a time. It shifts. And when the formal line has in some manner been exhausted, the vigor goes back to the base. The middle must put up with what it has: their flabby little songs, their attempts at reviving the "golden" American past; and their more ambitious flights: those attempts to combine autobiography with *post hoc ergo propter hoc*[3] comment on the world situation.

"The function of the great individual is to take up and transform what has been communally produced." For this function one must wait, when the folk material is in a transitional phase—unmalleable and too full of its own rough vigor to be handled, and when "great individuals" seem to be lacking. Even the artist may misjudge the time. In Eliot's "Sweeney Agonistes" and "Fragment of an Agon" the two lines—of formal treatment and "rough" material—are somehow artificially combined; the result cannot really move

Criticism

us. But there are times when the poet can deal with whatever comes to hand. And folk will not always remain ungraspable.

A FEW NOTES on the future direction of the poet:

The true hierarchic attitude as exemplified by some "inheritors of Symbolism" (Stefan George[4] and to a lesser degree Valéry and Yeats) seems to be exhausted. George's "willed rationalism toward the antique, his aesthetic and individualist humanism . . . which seeks in the universe the exaltation of man"—this line we have seen warped and corrupted; it now leads nowhere. The lesser task of the poet at present is satire. But satire cannot be asked to bear all of the weight of the diversified and subtle modern spirit. There is another development of this century's early period of aesthetic experiment and moral explanation. This proceeds from Rilke. "In Rilke (as opposed to George)," writes Geneviève Bianquis, already quoted above, "exists the most absolute abandonment to the law of the inanimate; the need to unknot, to detach the bonds of the individual; the need to love everything, to absorb everything into himself and to absorb himself in all; to channel toward God or toward things all happiness, all sorrow and all emotion." This is the contrast between the will which builds Ages of Faith and the act of faith itself; between compulsion and serenity; arrogance and humility; between the raw act of force and the more complex refusal of force but openness to spiritual power.

The foundation material is ready for this tendency. The only really usable and incontrovertible modern discoveries are in the spiritual field; and these have their everyday diagnostic and therapeutic uses. Truth has been told, experience undergone, and movement undertaken—"forward" as Eliot says; but this forward has not its old "progressive" connotation. The number of individuals engaged in writing poetry of this order will not be large, and, as is so often the case, may be unseen by their generation. The forms will be kept clear and the tone uninflated. No more rhetoric; no more verbalizing; no more exhortations or elegies or eulogies. No more conscious and affected investigations of dark corridors and deserted strands; no more use of the universe as a backdrop against which one acts out hope or despair. No more dejected sitting about. No more searching nature for an answering mood . . .

This exploration and movement can go on without having to search out the folk for refreshment. The more complex tasks have been neglected for a long time; attention to them is overdue. Compared to these at once subtle and difficult necessities the reiterated standardized demands of the bourgeois yearner sound incredibly stupid and outdated.

> Is it possible that despite our discoveries and progress, despite our culture, religion, and world-wisdom, we still remain on the surface of life? Is it possible that we have even covered this surface which might still have been something, with an incredibly uninteresting stuff which makes it look like drawing-room furniture during the summer holidays?
> Yes, it is possible . . .
> But if all this is possible . . . then surely, for all the world's sake, something must be done. The first comer, he who has had these disturbing thoughts, must begin to do some of the neglected things; even if he be just anybody, by no means the most suitable person: there is no one else at hand. This young insignificant foreigner, Brigge, will have to sit down in his room five flights up, and write, day and night. Yes, he will have to write; that will be the end of it.[5]

This was written at the beginning of the century; but nothing much seems to have been accomplished. Now that a good deal of the drawing-room furniture lies in ruins, there may be another beginning.

[1943]

1. The conductor Leopold Stokowski was crossed with Walt Disney in a work mixing film with symphonic music and cartoon called *Fantasia* (1940).
2. André Malraux (1901–76) is for LB a type of the artist whose energies stray into politics and explanations of culture.
3. *post hoc ergo propter hoc:* confusing earlier events with the causes of later ones.
4. In a 1943 review LB characterizes the German poet Stefan George (1868–1933), who studied in France with Mallarmé, as a poet whose ideas were simple and sincere, but whose expression was complex.
5. From Rainer Maria Rilke's *Journal of My Other Self,* also known as *The Notebooks of Malte Laurids Brigge,* 1910.

Isak Dinesen

WE NOW know Isak Dinesen to be Baroness [Karen] Blixen of Denmark. It was apparent from the first that the author who published, in complete pseudonymity, *Gothic Tales* in 1934 was a woman, a native of Northern Europe, and a person whose sources were in some manner attached to the feudal tradition. *Gothic Tales,* because of their exuberance (severely regulated as it was), their civilized bitterness, their brilliantly informed fantasy, were clearly an end product of some kind. They had the quality, under the surface classicism of their style, of that sparkling improvisation contrasted with melancholy revery so usual in Romantic music; the romance of the incompletely lighted and fantastic nineteenth-century "soul," at the end of one thing as much as at the beginning of another; caught back into nostalgia for the past and filled with premonitory anguish. But unlike Romantic music, these tales came to some sharp conclusions. Their intellectual underpinning was sturdy. They were highly conscious productions. The author behind them was not one to be taken in, least of all by herself.

Out of Africa (1938) brought the unknown author before us in the round. An autobiographical account of Baroness Blixen's life as owner of a coffee plantation in German East Africa, later Kenya Colony, it showed exactly what a feudal heritage had given this woman, and to what use she had put inherited ideas of responsibility. Her growth as an artist is also described; so that the reader, having read *Gothic Tales,* with only the information he could deduce from it, comes to any later work knowing more than one usually knows concerning a modern writer. He knows, for example, the writer's courage, both physical and moral, having watched it at work in rude and isolated surroundings. He also knows by the facts and their manner of presentation that she is as tender as she is courageous, as profoundly perceptive as she is sensitively humane.

Winter's Tales is not *Gothic Tales* repeated. The inventive extravagance has been reduced; the stories do not multiply, one within another, in the earlier manner. They share the simplicity and background, often, of the folk tale. But unlike the folk tale, they do not repeat some obsession of the simple mind —fear, desire for power or wealth, or luck, or freedom from restriction.

And it is interesting to see how completely they differ from those "fairy tales" composed by Isak Dinesen's fellow-countryman, Hans Christian Andersen. In Andersen the folk tale took on, for all his charm of treatment, elements of sentiment and "rise": the Ugly Duckling is a far more bourgeois character than Cinderella. The majority of the characters in *Winter's Tales* are not going anywhere, in the success-story sense. And those who have some selfish or insolent plans for themselves are soon taken down by unforeseen small circumstance. Destiny's plans, far more noble than any they could have invented for themselves, take over (as in the case of the young wife in "The Pearls" and the writer in "The Young Man with the Carnation"). These plans of destiny often have heavy justice in them and work on two planes. The cruel feudal despot who misuses his power ("Sorrow-Acre") is baffled not only by the selflessness of his victim but by the unfaithfulness of his wife, whose child by her lover will break the closed line of succession. And at the center of the book stands the child Jens, the pure poet and "comic fabulist" who knows his place in this world without having to be taught it; when he is transplanted from poverty to riches, he can look back on poverty with pleasure, accepting luxury the while, and remember the pleasing elements in the nature of his former friends, the rats.

The blunt and flourishing optimism of middle-class materialism could not have produced these stories. That we get them at this particular period of history is a remarkable thing in itself. They are, it is true, from time to time informed with the sharp bite of the civilized fable. But they are not fables, but parables. They deal almost entirely with inner themes of "love, hate, and reparation," with spiritual, not "practical" truths. The witty yet profound treatment of the artist and his public in terms of God and Job ("A Consolatory Story") sums up the author's view of one problem of reconciliation. Here light is thrown upon a situation by means of irony. Elsewhere Isak Dinesen prefers to irradiate mysteries of conduct by mention of other mysteries, as when, at the end of "The Invincible Slave Owners," the perplexed lover, realizing that certain human situations exist which nothing can change, contemplates the waterfall and thinks of the fugue. As in all good parables, the lines of meaning are not pulled tight. The reader is left with the threads in his own hands, and can examine and combine them according to his own experience.

The period quality is exquisitely managed. The publishers, it is true, have built up all the fustian possibilities of this atmosphere. The book is very nearly bound in seafoam and stardust; and one must grin and bear the book-jacket surrealism which runs over onto the end-papers. The little blurbs provided by the publicity department on the jacket for each story should be ignored; their facts are sometimes wrong and their interpretation almost always queer. These are by no means special or bizarre stories. They belong to an old and great tradition and are worthy of it. That they have been written in English is our good luck, the chance of contact with European tradition at present being what it is. It is good to be able to read them early, even though they are certain to be around for a long time.

[1943]

Detective Novels

THE MODERN detective novel originated in times physically, and perhaps spiritually, darker than our own. The *roman policier* was based on the invention, new and terrible to the French, of the political police, under Fouché and Napoleon. Later, Vidocq, an adventurer born under the Old Régime, managed under the new dispensation to make a transformation in which the chaos of the period is summed up: he became Chef de la Sureté [head of criminal investigations] and used his criminal career as a basis for his position on the other side of the law. His *Memoirs,* published in Paris in 1829, intersected the legend of the Byronic hero. Here was something new, a product of another social situation, the beginning of a new legend. Vidocq appears almost immediately in literature as Balzac's Vautrin. Meanwhile, and following closely in the steps of actual spies and *agents provocateurs,*[1] Eugène Sue began to produce, in the thirties, his series of *romans-feuilletons* [serialized novels], which included *Les Mystères de Paris* and *Le Juif errant.* Jean Cassou has stated that the development of the *roman-feuilleton* and the creation of the social sciences is parallel. The secrets of "sordid and terrible Paris" were sought out, in the first, under the cover of darkness. The rich and the poor, the intriguer and his victim, were linked together. "The poor adventurer, the pariah, the *carbonaro*,[2] the artist, the regenerator, the adversary of the Jesuits . . . these were the phantasmagoria projected by [the beginning of] the nineteenth century." They were symbolic of the strange desire that had manifested itself in the midst of chaos: "to pass beyond the political to the social revolution" [insertion LB's].

The earliest detectives worked by mystery and ruse rather than rapidity and force. Roger Caillois, in his intelligent study of the genre, *Le Roman policier*,[3] says that the detective is at first successful not through his logic but because of his disguises. He is, at the beginning, an inheritor of Fenimore Cooper, the infallible observer of the forest. The great city has become a new jungle, more dangerous than the solitudes of Canada. This pattern was soon abandoned, but it has returned in the spy and secret-agent stories of the present. But let us watch the closing in of the form, the development of "deduction," which at one point made the detective novel into an almost pure play of the logical faculties, a detached *jeu d'esprit*.

This tendency toward rules was observed in the detective novel while rules elsewhere in nineteenth-century literature were being progressively rejected. The detective novel splits off from the surrounding anarchy of form. And within its closed universe Poe further limits its locale by inventing the convention of the locked room. The detective now has completely rejected his bloodhound role. He becomes the scientist "coordinating indices," the artist-priest astounding the world at large as well as his rather stupid human foil. The crime becomes as isolated from life as a chemical experiment. Rules to protect the reader emerge: "Give the reader an equal right with the detective . . . no supernatural or scientific marvels . . . no tricky architecture . . . no factors brought in at the last moment." And the *acte gratuit*, the motiveless impulse, cannot function at this point; the diabolical machinery must work on the basis of accepted motives. Now, "the detective story must take from existence nothing but a frame. . . . It is not interested in passions or emotions except as a force to set the mechanism in motion. It is only interested in forming a complete and simple figure from incomprehensible and partial fragments. The novel attaches itself to the nature of man. This nature is a bother to the detective story, at this stage, and it supports it only unwillingly."

M. Caillois' analysis now reaches a crucial fact. Here is this new form, coldly opposed to everything literature stands for. But the pure exercise of the intellectual faculty, the detachment from emotion, the devotion of the detective to the penetration of "an artificial miracle"—all this is brought up against the unalterable convention that a detective novel must be based on a corpse. It demands a murderer—a person who has killed and risks capital punishment; no other sort of malefactor will do. And because of this anomaly between crude subject and skilled method, the detective story cannot remain a pure puzzle for long. "The cards must be shuffled." Suddenly "neither the murderers are real bandits nor the searchers real police." Variations multiply; here, in a late development, is Simenon's Maigret, a detective with a compassionate heart. "An obscure necessity obliges these policemen to make reservations in their role. They have a liberal attitude or a liberal profession. . . . They occupy a marginal place in regard to society, in the manner of the sorcerer or devil in the ancient tales who appears in the guise of a stranger, a horse dealer, a doctor, an itinerant merchant."

The closed circle begins to break. The puzzle begins to widen back toward the novel proper. Now the criminal has become anyone. "The most unexpected person" is now any man or woman, of whatever age or condition. And the elaboration of the setting becomes inexhaustible. *Everywhere* has become the scene of the crime. No situation, however sacred or cut off from life by money, power, or prestige, has been omitted. As in a fox hunt, every modern type and modern locale has been "blooded" by the detective novel. But the detective story has not by any means merged with the novel. It has, instead, drained off from the other form many of its residues of "sensation." While apparently working with the most icy logical detachment, the narrative breaks off "complaisantly to recount scabrous scenes of cruelty or eroticism. The ambition of the intelligence is flattered while the appetite for sensation is satisfied."

The mention of death and dissolution has almost disappeared from modern middle-class and "folk" literature. The detective novel does not reject one detail of the macabre. And it openly accommodates fear and aggression, open or disguised. Certain authors specialize in the frozen will of the nightmare— or the neurotic symptom; their characters may not escape even if they could. The rat-in-the-trap, the spider-and-the-fly motifs recur. The baseless fears of the folk tale or the psychiatric clinic are endlessly repeated. And the inveterate reader of detective stories can soon classify his reading into stories written by and for sadists, by and for masochists; into stories in which someone, under a pseudonym, is working off some obsession or perversion or fear that is sure to link up with similar aberrations in some reader. On a higher level we get a complete picture of paranoia in Kafka's *The Trial*.

The obscure religious undercurrent in these dramas of sin and retribution cannot be overlooked. "One of the strange phenomena of the nineteenth century"—I quote a modern clergyman—"is the spectacle of religion dropping the appeal to fear while other human interests have picked it up." The Gothic novel that began in the late eighteenth century bore the marks of a broken-down, secularized, floating religion. It is the supernatural that intervenes. The trappings are Catholicism's ruined abbeys; the fumes are those of a Protestant personal hell. Ritual has dissolved. The detective story, on the other hand, has all the marks of a live cult, developing from primitivism toward complexity. The victim is always there, whether the sign of a brutal sacrifice or a more human oblation. And the priestlike character of the detective was once very clear: Sherlock Holmes, in whose human reality many people believed, is the supreme example of this type.

"The present-day individual," writes a psychiatrist, "is more and more called upon to give up his aggressions. The repressed and therefore unconscious criminality of the normal man finds few socially harmless outlets: dream and fantasy life, the neurotic symptom, and some transitional forms of behavior. . . ." The breakthrough of the submerged Unconscious, the symbolic struggle between good and evil—in the detective story we find a re-enactment of these struggles. And the flight motif has returned, along with the tracking-down-of-the-fugitive role of the official or unofficial police. Graham Greene, one of the most intelligent and exciting writers of the modern "thriller"—because his imagination seems peculiarly sensitive to archetypal subconscious themes—has recognized the role of the conscience in these dramas; he gives one book in its English edition a title extracted from Francis Thompson's poem "The Hound of Heaven"—*The Labyrinthine Ways*. And it is Greene who has stated that the history of contemporary society is being written "in hundreds of volumes, most of them sold in cheap editions—the detective novels." The great and perceptive writers of the nineteenth century from George Eliot through Henry James accepted the material and announced the themes, in a period devoted to ideals of "progress" and bourgeois complacency. At the moment, continuous and sharp attention should be paid to this vehicle, in which every rejected and denied human impulse can be accommodated, from the petty but terrible *Schadenfreude* (joy in another's misfortune), bred from the poorer native qualities of the human heart as well as from the pressures of a competitive society, to larger evil schemes of power and ambition. The detective novel, now snobbishly cut off from the main stream of literature, reviewed flippantly if at all, may at this moment have within it secrets of what we are and shall be. And the future may look back to it, as it now exists, through great works engendered by it, as we look back through Baudelaire's poems to Sue's Paris, and back through Shakespeare to the crude horrors of the Tragedy of Blood.

[1944]

1. *agents provocateurs:* people hired to infiltrate organizations and incite members to illegal acts.

2. *carbonaro:* member of Italian revolutionary group, formed about 1811 to build a united Republican Italy, which met among the charcoal burners and spoke in their dialect.

3. "I have followed the analysis of M. Caillois' *Le Roman policier* (Editions des Lettres Françaises, SUR, Buenos Aires, 1941) very closely. I am also indebted to *Quarante-huit,* by Jean Cassou (Gallimard, Paris, 1939)." [Note by LB]

André Gide

Imaginary Interviews

IT IS a good omen that the first book to come through from France, in translation, after a silence that gripped that country from the 1940 invasion on, is a piece of literature—and one so fresh and vigorous that it might have been written by a man in his vigorous prime. It was written, as a matter of fact, by a man in his early seventies. André Gide was born in 1869, a date difficult to credit in this connection. Malcolm Cowley, who has done an excellent job of translation with these nineteen dialogues, two short essays, and a brief journal written at the fall of Tunis, brings out in his introduction to *Imaginary Interviews* the presence of certain passages concealing hidden fire to smoke out treachery. These passages exist, it is true, and no one can bring off such subtleties with the same ease and *brio* as Gide. At the same time, it would be a mistake to take this book as a piece of writing whose value lies solely in its hidden polemic. The remarkable thing about it is its openness. By comparison, much of the writing to which we have been accustomed in an uncensored American literature, these last heavy years, seems closed and stifling. It is the final answer to those opponents of Gide—and how numerous and vocal they once were—who prophesied for him final sterility. It is the final proof that his "Christianity without dogma," his belief in harmony and joy, his determined belief in individuality, had firm bases. It is also a proof, as Cowley says, that a wholehearted devotion to the literary art may in itself constitute political action. The *Interviews* appeared regularly from November, 1941, to the spring of 1942 in the literary supplement of *Le Figaro,* one outlet for serious writers in the unoccupied zone.

The works of André Gide have been presented to American readers in the most haphazard way. *The Counterfeiters* came out rather promptly after its French publication; but detached completely from Gide's career as a whole, it could not but puzzle many readers. *Si le grain ne meurt . . . ,* the key book to Gide and one of literature's great confessions, appeared in its first French public edition in 1924; it was published here in an expensive limited edition *(If It Die)* in 1935. The two lives of Gide in English to which Mr. Cowley refers in his preface are valuable, but nothing is so valuable as reading Gide himself, from beginning to end, in his proper order. He has, from the first, possessed the rare faculty of being able to make more or less disguised autobiographical material a continuing basis for his writing. This accomplishment—for autobiography is the most dangerous, and can be the dullest, material in the world—proves an actual underlying development. His vivid grasp of his own experience has been put into the service, moreover, of his moral ideas.

This man, whom readers without French will have to piece together from the scattered books available to them—they have his *Dostoevski,* his African travel notes, his books on Russia, and *The Counterfeiters,* as well as certain short pieces of prose—became a center of influence only after 1918. He had purposely kept his early productions small and varied, in what his opponents considered a perversely baffling manner. His opponents were intelligent and formidable. To Catholics especially he came to represent corruption and secret-keeping: the result of a truly demoniac possession. What was manifesting itself in Gide was showing up in several isolated individuals at the time—Freud, Havelock Ellis, Shaw. The fact of the Unconscious was breaking through European thought. Gide's basic tenets, upon which he acted with, to others, an infuriating tenacity, were actually rather simple. Combining in himself opposing elements of the most irreconcilable kind— a Protestant upbringing and a passionate nature the sexual organization of which differed from the "normal"—he early broke, through action, from the illness and misery imposed upon him by seemingly implacable forces. He refused to continue the endless and sterile struggle "against a conformity to which all nature was in contradiction." "It dawned upon me at last that this discordant duality might be resolved into harmony. And then I saw that harmony must be my supreme object, and the endeavor to acquire it the express reason of my life." Many years later he repeats his conviction—the conviction that defeated, for him, the anxiety which so afflicts modern man: "When I made the discovery that joy was rare and more difficult and more beautiful than sadness, joy became for me not only (which it is) a natural need but even more a moral obligation."

In order to give his "dangerous thoughts" some kind of circulation in the heavy pre-1914 world in which he found himself, Gide resorted to ruses. He wrote his books under the protection of the myth. It is difficult fully to understand Gide without a knowledge of these small early works. They are filled with a diffused wit, gaiety, and freedom. They brought into French literature something completely opposed to the heavy work of Barrès[1]—in its own way "mythical." They gave release from deadly compromise and pervasive hidden or open pressure. They "decompressed," in the phrase of one modern French critic.

It is this faculty for "decompression" which gives life and vigor to everything Gide writes. It is present in his criticism—in France the criticism which comes nearest to the warm humanism of Montaigne. It is a releasing touch that operates under the cool and pure classic style that Gide has made flexible, while keeping about it "an odor both resinous and dry." Under this serene surface exists an intellectual and emotional organization fully conscious of "the winds from the abyss." Gide has never allowed his need for reconciliation to blind or deafen him to the terrible contradictions of life, to the often insane tensions functioning in the human spirit. It is the appreciation of the force of these terrors that has drawn him to Dostoevski, Blake, Flaubert, and Shakespeare. He believes in the validity of the extreme, of the sincere, of intense limitation.

The crucial importance of Gide's thought at present is that he has discovered, and long acted upon, the fact of each man's personal responsibility
for evil.

> What a sad need for hatred [he wrote in his *Journal* in 1937] I see
> on all sides today! . . . the need to oppose all that should be under-
> stood, completed, enriched, united. These conflicts I have felt working
> in myself, before having come upon them in the outer world. I know
> them; and by this personal experience I know how one uses oneself up
> in the struggle. . . . [A day came] when I said: What good does it do?
> when I began to look, not for struggle and partial triumph, but for ac-
> cord: to understand that the more separate and different are the parts
> composing this accord, the richer the harmony. And in the same way in
> a state—it is a somber kind of Utopia, this dream of smashing one part
> by another: this dream of a totalitarian state where the subjugated mi-
> norities cannot make themselves heard: or, what is worse, where each
> and all think the same. It cannot be a question of harmony when the
> choir sings in unison. [Insertions LB's]

It is inevitable that this translation of *Interviews imaginaires* should bear
some marks of being printed for an immediate use; of being enlisted to a
hard-hitting purpose, with a special target in view. This sharp direction of
appeal has resulted in one or two faults. The first translation into English of
a set of Gide's essays should be more fully annotated. Some footnotes exist,
but not enough. Such annotation would tie these essays firmly into a background of reference, as well as stand as a reassurance that the time will come
when literature will again move freely over long open spaces, without fear
of traps or ambushes.

The sly, the sinuous, the demoniac Gide: can his opponents find him in
this book? I do not think so, any more than his admirers can find an infallible guide; for Gide can make mistakes in literary judgment. The important
thing is that they are never mistakes of sympathy. He can be wrong about
American writers, but for interesting reasons. And we search in vain for the
stiff old figure, loaded with years and evil—the end his enemies prophesied
for Gide long since. This man who, during the fighting in Tunis, walks the
streets happy in the radiant spring weather, who falls into a happy conversation concerning the respective merits of George and Rilke with the first
British staff officer he meets, who lies at night with his window open on "a

field of stars," is an aged man. It is impossible to remember this as we read him. His trust in life has not been an empty hope; he is free; and he hands an unambiguous key to freedom to us all.

[1944]

1. Maurice Barrès (1862–1923), French nationalist politician and author of propagandistic novels about the beauties of place and of a "trilogy of myself," in which the world divided into two kinds, barbarians and himself.

Journals: 1889–1913

THE PUBLICATION of this first of a projected three-volume American translation of Gide's *Journals: 1889–1939* should mark a fresh start, rather than a continuation, of Gide's reputation in the United States. The *Journals* draw Gide's other works into focus; but do many people now read the scattered American translations of Gide? The latest work published in America was Malcolm Cowley's translation of *Interviews imaginaires,* in 1944.

The *Journals* provide a firm basis for judgments of Gide's character and place in letters. For they are the central pier upon which the imposing edifice of his work is built. Gide from the beginning of his career has been a diarist. The regular, often daily record of thought and event has provided him with a form at once exigent and large, wherein his desire for stability as well as for movement and change, his detailed inquisitiveness as well as his wider curiosity, could be satisfied. Bored with the "big machines" of French literary form, incapable of filling in conventional backgrounds or of inventing stock figures, wary of technical tricks not based on actual emotion, happy to change his mind concerning the worth and direction of his material while that material was still in the process of composition, Gide has always preferred the short form, where effects can be brought off with full spontaneity, before the impelling emotion is exhausted.

Gide's most unfriendly critics have never been able to attack him in respect to his style. The present volume of the *Journals* shows us that style in the making, from the days when the young Symbolist had not yet decided to write "without metaphors," to 1913, when the accomplished man of letters had evolved a manner of writing so clear and flexible that it was a matter of pride to himself and of emulation to his disciples. The youthful admirer of Chateaubriand has "sharpened his beak" upon Stendhal. The *Journals* soon come to be based upon sincerity of feeling. In this way they never become a mere record of events. Neither do they fall into the errors and *longueurs* of the *journal intime,* since Gide effectually skirts the endless introspective self-indulgences of the intimate diarist. Experience and interest continually enliven the record: books read, music played (Gide is an "intellectual" who can use his hands with precision and speed), journeys undertaken, gardens planted, friends met, meals eaten, daylight walks and midnight prowls described, methods of work delineated with the same care as the most obscure of passing moods, the weather, and the scenery enjoyed. Gide's advance into maturity is by no means in a straight line, without forced detours or periods of circuitous progress. But he soon found his pace and his road. He writes, in 1905: "I escaped early from that world in which, to appear proper, I had to watch myself too closely."

Gide's courageous moral stand, which had so much influence on the post-1918 generation, is not indicated very clearly here: he has written his "confessions" elsewhere. The first exposition of his moral theories appeared in *Les Nourritures terrestres* [fruits of the earth] in 1897, in the last decade of the nineteenth century, at a time when, in French intellectual life, all that was not "determinist" or "finalist" was suspect. A rigid positivism had penetrated French thought to an excessive degree. The only escape for "sensitive souls" was into the refuge of an equally strict and confining religious dogma. In this situation, through bitter personal suffering, after a stay in North Africa and a friendship with Wilde, Gide dared to reconcile irreconcilables. He brought emotion over into the moral realm, declaring the experiences of the flesh to be of equal value to those of the mind and the spirit; and he affirmed that spiritual values could operate in a life-giving manner outside the rituals of religion. Always claiming a basic Christianity, he began his meditations on the figure of a Savior who stood for man's joy rather than for man's tragic and deforming frustration.

As the world of affairs begins to claim more of his attention, Gide meets people and events head-on; he does not take anyone's opinion as his own; he analyzes character and motive with a penetrating combination of intuition and acumen. His dislike of virtuosity in art parallels his impatience with the deviousness and pretentiousness of human beings. The tension between the oppositions within himself continues; perfect balance between impulse and scruple, asceticism and sensuality is never entirely achieved. There are break-downs, nervous crises, and capitulations, as well as spiritual and physical convalescences and reanimations. By keeping the poles of the tension clear, however, Gide escapes most of the enticements of self-deception. His life and relationships must be kept, so far as possible, vital and necessitous. All must be natural in the area of the senses while at the same time the will must function with a kind of "supple obstinacy." Gide's dealings with his colleagues and friends never lack an edge of critical sharpness; but shows of ambition, jealousy, rancor, and spite never occur, and small gossip and downright malice are relatively rare. His chief desire is to have friends who "exist behind and beyond what [they] reveal to us." He does not neglect "the insulted and injured."

> Take upon oneself as much humanity as possible. That is the correct formula. . . . Absence of sympathy equals lack of imagination. The most gifted natures are perhaps the most trembling. . . . As soon as an emotion decreases, the pen should stop; when it continues to run on just the same—and it runs on all the more easily—writing becomes detestable. . . . The wonderful thing on this earth is that we are forced to feel more than to think.

These are the words of a man and an artist who has detached himself from killing and "glacial" abstractions and moved into a world where the modern divided spirit is at least partially healed, where there are provable and classic linkages between the timeless and the time-bound.

Nothing has been spared—neither good-quality large paper nor an intelligent and meticulous editor—to make this American edition impressive. The French *Pléiade* edition (1939 and 1940) on which it is based still retains a peculiar charm, however. Complete in one volume, printed on thin paper, its 1,352 pages compactly yet flexibly bound, this French edition resembles some object delightful and usable: a convenient missile, let us say, against "the Philistine"; or a concentrated form of nourishment, on which one could maintain life over a long period.

[1947]

André Gide   305

Journals: 1914–1927

THE READER who advances into the second volume of Gide's *Journals* in English translation can be sure of a very nearly complete record of sincerity on all levels. The style takes its tone of truth from the material; the material is clarified by the style. In spite of our romanticisms the classic ring of absolute sincerity in writing is happily recognized by modern ears. The broad, generalized biographical work, as well as the emotional "confession," now leaves us more or less unmoved. We can easily detect that false smoothness and serenity which echoes a "maturity" achieved through the repression of a whole side of the personality. We also suspect, as Gide points out, the finicky style, as in Amiel,[1] or the self-satisfied style, as in the Goncourts.[2] Gide's *Journals* are one biographical work of our period where modern "truths" are discovered, and then openly presented in a manner equal to their complex demands.

The second part of the *Journals* also disproves the assertion of Gide's enemies that he is always ready with a specious formula that might at any moment be transposed into its opposite. We see only too clearly in the entries between 1914 and 1917 how Gide, harassed by the paradoxes of his own nature, as well as by the historical situation in which he found himself, and the object of critical attacks from all sides, was often compelled to improvise some way of life, and some means of spiritual survival, from day to day. It is one of the virtues of the *Journals* that these desperate improvisations have not been deleted from it. Gide often allows himself to sound like a lost soul—or like an ordinary human being whose control is snapping and whose will is petrified.

The search for equilibrium in a highly organized modern man, the theme which runs through the long work, is particularly apparent in this second section. Gide, at the beginning of the 1914–1918 war, was able to envisage his own worth and the moral and aesthetic tasks which lay before him, but only intermittently and in a partial way. He was forty-five, an age when the spiritual nature is impelled toward some comfortable orthodoxy, when the physical being begins to lose energy, and when the creative mind is assailed by fears of depletion and dryness. It is a period, moreover, when manias and compulsions may seize hold of the personality and force its acts into some repetitive pattern. It is an age when one must learn patience, without losing drive. "I cling desperately to this notebook; it is part of my patience; it keeps me from going under" (February, 1916).

The *Journals* at this time of doubt and loss become confused and begin to stammer. Long periods are filled with entries that are empty and dull. Gide finally consents to their mediocrity. He also consents to any diversion which will give him a little peace; piano practice, reading and translating, pets, botany, household tasks, and gardening. This is a time of the sharpest analysis of people. Whatever "life offers must be scrutinized with care"; and Bourget, Cocteau, Valéry, Proust, Maritain,[3] alive and in the flesh, are so examined along with crowds of the non-illustrious. We now recognize in these activities the attempts at "therapy" of a man whose more minatory side has taken the upper hand, and who is convinced that part of his nature is "abominable." Later Gide could write: "Arrogance and boredom are the two most authentic products of hell. I have done everything to defend myself against them and have not always succeeded in keeping them at a distance. They are the two great provinces of romanticism."

Gide finally made two decisions, with what difficulty the contemporary entries show. First, he rejected any sort of orthodox religion, in spite of his belief in God and the proselytizing efforts of his converted friends. Second, he decided to put down his "childhood recollections," in the first person singular, with as much frankness as possible. He also decided that the time had come to publish his study of the place and importance of homosexuality (*Corydon*) in a signed commercial edition. His dissatisfaction with his work continues ("it all lacks tremor, elasticity, and richness"); but soon the days of real desperation are over, even though the necessity for constant self-discipline continues. "I must go right on even if I have to write in the margin: to be re-written." By 1917 Gide has made himself capable again of love and joy. The periods "when my mind [is] much concerned with ridiculous anxieties that fatigue and dim it" lessen and then almost totally disappear [insertion LB's].

The Gide who in 1921 begins *The Counterfeiters* has come into that state of equipoise where original, because unfrightened, assessments of human nature and morals can be made. *The Counterfeiters,* published in 1926, begins where most novels leave off. The conventional theme of adultery becomes only an ironic detail in this survey of the neglected sides of human existence: the tragedy of senility, the sadism of childhood, the latent or real criminality of adolescence, the irresponsibility of the romantic. By 1927 all Gide's secrets were out. The man who had for a long time projected his ideas in the form of parables was now able to step forward with open statements.

This volume ends with Gide convinced, as one of his best critics has said, "that evil is a force which can become a factor of progress"; that "the real value is hardly ever the apparent value"; that "life destroys individuals, but, on the other hand, individuals bungle life." At fifty-eight Gide tells us that self-satisfaction on the anxiety level is both stupid and a waste of time. There is a world elsewhere. If he has not formulated the approaches to that world in neat metaphysical language—which he abhors—he has allowed us to watch the full spectacle of himself living them through.

[1948]

1. Henri Amiel (1821–81), Swiss philosopher, poet, and critic, whose posthumously published *journal intime* contained elaborate self-observation and sententious epigrams.

2. In the works of the Goncourts and in Emile Zola's novels, Henry James noticed a "Chinese quality," calling them "mandarins" in an enclosed world studying "warts rather than the beauties of man."

3. A list of the most estimable writers of Gide's time, including novelist, poet, and critic Paul Bourget and Catholic philosopher Jacques Maritain.

Robert Lowell

Lord Weary's Castle

RELIGIOUS CONVERSION, in the case of two modern poets writing in English—T. S. Eliot and W. H. Auden—brought an atmosphere of peace and relief from tension into their work. But Robert Lowell, a young American who has forsaken his New England Calvinist tradition for the tenets of the Roman Catholic church, exhibits no great joy and radiance in the forty-odd poems now published under the title *Lord Weary's Castle*. A tremendous struggle is still going on in Lowell's difficult and harsh writing, and nothing is resolved. These poems bring to mind the crucial seventeenth-century battle between two kinds of religious faith, or, in fact, the battle between the human will and any sort of faith at all. They do not have the sweetness of the later English "Metaphysical" writers; Lowell faces the facts of modern materialism more with the uncompromising tone and temper of the Jacobean dramatists, Webster and Tourneur, or of Donne, who (to quote Professor Grierson), "concluding that the world, physical and moral, was dissolving in corruptions which human reason could not cure, took refuge in the ark of the Church." (Lowell, it is clear, has not taken refuge anywhere.) He also bears some relationship to Herman Melville, the American with Puritan hell-fire in his bones. The more timid reader would do well to remember these forerunners, and the conditions that fostered them, when confronted with young Lowell's fierce indignation.

Lowell's technical competence is remarkable, and this book shows a definite advance over the rather stiff and crusty style of his first volume, *Land of Unlikeness,* published in 1944. This competence shows most clearly in his "imitations" and arrangements of the work of others, which he hesitates to call direct translations. "The Ghost" (after Sextus Propertius), "The Fens" (after Cobbett), and the poems derived from Valéry, Rimbaud, and Rilke reveal a new flexibility and directness. These poems might well be read first, since they show the poet's control of both matter and manner. The impact of the other poems in the book is often so shocking and overwhelming, because of the violent, tightly packed, and allusive style and the frequent efforts of nightmare horror, that his control may seem dubious. The extraordinary evocation of the sea's relentlessness and the terror of death at sea, in "The Quaker Graveyard in Nantucket" (an elegy to a drowned merchant seaman), is equalled in dreadfulness by the grisly emblems of "At the Indian Killer's Grave," a poem wherein successive layers of spiritual and social decomposition in the Massachusetts Bay Colony come to light through a descent into the King's Chapel Burying Ground in Boston. Lowell, again in the seventeenth-century way, continually dwells upon scenes of death and burial. He is at his best when he mingles factual detail with imaginative symbol; his facts are always closely observed, down to every last glass-tiered factory and every dingy suburban tree. To Lowell, man is clearly evil and a descendant of Cain, and Abel is the eternal forgotten victim, hustled away from sight and consciousness. And the modern world cannot reward its servants; no worthy pay is received by the good mason who built "Lord

Wearie's Castle." (The old ballad from which the book's title is taken runs: "It's Lambkin was a mason good As ever built wi' stane: He built Lord Wearie's castle But payment gat he nane.") These are the themes that run through this grim collection. Lowell does not state them so much as present himself in the act of experiencing their weight. It is impossible to read his poems without sharing his desperation. Lowell may be the first of that postwar generation which will write in dead earnest, attempting to find a basis for a working faith, in spite of secretive Nature and in defiance of the frivolous concepts of a gross and complacent society. Or he may simply remain a solitary figure. Certainly his gifts are of a special kind.

[1946]

Life Studies

THE ABILITY to face up to, and record, the raw contemporaneous fact has been one of modern poetry's great successes. Hardy was perhaps the first British poet who was able to use the everyday background of an industrial society (the railway station, the draper's shop) as a setting for his verse, at a time when most English poets were receding into a past—the Pre-Raphaelites into the Middle Ages, Browning into the Renaissance, and Tennyson into prehistoric Britain. (Whitman, in America, was, of course, superbly factual.) But it was Yeats who finally succeeded in getting himself, his ancestors, his enemies and friends into his work, and Auden learned from Yeats. This naming of names, once a device of satire (as in Byron's *Don Juan*), has given to modern poetry fresh liveliness and point. The modern poet's emotions have acquired emphasis by being attached to circumstance, and his memories, when kept strictly in line with actuality, have been freed from hampering nostalgia.

The poems in Robert Lowell's *Life Studies* gain much of their power and interest from the fact that they are almost entirely autobiographical. Lowell's need, at the age of forty-two, to reconstruct his past and his origins has been so strong that he includes an autobiographical essay, in prose ("91 Revere

Street"), as a center around which he has placed the poems. And he describes in both poems and prose not only himself as a child, an adolescent, and a grown man but his parents and his grandparents, his own and his parents' friends. Few poets have subjected their childhood and their family situation to a closer examination. Here great dangers arise. To write almost exclusively of oneself and one's setting, identifying person and place, is a task that presents troublesome problems of tact and tone. To deal in this way with the shifts and bafflements of experience and social change, as well as, in familial terms, with the ugly elements of personal dissolution, requires balance, detachment, and consistent moral courage. Lowell exhibits these difficult-to-sustain qualities; he has not glossed over the hard parts. We are left with the feeling that more than a family has appeared and vanished before our eyes; we have followed a way of life and have shared the poet's apprehensions of an era. Lowell's new book shows him vigorously taking hold of intractable material that lesser talents would be incapable of confronting, let alone putting down in words.

[1959]

For the Union Dead

PROOF THAT Puritan elements in the American character have never been entirely erased is the implicit demand from his audience that any American poet who at any time has shown signs of possessing a prophetic vein should continue with that vein, no matter what changes take place in himself or his situation. Robert Lowell's early poetry contained a good measure of Puritan brimstone. For the young Lowell, the seventeenth-century religious wars might have been fought yesterday, or, indeed, might still be going on. Lowell's later shift to closely personal subjects and looser poetic means has been deplored in some quarters. His latest book, *For the Union Dead,* is, in spite of its history-weighted title, largely a collection of personal memories, from which, evidently, much bitterness has been eliminated by the passage of time.

This turn toward the contemplation of one's past is natural at Lowell's age (the late forties), and he now is able to describe difficult transitional events with a compassion and humor that were totally lacking in his early writing. His later poems are expressed in loosened form quite different from his early high Metaphysical manner. A contrast with Larkin is interesting here; whereas the British poet was both formal and idiomatic from the first, and at ease in describing his environment, the American had to approach the present by working through circuitous avenues of history and religion.[1] Lowell, now the official poet of his generation, faces the various dangers of responsibility: the self-conscious attitude, the temptation to slip into a distorting nostalgia when dealing with the past, and the tendency to castigate every aspect of the present. Lowell, happily, has yielded to these dangers only in a minor way in these new poems. And if the custom of his country has eliminated for him the possibility of class pathos, it has presented him with the tragedy of race, which gives the book's title poem weight.

[1965]

1. LB paired this review of Lowell's *For the Union Dead* with a consideration of English poet Philip Larkin's 1965 volume *The Whitsun Weddings* (see below).

Near the Ocean

Is IT possible for one individual, in one life-time, to combine the roles of *poète maudit* [poetic outcast] and *chef d'école*? A nice little thesis could be written analyzing this question, with examples ranging from Verlaine's early choices[1] to the rare contemporary British and American poets who might just conceivably share both categories. A leader must remain on view, and he can have few secrets, "cursed" or otherwise. Robert Lowell, in his "confessional" poetry, has kept few secrets back. But confessions wear thin, and the attempt to keep them effective by artificial means must subject the talent of any poet, however gifted, to severe strain. The seven new poems (counting one in five parts) in Lowell's most recent volume exhibit a certain coldness and theatricality that often seem to spring from a will toward pure shock rather than from his earlier uncompromising intensity of presentation and courageous choice of subject. His translations—including three odes of Horace and Juvenal's "Tenth Satire"—are evidently meant to connect Rome ("the greatness and horror of her empire") to bruised and maimed aspects of America today. (Lowell has become more gentle toward the American past.) Sidney Nolan's horrifying illustrations (line drawings based on the text) rather disqualify the volume as a coffee-table object, although the large format and the perfectly acceptable and indeed rather romantic drawing (by Francis Parker) on the front of the dust jacket might help to place it in that class. An interim work in every respect.

[1967]

1. French poet Paul Verlaine (1844–96) early "chose" a life of poverty and alcohol in alternation with feverish repentance. His lyrics are considered pure and evocative.

Charles Baudelaire

A NEW TRANSLATION, by Geoffrey Wagner, of a selection of Baudelaire's poetry, called *Flowers of Evil,* has recently appeared. Enid Starkie, the English Baudelaire scholar, contributes an excellent short introduction to the volume. But the disparity in quality between Miss Starkie's prose and Mr. Wagner's verse is so great that it is a puzzle how the two came together into book form. Granted that certain insuperable obstacles to a feasible translation of Baudelaire into any language exist, it is still a disappointment to find Mr. Wagner making the most elementary blunders in choice, in tone, and in detail. The volume is, moreover, oddly lacking in the ordinary aids to the reader; it has no pagination, no table of contents, no notes, and no index.

Baudelaire's vocabulary and atmosphere constitute, without question, problems for translators. The vocabulary is filled with those splendid French abstract nouns and substantives that tend to come through into English sounding rather silly, and the atmosphere, particularly that of his early work, is rather repellent to Anglo-Saxon taste. It is the atmosphere of French

Second Empire luxury, morbidity, and eroticism. Baudelaire was a master of a whole rhetorical apparatus for evoking effects of horror and lubricity. The workings of this stylistic machine are now outmoded. And nothing is more tiresome than the reiterated subject—so usual in the early Baudelaire —of woman as puppet, as sinister idol of the alcove, or as erotic mannequin. Translators are attracted, however, to Baudelaire's more overheated and dated productions, and Mr. Wagner, no less than Arthur Symons and other searchers in the field, has chosen proportionately more poems from this side of Baudelaire's work than from any other. Yet, as Miss Starkie points out, the figure of Baudelaire as dandy and decadent has steadily diminished in this present century, to be replaced by the concept of a man whose insights were profound and valuable for a complex set of reasons. We now recognize Baudelaire as the first poet who saw through the overweening pretensions of his time. He stripped man's nature to its essentials, and he discovered, in an era when his contemporaries were still occupied with "rationalism" or with "romance," urban mankind's bitter loneliness and spiritual isolation. Baudelaire, as T. S. Eliot has said, learned everything for himself. He went from the confines of his early physical excesses into the streets of Paris; he drew portraits of the poor, the debauched, the senile, the obsessed, and the mad in a manner as uncompromising as Daumier's. He depicted the houses, the rooms, the roofs, the shuttered windows, and the chimney pots, and beyond this he re-created the look and the feeling of those times of day and of those turns of the seasons when the city's sadness is, as it were, distilled and the full, cold mystery of existence leaks through into our consciousness. These poems have the power to hit us like a blow. They are scattered through his work, and the beginner in Baudelaire needs guides to them. Mr. Wagner, in making his choices, has merely gone through the collected work and picked out a poem here and there, seemingly at random. The thirty-eight selections in this volume represent less than a quarter of Baudelaire's poetic output. To appropriate the title *Flowers of Evil* for it seems odd to anyone who remembers Baudelaire's careful sense of arrangement—"the inner architecture"—in his *Fleurs du mal,* in both its editions published during his lifetime. Miss Starkie's biographical summary and her short but penetrating analysis of the poet's present place in French letters, combined with the French texts (here included) of the poems, give this compilation a certain value, but the day when Baudelaire's translators match his critics in sensitiveness and understanding is yet to come.

[1947]

The Heart and the Lyre

THE RECORD of the verse written by women in the United States is remarkably full, for a variety of reasons. In the first place, the country became an independent republic, well equipped with printing presses and paper, during the period when American women began to write in earnest. Then, a new and eager periodical and newspaper audience, with the sort of pioneering background which holds women in high esteem, awaited bits of feminine sentiment and moralizing dressed up in metre and rhyme. Finally, the critical standard of the country remained for a long time rather lax and easygoing. A great mass of verse, good, bad, and indifferent, therefore managed to get published. Through this prolific feminine production we can trace, with much accuracy, every slight shift in American literary fashion, as well as larger changes of an emotional and moral kind. An examination of the rise and development of female poetic talent over a period of more than one hundred and fifty years in a society which, on the whole, encouraged that talent to function freely and in the open, brings to light various truths concerning the worth and scope of women's poetic gifts.

Before we survey the interesting, colorful, and frequently comic array of American women "poetesses" from Lydia Huntley Sigourney (1791–1865) through the youngest feminine contemporaries, let us look at some of the assumptions and prejudices that have long lodged in people's minds on the subject of women as poets. One rather hoary idea is that women put emotion before form and are likely to be indifferent technicians. Do they not usually, as well, imitate closely the poetic productions of men? A third dark suspicion concerning women's poetic powers troubled even the highly intelligent and ardently feminist mind of Virginia Woolf. Mrs. Woolf, in her delightful series of lectures published in 1929 under the title *A Room of One's Own,* is continually bothered by the thought that in spite of material and moral emancipations women may never write a work of wide and compelling force comparable, for example, to Shakespeare's plays. To exorcise this spectral doubt, Mrs. Woolf canvasses fully the history of woman's difficulties in the role of artist.

Women have always been busy and poor, Mrs. Woolf's argument runs; busy, because they are physically responsible for the production and early care of specimens of the human race; and poor because it seems that men's laws are often framed to keep them in that condition. Lack of education, the tyranny of families, the ridicule of society, as well as lack of independent means, have been factors which, perhaps, kept women from writing epic poems or long poetic plays. Mrs. Woolf gives every credit to the anonymous women who had a hand in composing folk tales, folk songs, adages, proverbs, and nursery rhymes (for it is, after all, Mother Goose, and *Ma Mère l'Oye*).[1] And she is happy to note that, when new freedoms arrived in Europe and England at the end of the eighteenth century, women novelists, at least, appeared in numbers and with brilliance. But what of Shakespeare's supposititious sister—ignorant, penniless, and fearful of masculine jeers, had she tried to carve out a career for herself in the sixteenth century? It is at this point in her argument that Mrs. Woolf begins to stumble against the doubt that any woman is ever going to write a great poetic tragedy in five acts. Perhaps after a hundred years or so this goal will be realized, if the creative woman is given five hundred pounds per annum and, behind a door with a lock on it, a room of her own.

It was a little old-fashioned even in 1929 for Mrs. Woolf to choose a five-act poetic play as the final test of a woman poet's powers. Her vision was somewhat clouded by an Anglo-Saxon literary point of view. Why should women, past, present, or future, remain fixed in the determination to out-Shakespeare Shakespeare? Can it be that there is no basic reason for women to excel in the art of poetry by producing the same sort of poetic structures as men? Men, as a matter of fact, stayed with the five-act poetic tragedy far too long. Perhaps women have more sense than to linger over an obsessing form of this kind.

We turn to the full and complete annals of American women poets hoping that we may discover facts that will lead to a new estimate of the poetic gift in women, as well as hints about its present and future direction. The first women versifiers who appear on the American scene were, it must be confessed, unendowed, grim, pious, and lachrymose. Mrs. Sigourney was provincial and naïve enough to glory in two titles: the "American Hemans"[2] and the "Sweet Singer of Hartford." She reigned, moreover, for a long period as the head of American female letters—from shortly after Washington's second term as president until just after the death of Lincoln, to be exact. She was fluent, industrious, and rather pushing; but she managed to put feminine verse-writing on a paying basis, and give it prestige; even Poe did not quite dare to handle her work too roughly. She gave simple men and women along the Eastern seaboard and in the backwoods of the West something to be proud of; it is pleasant for a young nation to have a vocal tutelary goddess.

During Mrs. Sigourney's lifetime the choir of female singers enlarged. Soon a series of anthologies began to appear, exclusively devoted to "songstresses." *The Ladies' Wreath* (1837), edited by Mrs. Sarah Josepha Hale, who also edited *Godey's Lady's Book,* was the first of these. Others followed; and by 1849 Rufus Griswold was able to make good profits with his collection entitled *The Female Poets of America.* This collection went through several editions and, after Griswold's death, turned up in the seventies with a new editor. We are now in a new world. The more depressing ante-bellum aspects of female piety and melancholy have worn off, and we are presented with the spectacle of women becoming ever more ardent and airy. The ardors of Poe's women friends, Fanny Osgood and Mrs. Whitman, are now surpassed by their successors. When we come to Edmund Clarence Stedman's *An American Anthology* (1900), an often unbroken phalanx of women with three (and sometimes four) invincibly Yankee names advances down the table of contents, and their work is now startlingly filled with evidence of culture, with whimsicality, self-preening, and affectation.

But although women's literary manners and, it would seem, their affections became ever more wayward and free, their grasp upon basic conventions remained firm. Even the Wisconsin farm girl, Ella Wheeler, who spiced her stanzas with hints of sin in *Poems of Passion* (1883) soon quiets down into marriage and respectability with a Mr. Wilcox. The list of these late-nineteenth-century women in Stedman, with their multiple names printed in chaste Gothic type, tends to become a blur. But if we search carefully for even the smallest sincerity and talent, personalities begin to emerge. Alice and Phoebe Cary; Celia Thaxter; the mill girl, Lucy Larcom, protégée of Whittier; Julia Ward Howe; Emma Lazarus, who was Jewish, and Louise Imogen Guiney, who was an "Irish Catholic"; Lizette Woodworth Reese of Baltimore and Harriet Monroe of Chicago; and, further back, crowded in with Mrs. Spofford, Mrs. Moulton, Thomas Bailey Aldrich, Joaquin Miller, and Edward Rowland Sill, we come upon an unpretentious name, easily overlooked, of a woman born in 1830 and dead in 1886: Emily Dickinson. Emily Dickinson represents the final flowering of a long Puritan tradition. Her genius has a hard, bitter, but real kind of civilization behind it; women poets share with men the need for some sort of civilized ground from which to draw sustenance. But it is apparently more difficult for women to throw off the more superficial fashions of any society in which they find themselves. The earlier history of women poets in America should stand as a warning to modern young women of talent. The special virtues of women are clear, in the same record. Women are forced to become adult. They must soon abandon sustained play, in art or life. They are not good at abstractions and their sense of structure is not large; but they often have the direct courage to be themselves. They are practical, intense, and (usually) both generous and magnanimous. They often have a true contemplative gift; and they are natural singers. They are capable of originality and breadth of emotional and intellectual reference as soon as their background opens to any breadth and variety. They are often forced to waste their powers in an inadequate milieu, in social improvisation; to tack back and forth between revolt and conservatism. Far from imitating men to an untoward degree, they often experiment boldly with form and language. Early in the twentieth century, Gertrude Stein, working indefatigably and alone, begins to examine words with the detached interest of the scientist and arrange them in abstract patterns. A little later H. D. [Hilda Doolittle] gives back to Greek themes some of the pure severity of Greek poetry in the original. Marianne Moore applies a naturalist's eye to objects of art and of nature, describing "with an extraordinary magnificence of phraseology" unlooked-for combinations and harmonies between matter and the spirit. These women have had their male, as well as their female, followers.

Young women writing poetry at present are likely to consider the figure of the woman poet as romantic rebel rather ridiculous and outmoded. The youngest generation of women poets is, in fact, moving toward an imitation of certain masculine "trends" in contemporary poetry. They are imitating, moreover, the work of male verbalizers and poetic logicians, rather than the work of men who have carried through, out of a profound urgency, major poetic investigations; there are few feminine disciples of either Eliot or Auden, in these poets' later phases. Even the greatly gifted Elizabeth Bishop, whose first book recently appeared, places emphasis more upon anecdote than upon ardor. The fear of some regression into typical romantic attitudes is, at present, operating from feminine talent; and this is not a wholly healthy impulse, for it negates too strongly a living and valuable side of woman's character. In women, more than in men, the intensity of their emotions is the key to the treasures of their spirit. The cluster of women lyric poets that appeared on the American scene just before and after 1918 restored genuine and frank feeling to a literary situation which had become genteel, artificial, and dry. Sara Teasdale's later verse; the best of Edna Millay's early rebellious songs and meditations; Elinor Wylie's ability to fuse thought and passion into the most admirable and complex forms; the sensitive, intellectual poetry of Léonie Adams—all these poetic productions helped to resolve hampering attitudes of the period.

The great importance of keeping the emotional channels of a literature open has frequently been overlooked. The need of the refreshment and the restitution of feeling, in all its warmth and depth, has never been more apparent than it is today, when cruelty and fright often seem about to overwhelm man and his world. For women to abandon their contact with, and their expression of, deep and powerful emotional streams, because of contemporary pressures or mistaken self-consciousness, would result in an impoverishment not only of their own inner resources but of mankind's at large. Certainly it is not a regression to romanticism to remember that women are capable of perfect and poignant song; and that when this song comes through in its high and rare form, the result has always been regarded not only with delight but with a kind of awe. It is a good thing for young women to bring to mind the fact that lost fragments of the work of certain women poets—of Emily Dickinson no less than of the Sappho quoted by Longinus as an example of "the sublime"—are searched for less with the care and eagerness of the scholar looking for bits of shattered human art, than with the hungry eyes of the treasure hunter, looking for some last grain of a destroyed jewel. Though she may never compose an epic or a tragic drama in five acts, the woman poet has her singular role and precious destiny. And, at the moment, in a time lacking in truth and certainty and filled with anguish and despair, no woman should be shamefaced in attempting to give back to the world, through her work, a portion of its lost heart.

[1947]

1. Charles Perrault's fairy tales, published in 1697, which included the French originals of "Sleeping Beauty," "Blue Beard," "Puss in Boots," and "Cinderella," were presented as though narrated by Mother Goose herself, or *"Ma Mère l'Oye"*).
2. Felicia Dorothea Hemans (1793–1835), an English poet deemed "exquisite" by George Eliot but "too poetical" by Sir Walter Scott; best known for her ballad beginning "The boy stood on the burning deck."

Marianne Moore

American to Her Backbone

IMPRESSIONIST CRITICS, because they have attributed to Miss Moore many of their own manias and virtues, have left her actual virtue—her "secret"—untouched. She belongs to a lineage against which the impressionist and the "modernist" have for so long rebelled that by now they are forgetful that it ever existed. In Miss Moore two traditions that modernism tends to ignore meet. She is, on the one hand, a nearly pure example of that inquisitive, receptive kind of civilized human being which began to flourish during the high Renaissance: the disciple of the "new" as opposed to the "old" learning, the connoisseur, the humane scholar—to whom nothing was alien, and for whom man was the measure of all. Her method, in her "observations," has been compared, and rightly, to that of Francis Bacon and Sir Thomas Browne. But we soon come upon in her work another, angularly intersecting, line. Miss Moore, child of Erasmus, cousin to Evelyn,[1] and certainly close kin to the Mozart who refracted Don Giovanni as though from a dark crystal, does not develop, as we might expect, toward full Baroque exuberance. She shows—and not to her demerit—a definite influence derived from that Protestantism against whose vigor the vigor of the Baroque was actively opposed. Miss Moore is a descendant not of Swiss or Scotch, but of Irish presbyters. She is, therefore, a moralist (though a gentle one) and a stern—though flexible—technician.

It is not an infrequent American miracle, this combination of civilized European characteristics in one gifted nature. Miss Moore, American to her backbone, is a striking example of a reversion toward two distinct kinds of heritage; of an atavism which does not in any degree imply declension or degeneration of the original types involved. She does not write *à la manière de . . . ;* she produces originals. She does not resemble certain seventeenth-century writers; she might be one of them. She stands at the confluence of two great traditions, as they once existed, and as they no longer exist. "Sentiment" and the shams of the *pasticheur*[2] cannot touch her, since she ends where they begin.

Examine her passion for miscellany: it is a seventeenth-century passion. "Academic feeling, or prejudice possibly, in favor of continuity and completion," she wrote in 1927, "is opposed to miscellany—to music programs, composite picture exhibitions, newspapers, magazines, and anthologies. Any zoo, aquarium, library, garden, or volume of letters, however, is an anthology, and certain of these selected findings are highly satisfactory. . . . The selective nomenclature—the chameleon's eye as we might call it so—of the connoisseur, expresses a genius for difference." There speaks a sensibility unmarked by the flattening pressures of an industrial age. Alive to the meaning of variation, Miss Moore can examine what the modern world displays, with an unmodern eye. This is her value to us. She sees as a specialist trained and bred sees. She is never, therefore, indifferent to what might strike her contemporaries as either precious or rubbish. Advertisements, travel folders, yesterday's newspaper, the corner movie, the daily shop and street, the fashion magazine, the photograph, and the map—these phenomena are gathered into her art with the same care with which she "observes" small mammals, birds, reptiles; or with which she microscopically examines details of human artifacts: "sharkskin, camellia-leaf, orange-peel, semi-eggshell or *sang-de-boeuf* [oxblood] glaze" in Chinese porcelain, for example. Unlike a magpie, she is not attracted by any kind of glittering swag. She is never in danger for a moment of appearing either a dilettante or a snob. She is occupied with the set task of imaginatively correlating the world's goods, natural and artificial, as a physician correlates "cases," or a naturalist, specimens.

The tone of her poems often derives from her "other," Protestant inheritance. Are not many of her poems sermons in little, preached in the "plain style" but with overtones of a grander eloquence? Are not many of them discourses which are introduced, or subsumed, by a text? Note the frequent cool moral that she extracts from her poems' complexities; and the dexterity with which, from disparate and often heavy facts, she produces a synthesis as transparent and as inclusive as air. Her sensibilities are Counter-Reformation; her emotion and intellect, Protestant.

She has immensely widened the field of modern poetry. She takes the museum piece out of its glass case, and sets it against living animals. She relates the refreshing oddities of art to the shocking oddities of life. The ephemeral and the provincial become durable and civilized under her hands. She is a delayed product of long processes. She is at once a contemporary

American, a seventeenth-century survival, and a native of those timeless and pure spiritual regions

> where there is no dust, and life is like a lemon leaf,
> a green piece of tough translucent parchment.

["People's Surroundings"]

[1947]

1. John Evelyn, late-seventeenth-century English art patron, court adviser, and author of a diary covering fifty-six years of his long life, also composed meditations on topics from Lucretius to gardening. He resembled the Dutch humanist Desiderius Erasmus (1466–1536) only in being well-traveled, a scholar of languages, and a proponent of scientific learning.
2. *à la manière de; pasticheur:* in the style of; writer of patchworks.

Johann Wolfgang von Goethe

A GENERAL EAGERNESS to wring some usable wisdom from Goethe, preferably in condensed form, on the two-hundredth anniversary of his birth, has pushed the great man from the company of the poets into the company of the philosophers, for the twin barriers of language and of time do not matter so much in the realm of philosophy. Metaphysics, by reason of its airiness, can seep from one period to another, and when one deals in abstractions, the partitions of language are fairly thin and yielding. But poetry, and particularly lyric poetry, is forever stuck fast in its original tongue. And although Goethe from youth on was surrounded by philosophers and knew them as close friends and as correspondents, and although his liking for abstractions, symbols, and enigmas steadily increased, he remained a poet *pur sang.*¹ Schiller, who, Goethe said, "cared more for speculation than for the direct vision of things," found him but an indifferent Kantian, and if

Goethe showed a strong sympathy for certain portions of Spinoza's thought, it is doubtful that he followed through to the end Spinoza's complicated and geometric arguments.

Being a poet, Goethe thought in images, trusted his intuition, and, in his own words, dwelt "in the truth of the five senses." This innate empiricism prevented him from being thrown off his course by the metaphysics all about him, and he boasts, in one of his lighter verses, of having achieved splendid results because he never lost his way "thinking about thought." We must not be led astray, therefore, into believing, because of the enormous range of his interests, that he possessed a variety of approaches toward his subjects. One approach—that of the interpretative imagination—underlies all Goethe's researches, from the theatre through the plastic and graphic arts, from the nature of the universe through the conduct of life, from religion and sociology through botany, mineralogy, and optics. Thomas Mann has spoken of the combination in Goethe of true naïveté with extraordinary intellectual power. Goethe's was the poet's naïveté, and this pleasing gift never dwindled.

Language is the insuperable barrier between Goethe and ourselves. Translations are not much help to the poetry, and Goethe's thought, at its purest and most forceful, is embedded in the poetry. "Goethe was particularly unfortunate in his English translators," D. J. Enright truthfully observes. "All along [his] natural, idiomatic German is debased into some or other kind of awful synthetic poesy. . . . The modern reader . . . after he has glanced at one or two of the *Faust* specimens [in English], may be led into abandoning Goethe on the ground that no really great poetry could ever look quite so dreadful in translation. But it can" [insertions LB's]. C. F. MacIntyre's version of the first part of *Faust*, published in 1941, has helped dispel this unhappy tradition. One way of getting at *Faust* is to get it onto the stage. The ideal celebration of Goethe's bicentenary this year would have been a full-dress production of *Faust,* in the exciting manner of [Max] Reinhardt's production of the Second Part in Salzburg in the early thirties. It would have put Goethe's poetry where it belongs—in the mouths of living and breathing characters.

The barrier of time is difficult to overcome. For Goethe is the epitome and one of the prime movers of a cultural period that was not only short-lived, in contrast to its importance, but, when it was over, was gone for good. It was the period between the charming yet rather sinister excesses of eighteenth-century German Rococo and, on the other hand, the "Biedermeier," a German version of English Early Victorian. It was the period of the informal "English" park, midway between the stiff, formal parterres of the past and the hideous, formal, geranium and begonia beds of the future. It was the period of "bourgeois classicism" so well described by C. L. Laing when, writing of Beethoven, he says:

> The sentimental irrationalism of the *Sturm und Drang*[2] emptied into the quiet world of ideas. . . . The genius [of the times] recognized the validity of objective norms; boundless humanism gave way to a humanism which recognized its own limits. This moderation and equalization ripened into a classicism of which the German phase is the very symbol. Classicism beautified life and gave it lastingness by viewing it from the heights of the ideal. . . . Its art was devoted to the ideal of plastic beauty which it believed to be absolute; its principal object was man living in consort with nature, man beautiful in body and soul . . . man who became aware of his inner harmony, and who was the measure of all things. The result was an aesthetic world-picture, a Germandom reborn from the spirit of Hellas. [Insertion LB's]

It was this idealism of an enlightened burgher class headed toward freedom that provided the climate for the time's "explosion of genius." Goethe, the young bourgeois from Frankfurt, all fire and temperament, was one of the constructors of this ideal and point of view. The gradual development of his feeling for classic depth, clarity, and equilibrium showed itself in his growing control over his life and impressed itself upon his surroundings. Far from being "a Prince's valet," he was the guide and teacher of his Weimar duke, and succeeded in making a humane man and ruler out of an irresponsible boy. We must look back at this period, of course, from across the Romanticist period that followed it (and that Goethe distrusted), and it is not easy to keep focus on the distant scene. That the period had its effect beyond the borders of Germany is proved by the reverence and admiration given it, during its brief existence, by the rest of Europe and even by America. It is the only cultural bridge between the eighteenth and the nineteenth centuries, at a time when France was exhausted by its fit of power and England had retreated from eighteenth-century "liberalism" into reactionary anti-Jacobinism and the small and dull frivolity of the Regency.

Goethe, except for Carlyle, made no great impression upon English thought or letters. English industrialism was a going concern long before Goethe's death. His point of view appealed more to Scotch moral idealism and American transcendentalism than to British hardheadedness. And soon, all over Europe and in America, Romanticist doubt, melancholy, and soul-searching began to negate the classic ideal. Goethe's age was at an end, and the poet for whom every living and evolving thing had importance, who was an enemy of the dry specimens of the museums, was turned over to the scholars and the commentators to be explained, ticketed, and mummified.

When we look for modern writers who have understood and profited from Goethe's poetry and ideas, we come upon an unexpectedly lively list. We find, to begin with, a young man who, visiting Rome in 1851, linked Goethe, quite naturally, with Dante, Shakespeare, and Michelangelo. This was Gustave Flaubert. We find continual references to Goethe in Flaubert's *Correspondance*. He defends Goethe against detractors, and everywhere tenders him admiration and praise, and one Goethian maxim helps him to run his life: *"Qu'est-ce que ton devoir? L'exigence de chaque jour."*[3] The influence of Goethe upon Flaubert was a creative one as well; the first *St. Antoine* derives directly from *Faust II,* and the first *L'Education sentimentale* from *Wilhelm Meister.* In our own time, we find Gide, in his *Journals,* constantly referring to Goethe. He reads the poetry with delight and attempts to translate it. He notes that "nothing in life so calms me as the contemplation of this great figure," and that "the greatest influence to which I have *submitted* is that of Goethe." We find among modern critics, philosophers, and historians who have submitted themselves to Goethe's intelligence and intuition the names of Santayana, G. Lowes Dickinson, Valéry, Toynbee, Albert Schweitzer, and, of course, Mann.

A Study of Goethe, by Barker Fairley, published in 1947, is the best modern critical work in English and should be consulted by anyone truly concerned with the poet's achievement.

To those who, although permanently baffled by German, can read French, a new and complete translation of *Faust,* published in 1947, can be recommended. It includes the Gérard de Nerval version of *Faust I,* together with *Faust II,* translated, with absorbing comments, by Alexandre Arnoux and R. Biemel. For those who can cope with German, a neat and well-printed pocket edition of *Faust,* in two volumes, has recently been published in New York.

The best introduction to Goethe's lyric poetry for the non-German reader is through music. Forgetting all the attempts of Romantic composers to deal with Goethe's work—from the sweetenings of Gounod, Tchaikovsky, Thomas, Massenet, and others, to the horrification of Berlioz—he can turn to three songwriters, two of whom were Goethe's contemporaries and one of whom is a modern. Beethoven's songs and incidental music for *Egmont*, and Schubert's songs written to Goethe's lyrics, bring us close to the poet's own music. The most extraordinary evocation of Goethe's power and poetic range, however, comes to us through the fifty-one songs written to his lyrics by Hugo Wolf. "Music as such," a learned critic says of Wolf's settings, "was never an aim to him, only a means to enhance the poem." Anyone who has listened to the wild longing of the Wolf-Goethe "Kennst Du das Land?" or to the noble and transcendent beauty of their "Prometheus" and "Ganymed" has experienced the only world it is important to share with any great poet —the world of his intense emotion and his piercing vision.

[1949]

1. *pur sang:* of pure stock, a thoroughbred.

2. *Sturm und Drang:* storm and stress. Period of literary ferment in late-eighteenth-century Germany identified with Herder, then Goethe and Schiller, who were briefly inflamed by the French thinker Rousseau's views of society, the merits of intuition, and the return to nature.

3. *"Qu'est-ce que ton devoir? L'exigence de chaque jour":* "What is your task? The demands of each day."

Wallace Stevens

The Auroras of Autumn

WALLACE STEVENS is the American poet who has based his work most firmly upon certain effects of nineteenth-century Symbolist poetry. The title of his latest volume, *The Auroras of Autumn*, indicates that his powers of language have not declined; here is one of those endlessly provocative, "inevitable" phrases that seem to have existed forever in some rubied darkness of the human imagination—that imagination with whose authority and importance Stevens has been continually occupied in his later period. This preoccupation was once implicit in what he wrote; his images performed their work by direct impact. Stevens's later explicit, logical, and rather word-spinning defense of the role of the imagination has weakened or destroyed a good deal of his original "magic." The whole texture and coloration of his later verse is more austere; his subjects are less eccentric; even his titles have quieted down. What has always been true of him is now more apparent: that no one can describe the simplicities of the natural world with more direct skill. It is a natural world strangely empty of human beings, however; Stevens's men and women are bloodless symbols. And there is something theatrical in much of his writing; his emotions seem to be transfixed, rather than released and projected, by his extraordinary verbal improvisations. Now that he is so widely imitated, it is important to remember that his method is a special one; that modern poetry has developed transparent, overflowing, and spontaneous qualities that Stevens ignores. It is also useful to remember (as Apollinaire[1] knew) that since the imagination is part of life, it must have its moments of awkwardness and naïveté, and must seek out forms in which it may move and breathe easily, in order that it may escape both strain and artificiality.

[1950]

1. The pen name of French poet Guillaume Apollinaris Kostrowitzky (1880–1918), who strove to bring the Cubist painters' dislocations and simultaneity over into poetry; known for his shape poems, or *calligrammes*.

Stevens and Cummings: *Collected Poems*

THE COLLECTED *Poems of Wallace Stevens* was published this October, on the occasion of Mr. Stevens's seventy-fifth birthday; and E. E. Cummings's publishers remind us, on the jacket of his recent *Poems 1923–1954,* that this year

Mr. Cummings has reached the age of sixty. Both these volumes are large; the Stevens runs to 534 pages and the Cummings to 468. One avant-garde tradition—sparseness of production—is thus broken, perhaps permanently. For these two veterans of little magazines and small or privately printed editions have been able to build up, over the years, a bulk of work without for a moment departing from their respective idiosyncratic methods. Neither poet has felt himself compelled to waste time in padding out his *oeuvre* with forms antipathetic to his gifts, in order to attract a wider audience or to prove his skill in manipulating what the French call "big machines." The continuing creative energy of both and the constancy of their aim are apparent, but the impressive quality of their production testifies, as well, to a shift in the American literary situation. The fact that Stevens and Cummings now have fairly large and appreciative audiences proves how firmly, at mid-century, modern poetry has established itself, to the point that it now quite naturally circulates around recognized masters.

The dissimilarity between the personalities and methods of Cummings and Stevens shows up dramatically when their entire lyric output lies before us. A revolution in the arts, we again realize, takes on power when it attracts a variety of temperaments into its field of operations. The revolt against nineteenth-century standards and practices gained impetus when poets, like other artists, began to lay bare their inalienable, and often opposite, gifts in a perfectly frank and direct way. Tensions were thus set up, and modern sensibilities began to function from more than one angle and over a range of subjects. Cummings, whose relation to the 1914–1918 war was close and cruel, brought into American postwar poetry a bittersweet mixture of satire and sentiment. His typographical experiments, which gave him an early notoriety, today seem less important than his persistent attempts to break taboos—to bring back into formal verse vital material that Victorian taste had outlawed. Today, as we read Cummings's lyric output from beginning to end, we are struck by the directness with which he has presented himself—his adolescent daydreams as well as his more mature desires; his small jealousies and prejudices, along with his big hatreds; his negative malice and his fears, beside his positive hopes. His awareness of tradition, too, comes out plainly; he has reworked traditional forms as often as he has invented new ones, turning not only the sonnet to his own purposes but also the ballad, the nursery rhyme, the epigrammatic quatrain, and the incantatory rune. His habit of projecting a continuing present, avoiding any expression of remorse or regret, gave a glitter to his middle period; nothing in it casts a shadow. The pathos of his later elegies is all the more remarkable because no one could foresee its occurrence. But it is his satire that remains focal and sharp as his main contribution to the reinvigoration of modern verse. His targets have been, for the most part, well chosen, and he has made his stand clear—for the rights and value of the individual as opposed to the demands of the crowd and the standards of the machine. He scornfully stuck to his guns in times of crisis, when many of his contemporaries were deserting theirs. It is this underlying passion for simple justice that has given Cummings the power to uncover, point to, and stigmatize those dead areas of custom as only a satirist can effectively do it.

STEVENS HAS never applied himself to the tasks of the satirist; he is by nature the contemplative poet *pur sang,* who distills symbols, meaning, and what he calls "ideas of order" from the crudity and the confusion of the actual. His ability to link the outer world of reality closely to the inner world of vision has been astonishing from the first. He never breaks into explosions of form or fusillades of feeling, but he is often lively and always in search of the ironic paradox. His poetry is securely based on reality; he was the first modern American, for example, to deal with the American scene in imaginative rather than purely topical or regional terms. Beginning with *Harmonium* (1923), Stevens used American place names with a sense of their awkward charm, and he has extracted the essence of American climate and atmosphere—of the American "spirit of place"—from Florida's subtropical abundance to New England's stern extremes of climate and contour. Stevens's later work (to the delight of the professors) contains elements of philosophical thought, but continually, as it were, in solution, for it is the full evocation of thought and emotion that he is after, not the cold, isolated, abstract idea. Taken together in these two formidable volumes, Cummings's and Stevens's talents, it is quite evident, complement and reinforce each other, and each poet in his way has indicated the imaginative direction, as well as outlined the complicated moral and spiritual exigencies, of our time. We must be grateful for Stevens's subtle discipline no less than for Cummings's boldness and verve, and be thankful that a native tenacity has allowed both poets to develop and endure.

[1954]

Ivy Compton-Burnett

THE NOVELS of Ivy Compton-Burnett owe much of their power to the fact that each of them is a nightmare into which we are drawn by degrees but from which we escape with reluctance. For these are high-comedy nightmares. Miss Compton-Burnett belongs to the company of artists who, with the aid of the comic spirit, are able to enlarge life by imposing inexorable patterns on it. Within a straight Victorian world—which escapes being "period" because it lacks any scrap of fashionable ornamentation—her three fixed circles revolve: masters, servants, and children. And although the members of each circle are vocal to a degree, communication among the groups is largely indirect. Children spy on masters and servants; servants, on masters and children; masters, on servants, children, and one another. Situation is built up by the intrusion of some shocking reality in the masters' world which soon filters, by eavesdropping, into the other two; and the only weapon available to the majority of masters is the weapon of convention. But natural reactions, suppressed in one quarter, are allowed to the servants and to the young. Thus, humane generosity and simple love are allowed to break through barriers of spite and hypocrisy; and the rigid pattern is at length changed. Sex, in this closed universe, keeps cropping up in terms of comedy. A prevalent background of illegitimacy exists; so that masters are frequently faced with the results of their early "stumbles" in the form of butlers who are their natural sons and housekeepers who are their natural daughters. In *Darkness and Day,* the world of the bastard impinges so closely upon the world of the family that one of the masters believes for a time that he has married his own cast-off child. The child's mother (a servant) proves that this is not the case. But for a moment all three circles are menaced; and the one remedy seems to be silence. "Oedipus lost no time in going the full length," someone remarks. "Anything like that would make it very public."

Miss Compton-Burnett is certainly fixed permanently at the emotional level of childhood's most "knowing" and disabused stage. This is a point of fixation which breeds a hostility to life that great gifts of intelligence and style alone can alleviate. Miss Compton-Burnett, in many ways a female Swift of our day, constantly proves her possession of these gifts.

[1951]

Caitlin Thomas

THOSE WHO are shocked not only by Caitlin Thomas's disclosures in *Left-over Life to Kill* but by her temper and style as a whole should try to imagine how tiresome and truly shocking it would have been if she had written out of a cold, not a warm and generous, nature, if a trace of apology or calculation or concealment had been involved. In this book, at once a memoir of her dead poet husband and an account of her desperate attempts to face up to the prospect of life without him, Caitlin Thomas puts herself down without extenuation as a childish woman and as a bearer of the terrifying Irish qualities of violence and rakishness. But she is neither a slut nor a fool; there is a conflict here that could not exist except in a woman who is conscious of her immaturity—who longs to grow up, be sensible to some degree, and find her place in the world. The basic good sense and the ability to discriminate are there, although often almost savagely repressed.

Innocence and violence are terrible things. The severe rituals imposed on adolescents in practically every tribe known to anthropology insist on two basic dicta: *Grow up* and *Calm down*. In maturity, it is necessary, mankind has discovered, to suppress outbursts of strong emotion—joy, rage, grief—that may, in their irrationality, disturb the general peace. The Greeks came to fear those who threw themselves against the will of the gods. The grave choruses of the tragedies continually warn, caution, and seek to make reasonable the man or woman in the throes of whatever overweening passion; the gods are sure to punish such pride. Yet it is true, and always has been, that innocence of heart and violence of feeling are necessary in any kind of superior achievement; the arts cannot exist without them. Caitlin Thomas here proves herself to be one of those rare individuals who have been able to keep hold of these dangerous qualities, in a pure state and to a highly operative degree, into the years when most people have lost them for good. This fact strikes the reader on the first page of her book. She immediately leaps into a state of "pure uncompromising abandon," and we are swept into it with her. And we at once believe what she says and keep on believing in spite of every obstacle she puts in our way. It takes foresight to lie, and Mrs. Thomas seems never to have heard of foresight.

She has at moments the aplomb and daring, the almost insolence in dealing with atmosphere and facts, of the born writer. She is always sentient,
wound up, nervously attentive; she is sometimes sharply witty and broadly
humorous. Her epithets crackle and sparkle; she moves into the most forbidding territory with ease; she jumps barriers and tears down walls. With
a child's heedlessness and headstrong courage, although she may know herself to be in the wrong, she sticks to her guns. Her despair rarely degenerates
into self-pity. She is able to put first things first, and to mix successfully time
present and time past, in what finally turns out to be a well-constructed
book.

She calls it a confession, but is it one? Confession implies a sense of
guilt, and to Mrs. Thomas it is God and life who are guilty, not harassed
human beings. It is, rather, a headlong descriptive analysis of herself and
other people. Dylan Thomas, man and poet, is here for the first time seen
very nearly complete—his dour origins, his deadly faults, his nearly as deadly
virtues, his poet's compulsions, his hidden yearning for respectability, his
household rules of behavior (no children at meals; the family *endimanché* [in
Sunday best] whenever possible), his consistent flight from reality, his un-
governable plunge toward death. The relationship between this man and
wife, whose tutelary goddesses were certainly the Furies, falls into place in
a line or a phrase: "He said he loved me. . . . I believed him, and still do . . .
my all-in-Dylan world. . . . He would flood me with a contempt of words;
there is no fury like the weak, against the weak." Then there is America and
the Americans, treated with alternate appreciation (for hospitality and generosity) and dislike ("the indistinguishable waves of gush"). Here is "the
Killer, poetry reading"—the murderous (for him) money-maker into which
role Thomas finally threw himself with frenzy, thereby arousing his wife's
latent desire to be appreciated in her own right. After Dylan's death, the inhabitants of Wales and the natives of the island of Elba come into view (with
few exceptions, totally repellent). Caitlin Thomas—brought up in Ireland
as a "guerrilla lady," improvident but not completely impractical; the wife
of an extraordinary man whose excesses and even triumphs filled her with
presentiments of disaster; a grief-stricken widow; a passionate mother; and,
finally, a woman newly in love—appears throughout, combining all these
roles with many characteristics of an outrageous and exhibitionist child. We
are not spared one detail of the background or foreground, and we are
treated to insights of the most cruel and penetrating kind. Everything is pre-

sented raw and quivering. All this took some doing. It is remarkable, under the circumstances, that it was done at all, and with so little querulousness and contempt.

For the child, a fairy tale goes forward from darkness to light. The deformed stranger becomes the radiant prince, and the ugly duckling turns into a swan. For the grownup *manqué* [the failed grownup] the story always unrolls in reverse. The kind, reliable, masculinely protective friend becomes a rogue; the happily remembered place, freedom's own, becomes a prison; and the hero or heroine is forced step by step from a position of some dignity and worth toward the status of the victim or the culprit. Caitlin Thomas's experiences on the island of Elba—a place so weighted, to begin with, with associations of detention and exile—bear many signs of a paranoiac nightmare come true. She returned to a scene where she and Dylan had once spent an "unspoiled" holiday. Time had passed; things had changed. She found ugliness and restriction where she had hoped for beauty and peace. The hotel-keeper, once her friend, becomes a tyrant; the lovely young boy to whom she loses her heart remains a playmate more than a lover. She is frozen by the winter climate; the sea rejects her; the very ground of the town and its environs becomes a difficult terrain, like the impeding surfaces we walk over in bad dreams; the mines in the district become "the cemetery of the earth"; and, worst of all, the endlessly attentive, endlessly suspicious natives become an audience of adversaries. The story that works itself out of this has little true drama in it, since it could be controlled only by attempts either to rebel against it or to wipe it out of consciousness. Situations keep lapsing into travesty and the grotesque, and the heroine finally flees the sought haven that had consistently rejected her. At the end of Mrs. Thomas's recital, it is hard not to feel that a little good sense or a drop of loving-kindness might have changed the outcome. But events seem to order themselves in this nightmare fashion for anyone who tries to face down life in general or his own destiny in particular. It would be a fine thing if Mrs. Thomas should go on to write another book, in which she tries not to kill life but to resurrect it.

[1957]

Caitlin Thomas

Juan Ramón Jiménez

WE MUST blame history, in part, for the fact that so little Spanish poetry has been translated, successfully or unsuccessfully, into English. England, in the natural way of things, did not, after Elizabeth, spend much time or consideration on the literary works of a defeated rival, and after the early seventeenth century there was little in the way of brilliance or power to be considered, either in prose or in verse, Cervantes, Góngora, and Lope de Vega being contemporaries of Shakespeare. Spanish poetry of any interest or intensity did not exist in the eighteenth century, and it was negligible or imitative up to the end of the nineteenth. No constellation of Romantics appeared, and the themes of doubt, soul-searching, and spiritual turmoil in general, which occupied the Victorians, had no counterpart in a country almost totally closed off from the Industrial Revolution. Only with Federico García Lorca, born in 1899, did modern Spanish poetry come to international attention.

It was left to the 1956 Nobel Prize committee to bring to international notice two other modern Spaniards whose importance might otherwise have been passed over—Antonio Machado, who died in 1939, after having helped defend the Spanish Republic, and Juan Ramón Jiménez. Jiménez received the Swedish medal, but in its presentation the committee, by also naming Machado and Lorca, evidently took into consideration the merits of these two Spanish poets, now dead. For, as the uninstructed then came to learn, Lorca was by no means an isolated figure; both Machado and Jiménez had been, to some extent, his masters—Jiménez particularly so, because he had explored, in his work, much the same territory and material, although in a quite different way. Lorca's poetry, dramatic and highly colored, had some of the "Spanish gaudiness" that is a striking but ultimately superficial element in Spanish art as a whole. Lorca had emphasized, moreover, folk (chiefly gypsy) intensity and abruptness, and his poignant refrains, his ballad feeling, came over with greater ease in translation than Spanish verse written in more conventional forms. And Lorca's closeness to literary Surrealism in its most flourishing period linked him to poets writing in a like manner in French and English.

But it is now generally conceded that Jiménez, of a slightly older generation (he was born in 1881), has had the strongest influence on Spanish poetry written in the twentieth century. Unlike Rubén Darío, who first brought French Symbolism over into Spanish verse, he was not so much an imitator of this French poet or that as he was a writer of the same kind of poetry. His first poems, published when he was eighteen, were close to the heart of a native Spanish Impressionism, what has been called the "shimmering extravagances" of his native Andalusia. Jiménez later developed a style and attitude that could accommodate direct and detailed observation of the world about him: like Yeats, he worked himself free from any device that resembled applied ornament; for him, to be modern meant to be free. His rhythms became more individual as he moved away from conventional metres toward a kind of patterned *vers libre*. He has never lost, however, his special power over language, which has become—in his later years— increasingly transparent, shifting, and luminous.

At its most subtle, such poetry, of course, defies translation. It nevertheless seems a pity that the first attempt to make the work of Jiménez available in any large way in America turns out to be more baffling than clarifying. *Selected Writings of Juan Ramón Jiménez,* edited (with a preface) by Eugenio Florit and translated by H. R. Hays, breaks so many of the rules we are accustomed to have modern translators follow that very nearly all of the savor and point of the poetry is lost, while the prose—which should present far fewer difficulties—comes through in rather a blunted way. Translation has offered, in our century, refreshment to the poetry of all Western languages. So many crucial discoveries of both difference and relationship, and so many fruitful exchanges of material and method, have been made that it is difficult nowadays to think what modern poetry in English, for example, would be like if it had not received the exciting impact of Pound's renderings from literatures ranging from the Chinese to the Anglo-Saxon, of Eliot's translation of the Symbolist St.-John Perse, of the various translations of Rilke and of the French Surrealists. Modern versions of the classics of antiquity have also been turned into acceptable and readable modern speech, from Homer and the complete canon of Greek drama through Virgil and Ovid. These have been demanding labors, carried out with several rules in mind—strict adherence to the spirit and tone of the originals and the utmost simplicity and accuracy in regard to form and language, the natural words in the natural order. In the case of lyric poetry, modern translators have also been meticulous, wherever possible, about presenting the original poems on facing pages.

We are given no originals for Mr. Hays's translations, so we have no notion of the poems' basic pattern and coloration. His unsuccess can be gauged, however, by the frequent awkwardness and the pervasive weakness of the English. Here all the old, bad literary words, which modern poets have worked so hard and so long at eliminating, reappear. And here are the little extra (and unnecessary) turns of speech, at the same time that important touches are left out. And the syntax is disarranged, so that telling emphasis is lost. Granted that the translation of lyric poetry requires the most delicate tact and the most varied gifts of ear and insight, and granted that the Spanish language presents special hazards to the translator, surely today, after so much achievement in the field, it is difficult to bear what seems to be deafness on the part of a translator not only to the Spanish he is taking the poem out of but to the English he is putting it into. Hays's versions, taken on their merits as English poems, would most certainly never have seen the light of print.

Eugenio Florit, a poet who in his youth, in the thirties, knew Jiménez in Cuba, gives a most sympathetic and detailed account, in his preface, of Jiménez's development and influence. Florit emphasizes the poet's critical powers and his gift of Goyaesque caricature, for Jiménez has a biting sardonic side. What seems to be most striking in Jiménez, apart from his lyric gift, is his persistence and endurance, his impulse to advance and to explore. He is again comparable to Yeats in his mature insistence on examining every level and facet of his experience, of refining his expression down to essentials, of contemplating both appearance and essence. These two men, both from "backward" countries (and both close to the most primitive regions of those countries—Yeats to Sligo and Jiménez to Andalusia, a province where an ancient pastoral life continues to exist), brought over into the modern, mechanized world a sense of poetry as a part of primitive ritual, and of the poet as one who is still able to touch at their source human gaiety, melancholy, and enchantment. Jiménez's travels in North and South America and his present "exile" in Puerto Rico (where he has lived and taught since 1952) have not blurred or distorted his sense of origins. It is a heartening fact that even today "sensibility" is more tense and durable than one might suppose; that Jiménez, for all his uneven health and sensitive nature, has been able to hold to unchanging human values in a world that seems to turn more and more toward the concept of man as machine-tender or puppet. The slightest lyric of such a poet is a positive act against disorder of feeling and the falseness of the second-hand. Platero, the tough little Andalusian donkey, the beast of burden who is Jiménez's most touching creation, was made "of steel and quicksilver." His master shares these qualities, and would have poetry share them.

[1958]

Philip Larkin

The Whitsun Weddings

LARKIN, ON the dust jacket of his latest volume, *The Whitsun Weddings,* disclaims any special love of form: "Form holds little interest for me. Content is everything." But it is at once apparent to the most casual reader that this member of what is now becoming a middle-aged British poetic generation possesses formal gifts that are not only perfectly controlled and strongly sustained but capable of wide and interesting variation. He is able to use such gifts as they are seldom used, to describe the tough realities of his time —those sometimes major and sometimes marginal uglinesses that seem unassimilable in art unless they are caricatured: the hideous, the cheap, the wrecked object; the desolate, the devastated locale. Larkin's realism (which has Hardy behind it) is not inflexibly dour. A profound pessimism exists, but this bleak background is often unexpectedly broken to let through some calm and tender emotion.

One aspect of Larkin's work that often adds subtle reinforcement to his moments of pathos is his open assumption of the British sense of class.

The title poem—one of Larkin's most striking successes—of the new book is based on a touching succession of insights into what must be taken as a working-class spring festival. Larkin reports with a direct first-person approach the phenomenon of young brides and their wedding parties as they appear at the railway stops during a journey he is making to London from the North. Written in stanzas large and free enough to accommodate minor variations in stress and speed, yet strict enough to give what can only be called an odelike dignity to awkward material, the poem releases, in its last lines, a restrained lyricism that reverberates in the classic manner. Touches and colorings of feeling keep recurring in Larkin, not set off in any sharp contrast but present as part of the general web of his response to the difficult details of his world—details he does not shy away from but attacks and resolves. And he openly examines his limitations. This frankness has troubled those of his readers who expect from him a more copious flow of work, perhaps more cheerfully expressed. And what about the disconcerting streak of wicked satire that appears from time to time? A great deal of truthtelling is projected by Larkin's intense dramatic lyricism.

[1965]

Dorothy Richardson

THE BEGINNING and middle years of Victoria's reign were marked in England by grotesque excesses of male control—social, political, and familial. One student of the period has given, in recorded statistics, the number of benighted governesses (21,000 in 1851) and of ill-paid and sweated seamstresses who struggled at that time for some sort of livelihood. We also have the number—in six figures—of the domestic servants who, in 1841, waited on the Victorian wives, whose husbands, quite generally, had forced them into an enervating idleness. Idleness had become, for the middle-class woman, a class badge; if you were the wife of a prosperous man, you did nothing. The demand of the Victorian male for innocence—and ignorance —in a wife left the Victorian woman untrained in the practical conduct of life. The "bustling Chaucerian housewife," the Renaissance manageress of estates, had largely disappeared.

Girls and women, except in the rarest instances, took on the servile, flattering manners of the slave. Women became past mistresses of the cosseting gesture and the seductive wile. Their insanely hampering clothes made them into puppets. They were almost helpless under the law, trapped by father and husband. But soon they began to break into open, or half-concealed rebellion. Florence Nightingale raised nursing to an honorable profession. Miss Barrett ran away with Mr. Browning. "George Eliot" entered into a long, fruitful extra-marital relationship with George Lewes.

And they began to write. A very nearly complete documentation of the life and surroundings of the nineteenth-century Englishwoman has come down to us. From the mills of the Midlands to the parlors of the high bourgeoisie; from the Yorkshire moors to the governess's shabby little realm, we have it all, written by women who were learning to cast brave and penetrating glances into their surroundings and into their own hearts.

Dorothy Richardson, in making her first break into the pupil-teacher and governess pattern at seventeen, was following the Brontë tradition. A season in Hanover, used in *Pointed Roofs* (1915), was followed by two later teaching stints in England, described in *Backwater* (1916) and *Honeycomb* (1917). She then, barely twenty-one, moved into the beginning of a career that was to hold her for over a decade: she became a dental assistant for a group of Wimpole Street doctors, oddly combining the duties of nurse and secretary. At the beginning of *The Tunnel* (1919), the fourth "chapter" of her long prose work, *Pilgrimage,* we find her established in this post.

Merely to get at Dorothy Richardson's novels—the twelve "chapters" of *Pilgrimage,* published separately between 1915 and 1938 and in a four-volume collected edition in England and America in the last-mentioned year —has, of late, become so difficult that the waning of her reputation may be partly put down to the absence of the books themselves and data on their author. Moreover, she gave the public, or the occasional inquiring journalist, little help. After her marriage in 1917 to Alan Odle, an artist and illustrator, she lived, evidently with the thought of her husband's frail health in mind, principally in Cornwall, with a few months in London lodgings each year. This marriage, it is clear, was a sustaining one, which brought out, until Odle's death in 1948, a latent maternal emotion of a particularly deep nature—an emotion which had appeared only fragmentarily in her account of Miriam Henderson (the *persona* she had assumed in the closely autobiographical account of her early years).

It now turns out that the account did not end with *Dimple Hill* (1938). A later manuscript, *March Moonlight,* was discovered after her death in 1957. The journey of "Miriam Henderson" from the point when she was "thrown out upon the world," at seventeen, to the moment when, a woman in her thirties, she is about to be given, by a patron, a year of freedom in which to write, is now complete. But at the moment when she has found, after many false starts, her subject and method, Dorothy Richardson becomes so absorbed in recovering the experience of her young alter ego that she herself vanishes from sight.

Early on, Richardson's method was described by the novelist May Sinclair, in a phrase of William James, as "stream of consciousness." Richardson herself, in later years, repudiated this label, and it is true that she did not hold to a single method after her first experiments. Impressionism in the novel was soon to be pushed to extraordinary limits; but Richardson owes nothing to either Joyce or Proust, or to Virginia Woolf, who took over much but invented nothing. Two innovations are truly Richardson's. She used Henry James's viewpoint person, and she made that person—unchangeably—a woman: herself, at one remove. The character of Miriam Henderson is the mirror in which all is reflected.

At first this reflection is exquisitely clear, with the senses of the female perceiver unblurred. Later, Miriam becomes more tendentious; the arguments multiply and the lines dividing pure creation and repetitive obsession begin to show. For there is no doubt that Richardson was obsessed, concerning what to her was the irreducible gap between the nature and motives of women and men. But there is also little doubt that her findings had truth in them; modern psychological insight has confirmed many. And Miriam, as part of her gradual enlightenment, is finally able to recognize and acknowledge her deep and compulsive psychic scars.

Her variations on the man-woman theme are often extraordinary. It is evident that she has heard of the myths, as well as the historical facts, of matriarchy, and of the worship of the Great Mother; and, to her, it is with the bonds of a strong secret sisterhood that all women are bound together. It is fascinating to watch her sensibilities operate in a region which, though at first glance seemingly frivolous, is undeniably women's: the world of clothes. She has written a whole grammar, a whole history, of the costume of the late nineteenth and early twentieth centuries; she builds up, little by little, what can only be called an elaborate mystique of dress. Not only the cut of garments but their differing fabrics are described, and she is often naïvely delighted with the details of what has come to seem the ugliest period of fashion known to Western man.

She often takes direct leaps from perception of character through dress to perception of character through height, weight, bone structure, and tricks of carriage. She is merciless to "the common"; and it is almost always spiritual commonness that repels her. And commonness had, of course, its own undeniable sound. She can detect the nuances of this sound in three languages (French, German, and English) with zones of *patois* in between. She can not only detect the smallest peculiarity of speech, but she can reproduce it in an almost ventriloquial manner. The reader will remember a minor character— come upon once, and never to reappear; Richardson is full of such characters —by the shape of a forehead, the manner of getting in and out of a chair, or a flattening of vowels.

All this is feminine. It is feminine "reality" she is after; and she soon finds that this reality can be most tellingly presented in a condensed, episodic form. She is not recounting it to us retrospectively; she is sharing it with us in a kind of continuous present. Not *this is the way it was,* but *this is the way it is.* Irritation caused by this condensed, elliptical approach has been repeatedly expressed by masculine commentators. A gap between male and female sensibility then exists? Not an abyss, as Richardson came to believe, but certainly a temperamental disjunction from which irritation and misunderstanding can and do spring.

BUT SHE receives high praise from men. J. C. Powys,[1] in a long study of her work published in 1931, says of her: "She works with memory, and what must amaze most people is the apparently willful choice of unpicturesque, unpromising, unideal and in many instances actually unpleasant aspects of reality. Yet all these queer things . . . are treated by her with their ramifications and convolutions as if they were carefully selected ideal symbols of human life." These "queer things" were the material circumstances of her youth, and she did not shirk any difficulty in outlining and projecting this portrait of a young woman living in an attic room on £1 a week. She is recording feminine heroism, as well as feminine insight and subjective perception.

Particularly subjective and feminine are the waves of euphoria that wash over her again and again. Sudden radiance will illumine some dull task; a London street—the line of its houses against the sky, its traffic, its people —will begin to open out into timelessness. As with all true mystics, her vision is based on the sharp apprehension of reality. Later in the work, it is true, the half-impression begins to replace the full delineation, and the hint and the veiled anecdote can become rather tiresome. She begins to bypass crises. That she evaded any direct description of her mother's suicide, at the end of *Honeycomb* (1917), we now know; it is one of the facts put before us by Mr. Horace Gregory's meticulous biography, *Dorothy Richardson: An Adventure in Self-Discovery.*

At the same time, she does not scant descriptions of certain hysterias and neuroses of the transitional time she is dealing with—pathological states which were to disappear, or take on another coloring, in the post-1914 world. Here is the "born spinster," the "born bachelor," the pathological child, along with morbid jealousy and emotional tyranny in various disguised forms. It is freedom Miriam is out for, not power. She is fighting every step of the way, not only for social justice, but for the right, as a woman and a growing individual, to stand clear from the shams which had tortured her as a child; from her father's double-dealing and her mother's subservience and final despair.

Her diction, from the beginning, is fresh and alert. There is no "period" or deadening language; she places, often, epithet beside epithet in her effort accurately to give the true innerness of people and events. She possesses, Powys says, "a certain obstinate, humorous, massive, deliberate approach to life which is not in the least ashamed of being pedantic." She is capable of slashing out at women; and she is never taken in by the then-prevalent feminist notion that men have been continuously, throughout history, out to conquer and enslave women. Women have a birth-right, which they should claim, as beings whose knowledge of, and intuitions concerning reality are profound.

Politics and the vote touch the surface only. "These women's rights people," she says in *Deadlock* (1921), "are the worst of all. Because they think women have been subject in the past. Women have never been subject. Never can be. The proof of this is the way men have always been puzzled and everlastingly trying fresh theories; founded on the very small experiences of women any man is capable of having. . . . [Men] must leave off imagining themselves as a race of gods fighting against chaos, and thinking of women as part of the chaos they have to civilize. There isn't any 'chaos.' . . . It's the principal masculine delusion. It is not a truth to say that women must be civilized" [insertion LB's].

Mr. Gregory's well-organized and perceptive study is extremely valuable in setting the rather confused record straight. He has had access to late correspondence between Richardson, her occasional patrons, and her many friends; and at last the dates are put right (1873–1957)—for at the time of her marriage, the forty-four-year-old woman had fibbed, in a rather endearing female fashion, about her age. Mr. Gregory quotes brilliantly from *Pilgrimage* and rightly describes it as a rare example of a woman's restless, yet profound, spiritual quest.

And in the beautifully printed, new complete edition, comprising, at last, the entire thirteen "chapters" of this remarkable and original prose chronicle of our time, we finally have Richardson through "Miriam" complete: the brave, if not entirely fearless (for she is often racked by fear), little wrong-headed-to-the-majority partisan of her own sex (and of living as experienced by her own sex), in her high-necked blouse and (before she took up cycling) long skirt, from which the dust and mud of the London streets must be brushed daily; working endless hours in poor light at a job which involved physical drudgery as well as endless tact; going home to a tiny room under the roof of a badly run boardinghouse; meeting, in spite of her handicapped position, an astonishing range of human beings and of points of view; going to lectures; keeping up her music and languages; listening to debates at the Fabian Society; daring to go into a restaurant late at night, driven by cold and exhaustion, to order a roll, butter, and a cup of cocoa; trying to write, learning to write; trying to love and yet remain free; vividly aware of life and London. And continually sensing transition, welcoming change, eager to bring on the future and be involved with "the new." And reiterating (on the verge of the most terrible war in history, wherein all varieties of masculine madnesses were to be proven real): "Until it has been clearly explained that men are always partly wrong in their ideas, life [will] be full of poison and secret bitterness" [insertion LB's].

[1967]

1. English writer John Cowper Powys (1872–1963) was one of three brothers, all of whom wrote novels; his best known were *Wolf Solent* and *Owen Glendower.* Among his critical essays was "In Defense of Sensuality" (1930).

Poetry Appendix

Uncollected Poems

A Night in Summer

> The restless sea before my window breaks
>> All night beneath the stars that bend to see;
>> Full of unrest, and sad and longingly,
> It sings its soft, sad song as day awakes.
> And, oh, the tender lullabies it makes
>> That seem so full of some sad memory,
>> Of cadences that come and swiftly flee,
> And leave a gentle murmur in their wakes.
> I cannot sleep with all its whisperings,

I lie wide-eyed and hear the tide's swift rush
Against the sand and seaweed of the beach—
    All through the night until the dawn it sings,
Each ripple sighing—fading each in each—
    And always, "Hush"—and always, always, "Hush!"

[1911]

The Betrothal of King Cophetua

When they had brought her at the king's behest
The courtyard dusk fell cool to her forehead's heat.
She silent stood, the sun on her bruised feet,
The evening shadow lay against her breast.
"Your name?" he asked—
                  "I have not any name."
Her round voice held the sound of windless streams
Fringed to the bank with grasses, of old dreams
His youth knew. His voice broke and he was mute,
But asked again, "You come from out what land?"
"I have forgotten."
              Under trees of fruit
He had seen her first, as they bowed in the ripening year.
Fragrant her lips with juice, and stained her hand . . .
He said "Come nearer" and she came more near.

A casket then he gave to her. Like flame
Beneath the lid, like flames into the dark
The jewels sprawled and looped and shot their spark
Star-wise: peridot, beryl, winy sard
And icy straps of diamond.
                 A dove
Beyond where to the sky the roof cut hard
Called, notes like heavy water to a wave
When falling, and with pain her heart knew love . . .
The box crashed, the heaped gems spilled to the pave.

Blindly through the dark to his side she came.
Her feet seemed shod with rain, so swift they were.

Like wings on her forehead folded lay her hair
And she was wild and sweet.
                              "I am a king"
He said, "But if I give you jewels, lands,
And you spurn all, I have no other thing,
No more to give, if it be not love you seek."
Leaning, he took her face between his hands;
She turned her eyes to him and did not speak.[1]

[1915]

1. LB's dramatized pre-Raphaelite tableau of the legendary African king, indifferent to
women until he sees a beggar maid dressed in gray rags. One of the ballads in Percy's *Reliques
of Ancient English Poetry* narrates the story, as does Tennyson in "The Beggar-Maid." Shakespeare and Jonson refer to the beggar maid, and Burne-Jones painted Elizabeth Siddal in the
role.

The Young Wife

I.

I do not believe in this first happiness,
But one day I shall know that love is not a fruited bough
Low bending to the hand;
One day I shall know that love is the secret wind
Rippling the grass
Along hillsides in the night;
That it is the tree in spring
Holding lightly in the air its shining twigs
And with its roots throbbing in darkness.

So I shall take less love now
And not think it as due me,
And I shall not watch the eyes of my lover, their every glance,
Nor take his day as mine, nor count the hours of his night.
Even though love comes hard
With all the labor of the spring,
Though I may wish to grasp that for which I have suffered
And crush it to me with a tight hand.

A day comes when all must go.
Love does not stand;
Love does not wait;
No man can follow after love—
A day dawns with a wild sky,
I have laid my hand to the earth and felt how it is cold,
I have seen the little leaves that the poplar tree lets fall upon the wind.

II.

Had I the sweet skin of Helen
And Deirdre's autumn-colored hair
I could not be as beautiful as all beautiful women.

I cannot have the voices of all beautiful women
Were my voice bright with the trill and quiver of water,—
Nor their laughter
Nor their speech.
Though I might choose delicate words
I could not speak so fair as they.

They have taken everything from me,
The beautiful women my lover has had before me,—
Gentle touches of cheek to cheek,
The embraces of passion and of terror;
They have given all to him before me:
Love in the night,
Tears,
Trust and suffering and long desire—
I can but repeat these, and say them over,
All love's thousand things.

He has kissed me with closed eyes,
Embraced me with a hidden face,
And I did not know whose kiss he took and whose face burned behind
    his eyelids.

And all women will bear me out in this,
All women now yielding to a lover,
And all of other years:

Ye, poor queens,
And ye, poor haughty ladies.

[1917]

Survival

I hoped that you would die out from me
With the year.
Between you and my heart I thrust
The glittering seasons.

I denied you with late summer,
Watching the green-white hydrangea change
To petalled balls of thin and ashen blue,
And nasturtiums, hot orange on stems like ice or glass
Shriveling by round leaves.

I went on to autumn
Without you,
Seeing hills burdened by trees colored unevenly:
Applered, pearyellow,
And leaves falling in ravines, through bitter smoke,
Falling indirectly,
A long wave and turn.
Those evenings came
High and shining over rivers like quicksilver;
And latest autumn:
The underbrush sienna, cut, twisted, carved,
Red berries shaken through it like beads
Scattered in barbaric hair.

Nothing moves in the fields that once had the grass.
To look upon the fields
Is like silence laid upon the eyes.
The house is shut sternly
From limitless radiance outside
In these days of afternoon stars.

The year dies out.
Who are you to be stronger than the year?
I have you like long cold sunshine in an empty room,
Through and beyond black thaws that rot the snow.

[1921]

Elders

At night the moon shakes the bright dice of the water;
And the elders, their flower light as broken snow upon the bush,
Repeat the circle of the moon.

Within the month
Black fruit breaks from the white flower.
The black-wheeled berries turn
Weighing the boughs over the road.
There is no harvest.
Heavy to withering, the black wheels bend

Ripe for the mouths of chance lovers,
Or birds.

Twigs show again in the quick cleavage of season and season.
The elders sag over the powdery road-bank,
As though they bore, and it were too much,
The seed of the year beyond the year.

[1922]

Resolve

So that I shall no longer tarnish with my fingers
The bright steel of your power,
I shall be hardened against you,
A shield tightened upon its rim.

A stern oval to be pierced by no weapon,
Metal stretched and shaped against you.
For a long time I shall go
Spanned by the round of my strength.

Changeless, in spite of change,
My resolve undefeated;
Though now I see the evening moon, soon to wane,
Stand clearly and alone in the early dark,
Above the stirring spindles of the leaves.

[1922]

Leave-Taking

I do not know where either of us can turn
Just at first, waking from the sleep of each other.
I do not know how we can bear
The river struck by the gold plummet of the moon,
Or many trees shaken together in the darkness.
We shall wish not to be alone
And that love were not dispersed and set free—
Though you defeat me,
And I be heavy upon you.

But like earth heaped over the heart
Is love grown perfect.
Like a shell over the beat of life
Is love perfect to the last.
So let it be the same
Whether we turn to the dark or to the kiss of another;
Let us know this for leave-taking,
That I may not be heavy upon you,
That you may blind me no more.

[1922]

To a Dead Lover

The dark is thrown
Back from the brightness, like hair
Cast over a shoulder.
I am alone,
Four years older;
Like the chairs and the walls
Which I once watched brighten
With you beside me. I was to waken
Never like this, whatever came or was taken.

The stalk grows, the year beats on the wind.
Apples come, and the month for their fall.
The bark spreads, the roots tighten.
Though today be the last
Or tomorrow all,
You will not mind.

That I may not remember
Does not matter.
I shall not be with you again.
What we knew, even now
Must scatter
And be ruined, and blow
Like dust in the rain.
You have been dead a long season
And have less than desire
Who were lover with lover;
And I have life—that old reason
To wait for what comes,
To leave what is over.

[1922]

Decoration

A macaw preens upon a branch outspread
With jewelry of seed. He's deaf and mute.
The sky behind him splits like gorgeous fruit
And claw-like leaves clutch light till it has bled.
The raw diagonal bounty of his wings
Scrapes on the eye color too chafed. He beats
A flattered tail out against gauzy heats;
He has the frustrate look of cheated kings.
And all the simple evening passes by:
A gillyflower spans its little height
And lovers with their mouths press out their grief.
The bird fans wide his striped regality
Prismatic, while against a sky breath-white
A crystal tree lets fall a crystal leaf.

[1923]

A Letter

I came here, being stricken, stumbling out
At last from streets; the sun, decreasing, took me
For days, the time being the last of autumn,
The thickets not yet stark, but quivering
With tiny colors, like some brush strokes in   5
The manner of the pointillists; small yellows
Dart shaped, little reds in different pattern,
Clicks and notches of color on threaded bushes,
A cracked and fluent heaven, and a brown earth.
I had these, and my food and sleep—enough.   10

This is a countryside of roofless houses,—
Taverns to rain,—doorsteps of millstones, lintels
Leaning and delicate, foundations sprung to lilacs,
Orchards where boughs like roots strike into the sky.
Here I could well devise the journey to nothing,   15

At night getting down from the wagon by the black barns,
The zenith a point of darkness, breaking to bits,
Showering motionless stars over the houses.
Scenes relentless—the black and white grooves of a woodcut.

But why the journey to nothing or any desire?   20
Why the heart taken by even senseless adventure,
The goal a coffer of dust? Give my mouth to the air,
Let arrogant pain lick my flesh with a tongue
Rough as a cat's; remember the smell of cold mornings,
The dried beauty of women, the exquisite skin   25
Under the chins of young girls, young men's rough beards,—
The cringing promise of this one, that one's apology
For the knife struck down to the bone, gladioli in sick rooms,
Asters and dahlias, flowers like ruches, rosettes...

Forever enough to part grass over the stones   30
By some brook or well, the lovely seed-shedding stalks;
To hear in the single wind diverse branches
Repeating their sounds to the sky—that sky like scaled mackerel,
Fleeing the fields—to be defended from silence,
To feel my body as arid, as safe as a twig   35
Broken away from whatever growth could snare it
Up to a spring, or hold it softly in summer
Or beat it under in snow.
                              I must get well.
Walk on strong legs, leap the hurdles of sense,
Reason again, come back to my old patchwork logic,   40
Addition, subtraction, money, clothes, clocks,
Memories (freesias, smelling slightly of snow and of flesh
In a room with blue curtains) ambition, despair.
I must feel again who had given feeling over,
Challenge laughter, take tears, play the piano,   45
Form judgments, blame a crude world for disaster.

To escape is nothing. Not to escape is nothing.
The farmer's wife stands with a halo of darkness
Rounding her head. Water drips in the kitchen
Tapping the sink. Today the maples have split   50
Limb from the trunk with the ice, a fresh wooden wound.

The vines are distorted with ice, ice burdens the breaking
Roofs I have told you of.
                              Shall I play the pavane
For a dead child or the scene where the girl
Lets fall her hair, and the loud chords descend   55
As though her hair were metal, clashing along
Over the tower, and a dumb chord receives it?[1]
This may be wisdom: abstinence, beauty is nothing,
That you regret me, that I feign defiance.
And now I have written you this, it is nothing.   60

[1923]

1. LB refers in these lines to two pieces of late-nineteenth-century music, Maurice
Ravel's slow *Pavane pour une infante défunte,* and a scene in Claude Debussy's "impressionist"
opera *Pelléas et Mélisande* in which Mélisande is combing her hair and Pelléas, who has come
to bid her farewell, takes hold of her hair and kisses it. LB knew this Debussy passage by
heart (see letter to Morton Zabel, October 9, 1937).

Words for Departure

Nothing was remembered, nothing forgotten.
When we awoke, wagons were passing on the warm summer pavements,
The window sills were wet from rain in the night,
Birds scattered and settled over chimney pots
As among grotesque trees.

Nothing was accepted, nothing looked beyond.
Slight-voiced bells separated hour from hour,
The afternoon sifted coolness
And people drew together in streets becoming deserted.
There was a moon, and light in a shop-front,
And dusk falling like precipitous water.

Hand clasped hand,
Forehead still bowed to forehead—
Nothing was lost, nothing possessed,
There was no gift nor denial.

2.

I have remembered you.
You were not the town visited once,
Nor the road falling behind running feet.

You were as awkward as flesh
And lighter than frost or ashes.

You were the rind,
And the white-juiced apple,
The song, and the words waiting for music.

3.

You have learned the beginning;
Go from mine to the other.

Be together; eat, dance, despair,
Sleep, be threatened, endure.
You will know the way of that.

But at the end, be insolent;
Be absurd—strike the thing short off;
Be mad—only do not let talk
Wear the bloom from silence.

And go away without fire or lantern.
Let there be some uncertainty about your departure.

[1923]

Epitaph for a Romantic Woman

She has attained the permanence
She dreamed of, where old stones lie sunning.
Untended stalks blow over her
Even and swift, like young men running.

Always in the heart she loved
Others had lived,—she heard their laughter.
She lies where none has lain before,
Where certainly none will follow after.

[1923]

Song

Love me because I am lost;
Love me that I am undone.
That is brave,—no man has wished it,
Not one.

Be strong, to look on my heart
As others look on my face.
Love me,—I tell you that it is a ravaged
Terrible place.

[1923]

Pyrotechnics

Mix prudence with my ashes
    Write caution on my urn;
While life foams and flashes
    Burn, bridges, burn!

[1923]

The Stones

Your hands that seek in my bosom to find what I am
May bruise on the old dark stones, the upper, the nether,
That have been ground and pressed and broken together,
That turned in the night, and made the morning a sham.

Guard your hands. They turned with a heavy moan.
They are silent now. Their grain is the torrent, the mist.
They are old stones. I have forgotten their grist.
They are mossed with the dark. Have done. We will leave them alone.

[1923]

Trio

Children come to be born;
Mirth is shattered with sense.
Summer lends passion and scorn
The light of its elements.

So take your kisses, give tears;
Savor the perishing minute
By the grave that you dug, my dears,
Even though I'm not in it.

[1923]

The Flume

I.

She had a madness in her for betrayal.
She looked for it in every room in the house.
Sometimes she thought she must rip up the floor to find
A box, a letter, a ring, to set her grief,
So long a rusty wheel, revolving in fury.   5
But all that she ever found was the noise of water
Bold in the house as over the dam's flashboard,
Water as loud as a pulse pressed into the ears,

Steady as blood in the veins,—often she thought
The shout her own life,—that she did not listen and hear it.   10

The fields had gone to young grass, the syringa hung
Stayed by the weight of flowers in the moving morning.
The shuttered house held coolness a core against
The hot steeped shrubs at its doors, and the blazing river.
She in the house, when he had gone to the mill,   15
Tried to brush from her heart the gentlest kiss
New on her mouth. She leaned her broom to the wall,
Ran to the stairs, breathless to start the game
Of finding agony hid in some corner,
Tamed, perhaps, by months of pity, but still   20
Alive enough to bite at her hands and throat,
To bruise with a blue, unalterable mark
The shoulder where she had felt his breath in sleep
Warm her with its slow measure.

                    In a mirror
Reflecting a barrow by a neighbor's barn   25
And a weathervane stopped between north and west
She saw her face, as she had thought to see it,
Tightened between the eyes. She sat down on the bed
So that a tree was thrust into the mirror
Behind her head, and moved there shadowless   30
Turning around her the green of its distant leaves.
She had her two eyes before her, giving her back
The young face, softly marred by its own derision,
A hand that settled combs in the heavy hair,
The willing mouth, kissed never to its own beauty   35
Because it strained for terror through the kiss,
Never quite shaped over the lover's name
Because that name might go.

                    The tree moved over
Its bounded space, and gave some sky to the glass
Mixed with its leaves. Although the branch rushed loud   40
A field off, it was lost within the steady
Leap of the dam to the flume, made to a silence
She had heard it so long. Nothing against the cold
Beat of her own proud purpose was noise or power.

She had some guilt in her to be betrayed,   45
She had the terrible hope he could not love her.

II.

The wind before storm was to her the wind before thunder.
She heard the break within it from the first.
She never was afraid to face the heavy
Sprout of the lighting, for one moment branched   50
Within the sultriness of the high pasture
A little like another tree for a moment
Gathering through the window not like danger.
She ran about to shut the windows, slammed
The doors that gaped along the wall like ears   55
And tried to keep herself from the first crash
To follow the stripped spasm that took root
On the rocky hill, in the field, or in the water.
She needed more than a house to keep it out.
She clung to the wall, and smelled the dusty paper   60
Beside her face, and counted out the figures
Into a spell, to keep her terror hushed,
And clenched herself so tightly that she thought
Nothing could make her hear that noise again,
And again heard, spun down throughout the valley,   65
The spill from the long sky, over the roof,
Mounting as surely as the beats in pain.
The thunder was like agony, a smother
Against her life: she thought never to stand
Out in the free still air again, and buy   70
A loaf of bread out of the baker's cart,
Or cut the lamp-wicks in the early morning,
Or carry in the biggest lamp at night
Shining and clean under the china shade
To light the dishes of the supper table.   75

—Still—still—everything quieter then
Than the very earth escaping under the plough,
The depth beyond seed of the still and deep-layered ground
Stiller than rock, than the blackest base of rock,
Than the central grain crushed tight within the mountain.   80
It would be still again. She could say tonight

"There has been a storm," as though he hadn't heard
The hundred breaks within the murderous sky,
And he would say that thunder couldn't hurt her.
"There's been a storm," she would say. "Trees have been struck,   85
"Maybe a man stunned in an open field,
"The milk in the cows' udders curdled sour."
One woman frightened in a dusty corner
Who bit her fist and wished to pluck the thunder
From its swinging tree, to throw it down forever   90
Against the pastures it could not destroy,
And after the thunder, run and stop the dam,
The endless fountainous roar of falling water,
And scratch her heart free from the itching love
So much like sound, never spending itself,   95
Never still, in any quietest room.
The thunder ended. She could hear the others:
The water that wrapped the house like a shawly vine,
Love like a rough wind mixing a branch's stems.
The thunder had stopped. Some day she could stand   100
Listening yet, with the others silent around her.

III.

At night his calm closed body lay beside her
Beyond her will established in itself.
Barely a moment before he had said her name,
Giving it into sleep, had set the merciful   105
Bulwark of spare young body against the darkness.
Her hair sweeps over his shoulder, claiming him hers,
This fine and narrow strength, although her hands
Lie, shut untenderly by her own side.
Her woman's flesh, rocking all echoes deep,   110
Strains out again toward ravenous memory.
He lies in sleep, slender, a broken seal,
The strong wrists quick no more to the strong hand,
The intent eyes dulled, the obstinate mouth kissed out.
Outside the dam roars. He is perhaps a child,   115
With a child's breath. He lies flexed like a child,
The strong ribs and firm neck may count for nothing.
She will think him a child. He is weak and he will fail her.

Again she remembers the girl on the edge of town
Who took her lovers out along autumn roads,   120
Under half-empty trees, and shouted her laughter
To hear an echo thinner, later than summer's,
Answer her from the fields. Again she remembers
The true hard cold that caught at the wild girl's body,
When night after night she felt the autumn break   125
And open the country she knew, when she gave her kisses
Beside rough field-stones piled into a wall
Cold as the wind in every particle.
She had been that girl, this woman in a house,
Who well might have no bed. He had given her walls   130
She wished to burn, his body she wished to tear
Ever upon the knife of another's body.
He was the dark, he was the house and sound.

One morning she saw how the first autumn had changed
The splayed repeated figures on the ground   135
Making them leaves, and not the shadow of leaves.

IV.

She has been away. She shuts the heavy door
Against the stars of the late afternoon.
The fine fire in the kitchen warms the hall
And has turned the stove lids golden-red. Such burning!   140
Oh, equal to the terror of the cold
Biting itself outside, like a maddened thing,
Its tooth and fury matched. The lamp flames clearly
Against its glassed-in air. Nothing has changed.
Table and floor have been swept clean enough.   145
She pulls the frozen patch of veil from her mouth
And stands, like a stranger, muffled from the cold
To which she may return. Where is this treachery
That she has come home earlier to find
Wide in her house? It has not tracked the floors   150
Nor strewn crumbs on the shelves. It is hid away.

Begin to turn, you whirring stone in the breast;
Beat again, unsated pulse of fury.

He will soon be here. Give her before he comes
Whet to the blade. Lie open to her eye;   155
Rustle against her ear; give her mean glory
Of treason found outside the treacherous heart.
—No moon is close against the empty windows
To fill the cold hand of the air. The cold stairs murmur
In all their boards and nails, under her feet.   160
Her breath shows white over the lamp she carries
And sets by the bed. The panes shine back
As though there were nothing but a precipice
Beyond the wall, and the house itself a shelter
Held over space. She stands within the panes   165
As in the room, coated, the veil on her cheeks,
Save that there darkness streams behind her body
And through it. She almost knows the change
She could not know until now, so recently
The whistling cold outside beat down her sense.   170
But now she is snared. She tries to take a step
Toward the clumsily smoothed bed, and waits half-balanced,
Even her anger checked. Now all is over.
Her blood still beats, but everything else is still.
She stands in an empty room, in a silent room.   175
The ear has stopped. Great quietude spells the throb
Expected, because here the water sounded,
Because of it the bed and chairs stood here.
She stands here, too, because she once heard water
Night or day, go down in a bristling swing,—   180
Water now like stone over the dam,
And in the flume below, that once ran black
And marked its current with the earliest stalks
Of summer broken, the water might be the ground.
No longer the echo of frenzy bound on itself   185
Answers her from below. She and the mirror
Can play no longer together their bitter game.
Here now is silence, over the earth as beneath it,
The rim of the cymbal frozen, the drum gone slack.

And here at last the lust for betrayal breaks.   190
Her blood beats on, and her love with her blood
Beats back the staring coldness that would kill her,

Laying a palm over the ebb and return
Of her warm throat, heard now for the first time
Within the room. Soon he will find her,   195
Still dressed for flight, quiet upon his bed,
When he has hurried from the weighted cold
Toward the faint lamp upstairs. She will lie there
Hearing at last the timbre of love and silence.

[1929]

Old Divinity

If you at length remain
Though all your garlands wilt—
Awake in me, like pain,
Afire in me, like guilt—

Not fading, as fades smoke,
Or snowfall, swift and serried—
Be pierced by one sharp stroke
And die thus, and be buried,

Cast in some unmarked spot
With granite that does not bloom
(Insensate, as I am not),
To serve you as a tomb.

[1929]

For an Old Dance

What can be said
When we depart?
What can begin
When we are over?
For love, no mouth,

For grief, no tears.
O, learn me now,
Hearing me beat
Like sound in the ears,
Blood in the heart.
Quick, come away;
Be my lover.

Nothing can wait:
Not spring, the wind,
Not light, the flower.
All loves abate.
And quieter lying
Than grass struck down
On a winter hill,
I shall lie,
You will be still—
Than the fallen branch,
The leaf in the cold,
Locked in the snow
By dark closed over—
Come, be my lover;
We shall grow old.
Come away now.

[1930]

The Engine

The secure pulses of the heart
Drive and rock in dark precision,
Though life brings fever to the mouth
And the eyes vision.

Whatever joy the body takes,
Whatever sound the voice makes purer,
Will never cause their beat to faint
Or become surer.

These perfect chambers, and their springs,
So fitly sealed against remorse
That keep the lifting shaft of breath
To its cool course,

Cannot delay, and cannot dance—
Until, wrung out to the last drop,
The brain, knowing time and love, must die,
And they must stop.

[1931]

Gift

All that's left of this season
You may have—
If time's for love's granting,
Dearest and brave.

And of fresh time's avowal
You may bespeak
The months of my year,
The days of my week,

Ash tree and beech,
The cinquefoil's measure,
The meadow's speech
And the furrow's treasure.

If summer ends
You may have for the sharing
Plots of corn and of rye
And the red tree bearing;

In another winter
Each bell-like night,
When stars and the fields
Break in their light.

[1932]

Hidden

I thought to make
The smallest possible compass for loveliness
For safety's sake;

To cheat the skill
Of any who might well measure or covet it
Against my will.

"They have big eyes;
This, if it be but a little seed-point of brightness,
They will not prize."

But you said "No;
It is the little thing that the marksman looks for
With his long, spliced bow.

The arrow takes
(With luck) a line to the target's center,
Holds there, and shakes.

If the archer be clever
The landscape about him is scattered with tiniest marks
Speared neatly forever."

What shall I do?
It cannot be small, so that any casual arrow
May rive it in two.

Beyond all size,
Secret and huge, I shall mount it over the world,
Before the bolt flies.

[1936]

New Moon

Cruel time-servers, here is the crescent moon,
Curved right to left in the sky, facing planets attendant.

Over the houses, leaned in the silent air,
Purest along the edge of darkness infinite.

Under it, men return from the office and factory,
From the little store at the corner of Eighty-eighth Street.

On the gnawed snow, or under the breezes of autumn,
With hope and fear in their hearts, and their arms full of groceries.
Above the trim suit, above the flesh starved or satiate,
Above the set hair, above the machines in the beauty shops;

Above the young men, thinking the popular song;
Above the children, who now in the dusk go wild.

Crescent, horn, cusp, above the clinics, the lodgings,
Sweet curve, sweet light, new thin moon, now purely at ease,

Above the old, going home to their deafness, their madness,
Their cancer, age, ugliness, pain, diabetes.

[1937]

Untitled

Tender and insolent,
Beware. Within this lies,
When little more is spent,
The crowded tears of the eyes,
Naked astonishment.

The pillow torn with pain,
The dogging agony
That could not happen again,
Once more will thrash at thee
Sharper than winter rain.

Beware, beware, beware.
Give thyself wider room
Than these sweet eyes can share,
Than the most cruel bloom
Of the false tall and fair.

[1937]

The Catalpa Tree

Words do not come to the old prayer,—only the rung names and the pauses.
An autumn I remember only by the pods of the catalpa tree that did not fall.
Tears were shed, sobbed to wild herbs in a field, whatever their causes,
And a house had a wall like a web of thorns about it. I remember that wall.

Only the long pods remained; the tree was drained like a sieve.
Perhaps the secret voice you hear under your mouth was all I could keep.
The burnished pods not claimed by a wizened month once said I should live.
They hang in my song of another autumn, in this hour stolen from sleep.

[1951]

Unpublished Poems and Drafts—Dated Works

Second Act Curtain

Had heaven and earth combined
To strike my life in two,
I should have, once, being blind,
Called upon you,—
If earth and heaven had striven,
You being earth and heaven.

If the vain thunder broke
And earth spewed up its dead,
In order to invoke
My due upon my head,
I should have cried, "My love,
Heaven splits, and corpses move."

I should have said, "My dear,
Racked mountains and the wave
Dispense their angers here;
Nothing can save,
If you, O strong beyond men,
Lift all not up again."

The tempest broke, but I
Was not its mark; the wrath,
The lightnings in the sky
Spilled not upon my path.
At night I woke to see
Stars range, fixed, bright and free.

My forehead cannot bear
The legendary scar

The cursed of heaven wear;
Yet all's at war
With what, within my breast,
Once called on love for rest.

All's safe, and all's forgiven.
Bone, blood, and breath remain.
No firmament has striven
To strike me down again.
Under wide sunny skies
The year, and I, arise.

Earth's creatures, with the year,
Will walk among their crowd,
Safe, holding themselves dear,
Laughing aloud.
—Though herd and swarm and flock
Seek shelter in the rock,

Free in the plain shall I
Reasonably know my kind,
And see the sun on high,
Smell honey in the wind,
And seek from all, not one,
To cure a mischief done;

And choose no one to spare
My skin from hell laid bare;
But, if hard weathers rise,
With my hand shield my eyes;
And, if the earth will move,
Summon not you, nor love.

[1933]

Lines Written After Detecting in Myself a Yearning toward the Large, Wise, Calm, Richly Resigned, Benignant Act Put On by a Great Many People After Having Passed the Age of Thirty-five

For every great soul who died in his house and his wisdom
Several did otherwise.
God, keep me from the fat heart that looks vaingloriously toward peace
    and maturity;
Protect me not from lies.
In Thy infinite certitude, tenderness, and mercy
Allow me to be sick and well,
So that I may never tread with swollen foot the calm and obscene intentions
That pave hell.
Shakespeare, Milton, Matthew Arnold died in their beds,
Dante above the stranger's stair.
They were not absolved from either the courage or the cowardice
With which they bore what they had to bear.
Swift died blind, deaf, and mad;
Socrates died in his cell;
Baudelaire died in his drool;
Proving no rule.[1]

[1934]

1. As Ruth Limmer points out, these lines from an October 16, 1934 letter to Edmund Wilson were later reduced to four and published under the title "To an Artist, to Take Heart": "Slipping in blood, by his own hand, through pride, / Hamlet, Othello, Coriolanus fall. / Upon his bed, however, Shakespeare died, / Having endured them all" (WTWL, 82).

The Lie

First met when I was young:
Within the sliding eye,
Upon the sidling tongue
I knew the lie.

Innocent, saw the look,
Dupe, heard the dreadful beat

When the beautiful eye and mouth
— Gave forth deceit.

Was truth bred in the bone,
Fast in the flesh, of that child,
And is it I alone
Whom shifts drive wild?

What curse, then, living truth,
Long upon me has lain
That I should seek the whole
Sound word, in vain?

My whole life, with the lie
Has lived. At night it moved,
In daylight, with a cry,
It loved.

Inchworm, O you, O crude,
Horrible mouth, abate;
Move from me, long withstood,
Lest I must touch your state.[1]

[1935]

1. "The Lie" was enclosed in a letter to Rolfe Humphries, July 2, 1935, in which LB
notes:

The first stanza is admittedly lousy. There's something terribly wrong with it; I don't
know what. I thought it would be fun to say—Within the sliding eye. Upon the sidling
tongue,—but that's too much like anagrams, I admit. It is rather a good trick though,
now isn't it?

The second stanza is good, except I wish to God I could get away from the word
beat. The book [*The Sleeping Fury*, 1937] will be sown with *beats*, one to a page, and sometimes two. The third stanza begins to get too noble for anything, and that's bad, I suppose.
As a matter of fact, I was a nervous, frightened kind of brat, with no particular claim to
truthful bones, but I did hate to have my mother lie to me, but all kids do. *Whom shifts
drive wild* is nice; I like that. I looked in the thesaurus for a one syllable word meaning
lie, and when I found *shift* I fell upon it like a mad thing. It's a superb word.

In the fourth stanza *whole* is right, but I wish I could think of something else. I'm
terribly fond of *whole*, as well as of *beat*.

I mean to repeat *whole*, in the fifth. An effect. What do you think?

Now, about inchworm. There's nothing particularly loathsome about an inchworm, is there; it's the dry rather attractive type of worm, as I remember. *Lugworm* is
the word at the back of my mind, of course; you remember the Yeats poem ["The Man
Who Dreamed of Faeryland"]. What is the kind of worm that raises itself up and looks

around, as distinguished from writhing forward all over? If that's an inchworm, then it's all right; this is a horrid kind of worm. The rest of the stanza I like: how it came out so well, I can't think.

I was shaking with rage when I wrote it. (WTWL, 89–90)

Elsewhere in the same letter she bursts out, "I hate a lie, O Christ how I hate a lie." References to Raymond Holden's falsehoods appear in three other letters above: July 1, 1935, to John Hall Wheelock, to Rolfe Humphries again on January 24, 1936, and in December 1935 to Theodore Roethke.

Lines Written on Coming To Late in the Afternoon

My God, Louise
Here it is night!
Snap on the light
And write out plain

Again with labor,
Written as heard,—
Set the fit word
To its fit neighbor[1]

[1935]

1. Enclosed in a letter to Theodore Roethke, September 9, 1935, in which LB commends Rolfe Humphries's services to *her*, to prepare Roethke for the critique she is about to give *him*. She explains: "To illustrate R.'s methods with me, I will quote you an eight-line and about fourteen-syllable lyric, torn off by me last month. In its first form, it had a lamp that had to be lit in it, and the 2nd line was different, *undsow*[*eiter*, German for etcetera]. Well, Rolfe attacked it, one evening when he was here, and for a week we wrote and rewrote it, knowing all the time that it was only an eight-line, fourteen-syllable poem, not much damn good in any case. Variant readings ran through the mail like wild, and after all this fuss, I put it in a drawer and forgot about it. But you see that such things can happen, and not be tampering. . . ." (WTWL, 101–4)

"I put the supposed"

I put the supposed
Enlightened, together
Into the mind

To endure its weather,
That's sharp with the past,
To see what's proposed,
And what has been lost.

Once under that clear
Look, they became
Not dreadful in purpose
For some pure belief;
But rather, they cast
Ragged shadow, at last.

If we break the measure,
Make bitter the air, —
The tight bemused circle
Breaks, and turns where?
O, faithless let us be,
Unruly in pleasure,
Since at length we must bear
The worst in each other.

—Nothing brings us here
But strong childish thought.
We turn, once that's caught,
To some heightened year
That yields up its token,
To find the best broken.

[1935]

"We might have striven years"

We might have striven years
For what now comes to us without our aid;
Time might have rung its changes, cast its shade
Between our bodies and above our tears.
But now, between our meeting and our kiss
Hardly the branch that stirred within the tree

In some light wind, has fallen back to rest;
And fast upon our first word follows this,
That speaks to you much as it sounds in me, —
Reverberant on the barrier of your breast.

Four Quarters

I viewed it from the north:
All that it did was burn;
The trees, between false calms,
Clattered and wept, in turn,
And fire fed, through the earth,
Spiny fruit, and the palms.

Now from the south I gaze:
With sanity extreme
Cold on the builded ice
The men and houses gleam,
Under the withering days,
Stricken to a device.

Eastward is hard to see
Because of the clearest light;
The curled wave rides beneath;
Time flies from left to right.
The soil is salt; the tree
Hangs low a salty wreath.

There is one quarter more,
That of the hills and grain.
Forests sever the skies,
Lifting them from the plain.
Father, there is a shore
Where some last ocean dies.

[1936]

"You labor long to fit the pearl"

You labor long to fit the pearl
Woman, within your learned art,
That long ago an ignorant girl,
Weeping, found in her heart.

[1936]

Entrance, with Harp and Fiddles

. . . But the musicians have arrived:
And now through music's lattices,
Throughout accompaniment and song,
We shall review what has gone wrong
With all that has been, all that is.

And you, my hollow lovely one,
Tall, with such eyes, too, speak and bend.
O not yet learned, not yet begun,
Still safe, before beginning, end.

How tall you stand, how gentle in
Your manly beauty, how your voice
Echoes the fineness of your skin,
Whereat my heart and soul rejoice.

But the icy fugue, within my ear,
Once held me living against death.
The poured scales hardened, against fear,
The shaken and fear-loving breath.

And now begin the flute and drums;
The woodwind, brass, are twinned and wived;
The strings in pizzicati hum.
Look, the musicians have arrived.

[1936/37]

Poem at Forty

Seek out the heartless from the great
And cozen them, and give them tongue.
I thought I knew of man's estate,
Its nobleness, when I was young,
In the broken chords
And the builded words.

Lay cheek on clever cheek, the flat
Voice on the shrill voice, seeking praise.
I thought to break the joy thereat
Even in my youngest and wildest days,
Hurling down the gage
Of my ignorant rage.

Having heard, in my young ears, the sea
Fall in its rhythm of nine, the tide
As quenching as its power could be
To flame in power along its side;—
Seen eyes and mouth
Symbolizing both.

What met and what dispersed I saw
And hoped from them what has not come
(Even though hard winters and great thaw,
Year after year, have given room):
Pity beneath;
And love till death.

[1937]

Mozart

To thee when I hear thy rainbow of summer:
Happiness began here, at the middle height of the moving air.
The swords of anger

Were sheathed by a thousand outpourings of cloud and bird,
A columbine in a field which pleases for a day
Was forgotten by the scythe,
Nostalgia set free bitter tenderness.
Do you know Salzburg at six o'clock in summer?
A light shiver of cold delight, the sun has set, drunk by a cloud.

A light shiver of cold—in Salzburg in summer.
O divine joy, you are about to die in captivity, O imaginary youth,
Live for a single day longer among these true hills.
It has rained, the end of a storm. O divine joy,
Appease these people with closed eyes in all the concert halls of the world.[1]

[1939]

1. Bogan's translation from the French of Pierre-Jean Jouve; her version of Jouve's prose "Kapuzinerberg" appeared in *The Blue Estuaries*. According to her biographer, these two renderings into English "belong to the unsystematic but passionate assortment of Bogan's responses to the contemporary panorama of fascism and cultural decay" (EF, 313).

Portrait of the Artist as a Young Woman

Sitting on the bed's edge, in the cold lodgings, she wrote it out on her knee
In terror and panic—but with the moment's courage, summoned up from God
    knows where.
Without recourse to saints or angels: a Bohemian, thinking herself free—
A young thin girl without sense, living (she thought) on passion and air.

The winds struck her; she flew abroad; what is this land wherein she wakes?
The armoire broods and the bed engulfs; the café is warm at ten;
The lindens give out their scent, the piano its scales; the trams rumble; the
    shadows in the formal garden take
The half-attentive gaze of the still-young woman, who will grieve again.

Everything falls to pieces once more; and the only refuge is the provincial stair;
People without palates try to utter, and the trap seems to close;
A child goes for the milk; the library books are there,
Generous to the silly young creature caught again in a month of the rose.

Is there a way through? Never think it! Everything creaks.
And here once more is the cold room, between thin walls of sadist and lout.
But at last, asking to serve, seeking to earn its keep, about and about,
At the hour between the dog and the wolf, is it her heart that speaks?
She sits on the bed with the pad on her knee, and writes it out.

[1940; revised November 20, 1956]

Leechdoms

Cocayne (T.O.), Editor. Leechdoms, Wortcunning and Starcraft of Early England;
Being a Collection of Documents for the Most Part Never Before Printed, Illus-
trating the History of Science in this Country Before the Norman Conquest. Lim-
ited to 500 copies, 3 vols. Buckram, board £ 16/10/

Item in Blackwell's catalogue
under Bibliography, Paleography & Typography

Wortcunning I know;
Starcraft I can find;
But a vision of leechdoms
Has taken hold of my mind.

Where are they found?
Are they forbidden?
Deep in the ground
In a kitchen-midden

With danegeld abandoned?
Crossed by Pict swords?
Mixed up with runes?
Leaking out of word-hoards?

By the salt Saxon sea,
In the blue Druid glade
We shall find leechdoms
(Don't be afraid...)

[1961]

The Castle of My Heart: A Rondel

Cleanse and refresh the castle of my heart
Where I have lived for long with little joy.
For Falsest Danger, with its counterpart
Sorrow, has made this siege its long employ.

Now lift the siege, for in your bravest part
Full power exists, most eager for employ;
Cleanse and refresh the castle of my heart
Where I have lived for long with little joy.

Do not let Peril play its lordly part;
Show up the bad game's bait, and its employ.
Nor, for a moment, strut as fortune's toy.
Advance, and guard your honor and my art.

Cleanse and refresh the castle of my heart.[1]

[1966]

1. Whereas the rondel on which this poem is based, by fifteenth-century French poet Charles d'Orléans, speaks only of *strengthening* the heart after its disappointment in love, LB provides a more psychologically inflected verb-pair, *cleanse* and *refresh*. The speaker of the original addresses the poem "To his Mistress, to succour his heart that is beleaguered by jealousy"; LB's speaker addresses some force in herself (*full power*), to which she is trying to break through. The original's *jealousy* is finessed into what could be internal threats, *Falsest Danger, Peril,* and *Sorrow*. LB has transposed the poem into her own key.

December Daybreak

Caught in a corner of the past
Wherein we cannot even weep
We only ask
For present sleep.

But the dream shoots forward to a future
We shall never see;

Therefore, in December's night, at the beginning of the morning
We must give over, and be

Once again the ignorant victor
Or the victim, wise
Within those proven but broken circles of wisdom
By which the living live
And the dead rise.

[1967]

Unpublished Poems and Drafts— Undated Work

Fortune-Teller's Pack

We might have escaped the Fiend,
The Serpent, the Tea Table's sound,
Distance, and Jealousy's round,
Had not brisk Time intervened.

The Ring, the Gift, the Surprise,
Clearly imprint their card.
What does not appear is hard
To tell of,—and it counts twice.

Double the count thereto,
And no sign of it on the table.
The Fan does what it is able,
But Time, what there is to do.

Fantasy

The women hang the clothes on the blocks of roofs
At the anonymous edge of the city: I dream to be here,
To mount this stair, put the key in the lock, to put down
The bundle full of tins and fruit; light the stove, pull the light on.

The old polished table, the desk and the books, the window
Facing the water; a quilt at night on the narrow bed;
The shut door; the scales on the piano.
I have fought through flood to have them; I have looked for them in dreams.

I have fought for the right to smell the cooking
And hear alarm clocks go off in the winter mornings.
I have fought for the peace to sit alone in a room.
I can only love the dead who brought me here.

It was where I never looked.
I wanted so much beside.
It stood in the plain streets
Close to this riverside.
It was three flights up the stairs
In this cold bare room.

Finally it was there
When I came in the door
The paper bag in my arm
At last in the smell and form
At last it was my thought
And the look of the pure young dream.

In the anonymous streets
Women hang the wash.
Hidden within the flats
Nameless and without hope
I learned how the heart beat.
I can only thank the dead
Who cleverly brought me here.

"In what still rays"

In what still rays
Does the sun draw water
On half-dark days
From the tracks of water invisible!

Over the wise township
From houses, from the stacked corn,
From fields of birds and grain,
Slowly is drawn

Silent and clear
In pure, divisible
Shafts built up in light,
The bitter winter rain,
The storm in the night,
That all shall hear.

Beginning of an Unpopular Song

Stopping wild love is (believe me)
    Like stopping fever in the veins.
What shall we do?
Shall we take it or leave it?
Shall we have it or grieve it?
Shall we make it what we can, or
    This moment start suffering it through?

Letter to Mrs. Q's Sister

Adulterers' letters, unfortunately, are always the same.
They speak of beautiful snatched experience, usually in a room shaken by trucks;
The walk later, until two in the morning; the tunnel to the last train;

Kisses in the shrubbery; talk by the monument;
They reach the clumsy bronze statues in the alleys of parks, shaded by the late
    leather leaf.

So she is killed and so she is taken.
So fire mounts and air breathes again.
So tedium is relieved and courage underlined.

O what woman should weep, because of this,
Safe with her dove, her fountain, her earth, her ilex?

Three Sonnets in Autumn

Those were my days, when change, a great bird, clapped
Its wing over wood and field. On a hope, all turned.
Half open and half shut, half free, half trapped,
The world lay, half still burning and half burned.

Under the sun, declining in the mind,
Blown over by great firmaments of cloud,
Those were my days, O many years out of mind,
When I looked up, and saw, and laughed aloud

At the big symbols of running dark and night,
Seeing time pass, most intent in its groove.
Without you, who, half darkened, half in light,
Stymied, forsaken, hold me now in love.

Love Severally Rhymed

Fool and wise woman alike
Ripple your stream,
Shallow, as in a dyke,
Running in a dream.

Easily surfeited
The fields your waters tread.

In this last pang shall I
Describe your way.
Once, in an even sky
I saw your day,—
Treacherous now in love
Like light the waters move.

"O come again, distilled"

O come again, distilled through the blood, the spirit, and the nerve,
Whisper and silence, articulate power. Symbolized by that shining curve of ad-
    vancing and retreating water.
The ocean at ebb never hears the wave. For an unnatural time the ebb has held.
    Give virtue again
To whatever lies among the shells and seaweed on the drying beach.
Curved glass wave and diamond foam
Come in, come in to the curved sand,
Come in with your great reward and power, your sliding root and your sliding curl.
Something still waits, not in the salt tear but in the salt blood. Come in at need
Great wave to the strong woman, as once to the gentle girl.

"When at last"

When at last we can love what we will not touch;
Know what we need not be;
Hum over to ourselves the tune made by the massed instruments
As the shell hums in the sea;

Then come the long days without the terrible hour,
And the long nights of rest.
Then the true fruit, from the exhausted flower
Sets, in the breast.

Index of Names

Numbers in **boldface** indicate included essays.

Debussy, Claude, xxvii, 250; *Pelléas et Mélisande,* 155, 355

Dekobra, Maurice, *La Madone des sleepings,* 26

Dickens, Charles, 242, 276n1

Dickinson, Emily, xxvii, xxxiii, xxxiv, xxxv, 61, 184, 236, 254, 317, 319

Dickinson, Goldsworthy Lowes, 279, 325

Dietrich, Marlene, 182; *The Blue Angel,* 183

Dinesen, Isak, xxviii, **293–95**

Disney, Walt, 267, 292n1

Dodge, Mabel. *See* Luhan, Mabel Dodge

Donaldson, E. Talbot, 236

Donne, John, 229, 309

Dostoevski, Fyodor, 300, 301; *Crime and Punishment,* 170

Dowson, Ernest, 201, 203

Dreiser, Theodore, *Sister Carrie,* 236

Drummond, William, of Hawthornden, 26

Dryden, John, 226; "A Song for St. Cecilia's Day," 135

Eliot, George, 298, 319n2, 339

Eliot, T. S., xv, xviii, xxvii, xxviii, 133, 176, 179, 201, 220, 226, 228, 230, 231, 232, 253, **255–259**, 274, 285–86, 287, 290, 291, 308, 314, 318, 335; "Little Gidding," xxviii, **258–59**

Ellis, Havelock, 301

Erasmus, Desiderius, 320, 322n1

Escudero, Vicente, 122, 122n3

Evelyn, John, 320, 322n1

Faulkner, William, 89

Ferguson, Sir Samuel, 204

Fields, W. C., 87n1

Flaubert, Gustave, xxvii, 62, 132, 214, 248, **278–83**, 283n2, 288, 301, 325; *L'Education sentimentale,* xxviii, 170, **278–83**; *Madame Bovary,* 170, 283n2

Florit, Eugenio, 336, 337

Ford, Ford Madox, 181

Forster, E. M., 167n1, 170, 231

Foster, Stephen, 284; "The Old Folks at Home," 155

Fouché, Joseph, duc d'Otrante, 295

Fowler, Henry W., *Modern English Usage,* 264–65

Frank, Elizabeth, xxxiii, 176n1, 176n2, 178n2, 379n1

Frank, Waldo, 89

Frazer, Sir James, 236; *The Golden Bough,* 104, 159

Freud, Sigmund, 144, 232, 236, 250, 301; "Ego" and "Super-Ego," 144; "Id," 144, 195

Frost, Robert, xxxiv, 236

Garrett, John. *See* Auden, W. H.

Gay, John, 226

George, Stefan, xxxiv, 291, 292n4, 302

Gershwin, George, 121

Gibbs, Wolcott, 123–24, 124n1

Gide, André, xxiv, **299–308**, 308n3, 325

Gilbert, Stuart, 267

Gilbert, Sir William Schwenck, 133, 220, 222n1, 226; *Iolanthe,* 135, 222, 222n1

Goethe, Johann Wolfgang von, xxv, xxvii, 49, 99–100, 124, 169, 174, 203, 216, **322–26**

Gogarty, Oliver St. John, 150, 202

Gogol, Nikolai: *Taras Bulba,* 26; *Dead Souls,* 118

Goldsmith, Oliver, 204, 235

Goncourt, Edmond and Jules, 278, 281, 283n1, 306, 308n2

Góngora, Luis de, 260, 334

Gonne, Maud, 148, 156, 207

Graham, Martha, xxxv, 183–84

Grattan, C. Hartley, 244

Grattan, Henry, 212

Greene, Graham, *The Labyrinthine Ways,* 298

Gregory, Augusta, Lady, 156, 202

Gregory, Horace, 131, 133, 342–43

Grieg, Edvard, 155; *Peer Gynt,* 236

Griswold, Rufus, *The Female Poets of America,* 317

Guiney, Louise Imogen, 317

H. D. (Hilda Doolittle), 318

Hale, Sarah Josepha, 317

Handel, Georg Frideric, 120, 229

Hardy, Thomas, 104, 216, 226, 310, 337

Hays, H. R., 335–36

Hecht, Anthony, 238

Hegel, Georg Wilhelm Friedrich, 124

Heine, Heinrich, 124

Helmer, Rufina McCarthy, 151, 152n1, 169, 189

Hemans, Felicia Dorothea, 64, 316, 319n2

Hemingway, Ernest, xxi, xxx, 153; *Death in the Afternoon,* 88–89

Herbert, George, xxxiii, 65

Herrick, Robert, 226

Hofmannsthal, Hugo von, *Der Rosenkavalier,* 165n1

Holden, Raymond (LB's second husband), xvii, xxxi, xxxiii, 64, 82n1, 100, 101n5, 103, 104, 105, 107, 109n1, 110, 111n1, 122, 125n1, 127, 128n1, 133, 177, 374n1

Homer, 274, 335

Hopkins, Gerard Manley, 129, 129n2, 162, 202, 236

Horace, 313
Housman, A. E., 129, 226
Howe, Julia Ward, 317
Huling, Betty, 193, 194
Humphries, Rolfe, xvi, xxxiv, 62, 90, 99–101, 100n1, 101n4, 108–11, 127–28, 128n1, 131–34, 134n1, 142, 146, 157–60, 165, 173, 193, 260–61, 261n1, 373n1, 374n1

Isherwood, Christopher, 64, 220, 221, 231

James, Henry, xxiv, xxv–xxvi, xxvii, xxix, 61, 62n, 83n1, 89–90, 101–3, 119n1, 137, 138–39, 141, 152, 185–86, 227, 229, 232, **241–55**, 257, 279, 298, 308n2, 340; *The Bostonians*, xxv, xxviii, 138, 152, 241, **251–55**; *The Princess Casamassima*, xviii, xxvi, 152, **241–47**; *The Turn of the Screw*, 26, 103 (filmed as *The Innocents*, 185–86)
James, William, 340
Jeffers, Robinson, 87, 87n1, 110, 135
Jiménez, Juan Ramón, xxviii, **334–37**
Jolas, Eugene, 266
Jonson, Ben, 226, 347n1
Jouve, Pierre-Jean, "Mozart," 379, 379n1
Joyce, James, xx, xxvii, 115, 148, 192, 236, 340; *Finnegans Wake*, xxv, xxvii, **264–71**
Joyce, Peggy, 87, 87n1
Jung, Carl Gustav, 136, 147, 212, 227, 250, 256

Kafka, Franz, 227, 298
Kenyon, Bernice Lesbia, 135
Kern, Jerome, 121
Kerr, Deborah, 185–86
Kierkegaard, Søren, 227, 231
Kinnell, Galway, 194n3
Kunitz, Stanley, 65

Lamb, Charles, 226
Laing, C. L., 326
Landor, Walter Savage, 203, 226
Larkin, Philip, 312n1, **337–38**
Lawrence, D. H., 87, 87n1, 119, 192, 202, 226, 288
Lawrence, T. E., 119, 120n2, 151, 154
Lazarus, Emma, 317
Lear, Edward, 226, 264
Leavis, F. R., 241
Lenin, Vladimir Ilich, 124, 137
Leschetizky, Theodore, 120
Lewis, C. Day, 202, 237
Limmer, Ruth, xv, xxxiii, xxxiii, 68n2, 68n4, 96, 183, 183n1, 185, 190, 193, 194, 196, 372n1

Lindsay, Vachel, 226
Lloyd, A. L., 260, 261n1
Lloyd, Marie, 285–86
Longfellow, Henry Wadsworth, 236
Lorca, Federico García, xxviii, **260–61**, 261n1, 284, 334
Louis-Philippe, king of France, 279, 280
Lowell, Robert, xxvii, **308–13**
Lucretius, 65, 322n1
Luhan, Mabel Dodge, xxx, 87, 87n1

Macaulay, Thomas Babington, 204
Machado, Antonio, 334
MacIntyre, C. F., 323
MacLeish, Archibald, 64, 157
MacNeice, Louis, 64, 202, 222–24, 231
Mahler, Gustav, *Das Lied von der Erde*, 164
Maidie (LB's daughter). *See* Alexander, Mathilde
Mailer, Norman, 194
Maistre, Xavier de, 92, 92n1
Mallarmé, Stéphan, 65, 239, 268n3, 292n4
Malraux, André, 288, 292n2
Mangan, Clarence, 204
Mann, Thomas, 144, 161, 323, 325
Mansfield, Katherine, 199
Maritain, Jacques, 307, 308n3
Marlowe, Christopher, 235
Marshall, Margaret, 193, 194n1
Martyn, Edward, 205
Marvell, Andrew, 235, 266; "The Definition of Love," 175–76, 176n1
Marx, Karl, 124, 126, 155
Masefield, John, 121, 122n1
Matthiessen, F. O., *Henry James: The Later Phase*, 248–50
Maxwell, William, xxiv, xxx, xxxi, 161, 162n1, 164, 166, 167n1, 169, 169n1, 170, 171n1, 182, 195, 196
Mayer, Elizabeth, xxv, 82, 174, 175n2
Mead, Margaret, 107n1, 227
Melville, Herman, 236, 309
Merwin, W. S., 194n3
Meynell, Viola, xxx, 137
Michelet, Jules, 124–25
Middleton, Thomas, 26
Millay, Edna St. Vincent, 185, 319
Miller, Henry, 176
Milton, John, 203, 235, 372; *Samson Agonistes*, 236
Monroe, Harriet, 111–13, 112n1, 119, 123, 145, 317
Montaigne, Michel de, 26, 301
Moore, George, 205, 206, 211

Moore, Marianne, xv, xvi, 168, 187, 318, **321–22**

Moore, Thomas, 204, 226; "The Last Rose of Summer," 171

Moore, T. Sturge, 202

Moreau, Jeanne, xxxv, 186–87

Morgan, Charles, *The Fountain,* 89

Morris, William, 63, 203, 207

Mozart, Wolfgang Amadeus, 36, 38, 84, 119, 120, 129, 143, 320, 378

Murnau, F. W., 182

Musset, Alfred de, 141

Nabokov, Vladimir, *Lolita,* 181

Napoleon (Napoleon Bonaparte), 279, 295

Napoleon, Louis, 280

Nation, The (Ireland), 204, 205, 213n2

Nation, The (U.S.), 119n1, 163n1, 173, 194

Nazimova, Alla, 182

Nerval, Gérard de, 325

New Republic, The, 108n2, 193

New Yorker, The, xv, 101n5, 120, 121n1, 124n1

Newman, John Henry, *Apologia pro Vita Sua,* 26

Nicholl, Louise Townsend, xvii, 107n1

Nietzsche, Friedrich, 63

O'Connor, Frank, 202

O'Flaherty, Liam, *Mr. Gilhooley,* 148, 148n2

O'Grady, Standish James, 205

Orléans, Charles, duc de, "Castle of My Heart," 381, 381n1

O'Leary, John, 207, 209

Ovid, 100n1, 335

Owen, Wilfred, 136–37, 202, 237

Parker, Dorothy, 172

Parnell, Charles, 205, 217

Pater, Walter, 63, 201

Pears, Peter, 191

Pearson, Norman Holmes, 234–36

Percy, Thomas, *Reliques of Ancient English Poetry,* 59, 347n1

Perse, St.-John, 335

Perrault, Charles, 319n1

Phelps, Robert, xxxiii, 180, 180n1

Plath, Sylvia, 191

Poe, Edgar Allan, xviii, 61, 135, 176, 235, 296, 316, 317

Pope, Alexander, 179, 226

Porter, Cole, *Fifty Million Frenchmen,* 110, 111, 111n1

Potter, Stephen, 166

Pound, Ezra, 202, 239, **272–78**; "Rock-Drill 85-95 de los Cantares," xxvii, **276–78**

Powys, John Cowper, 341–42, 344n1

Praed, Winthrop Mackworth, 226

Propertius, Sextus, 309

Proust, Marcel, 139, 197, 288, 307, 340

Pushkin, Aleksandr, 226

Rabelais, François, 268n1

Rahv, Philip, 62, 253

Ransom, John Crowe, xxxv, 117n1; *The New Criticism,* 165, 166

Ravel, Maurice, 355n1

Read, Herbert, 202

Reese, Lizette Woodworth, 317

Richardson, Dorothy, xxviii, **338–344**

Ridge, Lola, *Firehead,* 111–12

Riding, Laura, xv

Rilke, Rainer Maria, xxxiv, 127, 130–31, 131n1, 140, 227, 230, 231, 232, 291, 292n5, 302, 309, 335; *The Notebooks of Malte Laurids Brigge (Journal of My Other Self),* 291–92, 292n5; *Sonnets to Orpheus,* 140–41, 141n1

Rimbaud, Arthur, 10, 65, 309

Robinson, Edwin Arlington, 191n1, 122n1, 238

Robinson, Henry Morton, 269

Roethke, Theodore, xix, xxx, 83n1, 90n1, 125, 126n1, 130–31, 134–35, 136n1, 138–39, 140–42, 145, 154–55, 175n1, 192, 222n1, 374n1

Roosevelt, Theodore, Jr., 122n1

Ross, Harold, 123, 124n1

Rossetti, Dante Gabriel, 63, 185, 207

Rossetti, Christina, 154

Rousseau, Jean-Jacques, 326n2

Sand, George, 89, 90n1, 101, 132, 141, 278

Santayana, George, 95, 325

Sappho, 64, 139, 319

Sardou, Victorien, 58, 58n1

Sarton, May, xxx, 175n2, 177–80, 184–85, 190n2, 193n1

Schaefer, Josephine O'Brien, 192–93, 193n1

Schiller, Friedrich von, 322, 326n2

Schubert, Franz, 5, 122n2, 326; *Gruppe aus dem Tartarus,* 164

Sexton, Anne, 191, 194

Shakespeare, William, 64, 65, 129, 129n2, 185, 226, 228, 229, 232, 235, 299, 301, 315, 316, 325, 334, 347n1, 372, 372n1; *Antony and Cleopatra,* 236

Shapiro, Karl, 176n2
Shaw, George Bernard, 301
Shaw, T. E. *See* Lawrence, T. E.
Shelley, Percy Bysshe, 39, 82, 252
Sidney, Sir Philip, 185
Sigourney, Lydia Huntley, 315, 316, 317
Simenon, Georges, 181, 297
Sitwell, Edith, 202, 221
Sitwell, Sacheverell, 191, 221
Smart, Christopher, 236
Sontag, Susan, xxxv, 188–89
Sophocles, 203, 256
Spender, Stephen xxvi, 237, 244
Starkie, Enid, 313–14
Stedman, Edmund Clarence, *An American Anthology*, 236, 317
Stein, Gertrude, 236, 238, 318
Stendhal (Marie-Henri Beyle), 65, 247, 247n2; *La Vie de Henri Brulard,* 198
Stephens, James, 150
Stevens, Wallace, **326–30**
Stickney, Trumbull, 238
Stokowski, Leopold, in *Fantasia,* 287, 292n1
Strauss, Richard, 265; *Der Rosenkavalier,* 165
Sue, Eugène, 295, 299
Sullivan, Sir Arthur, 222n1
Swedenborg, Emanuel, 204, 212
Swift, Jonathan, xxiv, 10, 65, 84, 115, 116n2, 133, 204, 212, 221, 226, 330, 372
Symons, Arthur, 61, 63, 314
Synge, John, 156, 202, 213–14; *The Playboy of the Western World,* 213–14, 216n1

Tate, Allen, xxv, 60, 116–17, 117nn1–2, 133, 144, 162, 163n2, 168, 176
Tchaikovsky, Pyotr Ilich, 126, 326
Teasdale, Sara, 319
Tennyson, Alfred Lord, 201, 235, 310, 347n1; "The Lotos-Eaters," 171n1
Thackeray, William Makepeace, 170
Theresa, Saint, of Avila, 64, 171
Thibaudet, Albert, 268n3
Thomas, Caitlin, xxviii, 182, **331–34**
Thomas, Dylan, 332
Thompson, Francis, "The Hound of Heaven," 298
Thoreau, Henry David, 61, 92, 120, 236; *Walden,* 26
Thucydides, 227
Torrence, Ridgely, 108, 108n1
Tourneur, Cyril, 309

Trollope, Anthony, 15–16
Trotsky, Leon, 155
Turgenev, Ivan, 62, 181, 242, 253, 263, 279
Twain, Mark, 236, 236n1

Updike, John, xxxv; *Rabbit, Run,* 183

Valéry, Paul, xxviii, xxix, 291, 307, 309, 325
Vega, Lope de, 334
Verlaine, Paul, 49, 312, 313n1
Vico, Giovanni Battista, 124, 264, 266–67, 269
Vidocq, Eugène François, 295
Virgil, 335

Wagner, Geoffrey, 313–14
Wagner, Richard, 63
Waller, Edmund, 26
Walton, Eda Lou, 129, 129n1
Warren, Robert Penn, 117n1
Webster, John, 309
West, Rebecca, 103
Wheelock, John Hall, xxix, 106, 106n1, 114, 126–27, 128n1, 135, 137–38, 165, 374n1
White, Katharine S., 120, 121n1, 124n1, 174–75
Whitehead, Alfred North, *An Introduction to Mathematics,* 26
Whitman, Walt, xxix, 61, 62, 239, 310
Whittier, John Greenleaf, 317
Wilcox, Ella Wheeler, 127, 317
Wilde, Oscar, 201, 304
Wilson, Edmund, xvi, xix, xxxiv, 90n1, 101–5, 101n1, 103n1, 105n1, 115, 116n1, 121, 124, 125–26, 138, 150–51, 156, 161, 163, 166, 212, 372n1
Wolf, Hugo, xxvii, 326
Woolf, Virginia, xxxiv, 192–93, 193n1
Wordsworth, William, 202, 216, 222
Wylie, Elinor, 185, 319

Yeats, William Butler, xxviii, 61, 62, 65, 82, 114n1, 133, 150, 156, 161, 179, **200–219**, 225, 226, 235, 260, 284, 291, 310, 335, 336, 373; "Men Improve with the Years," 23

Zabel, Morton Dauwen, xxv, xxxi, xxxiv, 118–20, 119n1, 121, 124–25, 136–37, 139–40, 142, 144–45, 146–49, 147n1, 153–54, 155–57, 164–65, 168, 172, 175, 182–83, 268–69n3, 355n1
Zola, Emile, 308n2

Index of Prose by Louise Bogan

Boldface indicates included fiction, memoir, and essays.

Index of Poetry by Louise Bogan

Boldface indicates included poems; initial phrases are given for untitled drafts.